D1109556

The Education and Treatment of
SOCIOEMOTIONALLY IMPAIRED
CHILDREN AND YOUTH

The Education and Treatment of
SOCIOEMOTIONALLY IMPAIRED CHILDREN AND YOUTH

WILLIAM C. MORSE

SYRACUSE UNIVERSITY PRESS

1985

Library of Congress Cataloging in Publication Data

Morse, William Charles.
   The education and treatment of socioemotionally
impaired children and youth.

   Bibliography: p.
   Includes index.
   1. Mentally ill children—Education—United States.
2. Mentally ill children—Care and treatment—
United States.   3. Mentally ill children—United States
—Psychology.   4. Socially handicapped children—
Education—United States.   5. Socially handicapped
children—Care and treatment—United States.
6. Socially handicapped children—United States—
Psychology.   I. Title.   II. Title: Socioemotionally
impaired children and youth.
LC4181.M67   1985   371.94   85-2842
ISBN 0-8156-2268-6
ISBN 0-8156-2269-4 (pbk.)

Manufactured in the United States of America

Contents

List of Figures

WILLIAM C. MORSE is Professor of Educational Psychology and Psychology, University of Michigan, Ann Arbor, co-author of *Learning Disabilities: The Struggle from Adolescence toward Adulthood,* and editor of *Humanistic Teaching of Exceptional Children* (both Syracuse University Press).

"Does life come to be felt as a basic ground of satisfaction temporarily interrupted by periods of discomfort which are reliably relieved, leading thus to a feeling of trust in and hopefulness about the biological enterprise? Or is life essentially 'one damn thing after the other' broken up by periods of calm from which no real satisfaction can be taken since one knows that at any moment the basic fact of life's discomfort will reassert itself?"

Kegan (1982)

Preface

THIS IS A BOOK about the education and care of Kegan's "one-damn-thing-after-the-other" children and youth. What can we do to convert the lives of these youngsters to "a basic ground of satisfaction"? When one knows the difficulties that teachers and other mental health workers face in this enterprise, it is easy to be disheartened. And yet the only hope that can sustain a professional career is built upon a realistic awareness of the situation and sound knowledge of how one can confront the condition.

The number of children who are in need of special help because of social and emotional impairments that confound their lives is between 10 and 12 percent. Some 3 percent are very seriously impaired. Yet the federal government states that only a total of 12 percent of the total child and youth population are candidates for all types of special education, with 2 percent assigned as the total for the emotionally disturbed. The estimate for the actual number being served by special education is 1 percent. Grosenick and Huntze (1980) found that 20,000 added teachers would be needed to adequately serve even the currently recognized numbers of emotionally disturbed children.

At the same time social changes are eroding the support systems for normal development of children. Although divorce and poverty do not directly produce social and emotional disturbance, we know that they do increase the risk of disturbance. Sexual mores have changed, placing new responsibilities on adolescents. The consequence of these and many other societal changes are reflected in more than half-a-million teenage mothers each year; the increase in depression and suicide; and the prevalence of delinquency, alcoholism, and drug abuse. Currently a million youths run away each year. Although youth violence is a mirror image of adult behavior, it has reached epidemic proportions in some schools. All of these children are legally bound to attend school; more than that, the school is responsible for providing all of these pupils with an appropriate education. It is a sad commentary that over half of the robberies and assaults on youngsters actually occur in school!

It would be easy to give up; in fact, many mental health workers and teachers have given up. Some have left the field while others perform zombielike rituals and collect their pay. Others pursue naive anticipations about changing behavior. The files are filled with Individual Educational Plans (IEPs) that no one takes seriously. At the same time the modal behavior of our profession is quite otherwise. There are teachers both new and experienced who are committed, who continue to stick in there working diligently to help these children. What the professionals seek is a sound psychology on which to build the best possible special education for *SEI* children, which is the general term we shall use for socially and/or emotionally impaired pupils. Special education in the decade of the 1980s is dedicated to improvement of the *quality* of special education. This is a tacit recognition that we can and must do better. How can this come about? To be sure, given the high risk of most of our clientele, one does not expect total success. At the same time much can be achieved, as exceptional teachers demonstrate every day. These teachers have a more profound understanding of their individual pupils and have advanced skills in intervention. What we all need is a deeper understanding of the psychology that undergirds the performance of these master teachers.

It is time for a new psychology of the socially and emotionally impaired that can match the new expectations for special education. Legislation trained our focus on the individual, but the old psychological modes often fell short of providing the help a teacher needed to do this. Special education was to be infused with a more humanistic approach to children and families. But the psychology did little to engender an appreciation of the world as children perceive it. The phenomenological world of children and adolescents remains opaque to many adults. Although we have recognized that the pupil is not an island, schools have had little help in conceptualizing the systems that held the disturbed child in bondage or what to do about these systems.

The psychology that offers the most promise and is coherent with the IEP is individual psychology, the study of the unique individual-environment complex that best represents each human being. Teachers recognize that their efforts depend upon knowledge of individuals; they relate to and teach individuals even when these individuals are assimilated into groups. The beauty of individual psychology is freedom from restrictive views of human beings through the lens of one or another particular school of psychology. When one concentrates on the individual, it becomes apparent that concepts from many schools of psychology have a place in planning. The tenets of individual psychology will be enumerated in the first chapter. But euphemisms that speak of the "whole child" can lead to a diffuseness with limited value to the special teacher. There must be an integrative force that will draw together, in a meaningful way, the myriad of informational strands that make sense of the individual person. To bring about this synthesis, the study of the self-concept becomes the core of individual psychology.

For special education, the IEP must become the central force. Decisions rest upon what an individual is like and how that individual can be helped to learn new behavior. Because teachers commonly think of their pupils in terms of self-concept attributes and self-esteem, this is the natural way to blend psychology with special education of SEI pupils. Above all, this approach recognizes the subtle and gross diversities that come under the rubric of SEI children. This is the key to increasing the quality of special education.

We start with the federal mandate, PL 94-142, and other pertinent legislation (Ballard and Weintraub 1982) supported in the courts. Public schools have the responsibility of providing free education for all special pupils, appropriate to their needs, and in the most normal school setting possible. Recent efforts to weaken this mandate by changing the legal obligation have failed. At the same time budget reductions and the lack of adequate programs are a bigger threat. Legal and economical concerns mean that the improvement of quality of SEI education has to take place in the delivery of direct services by special teachers and related mental health personnel.

The Education and Treatment of
SOCIOEMOTIONALLY IMPAIRED
CHILDREN AND YOUTH

1

Individual Psychology

ONE'S PERSONAL PSYCHOLOGY AND PROFESSIONAL PRACTICE

THE PSYCHOLOGIST George Kelly (1955) wrote that every person is a human behavior scientist; however he did not comment upon each one's level of competency. Youngsters develop psychological understanding in order to survive in the social milieu. Many children become astute at manipulating others, especially adults. Sometimes we think we are interviewing them when in actuality they are "interviewing" us. Many children learn only too well how to manipulate their parents. It is interesting that, when an older child tutors a younger one, he explains his tactics of motivation and management as if he had read a college text.

Adults, too, have their explanations concerning the behavior of others, and sometimes even their own behavior. As teachers we put these explanations together as a set of premises that we use to guide our decision making. Teachers accumulate generalizations and convictions about SEI children. These convictions—Kelly calls them constructs—deserve scrutiny because they constitute our theory of why disturbed children behave as they do and what we can do to change their behavior. The late Nicholas Hobbs (1981), said that premises (convictions) must make sense of life for the disturbed person, somehow putting order and meaning into the chaotic nature of human experience. Otherwise, as is quoted in the epigraph, life is just "one damn thing after the other."

Practitioners are usually impatient with "theory," considering it alien to their everyday work. And yet, teaching SEI pupils requires hundreds of decisions about a variety of pupils in a single day, and a continuing stream of decisions day after day. There are on-the-spot

1

decisions in response to ad hoc pupil behavior and there are embedded decisions found in the rules and practices that are set up to guide the classroom. What we think works constitutes the theory behind our practice. Recognized or not, each one of us has a theory of human nature—how children develop and how they learn—with a subset of ideas that are applied to the SEI youngster. Just as the notions of child raising that our parents held were of great concern to us as we grew up, so the beliefs of a teacher are high priority for pupils assigned to that classroom.

Some of the theoretical constructs that orient our practice are basic assumptions about human nature. For example, some teachers assume that human beings are naturally antisocial, and that educators must counteract the inclination toward aggressiveness and social exploitation. Others see human propensity as prosocial until distorted by experience. Consequently, they have a profound trust in youngsters but not in institutions. Another common stance holds that we are not innately antisocial or prosocial, but only reflect what we are taught. In addition to the theory one holds about human nature, there is the counterpart theory of how children learn, what behavior can be changed, and how it can be done. Can teachers make significant or only minor changes in pupils? Do we "punish" to normalcy? Is behavior dependent upon inner wellsprings, which are largely unconscious, or is behavior a consequence of rational decision making? Are there biological predispositions that shape our ends? What is the impact of developmental periods such as adolescence? The wide divergency of concepts about these matters found among groups of teachers is apparent when the scores of scales concerning human behavior are compared (Wrightsman 1964). One's personal theory about these matters becomes consolidated and dictates practice. For example many schools seem to have a central concept, "punishment makes perfect." The theories the teacher and the pupil have about behavior, and behavior change, are of utmost importance. It is common to have one set of premises to explain our own behavior and yet another set to explain "their" behavior. There is also the possibility that we say we believe one set of premises while the way in which we actually respond suggests we hold a different set of assumptions. Professionals are obligated to clarify what concepts they use and what they believe. When one considers how many different perceptions of these matters a group of professionals may have and then one adds perceptions of the pupils and the parents, many different languages may be spoken in one IEP meeting.

Professional training frequently attempts to define one theoretical stance or set of givens that is presented as pertinent to all children and all circumstances. Teachers come out of training identifying themselves as behaviorists, dynamicists, developmentalists, humanists, or followers of some other school. They then religiously fit the complexities of teaching SEI youngsters into their own format. Conversely, a teacher may be admonished to select "what works" from various theories, and to formulate an eclectic composite.

An alternative direction is taken in this book. First, we are to look as deeply as we can into the natures of our pupils, noting their similarities and differences. Second, we look with equal intensity at ways we can help them change; this is the helping process. The psychological position that fosters such a process is individual psychology—the next major topic. A unifying conceptual system emphasizes the uniqueness of the individual while at the same time providing a core; it is the study of the self, which is also to be discussed in this chapter.

Before turning to individual psychology and the study of the self, there is one confusion which enters into teacher decision making as a powerful modulator of practice. This is the ofttimes hidden agenda of goals. there are multiple goals—immediate and long term—that direct classroom practice. Sometimes achieving one goal for a child conflicts with achieving another goal for the same child. What is our aim for the pupil? Conforming to school and societal standards enforced by external contingencies? Acquiring internalized controls and guiding values? Sitting in a seat? Learning to read? Eventually being able to get a job? Surviving in a lethal home or community environment? Returning to the mainstream? Existing in the least extruded special environment? Maximizing potentials? Acquiring self-esteem? Being happy? Being "adjusted"? We have overt and covert goals for each pupil. We may have very different goals for different pupils. There may be a sequence or hierarchy of goals that anticipate a change in tactics over time. The regular school may have keeping a frustrating pupil out of the mainstream as its goal. Thus we have system goals and teacher goals, to say nothing of pupil and parent goals. A special-education teacher recently commented, "If the student doesn't share my goals, I know nothing can be done so I don't waste time on him." And yet the pupil is in the classroom. When Kelly wrote that every person is a human behavior scientist, he might have added that we are all philosophers as well. Our goals imply our values. IEPs are philosophical statements as well as educational and psychological ones.

ASSUMPTIONS OF INDIVIDUAL PSYCHOLOGY

The Nature of Individual Psychology

Our problem is, which psychology is most useful in understanding our pupils, and what we can do to help them? In the face of the complexity of the task, most books in our field present one of two solutions. They push one theory and try to make all behavior fit this one pattern or they present each theory—behaviorism, Freudianism, humanism, ecological theory, for example—and suggest borrowing here and there on an eclectic basis. The shortcoming of the single-theory approach is that no single school of psychology provides answers for the many situations a teacher must face. Although it is certainly of considerable value for a teacher to study the various theories, holding an eclectic position is like participating in a lottery. Bits and pieces of various theories are not sufficient.

There is a third alternative, coherent with the philosophy of service to special pupils evolving from PL 94–142. The new special education is based upon study and planning for *individuals,* through the *IEPC* or Individual Educational Planning Committee. The obvious parallel in psychology is individual psychology, the concentration on the growth of the self. Human beings have a great deal in common, although it is their uniqueness that must be addressed. The personhood of each one of us is as unmatchable as our fingerprints. The study of this uniqueness characterizes personologists or individual psychologists. There are a number of prominent psychologists of this persuasion. We saw that Kelly dealt with individuality through the study of personal constructs—the roles each person evolves. Murray (1938) emphasized the major "themes" that are woven together in unique patterns in each individual. Allport's (1968) major contribution was *The Person in Psychology.* Lecky (1961) emphasized self-consistency. Jersild (1952) was a pioneer in centering on the self-concept. Most recently, Leona Tyler (1978) has emphasized the multiple dimensions essential for understanding individual differences and has brought together cognitive, developmental, social, and learning processes in a new approach to psychology of individual lives (1983).

The emphasis of individual psychology is currently undergoing a metamorphosis, illustrated by the recent work of Kegan (1982) and Babad, Birnbaum, and Benne (1983). This metamorphosis is a result of the blending of developmental and learning psychology with a balanced attention to both the affective and cognitive aspects, which is sometimes called social cognition (Lewis and Brooks-Gunn 1979). The growth of normal and atypical selves is seen as emerging from common processes (Guidano and Liotti 1983). In turn, the result of the progress in individual psychology is a functional way to integrate psychological knowledge as applied to the growth of the self. We are no longer subject to choosing one school of psychology; we utilize whatever any school can contribute to conceptualizing the self.

Thus the emphasis is on the process of comprehending the nature of the pupil's self—its evolution, its current structure, and its amenability to change. Individual psychology functions within a broad set of general concepts that set the parameters of the exploration of selves. These concepts are discussed in the following section.

General Parameters of Individual Psychology

"What you see is what you get" is equivalent to "what you look for is what you find" (Bandura 1974). Our selectivity limits the aspects we consider when we make our image of another human being. The more constricted our viewpoint, the more incomplete our picture of the child will become. If our understanding of the child is superficial or distorted, our efforts to help will falter. Individual psychology puts a premium on utilizing a broad spectrum of concepts in the study of selves. These concepts may appear to be self-evident generalizations, but the reader has a right to know the premises embodied in this book. The following are basic constructs that are employed throughout the text, and they provide the reader with a scan for checking his own assumptions.

Meaning of Human Behavior Is in the Synergy and Pattern of Attributes

The pieces of information we know about an individual take on meaning only when they are seen as part of the pattern that makes up the whole person. The integration of the elements must be considered. For example, an IQ of 85 has a different significance for a child who has a high need for academic achievement than for a child who follows another channel to self esteem—say such as physical-skill performance. A youngster with high anxiety and well-tuned coping mechanisms is not the same as a youngster with high anxiety who panics because he cannot cope. It is the way the attributes combine that produces the personality pattern. As a consequence, individual psychology seeks to know as much as possible and does not rely on isolated, single theories for knowledge. The result is an emphasis on the intensive study of a person, an emphasis that tries to do justice to the complexity and uniqueness of human behavior through ideographic studies.

Biological Predispositions Underlie Much of an Individual Pattern
(Eyde and Fink 1979)

We differ in temperament and disposition, in cognitive and affective potentials, and in rates of growth, to list but a few of many individual differences. These givens of human nature do not in themselves insure either positive or negative socialization. The quality of the learning experience becomes a critical factor, even though certain biological predispositions increase the chance of failure while others increase the chance of success in life. In extreme conditions, individual differences predetermine a limited prognosis—as in the case of true autism—though again there is a range of possible adaptation. Cognitive capacity, the key to so much, may be severely constricted; neurological integration may be deficient. The existence of such limiting factors is in no way an excuse for not providing education to insure maximum progress. There are temporary and sustained biological deficiencies in certain individuals that may be the result of food intake, medication, illnesses, and chemical imbalances, and these can affect their behavior. Growth—normal and delayed—brings profound physiological and psychological changes at all ages, particularly at adolescence. Thus the original and ensuing biological substrata are of essential concern in individual psychology. What we become is the product of the interaction of our given potentials and the particular environment to which we are attached.

Normal Growth Processes Have a Significant Impact on Behavior

Quite apart from planned interventions, growth produces changes in behavior. As a child increases in mental age he makes additions to the storehouse of information—his memory—and thus his capacity to analyze and predict consequences of behavior increases as well. Cognitive mediation increases. Counter to these anticipated developmental changes are the unforeseeable events in life that, as Bandura has stated

(1982), may be most potent determiners of one's future directions. Adolescence combines both biological and social forces as the most dramatic example of developmental conditions that envelop youngsters. Individual psychology takes into consideration the factors of developmental phases in the study of children. Common developmental schemas are those of Piaget (1948, 1952) on intellectual and moral development, Erikson (1963) on affective development, and, Kohlberg (1976) in moral development. Havighurst (1953) sees development as a series of environmentally induced tasks. It is crucial to think in terms of developmental lags in contrast to aberrant development when appraising an SEI pupil.

Children and Youth Are Both Proactive as the Dynamicists Hold, and Reactive, as Behaviorists Espouse

Human beings are proactive in the sense that they are not just recipients of external events; they have inner drives and are selective and searching in efforts to make their way in life. Drives include not only basic biological needs but a wide range of motivations such as curiosity, achievement, and the security of human relationships. Again, the range and patterns are multiple. Children's behavior reflects their efforts to meet these needs; the nature of the self can best be understood in terms of need fulfillment (McCandless 1964). There is considerable strength, direction and vitality in the growing person. The human organism is robust.

At the same time children are also reactive to both subtle and major cue systems in their environments. There are many ways children are taught by cue systems: contingencies in behavior modification as well as modeling and identification are examples of responses to external conditions. Thus ecological forces, the impact of the milieu, and unforeseeable events (Bandura 1982) must be considered to understand the nature of the self. There can be external overloads of such intensity that an individual is overwhelmed and cannot function effectively. Another individual may lose the capacity to cope or follow self-defeating channels in an effort to have his needs met. Susceptibility to the impact of experience differs from person to person. While some children collapse under what objectively seems to be little stress, others survive under seemingly impossible odds. The impact of particular experiences on a given child is a major focus of individual psychology. The same punishment may be seen by one youngster as help for self-control and by another as a reason for rebellion. The meaning of events can be known only through the individual. For example, there are many processes of learning utilized by children. They model; they avoid punishment and seek rewards; they anticipate the future. An individual's choice of process is based upon individual meaning. To appreciate the choice we must know the individual.

The Inner Life of Children and Youth is a Blend of Both Cognitive Processes and Feelings

Thinking enables the use of language and symbolic expression. In cognitive mediation we stop to consider and attempt to organize a plan to resolve the problem we face. But not all of our operations are cognitive or even conscious. The capability of children and adolescents to feel affect is equal to that of adults: they are fearful, angry, helpless; they feel injustice as well as joy, excitement, and love. Emotions have great strength in children even as they do in adults. Anger can motivate violent actions, and the feeling of being uncared for can lead to panic.

Understanding a "self" anticipates knowing not only what the youngster is thinking but what he is feeling as well. The study of individuals puts emphasis on the phenomenological world of the youngster equal to "objective" measures. We may know the child's IQ, but we must also know his self-perceived IQ, and the significance of this to the individual. Children try to make sense of and explain their world and in doing so create rationalizations as to why things happen.

The Continuity Hypothesis

Were there no continuity to behavior, there would be no predictability; if continuity were all-powerful, efforts at change would be ridiculous. Individual psychology pays attention to what behavior resists change and what behavior can be altered. Change refers both to the person and the system in which the person functions. Life history is important in predicting individual behavior but no more so than the current field of forces operating on the individual and the goals the individual envisions for the future. Anticipations as well as past experience shape behaviors. We have probably underestimated the resiliency and verve of the human organism for survival if we give past experience sole credit for shaping an individual. While this view engenders hope for the efforts of intervention, it is impossible to overestimate the energy necessary to replace an atypical continuity with a typical one. Ofttimes failure results not because we are unaware of what should be done to insure a healthy development, but because as a society, we do not invest the time and psychic energy needed to produce the desired change.

Deviance and Normality

Compared with the SEI children we seek to help, most teachers and other professionals have experienced supportive conditions leading to normal development in children. Given their past and current living conditions, the oddity is not how aberrant the SEI pupil's behavior is but how they can hold together at all. The nature of the deviant self is not foreign to the nature of the normal self. The processes producing both are shared; differences are a matter of degree, not of kind. What so-called normal person has not suffered periods of acute anxiety or depression, never once indulged in thoughtless sociopathic behavior, or felt alienated and apart? In the so-called normal, the deviation of periods of anxiety and depression are less severe and extensive; we bounce back because of adequate coping skills and compensatory attributes. But we must recognize that SEI impairments are part of the essentially human condition.

The Self-Concept as the Core

Individual psychology perceives the self-concept as the distillation of experience. Behavior is a product of the self operating under a given condition. Depending upon the individual, there are many ways to enter a pupil's life space to produce change. The choice of method depends both upon the nature of the self, and upon the malleability of the attribute we wish to change. Because the "support system" surrounding the child is crucial in maintaining and altering the self-concept, the children's immediate environments are where interventions can best be applied. Of the three areas where children spend many hours—school, home, and neighborhood—the school is the only environment that is professionally monitored. The school has vast resources with access to the self through the social components, the wide variety of learning experiences which can be introduced, and the presence of a sensitive, caring adult who is in charge.

Implicit Goals

Psychologists are reluctant to take an explicit stand on their goals for human beings, but as we have seen, goals are an underlying condition in work with SEI children. Two sets of goals, individual and social, are important in our efforts. For the individual, we have objectives such as the elimination of chronic psychological pain and discomforture. We can even aim for periods of calm, enjoyment, play, and pleasure in life. Further, we would enhance relationships with others, and cultivate potential in all areas of scholastic skills. There are social goals as well; remedial education hopes to encourage a set of values that reflect the rights of others to their person, property, and dignity. In short, the social goal is a reasonable conformity to social norms so that SEI pupils can live in the real world. Some SEI pupils need help in both individual and social areas. Others have specific aspects of impairment. Inevitably, because of the severity of biological and experiential limitations, some of these youngsters will not achieve an average status, nevertheless the goals remain.

INDIVIDUAL PSYCHOLOGY AND
THE SCIENTIFIC STUDY OF THE PERSON

The essence of individual psychology is the study of the person. One seeks to know as much as it is possible to know about the individual over time and in multiple settings. Consistency of a person's behavior is revealed by the intraindividual complex combined with the significant characteristics of the external situation. This is not to deprecate the importance of classical studies, which contrast the *average* difference between the performance of a "control" group and an "experimental" group. The problem with any classical study is that teachers do not teach the hypothetical average pupil. How does one apply "average" results to an individual? The striking psychological fact is the large individual variance in the responses of SEI pupils. What works for one youngster fails with another. Teachers come to know their pupils and compensate for such differences. Some pupils defy predictability even after extensive multiple-discipline study. Nevertheless, the efforts of group experimental studies have produced and continue to produce valuable psychological knowledge concerning the general relationship of variables. However, individual psychology is less concerned with the general relationship of variables such as say intelligence, anxiety, self-efficacy and achievement *between* large groups of pupils, than in the various relationships of intelligence, anxiety, self-efficacy and achievement *within* particular individuals. The intraindividual pattern is the key to understanding, and subsequently, to the IEP.

Originally individual psychology was dependent upon the case study as its primary tool. Case studies, including objective and projective findings, are still important, but the technique is subject to risk. The richness of information and the effort to examine many different aspects are valuable. The risk is the possibility of a vague or imprecise interpretation, because interpretations are left to teachers, clinicians, or more complicated still, group case conferences. There is a very high probability of personal bias in such interpretations. The data assembled vary from case to case. In general, case studies are better at "explaining" past development than in "predicting" future behavior.

Individual psychology makes use of "N of 1" technology for scientific studies (Kazden and Tuma 1982; Hersen and Barlow 1976). There are two styles of N of 1 rigorous examination of individual behavior. One style is the behaviorists' charts where a baseline for given behavior is recorded, an intervention imposed, and a change in frequency of the given behavior noted. The intervention may be removed to check the continuance of changes in behavior. Usually highly specific behaviors are observed, isolated from other aspects of the individual.

The so-called clinical N of 1 studies are of a different nature. They employ multiple attribute measures of each individual to make behavior predictions. When two individuals have the similar profiles of measures, the predictions for behavior are the same. Such multimeasure profiles can be subjected to statistical tests (Lorr 1983).

If there are several measures they can be analyzed for subgroups of similar individuals, rather than stopping at the large-group averages. Each subgroup is made up of N's of 1 that are alike in certain salient characteristics. Then the behavior of various subgroups can be tested against a dependent variable. The situations must also have similar attributes for the individuals under study. Studies employing profile analysis or cluster analysis that test out assumptions on groups of individuals with like characteristics are appearing with increasing frequency. Teachers have done this since time immemorial or in an informal way: "Jimmy is just like George, whom I had last year. He behaves in just the same way." Eventually, true typologies may replace the present special-education categories that are far from pure types and contain much overlap.

For several reasons individual psychology offers no panacea. First, psychological measures are far from definitive. Measures of anxiety, for example, lack adequate reliability and validity. Second, we have even less ability in assessing the ecological conditions than we had in assessing emotional conditions. A given classroom structure does not necessarily have the same meaning for all pupils. Objective and subjective reality differ. Third, there is as yet no methodology capable of analyzing the complexes of internal and external attributes that interact as a system to produce the behavior we are seeking to understand (Kahle 1979). We are far from precise. Nevertheless, special education, with the focus on the individual pupil through the IEP, is dependent upon individual psychology.

My purpose in this section has been to indicate, in a very general way, some of the particular emphases of individual psychology and the emergence of an applicable scientific methodology. We turn now to the central integrating concept of this psychology, the study of the self.

INDIVIDUAL PSYCHOLOGY AND THE DEVELOPING SELF

Teachers, and other nurturing professionals, interact with specific individual pupils; an abstract, theoretical child does not exist. Their goal is to understand the nature of that individual pupil, what he or she thinks and feels, and to assess what tests and observations reveal about the nature of the pupil's life. The objective is to know this other human being well enough to plan useful interventions. We can neither relate usefully to nor plan effectively for those we do not understand, though—at best—knowledge of another is always limited to some degree. Though theoretical information is useful to appreciate the nature of an individual, the knowledge of theory per se is not the goal.

Kagan (1982) asks the question "Why is the state of a person's evolution so crucial to understanding him or her?" (p. 113). His answer is that the way in which a person settles what is self and what is other is the key to personal meaning. We understand another not only by knowing his or her life experiences, but by knowing what those experiences have meant to the individual. This the phenomenological condition of how each individual constructs the truth of his or her life.

The propositions of individual psychology enumerated under the section on general parameters provide guidelines for considering how individual selfhood comes about; no two of us are precisely alike. Our patterns are woven from different biological and experiental elements, somehow merging into a more or less integrated whole. Brewster Smith (1978) holds that achieving selfhood is the universal human quest. Normal self-growth is the organization of successful patterns of coping for the individual who is compliant with social standards. Aberrant self-growth is the organization of patterns that are linked to excessive internal and external conflict (Wylie 1961; 1979).

The term *self* is generally equivalent to personality and consists of the central characteristics we assign to an individual as well as the individual's overall dominant nature. A great deal of effort is spent in order to describe the nature of an SEI pupil. We test, observe, and interview in order to construct our idea of what the pupil is really like. We do well to remember that our description may or may not coincide with the child's own self-perception, termed the phenomenological self. William James once remarked that when two persons meet there are really six selves: each as he or she thinks he or she is, each as seen by the other, and each as he or she really is. The confusion among the various selves as seen by pupil and teacher make for much of our difficulty.

The *self-concept* consists of salient characteristics of the person. As indicated above, phenomenological self-concepts are the characteristics that an individual accepts as or is willing to admit belong to his being. The observed self-concept is the self assigned by external tests and observations. Coherence of the observed and phenomenological self-concept varies considerably from person to person. In describing their attributes, most children include elements of their social role within their families, with their peers, and with authority. Another category is their physical nature and sexual identity. The achieving sphere includes accomplishment in school, unique skills, and special talents, in other words, the "I can do" self. One of the important cues here is the accuracy of "what I can do" and actual test information. Another segment of the self-concept consists of a child's code, or moral beliefs.

Self-esteem (often confused with self-concept) is reserved for one's appraisal of the self-concepts one has (Rosenberg 1979). If one judges his attributes to be satisfactory, one feels good about himself or herself. We say he or she has high self-esteem. Many SEI pupils have low self-esteem. When they evaluate their characteristics they feel helpless, inadequate, "bad" or unworthy. They are self-perceived failures. Some individuals are quite independent in making self-evaluations, caring little for what others may say. However most of us, and certainly most children—who are after all dependent on others for survival—use external reference persons to ascertain how well they are doing, looking for corroboration from parents, teachers, and peers.

If the teacher were allowed to know only a single condition concerning a pupil, he or she would ask about the pupil's self-esteem because this self-evaluation is a central aspect of any individual's selfhood. Bandura (1974) has written that self-esteem is the central aspect of a person: most individuals will do whatever is possible in order to maintain the semblance of high personal self-regard. We deny and defend ourselves against low self-esteem; depression results if we capitulate.

Over time, certain aspects of the self gradually permeate one's selfhood. These attributes underlie one's being as elements of one's *identity*. For example, as the individual becomes aware of being a creature apart from others, his body image emerges. In this case, identity is based on physical strength and motor competency. Adults are continually describing children with reference to these attributes, and these judgments become lodged in the child's perceptual system. In a way, what adults put into a child's identity becomes a self-fulfilling prophecy; the child will tend to select things that fit adult expectancy and avoid activities that do not. Very early and forever, one's sexual identity and feelings about this identity are formed. Also, human beings come to be identified as having a general style or temperament. People accumulate identity elements as part of a certain family, ethnic group, social group, socioeconomic level, and religious or political group. Sometimes identity is reinforced in ceremonies and rituals whose intent is to label. Other times the message may be obtained only through subliminal innuendo. As children develop they may accept and take pride in or rebel against the implications of having a given identity.

Most of us also develop an *ideal self-image,* what we would like to be if our dreams were to come true. If this ideal self is not too distant from our real self and is comprised of real possibilities, it serves as a guide for effort. When there is considerable disparity between what we are and what we would like to be or think we can ever be, or what parents or others hold up as what we should be, we can become anxious or depressed. Life seems hopeless. Some adolescents are driven to suicide by the impossibility of reaching these expectations.

Now it is crucial to remember that adults may hold very inaccurate judgments about a youngster's self-concept and self-esteem. Not everything is of equal importance to an individual, and aspects of major concern to a teacher may be seen as low priorities by a youngster. Self-esteem is responsive to characteristics that are of significance to the person. If a pupil cares about reading and thinks he is performing poorly, his self-esteem will diminish. Adults usually assume that children echo their own hierarchy of values; nothing could lead a teacher further astray. For example, a successful delinquent may have high self-esteem in spite of his delinquencies and regardless of his failure to read.

Sometimes a youngster's self-esteem or personal regard becomes dependent upon a specific issue. Even though there are other positive life experiences, they do not compensate. Teachers may like you, mother may like you, and peers may like you; but father cared so little that he deserted you, and this single condition makes you feel both unloved and angry. We can all remember how not being liked by a particular member of the opposite sex during adolescence affected our competence level, bringing on devaluation and depression.

The manifest behavior of the child we teach is the visible evidence of the given self interacting with external conditions and struggling to maintain self-esteem. We shall later see how even accepting help can be deprecating. The psychology of normal self-development provides a base from which we can study so-called abnormal development. All of us try to behave according to the model provided by our phenomenological self-concept, our self-esteem status, and our (perceived) essential identity. The moment-by-moment flow of behavior is modulated by what we think we are as we confront the external world. If we think we are "born losers" we give up, because there is no use trying. If we have low self-esteem we may capitulate, deny, or struggle. If we think persons who are like us (with similar identities) are always being cheated we generate certain protective responses toward others. If our moral self dictates that it is all right to steal if we don't get caught, we act accordingly. Sometimes the self-image is evident and the linkage to behavior direct. More often the nature of the true self is hidden or not even part of the conscious process, and the linkage is obscure. The point is that our behavior reflects our "self."

The purpose of the study of the self is to come to know the essential nature of the pupil as a totally functioning person, which is never an easy task. Each of us remains to some degree a mystery to all others; however, it is possible to gain a working understanding of a pupil's self. The final goal is the use of this understanding to effectively relate to and assist the pupil toward a more adequate self-concept, a more positive self-esteem, and a sustaining identity.

ACQUIRING A SELF

It is our purpose now to explore the evolution of this complicated entity, selfhood. What is normal expectation and what threatens social and emotional development during childhood and adolescence? We are interested both in what should happen at various ages and what can go wrong.

The infant begins the self-formation process; this is continued as the young child individuates and moves through the consolidation period of preadolescence. Many self-changes occur at adolescence. The evolution continues at young adulthood where the work-world identity is added. Erikson demonstrates that throughout adulthood new aspects of selfhood come into being. Conditions can occur that warp the self at any of these stages.

Preschool Self-Development and Problem Areas

The Infant

Special education services play an active (and in some states mandatory) role from birth on. Much of the work will be in cooperation with medical disciplines, where the goal is prevention of problems in the future through genetic counseling.

The neonate begins life biologically endowed with a capacity to respond, an ability to learn, a high attentiveness to the human face and human speech, and a given temperamental disposition. Autonomous self-regulatory systems take care of bodily needs. Social interaction begins at once, and with it, social learning (Lamb and Sherrod 1981).

The early years are characterized by a symbiotic relationship between the infant and his or her caregivers. As Kaye (1983) so aptly puts it, parents create people. Affective life, for the most part, is a transaction that takes place during feeding, other care giving, and mutual play. To Kaye, parents are as much a part of the child's endowment as the child's own genes. Attachment is a mutual condition of both baby and caretaker. The infant is provided with opportunities to grow in a cultural microcosm of conventions designed by the caretaker. Learning is mutual; the patterns that emerge are a joint product of baby and parent. Both are learning new behaviors. Nothing changes the family operation as much as the newborn. An infant's dependency is not the same as helplessness, as anyone who has been a provider knows. In fact the power of the infant on parents provokes strong reactions ranging from intensified love to abuse.

If there is consistency in care, the face of the caretaker and the routines of exchange become sorted out during the first year. Self knowledge is acquired through social interaction. The infant learns that certain behaviors produce given reactions. Along with the formation of bonds that is taking place, individuation also occurs.

Gradually, as motor control and eye-body movements consolidate into more coherent sensorimotor behaviors, the infant explores what is of himself and what is of another. Sometimes this is accomplished by biting the self, or sucking a foot. Gradually the physical self emerges. This is the start of the body image, the *me*.

Popper and Eccles (1977) make the essential point that *I* is central to experience and interpretation because sensory input is processed by the self. When the infant has the capacity to experience and interpret, the self-conscious person gradually emerges. Interpretations involve memory and thinking processes and result in assembling cues for appropriate action. Thus it is evident that limits of the processing ability (intelligence level and brain malfunction, diverting effects of overwhelming stress, as well as temperamental inclinations) can lead to disturbance in the self. The development of language and of symbolic thought enable the ordering of reality, including self-knowledge.

The presence of trust in the infant at the end of his first year indicates two things. He cannot trust the environment unless it embodies considerable consistency. A little one has difficulty in consolidating responses (and thus a concept of self) to widely variant caretaker styles. The other aspect of trust is feeling good, being well taken care of, learning that his needs will be met from milk to "mothering," that he will be stimulated and played with. Feeling good is the beginning of high self-esteem. It has been said that it is impossible to spoil a one year old.

What then constitute risk factors (Fraiberg 1980)? Obviously, in a symbiotic relationship there are two sources of risk: those of the caretaker and those of the infant. Many SEI children and youth reflect histories where parenting was inadequate, deficient, almost totally absent, or even abusive. Sometimes there have been a series of caretakers. The danger inherent in these conditions is a result of the interactive nature of early selfhood formation (Anthony 1974; 1978).

The caretaker must be able to spend time with and give affection to the infant, finding delight in their exchanges. The exciting times of learning to walk and talk are celebrated in a supporting family. Here again, biologically ordained significant developmental delays or aberrations can cause tensions while advanced accomplishments are fed back to the growing baby as great successes. Obviously economic and emotional stress adds stress to an individual caretaker's personal inadequacies. Interventions at this period range from therapy and support groups for the parent to economic aid. On the other side, the good baby at this period is one who eats and digests well, sleeps according to pattern and who responds in a way that gives pleasure to the adult. Babies who do not respond positively to cuddling and who do not interact socially are twice at risk: once from whatever biological limitations lie behind the behavior and once from the strain that this puts on positive interactions. A case in point is child autism, a biological disorder where the child does not respond normally to social stimulation and appears unable to learn useful social responses or the symbolic use of language.

As Thomas and Chess (1973) and Thomas (1981) point out, some children are easy to raise, some difficult, and some next to impossible due to arrhythmic and other temperamental disaffinities. Added to the differences in child potential are the equally influential differences in parenting potential. Abrasive interactions can set the stage for persistent stress early in life. Adjustment can go from bad to worse. Cameron (1977) has studied incompatible child-parent combinations and finds they are precursors to much problem behavior. Parents are frustrated when the basic lessons of the age-level are introduced and the child fails to learn them at an acceptable rate. Difficulties surround management of eating, sleeping, elimination, and impulse control. To reduce the risk of establishing an embedded, exacerbating relationship, both parent and infant are considered in treatment. Are there better ways of responding to the difficult temperament? Is there a physical problem such as a food sensitivity or allergy? The major intervention comes through diagnostic centers that provide a total assessment and an analysis of actual behavior in significant interactions (playing, feeding, etc.) so that alternative behavior can be introduced to alleviate parental frustration. Because of the number of high-risk infants now being saved and identified by new medical techniques, special education intervention can begin at birth.

The Toddler

Kagan (1982) finds that appreciation of standards of behavior, recognition of ability to achieve goals, anxiety about failure, and awareness of one's feeling states normally appear by the last half of the second year. The skills of locomotion and speech make a vast expansion in learning possible. Control of bodily functions marks a huge developmental step in most children's lives and in all parents' lives. If the toddler has learned to trust, the next step will be in establishing a sense of independence. There are new vistas for both mutual enjoyment and conflict with caretakers. Sometimes, before an infant has "learned" his parents, he may have had to deal with additional child raisers in child-care centers or nursery schools. He may spend more of his waking time away from home than with either natural parent.

In early childhood we see the emergence of the concept of self—the independent "I am"—and even the beginnings of positive or negative self-esteem. Little children see themselves as being "bad" or "good." One observation session of mothers and tots in a supermarket will demonstrate the pervasiveness of this perception. Affective states begin to be defined. While thinking is egocentric, the increasing use of symbols and language enable the organization of the external world and communication skills. With age comes differentiation and the struggle for an independent existence.

People are always talking about how a child is growing: a favored activity is recording the height marks over time on the back of a closet door. Teachers of small children help them to define the physical self by tracing outlines of their bodies on wrapping paper, identifying the drawings by name, and hanging them up; this may be a source of pride or embarrassment. One of the first aspects of identity to become clarified is that of sex. Being a little girl or boy begins to define many things about your life and what others expect of you. Siblings, if you have them, are another social laboratory; they often are vigorous definers of who you are. Certain clothes, a favorite toy, or even a blanket are extensions of yourself. Kegan (1982) sees growth as centered upon the "two greatest yearnings of human life," which are in opposition: the need to be included, connected, and attached to others, and the need to be independent and autonomous. The self who does not have the proper balance of these yearnings is in a problematic state. However, when we say that the child needs limits, the child does not need an arbitrary, overpowering adult but rather involvement with adults in the personal struggle over limit keeping. According to Kagan's studies (1982), during the last half of the second year the child will show smiles of satisfaction at mastery, recognize achievable goals, and show anxiety over potential failure. There is an awareness of self-feeling states; self-consciousness appears and aggression is recognized as prohibited behavior.

Children are usually admonished with evaluations, such as "you are a good girl" or "you are a bad girl." With these admonitions adults are also making value judgments and comparisons about sexual preferences, appearance, skill levels, general behavior, and whatnot. Adults are teaching self; they are creating human beings. As a child reflects on these evaluative statements he creates his own self-esteem. This is his judgment about his success or failure in meeting parental expectations. At early stages the natures of self-perception and judgments tend to be diffuse and unstable, but out of hundreds of evaluative statements certain generalizations gradually emerge.

Small children's mental processes are imperfectly understood. Sometimes the bits and pieces of experience are adhered to in rigid ways: sequences of behavior must be replicated exactly, specific toys must be available, particular clothes or foods are enthusiastically sought or vehemently rejected, a "golly" blanket to drag around as Linus does in the "Peanuts" comic strip may become an essential part of existence. Age and birth dates are attributes of high value. "I am four and I can ride a trike" helps to establish self-identity.

For the first few years a child's self-concept is rudimentary. Cognitive schemas are primitive but organization is beginning. The child is egocentric and narcissistic; moral concepts take the form of fear of disapproval or punishment. Locomotion and coordination and simple motor skills mean autonomy. If things do not go well, shame and doubt will result as low self-esteem.

Keller, Ford, and Meacham (1978) studied the self-descriptions of normal preschoolers through "tell about you" (I can, I am, I have), as a sentence completion. The most salient response categories were action items, habits, and competencies—or things the child could do. Body–image references and references to possessions were less frequent.

A direct question will usually elicit a response which refers to being good or bad. The SEI child, when asked how his parent or preschool teacher sees him, will often reflect on being "bad" or "good."

Many professionals see the seeds of later selves in this early period. Mahler (1968) believes problems of separation from the mother is a primary progenitor of later difficulty. Parens (1979) looks to the first three years of life as the start of aggressive behavior. We can agree that there may be self-concept developments at this early period that require intervention. If reasonable expectations are set and encouraged by gentle but persistent persuasion, the child's necessary stage of narcissism should become muted with the advent of socialization.

These processes would be hazardous for even the normal child were it not for the resilience of most children. If there were but one way, one perfect way, to be brought up, very few children would ever make it. But significant human flexibility enables the expansive learning that takes place by the time of toddlerhood, with each child possessing a unique pattern of development.

Self-development can become impaired as a consequence of birth defects, genetic factors, and—of course—by poor parenting and poor teaching. Feeding and sleep problems may result. Some little ones are always driven or hyperactive. Others experience high anxiety when mother is not visible; overfearfulness may be characteristic of these children. Communication disorders are diagnostically important. Toilet training can be the setting for intense battles. Compulsive masturbatory activity, hair pull, and "raw" thumb sucking are cues that expert consultation is necessary. Normally, one expects some assertive temper outbursts and a gradual gain in control. Considerable variations in rate and style of self-consolidation are normal, but persistent and sustained failure to integrate a self deserves scrutiny. One helpful method of evaluation is available for young children who attend a child-care center or nursery school. If, in the hands of a good teacher, given a period of some weeks, overshyness, aggressiveness, and fears of separation are not mitigated, it is appropriate to seek consultation.

Possible interventions center around changes in the interaction patterns between the child and significant adults. Special diagnostic preschools, home visiting, and parent counseling may be utilized. However, at the same time, the child's need to make his own explorations and to interact with toys in play, must be emphasized as well. There is the "thing world" as well as the "people world" to explore and organize.

One of the important methods of resolving SEI complications for the preschool child is the diagnostic preschool. In such a nursery school a competent teacher works with mothers who participate with their children. A full complement of mental health professionals is available. Individual assistance and group sessions are provided to discuss problems and strategies. At the same time the child has both the nursery group and individual play and talk therapy as indicated. Disturbed children show many fears such as fear of desertion or fear of the bogey man (the latter is a threat used to control many children). They may be very anxious and ofttimes are angry. Their self-concept reflects an inadequacy to cope as well as "being bad." Again, diagnosis is of the matrix of social relationships, not of the child alone (Anthony 1974; 1978).

Questions that even young children ask are more simple versions of questions adults ask throughout their lives. Looking at family photographs where he or she is missing often brings the question Where was

I? Not born yet while others were here? These are versions of questions of from where we came, how, and why. What are we about? What is the purpose of it all? When a pet or relative dies, where do they go? These questions have to be answered at some level that seems reasonable and makes sense to the child. The young child has a limited grasp of abstract concepts to be sure, but understanding will grow as cognitive power develops. For a normal youngster, the self evolves through digesting experience with the help of reasonable adults and peers who serve as guides.

Those who focus on infants and preschool children will know that this is but a brief excursion into the psychology of early self-development at a fascinating and complex age. Details of early emotional life are set forth in Plutchik and Kellerman, *Emotions in Early Development* (1983). For those who deal with the consequences of this age in later years, attention to what has gone before—as the self emerged—may give clues that will resolve what appears at a later time.

Self-Concept–Self-Esteem in the Elementary Years and General Problem Areas

By the start of formal schooling, the child is usually a multiactive going entity. There is (more) stability and relationship among the concepts that are used to deal with the world. If family socialization has been adequate, and school is reasonable, school becomes an invigorating place for new exploration, companions, and activities. Each accomplishment is enjoyed and welded onto the expanding self.

In the elementary years the child learns much about logical operations by using cognitive processes to solve problems and generalizes about rules. If things progress favorably this period leads to Erikson's period of industry where the self is now able to invest in learning, mastery of the three R's, and other skills. Self problems develop around the inability to learn and do things—a condition that results in a sense of inferiority and weakness, visible in many special pupils. Normally, dependency on parents lessens, and relationships with peers begin their course to eventual dominance. Sex roles intensify. By the end of elementary school, we have a far more complicated child self with which to deal.

There are several added facets of the self at preadolescence—the *public self,* how you want to appear to others, and the *ideal self,* what you would like to be. The ideal self comes from watching older children, parents, and television. The quality of the models children adopt is often a source of adult anxiety. By now a child has also learned that it does not pay to tell adults everything—the *private self* is emerging. At all costs a child will attempt to maintain his self-esteem.

It is regrettable how remote most adults are from the selves and lives of the preadolescent. Young gives a child's eye–view of grown ups in *Life among the Giants* (1965), which should be required reading for elementary school teachers once every year. Young points out that the adult sense of children's inferiority makes it difficult for children to communicate with adults because adults don't listen to children. Children are concerned with concrete specifics and with their own needs. They live in the present hour and struggle for control of their emotions. Adults are seen as omnipotent masters of a strange world of capricious power. A few youngsters become dedicated "giant killers." We have difficulty helping preadolescents because we have forgotten what it is like to be a preadolescent.

Sometimes the blatancy and frankness of preadolescents belies their subtlety. Just as the infant demonstrates deep emotional activity, the preadolescent is fraught with profound feelings of joy, fear, love, hate, anxiety, pride, and hope—the fundamental stuff of emotional life. Certain identity factors become incorporated: sex identity, race or ethnic base, general temperament, and being a winner or loser.

The cognitive processes have reached a more sophisticated stage of universal questioning. What is alive? What is me? What is death? Who are you? What will happen if . . . ? What was I like when I was little? These questions have to do with the comprehension of the human journey. An excellent way to identify with the preadolescent and adolescent youngster is to know the questions that children ask. Byler, Lewis, and Totman cover this area in *Teach Us What We Want to Know* (1969). To the preadolescent, a dead pet is a philosophical, religious, and personal experience. Also, adults are always giving him messages, reading his mind, and making him do things. It is as if they know him before he knows himself.

As a younger child, there is much about the world and yourself that is incomprehensible; emotions are especially difficult to understand. It gradually comes about that you think you are better known by those outside yourself than by you. Adults always seem to know everything and seem to have all the answers, even about you. Big people outguess you and predict what you are going to do even before you do it. They also interpret to you how you feel and what you really mean. They tell you that you love your brother when you think you are angry. They say they know when you are joyful, sad, or mad and tell you so.

They tell you how you are and how you should be. Most of all, your mother knows you inside and out. Your mother can tell what you are thinking and when you are lying. Teachers can, too. They can see right through you. They might discover your secrets—until you have no more. Yet, you are dependent on adults for your existence.

It is often frustrating, being in the power of adults. However, if the adults are kind, if they respect you, and protect you, you have a sense of security that you do not wish to upset by defying them. Dependency and comfort serve as a background while you work on your independence. Asking riddles is one delightful way of showing off information you have that others do not. You experiment with knowledge that is your own, or which is shared with a best friend. When asked Where were you? Who were you with? What were you doing? it is best to answer ambiguously Playing, with the kids, just around. Certain words you learn are not for use with adults. Your "collections" are an extension of yourself and are not to be cleaned up. They are not junk.

There are certain aspects of life that are so important that their management will determine whether or not a youngster will succeed or fail. Are you minding as you should? Are you getting your schoolwork? Are you happy and do you know how to play on your own? Do you get along with other kids and have friends? If you fail in these tasks, someone will complain.

The conditions necessary to maintain trust are still essential. The child remains dependent upon adults and their love for subsistence and psychological welfare, although there is a big move to coparallel peer reliance by the middle of preadolescence. Central features of the self, general characteristics and unique aspects that are the most "me," are recognized. Certain values have become articulate as part of the self. Values usually reflect those of adults who were important at the start. By the end of preadolescence, values are internalized into rules of right and wrong. A child who has not developed an acceptable code is cause for concern. The self-tasks of this age are essentially acquiring a satisfactory school role, family role, and peer role in order to maintain self-esteem. Comparative school performance makes evident to the child whether he is a successful, an average, or a low performer. Children make their own judgments regardless of what the achievement tests say. (The results are not likely to be shared anyway). Aspirations that you have or that others have for you, enter in. For some there is much joy in mastering the basic school subjects. For others, it is a massive frustration with low personal yield. But escape is impossible: if you are not learning, there are special people who will inflict intensified "help" upon you.

Body image continues to be critical. "He looks like a real boy"; "she is a cute little girl—so feminine." Then there are the "failed" ones: the obese ones, the frail and sick ones, and those with socially unattractive physical characteristics.

Sex-role identification becomes more significant at this period and can be the source of problems or pride. Those who are confused, unhappy, or in conflict about their sexual nature need help. It is sad to see some youngsters become a "real boy" or "real girl" by rejecting behaviors that have no intrinsic sexual identification but are culturally devalued. The family's attitude toward sex identification is often confused and filled with covert messages of sexual preference. You may see that Daddy always wins arguments even if he has to use physical threats. Male comes to equal macho. Fortunately, severe gender problems are not a common difficulty, although the general value and perogatives of one's sex may be an issue.

There is one's role in the family to consider, including sibling relationships. The significance of being oldest, middle, or youngest; of being a boy or a girl; of being the quick one, or the slow one, find their way into the self concept. The child's nature and character are being defined by parental expectations. Certain children become a family scapegoat; others are imprinted with a goody-goody self-image. Family roles embody expectations; expectations get built into both self and self-esteem. Individual psychology emphasizes the unique way that each person works out such matters. There are tremendously different patterns of coping that are normal and healthy. It is normal, though puzzling, when a quiet child grows up in an energetic family or a child who enjoys fantasy and reading grows up in a pragmatic environment. Just as cultural variation is normal, so is personal variation. In such a circumstance the problem begins if someone in power judges the reasonable to be unsatisfactory. Peers label some different children "freaks." Parents fear for the future of some children and openly predict disaster or unconsciously provide cues that express the same message.

Peers normally become important at this age, equal to and sometimes predominating over family ties. If there is no adequate family support, peers may serve as a substitute for family. If there is family security then the youngster is free to move out and explore peer relationships in a positive way. Failure to develop an adequate social self is a major behavior problem at this age. Both withdrawn behavior and aggressive behavior indicate this problem and are causes for referral, although the most prominent reason for referral is failure at school tasks. Having no friends, and no special pal, is a defeat that requires defensive reaction. Social skills to get along with adults and peers are survival skills. How do you negotiate with others? Are you to be a leader, follower, or rejectee? Do you buy, beg, or pretend about social acceptance? A child who is happy at home may find his nemesis in the peer culture. He may find his family's ways fail to fit the peer culture. This can make a child the target of cruel behavior. Being big or little for your age, attractive or disfigured, all of these are important because of the social references they induce. Children are labeled by peers and adults long before the psychologist affixes a label.

At this time, too, since the child's world expands, matters of ethnic, racial, and socioeconomic condition have to be dealt with. Television, the master communicator, gives the child a new awareness of differences. It supplies primitive fantasy to substitute for the lack of power you feel. Fairy stories, as Bettelheim (1976) so aptly describes, portray the victory of the chid over the adult in a make believe way. Television superheroes have the attributes the child wishes for: power, intelligence, resources, magic talents. Television heroes serve as primary role models for many children who have no close adult identification figures of good character or who lack heroes with fine attributes. Unfortunately, there is an oversupply of aggressive quack television heroes. The child who does not distinguish between the fantasy and reality in this matter will have significant difficulty. A precursor to future aggressive behavior is an addiction to television violence. However, living in a dream world is different than having dreams. There are times where the real world is too oppressive and demeaning; one then substitutes a world-of-pretend as an escape.

At this stage, self-esteem is still external to a considerable extent, a reflection of family opinion or, now, peer opinion. Other adults, relatives, and teachers make contributions too. For example, a fourth-grade girl shared with me a problem in self-esteem, wondering what was the matter with her because her teacher had given her none of the special favors given to her classmates. There is also some internal evaluation that stems from one's own judgment of one's performance. Helping a youngster with self-esteem means changing the attributes of the self and/or the evaluation of the self. The various combinations of self and self-evaluation that create the same problem—failure in school for example—are endless. A child can be an effective student but not care much about it, or be a poor student and not value achievement; he may maintain high self-esteem based on the other abilities. The essential thing to remember is that self-concept and self-esteem form an idiosyncratic complex. There is often a tendency to devaluate failure areas in to order to avoid low self-esteem. The child who is at the mercy of low self-esteem is depressed and defeated. There is no hope, or the false hope of great success, which is not really believed. The fact of childhood depression is only recently being recognized. If I pretend to be smart but in truth feel I am stupid, a great deal of energy is needed to keep up pretenses as well as to deal with the fear of being found out. Failure in sports may override the successes in the other 85 percent of life in the child's view. With equal intensity an area of high achievement may diminish the desire to do well in other segments. Some children cannot have high self-esteem until a particular condition is met—until they learn to read, for example. Others compensate across areas of success and failure, so that being good at games makes up for poor reading.

When one looks at the self-concept complex at preadolescence, it becomes clear why there are so many avenues of intervention to assist the inadequate child. It also becomes clear that there are many places and ways in which deviation may take root when we consider the effects of biological limitations and chaotic life conditions upon the self-concept in this formative period.

We have observed that increasing numbers of children are coming to school at risk because their self-development remains immature. School is a place designed for children who have absorbed the lessons from an effective primary group. The normal family, by providing security along with food, clothing, and shelter, has prepared its children for school in three major ways. Children are ready to trust because their parents have been trustworthy. They are ready to meet social expectations because the family has set and maintained standards. They have a sense of their selfhood because of their positive role in the family and the regard in which they are held. For such children, school is a new, extended world of promise for which they are ready.

But the child who comes without these accomplishments will be compelled to work on them even though the school is a secondary group, rather than a family group. In seeking the answer about trust, the child will subject the teacher to testing again and again. Behavior codes will be ignored because the precursors were never taught to obey codes in the family. The schoolroom has so much less to give than a good family, and so many "siblings" to care for, that a deficient child is likely to lose out in his effort to develop the self, which certainly takes precedence for him over learning the school curriculum. The confrontation between child needs and school expectations in such a situation usually results in defensiveness on the child's part. This acting out exacerbates and the result is a *problem self*, so labeled early in the school career.

When self-development becomes impaired at the preadolescent age, achievement problems often occur. Aggressive outbursts, anxiety (excessive fears and nervous habits) and withdrawal are signs that the self-concept is impaired (Kaplan 1980). Sarnoff (1976) sees children of this age as labile and quite reactive to external conditions. One first seeks to amelioriate the conditions that are producing the stress. Talking therapy, relationship therapy (big brothers/sisters), therapeutic activity groups, and academic therapy are other channels for giving help. Parents, or parent substitutes, are to be included in the treatment efforts; the child is still of the family whether or not his problems are related to the family.

Children may use different terms, but they are well aware of the self and self-esteem. For example they know the meaning of racial discrimination. A third-grade black boy demonstrated this when he said, regarding his lack of motivation to do arithmetic although it would help him get ahead in the future, "It doesn't matter. Who would hire a nigger anyway?"

Many children also feel a high responsibility for their lives. A sixth-grade girl told her teacher, following a discussion of her gang of kids who went to various houses to fool around after school, getting into liquor and experimenting with sex, and of her "lousy parents" (professionals who were never home after school), "I know what you're going to say and you shouldn't say it." The teacher asked what she expected to hear. "You are going to say how bad it is my parents aren't around. But you should tell me it's up to me. I can get into trouble or not. I know what I should do. It's up to me." There are other times when the preadolescent youngster feels responsible for conditions over which he or she has no control.

When things go well—which is not to say smoothly, for normal growth is fraught with periods of distress and reintegration—the result is a healthy self. The child develops the capacity for an age-appropriate affective life, a sense of self-esteem, and the ability to cope with reasonable expectations. The capacity to care for others emerges. Age-appropriate tasks are conquered. One learns to defend one's rights and integrity.

When things do not go well and the self-concept becomes deviant, or self-esteem falters at preadolesence, it is time to intercede and provide assistance. With adolescence ahead, one does not wait and hope for self-correction. Creating an opportunity for interaction with trained professionals who understand preadolescence is the obligation of special education.

Adolescent Self-Development, Normal and Problematic

It is interesting that, in contrast to earlier periods, most of us have vivid recollections of our adolescence. Many would not elect to repeat it unless they could change significant parts. There is a tendency to generalize about this stage in life in terms of our own personal experience and if it was a highly satisfying time we may not find it easy to identify with youths who find it a painful time (Cruickshank, Morse, and Johns 1980). Certainly neither regular nor special education—nor for that matter society at large—has found the key to assist adolescents effectively. Erikson sees the self at this period as struggling with identity problems. The task is to integrate one's past with new biological drives. Dangers are the possibility of fixations on negative self-identities, or failure to integrate an adequate self.

With adolescence comes increasing independence from adults and, one hopes, a more solid sense of one's identity. Values become assimilated into a personal code. Cross-sex relationships and, in general, more meaningful relationships normally emerge. Conceptual, logical, and symbolic thinking change the nature of the worldview and judgments of personal experiences. The individual has expanded abilities. How much adolescence is a special period of devastating storm and stress and how much is just one of life's series of stages is a matter of current debate, but there is no doubt that powerful forces are at work. While each individual follows an internal time clock, the effervescence of the early adolescent period—usually coming at the middle school level—is far more explorative in nature than the crucial decision-making time of high school adolescence is. Adolescence starts with body changes that draw attention to body image. The cultural stereotypes of the desirable male and female habitus leave no room for obesity or homeliness. The adolescent effort spent on diets and muscle exercises indicate the power of the prototypes. Inevitable though they are, secondary sexual characteristics can be a source of pride or shame. There are new body feelings and a reworking of the body image. The fact that girls mature earlier than boys creates certain difficulties in our school groupings which are determined by chronological age.

Adolescent self-concept–self-esteem is but an extension of the development already outlined, with a magnificent exception. While building on the foundation of preadolescence, the self undergoes a metamorphasis in adolescence. In early adolescence there is a mixture of both preadolescent and adolescent behavior, often loud and fluid.

One often deals with two levels of self at the same time in the same person.

Normal and disturbed early adolescence has been a highly neglected area until recently (Lipsitz 1977; Morse 1981). It is a time of particular change often producing consternation in adults. Compelled to seek and explore, adolescents try new selves on for size. A brash attitude is often used by the adolescent to gloss over initial struggles for an independent identity. Submitting to adult codes can be seen as personal defeat. Early adolescent frankness is like a sword; this age can be frank to the point of cutting. The impulsive behavior of the age is born of pervasive emotional feelings. Malmquist (1978) has pointed out the pattern of "episodic dyscontrol," periods when there seems to be no control alternating with periods in which reasonable control is exhibited. There is a penetrating loneliness and alienation for some adolescents at this time until intimacy with others can be established.

The ability to work at school tasks sometimes disappears, which is frightening to the student-self. Adult helpers can become the enemy. Often children who were motivated in elementary school because of the more simplified school environment where they were monitored, have their first real crises in the diversified middle school (Simmons, Rosenberg, and Rosenberg 1973).

For the normal early adolescent, given understanding parents and reasonable teachers, the time is one of expanding progress, one of exploring new academic and social meanings and trying out new behaviors. For those with low self-esteem, the struggle for independence becomes manifest as irrational risk taking and an overdependence upon peers. Impulsive behavior becomes chronic. The underlying confusion about authority results in resistance to expectations, adults become interpreted as the opposition when they attempt to exert demands. Anger and panic build up.

All the time there is a fixation on the changing physical nature. Regardless of their social participation, many adolescents feel alone and some are genuinely isolated. Getting help is often perceived as weakness and hence help is rejected.

The early adolescent period merges into mid-adolescence, when there should be a moratorium, a time for more extensive exploration, and for making decisions about one's future. This normally leads to the consolidation of the young adult self when the winnowing out process is fairly complete and the direction of one's destiny is clearer.

Erikson contrasts the temporary restructuring and role confusion of adolescence with the identity seeking that culminates in the young adult who has the capacity for forming reciprocal intimate relationships on a sustaining basis. The present society exploits the adolescent period by manufacturing a commercial subculture an adolescent cult which emphasizes its own music, mores, television programs, fashion, and literature. The adolescent longs to belong and to be "with it." It is not uncommon for the intense experiences of the sensitive adolescent to make a self-concept imprinting that will significantly alter the individual's life.

Typically, what is happening to the adolescent self-concept? Identity factors become more apparent, including nonverbalized attributes recognized from antecedents—one's place in society, one's cultural heritage. This may be accepted as a matter of pride or resisted. Black is beautiful or black is a handicap. Machismo is a strength or an aberration. These are phenomenological self-perceptions.

Usually by this time self-esteem includes self-generated judgments, but seldom without reflections of input from others. If what the adolescent feels and what the helping person sees do not match, interventions may be rejected as inappropriate. Defensive behavior, designed to hide negative self views from others, is common. Subgroups of adolescents with similar values reinforce each other to substantiate a self-image that may be at variance with the larger social context. This provides the motivation for gang solidarity, and alienation from the conservative or "square" adult culture.

Signs of physical growth can produce joy and satisfaction or generate fears and anxiety. One thing is certain, biological change does take place and has a significant impact on the self-image. This change brings with it a new and strong impulse to manage, namely, the sexual drive with all of its derivatives. Both heterosexual and homosexual arousal may develop, sending the individual into confusion and panic. Uncertainty over restraint or indulgence is not aided by cultural permissiveness nor stimulating movies. Physical relationships may occur without any psychological caring or may be a substitute for being cared about by parents. Experimentation often produces guilt. In some instances fear of growing up, and fear of impregnation or the loss of the sex object may result in severe problems. Child–mothers and child–fathers are almost epidemic, but their large numbers does not mean it is simple for the girls and boys involved.

Because of the implication of the future, the adolescent is playing for keeps. Many decisions must be made that will have long-term significance, and many of these will have heavy value connotations: What are *my* values? What will *my* life style be? What work role must *I* (can I) aim for? There is the contrast between "schoolwork" and work for money. The large role of vocational education in SEI programs becomes evident. What can I be, given my talents and resources? Will there be any jobs? Will I be able to hold a job? There are always questions and decisions to be made as the certainty of childhood is replaced with anticipations of adulthood.

The self in relation to family role undergoes alteration and frequently results in exacerbation of problem areas. An adult's worry over "what might happen" accentuates the need to exert control over the adolescent just when traditional control is least productive. For the adolescent, conflict abounds: How can you be independent at all when you have to live at home? What choice have you unless you run away? You must have your freedom and privacy even though you still need guidance. Parents, reliving their own "ancient" adolescence of a past generation and fraught with fears, resort to power plays in order to gain control. They don't let you grow up in some ways and expect you to be too grown up in others.

One's own self-decision and executive independence are important, especially in adolescence, as can be illustrated by the story of a youngster who referred himself to an SEI class by asking the teacher if he could join. It was discovered that his history with behavior problems was more severe than most of those classified as SEI and in the class. But he had a strong ego and was intact and was declared too normal to be diagnosed as disturbed. After some negotiations he was "permitted" to join. Immediately the other members of the class tried to induce this easily recognized "brother" to follow them and not do his work. He tolerated their efforts for a while, then he turned on them, saying that he was here as a last resort. He had been expelled most of the previous year; he had decided he wanted to graduate but always kept getting messed up because of his short fuse, but if they didn't leave him alone and let him work, he promised, he'd "beat the shit out of all of them." That was that. The others were rejecting the help but this one had made *his* choice. The others had been given the "opportunity" without self-commitment. They were surface look-alikes but with one very significant difference. Self-decision and executive independence can lead to success.

Alienation can become acute at this age. No one knows you, not your mother, not even yourself. Long discussions with chosen peers are necessary to clarify values and organize attitudes. Adolescents living in corrective institutions have a hard time with these situations. Adults are very fearful when these adolescents get together, sometimes rightfully so, because violence may result. Adolescent "crowds" simulate socialization, but the real need is for an in-group of peers to run with and use as a reference group for setting your same sex behavior, as well as an attachment to a member of the opposite sex. A crowd provides an audience and anonymity.

The range of adolescent tasks and their rate of accomplishment is great. For every belle of the ball there are the many wallflowers. For every athletic success there are many who can only watch. Some youngsters are the center of the social whirl, while others have no social life at all.

Our society does a poor job at helping adolescents. As it is presently organized, society does not need adolescents, except to fill secondary schools, menial job openings, and then, the colleges and universities if they are able. Even low-paying jobs open to the adolescent are scarce or nonexistent. Society is not organized to use their talents, their energies, or to respond to their need to participate. Many adolescents will willingly give time and care to younger children and to senior citizens. Others hope to work in order to be partly financially independent in our money-dominated world. For the majority, families, schools, churches, and communities meet these needs, and the ebullience and excitement of adolescence is both a delight to experience and to behold. Adolescents may even maintain their idealism in the face of the many poor models they see in public and private life. Their abhorrence of war, poverty, unfairness, and inequality are assets to our society.

Just as the baby changes the life of his mother and father, so adolescents provide growth opportunities for their parents and teachers. Granted, even the normal adolescent is a difficult companion at times, and the SEI adolescent is difficult almost all of the time. Parents cave in. Some become very anxious. Others give up. The feeling of helplessness that parents feel when they cannot "manage" the adolescent results in violent interaction and deep fears of impulses that—it is implied—no one can control.

Self-esteem at this stage is vulnerable. A rejection by a friend, especially one of the opposite sex, can be devastating and result in depression. A cutting remark from a teacher or parent can destroy hard-earned self-esteem.

The behavior resulting from temporary adolescent identity diffusion may look like a more serious deviation. It is helpful to remember that self-esteem vacillates. Although one does not expect deep and sustained confusion to be present in normal adolescents, discretion is needed; one cannot interpret each episode of adolescent behavior as a serious one. There is often a temporary loss of both motivation and confidence. School skills suffer; assignments are neglected. Moodiness dominates. Time, the basic motivation for many of us, loses its power:

"There's lots of time to get my work in," or "Why wait, now's the time to enjoy, enjoy" are characteristically adolescent comments. However, when such states continue over a long period of time they warrant serious concern.

In adolescence there is considerable role-playing of different life-styles. The adolescent who discovers ecology or religion can be absorbed in his new life to a degree that astounds and can even frighten adults. The unresolved adolescent need to belong is seen in cult attachments and their demand for infantile dependency. The struggle to be an independent person is given up.

The image of the young scientist, the prima ballerina, the race driver, the rock band leader, and other images become pseudoself roles. Groups also designate roles. "Smart Ass" with the brains, "Muscles," "Sexpot," and titles pertaining to the subculture diagnosis of the moment become labels. There is the strong appeal of the superficial, well known, though not approved of pop cult heroes. If the famous can get high, why shouldn't I? There are the pushers who have big cars and the opportunists who make a hit record. The dream supporting these images is one of being catapulted from ignominy to stardom and wealth without effort. These public models provide a glamorous alternative to working your way up from the bottom. Many SEI adolescents cling to a belief in an easy magic, way out.

For all their relating, it has been evident that many adolescents have difficulty in establishing meaningful, mutual, caring relationships. The casual and temporary cultural models advocated by some of the so-called stable adults say to the adolescent that one should not invest in long-term arrangements. Play it cool. Sleep with whom you please on a first-name-only basis. You don't have to be responsible. This ethnic is part of our age stemming from the narcissistic cult to do-your-own-thing. For the adolescent, this ethnic constitutes a very appealing indulgent model for the self. This mode of non-relationship is a substitute for more gratifying but more demanding social adjustment.

Adolescence can be the precipitator of a great deal of maladjustment because of the strain it places on identity dissolution and reintegration, especially if one has a history of failure in mastering previous age tasks. We should separate the youngsters taking a temporary moratorium for exploration from others destined for a tragic career of deviancy. The normal adolescent with internalized values and reasonable skills will succeed, though sometimes only with judicious crisis support and good preventive mental health programs. To react to each change one sees as a representation of deep character defect or pathology would be a mistake; most of our young people maintain or migrate toward purposeful and acceptable patterns as the self reintegrates.

Kaplan (1980) outlines the relationship between self-concept and behavior. Deviant patterns are responses to self-attitudes. They can be seen as defensive behavior to protect the self-image and maintain self-esteem. Thus the nature of adolescent deviant self-concept is the key to understanding and treatment. There are those for whom negative models in the family, the gang, or the neighborhood prove too seductive. The critical risks for the adolescent are evident. Failing in school can reduce opportunities for the future. Sexual activity without contraception can lead to babies; having a baby to love is not the long-term solution to feeling alone and unloved. Delinquency can suggest an easier way to money than legitimate work. Escape and self-destruction with drugs may become chronic. Paralysis of effort can atrophy a potential talent. Running away has become the solution for over half a million adolescents a year (Brennan, Huizinga, and Elliott 1978). The amount of severe depression and suicide during adolescence makes clear how destructive feelings of failure and loss of hope can be at this age.

The role of the self-concept in deviant adolescence has been detailed by Masterson and Costello (1980). The so-called borderline patients always reflect a self-image–self-esteem difficulty. They seem unable to define themselves, cannot regulate their self-esteem and cannot assert themselves. Some have only a very vague self-image, some a false image. Masterson and Costello see depression as the most common adolescent problem. Suicide attempts increase, school attendance and achievement problems increase, and delinquency is a particularly serious matter at this age.

Adolescent self-esteem revolves around a sense of executive independence—the inner capacity to make my own decisions and outer acceptance of my ability and right to make my own decisions. Adults, the peer reference group, and close friends should collaborate to provide security in this new self-independence. Jessor and Jessor (1977) show that the peer referent group selected by the adolescent usually reflects the values the adolescent is attracted to at this time, leaving those with other values relatively powerless to enter into the influence circuit. Low self-esteem can result from a lack of real accomplishment in given self-segments (such as school) or from a sense of weakness relative to one's own standards. In one institution for delinquent SEI youth, the youth have their own term for low self-esteem—*the smalls*. When someone is feeling down, they try to help him and describe the condition as having "a bad case of the smalls." There is a recognition of different categories of selves by adolescents. Mixing them, even if all are categorized as SEI, may provoke group reactions of a negative type. In a public school, a teacher was trying to generate group discussion with an adolescent SEI class, to no avail. Then the tough ones said, "Get that 'soft gel' out of here. He ain't like us. We won't talk with no 'soft gels' around. We're 'hard gels.' " These statements contrast tough ego-intact, or delinquent selves with inadequate, or neurotic selves. Youngsters are often astute diagnosticians; they recognize the different worlds of childhood and which world they belong to.

The solutions the adolescent may see demonstrated in the adult world around him look easy: drugs bring instant joy; it is possible to get your easy money no matter how; and violating values one is elected to uphold is o.k. The fun ethic replaces the work ethic. You get ahead by whom you know, not what you know. The list of easy solutions is endless and persuasive. This adolescent ability to rationalize astutely is a reflection of their intellectual capacity to think. Because their "reasoning ability" serves impulse so often, adults forget that adolescents are capable of reasoning on an adult level, though they have not had much experience. Were they not as astute, they would not be so difficult for us to redirect. A gang of slum kids was addicted to a television show of crime-cops, but they knew that real life was not like the show, where so few got hurt by the encounters. Wounds cannot be cured in one week. As they knew from their own bitter experience, such was not at all the reality. In real life they knew friends who were killed.

As we think of possible interventions for SEI adolescents, attention has to be given to the particular way each individual self can be reached. We must discover what will provide the youth with a better solution for the self-concept–self-esteem problem that exists. Is drug use a sign of defeat in a hopeless life situation or is it the answer to a hedonist's prayer? Will skill learning improve self-esteem? Is a job the best way to teach new behavior? Will new role models help? Many times the right girlfriend or boyfriend has done more for an adolescent than hours or professional counseling. Because many youths have not resolved their dependency = rejection quandary over authority figures, there may be cases when traditional therapy will yield little. In fact, some hold that only group interventions can provide the mental unraveling and peer identification that the adolescent needs. The key to planning a productive intervention is an appreciation of the individual's self-concept, and of the effort needed to deal with the adolescent as an equal. Adolescents are neither children nor full adults. They are at once the most difficult to help and the most in need of help, yet programs to help the adolescent are the most inadequate. In a recent survey of all the states, Hirshoren and Heller (1979) report a rapid growth in programs for adolescents but the formats are typical— special class, resource rooms, and vocational orientation. Obviously, concentration on schooling only is not sufficient. By adolescence, the self-concept has consolidated and changes are not achieved by simple interventions.

Vernon Jones (1980) has written one of the few books that blend the educational and psychological perspectives in dealing with SEI pupils. As he sees it, much adolescent acting out behavior is a normal response to the failure of schools to provide the adolescent with an opportunity to experience significance, power, and competence. He describes classrooms based on respect for these young adults that can escape the typical school failure. He also thinks that interventions must include parents, because adolescents remain dependent upon parents for such a long time in our society.

The sad state of many adolescent programs is not without cause. These youngsters are very difficult to help. Even those who are ready to change or make incipient changes are usually enmeshed in, or return to, the social setting that provoked the original problem and without the needed follow-up and support systems. Alternative schools and adult night school may be helpful in given cases. Counseling, especially if it is crisis oriented, may also prove helpful. Classical therapy is not the easiest method to employ at this age.

One must understand how life looks to the adolescent. As a young adult, you know a lot about the world and you know things about yourself that no one else knows. Still others keep trying to explain your inner life to you. The evolution of your own separate identity has reached the level where you are now a self, different from all other selves, a person in your own right, a separate human being. Usually such a person gives away only little pieces of the secret self from time to time. Yet you don't even know your new self really, or why you do certain things. This uncertainty can make one very uneasy. When asked why you do things, the answer, "because," is a convenient and safe putoff.

"But *I am* an independent being. In the whole world there is no other like me. I exist. I am private." Good. The possibility of power and control is in this new statement "*I* am." Adolescence ends when the ability to mesh with other human beings, to joining other independent selves, has been reached. This is the capacity for deepened friendships. Friendship pushes back loneliness. The symbiosis of love refutes alienation and results in a closeness not known before. Adolescents may rediscover and reaffirm relationships with their parents as people. For many, this new capacity to love will eventually lead to a family and children, and then the whole process starts over again. SEI adolescents are adolescents as well socially and emotionally impaired. For those interested in detailed analyses of adolescent pathology, see Feinstein and Giovacchini *Adolescent Psychiatry* (1983). Adults who influence the next generation sense the marvel, depth, and range of possibilities in adolescent growth. Because of the malleability of the self at this period, many consider adolescence to be our last opportunity to redirect a life.

SELF-CONCEPT AND THE TASK OF THE SEI TEACHER

The role of the self-concept–self-esteem identity complex in behavior changes is critical. Interventions may have a direct impact on given self-concepts, although most often the impact is indirect. Feelings of worthlessness can sometimes be assuaged by the acceptance and respect of an adult. The anxiety and guilt accompanying self-perceived inadequacies may be reduced through therapeutic counseling, which produces insight into the irrational causes of these feelings. Low self-esteem may be a consequence of inadequate coping; this can be altered. A pupil who cannot read, play games, or make friends may have deep problems steming from longtime experience. It will take time to change feelings as well as to learn new skills.

But it is evident that many youngsters improve in self-concept–self-esteem without ever dealing with the core problem directly. If all of us had to specifically resolve all of our emotional problems in order to function reasonably well, the world would be an asylum. Although there are times when we cannot progress without assessing and resolving the past, we often are able to cope without doing so.

Thus it is that when a pupil learns to read, is able to manage an impulse with the expectation of a token, or is put into a positive social peer role by the teacher, the whole is more than the sum of its parts. Not only is the useful skill built into the self-concept, making life more productive, but self-esteem is elevated at the same time. This self-esteem induces the feelings of well-being, worth, and ability to meet life. It is evident in some persons that the feeling of inadequacy (learned helplessness) is so pervasive that the opportunities for new and real accomplishments are avoided, or if they are achieved, they are disregarded because of low self-esteem and a lack of hope. Especially with children—who normally learn new things constantly—motivating concrete accomplishments is a major method of therapy. Teachers reflect on this and reinforce the satisfaction a youngster feels or may even prompt the recognition of a job well done. Unfortunately, there are children to whom concrete achievement means nothing; they are desperate for, say, positive parental regard, for which nothing else will substitute. Others are so severely damaged that a total reconstruction of the self is required. As a further complication, youngsters do not always comprehend the instigating elements which produced their feeling; some abused children blame themselves. To make life better (after preventing the condition) it may be best to teach a child that adults can care and then to get on with the tasks of the age. Understanding self-concept–self-esteem development helps to explain why assistance that is not related to the core problem often has the power to change the direction of a life.

In a recent article, Bandura's data suggests that the self-concept perception that has the largest value is the sense of self-efficacy (1982). Those individuals who have or with support can have a sense of self-efficacy will persist in efforts to cope until they have in some manner coped with their problem. When we consider interventions it will be important to explore in depth the expectations our pupils have about their future. SEI youngsters often have a self-concept that defines the self as a born loser and as helpless. It is small wonder so many present low self-esteem.

If a teacher does not know the pupil's self-concept, helping efforts are made by trial and error at best. Sometimes we can attempt to replace elements of the self-concept, substituting a socially approved section for one that is antisocial. We may change the social roles and values of certain selves. We may minimize discomfiture by actual successes. Our caring would enhance self-esteem. The chapters that follow deal with how these self-concept–self-esteem changes can be cultivated, and especially with the ways in which teachers and schools can function to accomplish these changes with SEI pupils.

2

Definitions and Descriptions

TRANSITION

THE GENERAL NATURE of normal and aberrant self-development
was depicted in chapter 1. Special education for the SEI pupil
begins with an understanding of the individual pupil, which leads to the
eventual development of an individual plan for education and related
interventions. Individual or ipsative psychology examines the
uniqueness and consistency within an individual's self functioning in a
given milieu or set of milieus. The purpose is to grasp the sense of this
life as seen by the individual as well as by external information from
tests and observations. We all behave as we do for reasons, private
reasons coming from our unique set of experiences.

There are several parts of this quest to understand the SEI pupil.
First, who are these children as a particular group within the totality
of special education? Second, what sources of information should be
considered in ascertaining the nature of an individual SEI pupil? Third,
how can this information be utilized? What schema of considering the
information is most appropriate for the educational setting?

THE KNOTTY QUESTION: WHICH CHILDREN ARE
SOCIOEMOTIONALLY IMPAIRED?

Societies have always had a problem in ascertaining who are the deviants. Gorenstein (1984) reminds us that we have been debating the
existence of mental illness for decades with no real progress. Disagreements include the variables used to define deviant behavior and

how society should respond to it. He sees essential disagreements over professional roles and the legal/ethical status of the behaviorally aberrant. The Russians have used mental illness as a way to punish political deviants. Proponents of special education were accused of using similar tactics for removing difficult children from the mainstream until the legal sanctions of PL 94–142 set up protective procedures. But all of the problems have not been solved.

Before a youngster can get special education services, he or she must be categorized with a label to fit the matrix of services created by special education. Is the pupil mostly SEI or learning disabled (LD) or mentally retarded (MR)? Forness, Sinclair, and Russell (1984) point out the conflict in this matter of categorization. We have to "fit" the child into the category through extensive and expensive differential diagnoses and yet we are to build the educational program on the idiosyncratic nature of each child. Would it not be more appropriate to use a noncategorical approach in the first place, focusing attention on the pupil's need for special assistance? For the special-education teacher the reality is obvious: children do not come in the neat categories that the field has constructed. Using "children in need of special education" may also solve the problem of parents and schools using LD as a more comfortable designation, ignoring the many such children who also have SEI problems. Generic special education certainly fits the individual psychology of our last chapter. It is well to remember that the child is the same child regardless of the name we bestow upon him, but that the services provided are often restricted by virtue of the designation. Still, at present we must face the definitional issue of SEI.

How is the category to be defined? An excellent exercise is to stop for a moment and write out one's personal criteria to check against the various current concepts employed today. Except for the few places that have circumvented the definitional dilemma by using "children in need of special services" (Garrett and Brazil 1979), the pupil is supposed to fit the national, state, and local definition for the category. Although the categorization brings hazards, on the positive side it does prevent circumstantial placement because SEI labeling requires a painstaking diagnosis.

Kanner (1962), in his historical review of emotional disturbance in children, noted that there is no circumspect definition of the condition. Although the term has been used for over a generation, it lacks specificity and includes a broad range from children with behavior problems to those who are psychotic. In an early survey (Morse, Cutler, and Fink 1964), the absence of any coherent definition of the clientele and a wide divergency of program approaches was revealed. In

1971 Schultz et al. made a national study of state-employed terminology and found that there is still no consensus. The main change is consideration of manifest behavior disturbances apart from internal emotional states.

Epstein, Cullinan, and Sabatino recently (1977) examined the definitions used by various states. In all, forty-nine definitions were analyzed through the use of eleven components. The components and frequency are as follows: (1) disorders of emotion/behavior (100 percent), (2) interpersonal problems (69 percent), (3) learning or achievement problems (55 percent), (4) deviation from norms (47 percent), (5) chronicity (38 percent), (6) severity (43 percent), (7) etiology (11 percent), (8) prognosis (8 percent), (9) absence of retardation, etc. (37 percent), (10) in need of special education (63 percent), and (11) certification by a designated individual or group (35 percent). They found the modal number of components in a state definition to be 5, with a range from 2 to 9. The major conditions were disorders of emotion/behavior, interpersonal problems, and learning/achievement problems; but the variety of language used belies actual agreement. As Epstein sees it, the two items *in need of special education* and *certification* are of a different nature. The remaining six characteristics become qualifiers of the major three components. The state definitions are vague, ambiguous, and even at some points contradictory. A teacher trained to teach children with one set of characteristics may end up teaching quite a different group, depending on geography. Definitions were found to be more psychiatrically than educationally oriented. The Joint Commission for Mental Health (1970) definition concentrates more on a combination of attributes: impairment in capacity expected for an age and personal endowment, inaccurate perception of the world, lack of impulse control, a lack of satisfying and satisfactory social relationships and learning inability. The text of PL 94–142 specifies *seriously emotionally disturbed* as a condition exhibiting one or more of the following characteristics over a long period of time and to a marked degree, which adversely affects educational performance:

A. An inability to learn that cannot be explained by intellectual, sensory, or health factors;
B. An inability to build or maintain satisfactory inter-personal relationships with peers or teachers;
C. Inappropriate types of behavior or feelings under normal circumstances;
D. A general pervasive mood of unhappiness or depression;

E. A tendency to develop physical symptoms or fears associated with personal or school problems. (*Federal Register,* 1977, p. 42478)

This is essentially the definition that Bower produced in 1960. Note that a definition including educational performance leaves out those who have no school problems or problems that do not affect achievement, and this can be a significant number. The idea that all disturbed children must have an educational problem in behavior or achievement is a significant error. The other error lies in implying that even when children have problems in school these problems are primarily school-related. The fact is that problems are often generated outside of the school environment and brought to school. Children who are schizophrenic or autistic are included, but not children who are socially maladjusted, unless it is determined that they are seriously emotionally disturbed as well! Subsequently the autistic have been removed from the seriously emotionally disturbed category and placed in the otherwise health impaired category. The reasoning is that although there may be emotional overlay because of life experience, the essential causative factor is biological. This ends the blaming of parents, especially mothers. Kanner (1962) had seen mothers as the cause of autism: he stereotyped them as cold or "refrigerator" mothers. Because many researchers see schizophrenia and many other maladjustments as biological in nature or with a significant biological component, there may be other changes in classification in the offing. There is also the condition of "behaviorally disordered" who have no intrapsychic problem but act out in school. In all probability these constitute the largest and most difficult subcategory of the socioemotionally impaired. This is where the schools and the children need the most help, and considerable attention will be given to these pupils subsequently. Regardless of supposed elimination of this group, there is no question that they appear in significant numbers in programs.

The state of Florida has taken what it believes is a new approach (Algozzine, Schmid, and Conners 1978). Two emotionally disturbed categories are enumerated, the regular emotionally disturbed (ED) and clinically emotionally disturbed. Decisions are based on *where* treatment is to be applied! For regular ED, mainstreaming has not been effective, deviations persist and are shown in a variety of settings, academic achievement is one standard deviation below school norms, and social relationships are inadequate and no other primary disability can be applied. For the clinical ED, the list is similar but more extreme:

achievement is two standard deviations below the mean, and current school relationships are disrupted. The developmental history delineates a clinical syndrome.

Wood and Lakin (1979) have contributed to and edited what stands to be the most authoritative and comprehensive study of the topic, entitled *Disturbing, Disordered, or Disturbed.* They list the elements of a good description as (1) What or who is the focus of the problem? (2) How is the problem behavior described? (3) Where does the problem behavior occur? (4) Who regards the behavior as a problem? (5) How is the differentiation of disturber-nondisturber made? (6) Does the definition provide the basis for planning beneficial activities?

There are, to be sure, certain common behaviors of MR, LD, and SEI children. Gajar (1979) has written that the IQs of the MR children were significantly lower than those in the other two categories, as would be expected. The MR were the lowest, the LD were next in order, and the ED were highest in reading achievement, although the order varied in arithmetic and spelling. So far as the affective dimensions are concerned, the ED were significantly higher in acting out behavior, personality problems, and on immaturity-inadequacy. Two observations are in order. First, regardless of label, many categories of special children have accompanying SEI attributes. Second, there may be individual profile differences within the category greater than mean differences between certain categories. Boucher and Deno (1979) found significant overlap in typical child characteristics of LD and ED when teachers did the labeling. Also, achievement goals and integration recommendations were not different for the two labels. Regardless of our efforts to categorize, children just do not fit the labels we invent. Thus the SEI clientele will differ greatly from place to place. A child may be eligible for help in one locale and not in another.

The time has come to change our direction from either an etiology or status basis to a needs basis. If we cast the assessment in terms of what we see as the *needs* of a pupil rather than concentrating on history, impairments, disabilities, or current problem behavior, we would be coherent with the approach taken in this book. Although help rests upon the pupil's problems, concentrating on the needs implies a different emphasis than concentrating on the disability.

Also the school setting that generates the decisions has an impact. A regular school with high pressure for academic achievement is going to produce a different set of "misfits" than is the psychiatrist on the basis of an interview, the social worker looking at the family, or the psychologist with a set of tests. And yet the child is but one child.

Fremont, Klingsporn, and Wilson (1976) used a Q-sort to study professional differences in perceptions of behavior problems between teachers, school counselors, school psychologists, clinical psychologists, and psychiatrists. It is no wonder these personnel have trouble consulting together, for they live in different worlds where childhood is concerned. The authors were interested in the differentiation of what they termed personality disorders (anxiety, depression, tense inner conflicts) and behavior disorders (disobedience; destructive, antisocial behavior). Teachers did not distinguish the terms; psychiatrists, clinical psychologists, and school psychologists did. This is another in a long line of studies from the twenties contrasting teachers' and mental health workers' views. These studies are based on a false assumption that a particular symptom is singularly correlated with a psychological label. Also, if you are a teacher dealing with groups of children and trying to teach them, you respond to the behavior which you have to deal with from this group context, which is quite a different context than the individual interview.

According to the law, teachers, parents, and school psychologists must meet together to decide the status of a youngster. Morris and Arrant (1978) found there were significant differences in their perceptions. However, we do not always see different children. What we see are different parts of the same child because our purposes and arenas of action make for differences in what is critical behavior. Bloom (1976) holds that school behavior problems and emotional disturbance are separate nosological entities. There are intraprofessional differences as well as interprofessional differences: one teacher's problem child is not a problem to another; one clinic sees schizophrenia and another sees retardation.

The studies on differential professional perceptions do not deal with three other potent sources of evaluation of behavior—parents, peers, and the child. We know that there are times when the school sees a problem and the home none or vice versa, and both may be accurate in either instance. A pupil may be a problem in the classroom and at the same time be a peer leader on the playground. Part of the matter is judgment and part is ecological. Swap (1973) found that personality and the nature of the setting both influenced the behaviors; nonacademic settings such as art and swimming produce different behavior than academic seatwork where teachers were particularly sensitive to behavior that interfered with others.

Harris, King, and Drummond (1978) indicate that teachers nominated as emotionally disturbed those pupils who report themselves as more insecure, apprehensive, and worried. Quiet and withdrawn pupils were favored over those who were aggressive and acting out. In contrasting pupil self-reports with parent and teacher ratings of pupils referred for clinical services, student self-reports were more positive than parents' ratings and parents' ratings more positive than teachers'. One could say either that this fits the order of sophistication and expected defenses or that it represents biases. What we do learn is that the worlds of the self, the family, and the school make for different appraisals of who is disturbed.

There is a solution to the confusion and this is to start with Rhodes's definition of disturbance. He defines disturbance as a person and a system in dissonance and pain—"a disrupted pattern of human-environment exchanges" (Rhodes and Tracy 1972, 23). It is a systems approach and is based upon the interactive nature of behavior. In an interesting study showing the importance of school environment on behavior, Rogeners, Bednar, and Diesenhaus (1974) found that a high level of problem behavior in an inner-city school could be substantially reduced when a stable faculty and smaller classes that were half the usual size were the interventions. From this view, considerable problem behavior is produced and maintained by the particular in school social system. Of course family systems also maintain certain behavior deviations.

In conclusion, how we define the SEI population and who decides the appropriateness of fit is a never-ending question, and no solution will be satisfactory to every reader. There are behaviors that a democratic society cannot tolerate because they interfere with the fundamental rights of others. There are other behaviors that make it difficult for the individual to negotiate the society in which he must live. And there are behaviors that persons themselves recognize as self-defeating and that result in personal pain. All are products of the biological and experiential base and environmental press of children's lives. We will subsequently indicate major subcategories of socioemotional impairment to complement individual diagnosis.

HAZARDS OF THE SEI LABEL

There are many problems with the use of labels, especially the SEI label. Parents, teachers, and other professionals start with an overall negative stereotype to the label socioemotionally disturbed (Foster, Ysseldyke, and Reese 1975; Critchley 1979). Even students in training to teach SEI pupils react adversely to the label. Using the semantic differential I found that SEI children were perceived as both "bad" and "powerful." The force of such negative halos on selective attention or observation is well known: we find what we expect. A study by Ysseldyke and Foster (1978) revealed that behavior of both emotionally disturbed and learning disabled was subject to the labeling distortion. It is the moral overtone that is most discouraging because it implies that youngsters are "bad" and could and should behave better if they only tried.

While labeling a SEI pupil is decried in almost all quarters, in most programs it is no label, no service. A youngster must be categorized (a harmful thing) to be a candidate for special education (a presumedly helpful thing). There are several crucial issues in this involved and emotional debate.

1. Children are usually labeled long before the diagnostic personnel enter the picture. Peers, parents, and neighbors are active in assigning descriptors. The soiler is "stinky" before he is encopretic.

2. The purpose of any categorization is to define a pattern, a syndrome or a self-configuration that will present general cues for what the corrective efforts should be. Seldom, however, does a person represent the abstract classical description on which the category is based.

3. While the label, accurate or not, does not in fact change the nature of the pupil so described, the name can and often does start expectation cycles. These cycles can have significant effects on what the person expects from himself based on his self-concept and even more on what others expect. It has been demonstrated that teachers change their responses negatively to the same behavior when a particular categorical label is attached. Labels such as sociopath, schizophrenic, neurotic, or autistic carry with them more than descriptive substance. They contain the emotional connotations of being mentally ill, being essentially different than the rest of us, and in many cases in a hopeless condition. Every professional worker who is in the business of "helping" had best search out conscious and unconscious attitudes regarding these matters.

If indeed labels are condemnations, then even professionals should not use them. Certainly, with the known attitudes of the community, we would be well advised to talk about the internal and external behaviors that need changing than to use shorthand of labels. Better still we should discuss needs rather than labels.

4. Neither a list of specific behaviors nor a label can provide a simple answer to individualized interventions nor can it prevent a poorly trained worker from gross misuse.

5. Not only is there the problem of goodness of fit within a label such as socioemotionally impaired, there is also an across-categories problem (Hallahan and Kaufman 1977). Children may have a complex of socioemotional problems and still have another primary special-education label. The LD pupil is seldom free from emotional disabilities. The retarded child too builds special defenses to deal with the assault on self-esteem. The dual impairment issue may well be one of the next to receive national attention. There are very few programs for dual difficulties such as the deaf or visual emotionally impaired, for example (Naiman 1975). All special-education conditions present growth hazards. It is said that multiple handicapping is the actual fact with at least two special education categories per child. A child treated on the basis on the primary label with the other categories ignored is being maligned. Of course, just because you lack mobility or sight or high intelligence does not signify you will have emotional disturbance, although these stereotypes exist. Many people still stereotype the MR as being also socially aberrant.

6. The SEI label sometimes induces a tolerance for "expected" behavior that, in a permissive sense, reduces the expectations needed to produce change (Algozzine, Mercer, and Countermine 1977). It is easy to give up, commenting, "Oh well, that's Norman's schizophrenic process again, asking the same old question."

CASE FINDING: SCREENING

Not only are we legally obligated to serve special pupils who turn up, we are to *find* those who fit the definition who are of preschool as well as school age. In essence, for those in school, it means screening the population to be certain we locate all who should be studied and subsequently helped.

There are many screening devices, some of which are very complicated and time-consuming. Before looking at these, a simple and yet effective procedure was developed by Rezmierski and Shiffler (1983) for the project "Intervention by Prescription." They used a four-point stress scale for teachers to report on pupils' needs: (1) of concern, needs watching; (2) substantial, needs study or attention; (3) pressing, needs prompt attention; (4) urgent, needs immediate attention. Eighteen percent of elementary pupils and 10 percent of junior high pupils were identified as stressed, with nine and five percent at the pressing and urgent levels. Boys were double the number of girls. Subsequently four major patterns were found from administering the Hahnemann Behavior Rating Scale, a common screening device, to all levels of pupils who were under stress: *negative,* disruptive, critical, blaming (45 percent elementary, 54 percent junior high); *withdrawn* (24 percent elementary, 25 percent junior high); *social overinvolvement with peers* (21 percent elementary, 9 percent junior high); and *anxious, insecure* (10 percent elementary, 12 percent junior high). Such figures far exceed the special-education allotment to the SEI category. Rezmierski points out that this method does not say whether or not the "true" problem is the pupil or the teacher, although there is evidence that well over 50 percent of the problems maintain with new teachers' ratings (Elitov 1984).

At the other end of the "find" process are the more complicated Bower and Lambert scales, which provide correlated information from the child, peer, and teacher (Bower 1982). There are separate scales for young elementary and secondary children. The peer role information comes from a clever procedure where fellow students are nominated for various parts in a play or types of jobs. With the preschoolers, picture situations are associated with names of children in the group. Preschool screening for risk has been developed by Anthony and Koupernik (1974).

One teacher instrument that has undergone extensive research is the Bristol Social Adjustment Guides (Stott, Marston, and Neill 1975). The advantage here is that the items relate to school situations in the classroom and on the playground. The Quay-Peterson (1979: Quay 1983) Behavior Problem Checklist categorizes children into conduct problems (delinquent-sociopathic), inadequacy (immature), and personality problems.

Rutter and his colleagues have devised screening devices covering five years through adolescence for behavioral and emotional disorders for parent and teacher use (Anderson 1973; Behar and Stringfield 1974). There are also screening devices for risk, autism, language, motor behavior, and many other specifics. An excellent analytical study of behavior checklists is found in Cone and Hawkins (1977).

It should be emphasized that screening is only the first step in SEI case finding. The population that is at risk in such scales must then be studied in detail to sort out those who really fit the definitions used in a particular district.

SEI Incidence

Depending upon the definition of SEI, its incidence goes up or down. The 12 percent of the total population given for *all* of special education does not accommodate what we know of the SEI category. A variety of studies and the generalizations indicate that 10 to 12 percent of children and youth have social and emotional problems at a level significant enough to warrant planned professional help. This is in keeping with the estimates of the National Commission on Children's Mental Health referred to previously. Reliable estimates indicate that at least 3 percent are severe enough to require immediate, expert intervention. A survey, *Special Education Programs for Emotionally Disturbed Adolescents* (1978), conducted by the National Association of State Directors of Special Education, shows various prevalence figures from .005 percent to 6.5 percent. Professor Kristen D. Juul, of Southern Illinois University, is a specialist in the international matters of special education for behavior disorders. In a personal communication he reported prevalance figures from several European studies. Totals in eight countries ranged from about 7 percent to 30 percent, all far exceeding the special education of the 2 to 3 percent prevalent in our literature. An extended discussion of prevalence figures from various studies can be found in Long, Morse, and Newman, *Conflict in the Classroom* (1980).

If we follow the federal interpretation and put the top level of SEI eligibility at 2 percent of the school population, we reduce the obligation of special education but we do not eliminate the number of children who need this help. The total group combines the very serious 3 percent and the additional up to 10 percent who still require some special services. If special education were to be generic, that is, take responsibility for all who need more than is available through good general education, then 12 percent would be a reasonable responsibility figure. As it is, those who do not fit whatever the SEI categorization in use are declared someone else's responsibility. Many of these children fall into the cracks between the educational and community services unless the parents have money and an inclination to get help. Because of the restrictiveness of who is special, regular education is left with the greater number of disturbed children than the number under surveillance by special education. Some of the so-called mildly disturbed are most disturbing in a school setting. The neglect of these youngsters by special education is a source of considerable conflict with regular education. There is little attention to prevention to reduce the number of children who will need additional service.

In Jessor and Jessor's (1977) study it appears that "problem behavior" is common in "normal" adolescents depending on one's definition. Over a third of twelfth graders were using marijuana, had engaged in premarital sex, and had serious problems relating to drinking! Grieger and Richards (1976) found that the ratings for regular and special-class pupils on the Behavior Problem Checklist were structurally similar but special children scored higher on all three dimensions (conduct disorders, personality, and immaturity-inadequacy patterns) and on almost all of the fifty-five individual items. There is an important lesson here: disturbed children and youth are not a unique category. They are like their peers and adults in kind but not in degree. The point is, schools do need assistance of some type for a much larger proportion of pupils than the 2 or 3 percent identified as very serious by the specialists.

Kelly and his colleagues (1977) note that incidence reports of behavior disorders by teachers range from 2 percent to 69.3 percent of given child populations, with a mean percentage of 20.4 over the grades. Of the 20 percent, 12.2 percent were assigned the category "mild," while 7.8 percent were characterized as moderate or severe.

One of the most careful incidence studies has been conducted at the Institute of Psychiatry of Maudsley Hospital in London (Rutter et al. 1976). The children born during two years in a relatively stable population on the Isle of Wight, have been studied for evidence of psychiatric disorder. Parents and teachers provided initial screening data, and on this basis 13 percent of the children were selected for intensive study. It is interesting that parents and teachers indicated similar percentages, but on largely different sets of candidates! A number of the disturbances were "situation specific." The final percentage for whom psychiatric help was finally indicated was 6.3. There were almost twice the number of boys. Boys tended to be more antisocial, and girls more neurotic. About two-thirds of the 6.3 percent needed treatment, while the others needed diagnosis and advice only. The rate for severe disorders was given at 2.2 percent. The group actually receiving treatment at the time of the study was only .7 percent. A group of London children was surveyed as well. Here the incidence figures were twice that of the Isle of Wight group. This was attributed for the most part to "family disadvantage," which was an index of various negative family influences.

A most analytical presentation of problems in identification, classification, and intervention is found in *The Ecosystem of the "Sick" Child,* edited by Salzinger, Antrobus, and Glick (1980). As is evident from the title, they take an ecological stance, defining disorder as a set of behaviors that are accepted or rejected with reference to different social contexts. Thus interventions are directed at variables in systems, not symptoms of the child as personal attributes. These authors propose a multimethod and multistage approach—that is, more than one nominating source for the potentially disturbed (parents *and* teachers for example) and then intensive psychiatric study of these. While this can eliminate false positives, there are still children who are overlooked. In a meta-analysis of many studies, these authors report the rate of clinical maladjustment as 11.8 percent for United States and 13.2 for Britain with considerable variation across age, class, and social setting.

One look at these difficulties and it is no wonder why we have no reliable index of the incidence of SEI problems. There is no agreement on the definition of the impairment. Age differences make for complications in differentiating the normal and atypical even if we agree on methods of assessment. Symptoms are difficult to evaluate. Some child behavior is transient, while others (sociopathy and psychosis) are most likely to exhibit continuity. Different experts and/or different professionals will not always agree about the state of disturbance, even when they are using the same definitions. And various settings make for differential behavior, further confusing the issue.

Wood and Zabel (1978) have analyzed the incidence reports. Their thoughtful and thorough examination covers the many reasons for the incidence variations and the implications for education, making it clear that although special-education programs are not required for any 30 percent of the school population, some other resources must be provided. They believe special education for SEI will be required for 2 to 3 percent of the students.

For our purposes, we will take the prevalent figures of 10 to 12 percent for the total SEI population and 3 percent for the very seriously disturbed, the clientele for special education, recognizing that the federal estimates are only 2 percent. The importance of the low accepted figure for the special SEI teacher is that the general education personnel will continually be seeking help for a much larger number and resenting our restrictiveness.

CONTINUITY OF PROBLEM BEHAVIOR

Teachers read of their past pupils in the horror reports in the newspapers. They will also have visits from past problem pupils who are now leading exemplary lives in which sometimes the crucial turning point was the teacher.

Continuity of problem behavior, a seemingly innocent matter, turns out to have both political and educational implications. Is disturbance a chronic condition, or a response to stress periods such as adolescence? If indeed problems disappear without special interventions, why invest in help, which is incidentally an argument used against Head Start based on faulty research. From the humanistic standpoint continuity is not relevant: *if at any point in time* there is a person-system in distress, the goal is to reduce the pain regardless of what may be the future course of events. One should be given the best possible life at any time.

In the study of a total child population on the island of Kauai (Werner, Bierman, and French 1971; Werner and Smith 1977, 1981), the continuity issue was clarified. The study started at the prenatal period and ended at age eighteen. Those suffering from prenatal stress had a very high incidence of serious behavior problems. Of those seriously acting-out children in preadolescence, only one-third improved by age eighteen. One half of those having mental health intervention improved. Shy, anxious children showed improvement even without intervention much more than the anxious, acting-out group.

Lewis (1965) concludes that it is the acting-out child, rather than the shy withdrawn one, who is likely to become the seriously disturbed adult. He makes the interesting observation that if one takes the adult patients, one is likely to find childhood problems; but the evidence is mixed if one follows the group of disturbed children to adulthood. He concludes that there is only mild support for the thesis that emotionally disturbed children will become mentally ill adults.

Rutter, in the Isle of Wight studies (Rutter and Graham 1966), resurveyed the 7 percent of psychiatrically disturbed ten- and 11-year-old children when they were fourteen to fifteen. Acting out conduct disorders were most persistent: three-fourths of these maintained. The outlook for children with emotional disturbance was much better but almost half still had problems. No sex difference was found. There was a slight increase in the rate of psychiatric disorder at adolescence. Overall, three-fifths of the psychiatric disorders at fifteen were newly developed while two-fifths were continuations, a preponderance being boys. The persistent cases had academic retardation and family difficulties not generally found in the new cases. Zax and his colleagues (1969) in a follow-up study found support for the hypothesis that early disturbance is predictive of later difficulty. Kupfer and others (1975) found links between childhood difficulties and lifelong personality traits. One of the best predictors of aggressive behavior at the close of adolescence is the choice of violent television programs at eight.

Richman, Graham, and Stevenson (1982) report strong continuity in a longitudinal study of behavior problems from age three to eight. Continuity was stronger for boys. Reading problems at eight were found linked to adverse family conditions at the early age. Bandura (1982b) makes an interesting point that fortuitous events are responsible for significant changes in one's life, which deemphasizes the expectation of continuity.

Kagen has argued for the reversibility in cognitive development, and he and Brim have edited a comprehensive volume on the subject (Brim and Kagan 1980). One of the ideas proposed is that there may be high continuity for some domains of behavior and low for others, which is what we have just observed. As Kagan sees it, the belief in continuity is part of man's wish to believe in a rational order of things. Another important factor is individual differences: just as some individuals are consistent over time, others change. Hedging seems to be the current general reaction to the continuity issue.

Most of the attention has been on continuity of problem behavior. Recently attention has also been given to the nonvulnerable, or, as they are called, resilient children, and what we can learn from them. Werner and Smith (1981) have studied high-risk children who did not succumb and note the importance of at least one stable caregiver in concert with other surrogate caregivers, and the formation of strong attachments balanced by independence. Some children can withstand strong shock. Macfarlane (1963) reported that half of those who were confronted with difficult childhood and adolescent situations became successful adults.

Overall we can say that certain behaviors have more probability of continuity than others. Also we should consider the continuity of the life situation as well as continuity of the child's behavior. There is little evidence that most SEI youngsters cure themselves over time, but there are great individual differences. Growth factors (as well as external factors) do change matters, and some youngsters will not persist along an early line of deviation. None of the continuity arguments should be used to delay giving help to pupils when they need it.

MOVING FROM CASE FINDING TO DIAGNOSIS

It is the law that no pupil should be signified SEI without an adequate diagnosis. There are severe criticisms of current diagnostic procedures. Some would abandon the rituals we have and just start teaching or working with the child as a different style of diagnosis. Whatever the style, the professional individual or team comes to certain hypotheses (tentative, we hope) that guide intervention efforts. Otherwise every helping exchange with the pupil would be an ad hoc one.

It is said that current diagnostic methods emphasize tests that tell the teacher nothing and psychiatric studies that have no relevance. What we need, it is said, is an educational diagnosis. Whatever we call it and whatever we do, we are talking about understanding a child.

There are good reasons why the law requires explicit diagnostic plans with appropriate personnel. Far too often the major effort of diagnosis is to label, asking only whether the pupil fits the SEI special education category. It is What do we call him? as if one knew what to do once such a label was assigned. Finding out *where* the child fits has too often become the major preoccupation of special education. For all the arguments against labeling, it still flourishes as usually the only door to obtaining help. Money follows the category, not the child. Also, some parent groups fear losing their share of help if categories are abandoned.

However, there are other even more significant arguments against diagnosis for the sake of labeling. A label is psychological stereotyping. It is illusionary. It denies the individuality that we must know. The most significant criticism is that a label, as a shorthand device, implies that the child fits a theoretical image. We know that the image of SEI has no given set of attributes.

The results of contemporary diagnostic procedures are usually more highly regarded by the clinical people who conduct them than by the educators who try to use them. Walter Mischel (1977) makes it clear that measurement of personality is confounded by multiple determinants of behavior and the role of the environmental context, as well as the function of a particular measurement scale. Procedures are often ritualized and easy answers are sought from the use of a mandated set of tests. Often the child gets lost in the pile of data: if you have ever read a case file and then met the youngster, you may have had the shock of comparison.

"Why Won't They Listen to Me?" This is the subtitle of Shectman's (1979) discussion, "Problems in Communicating Psychological Understanding," in which the problems of interdisciplinary communication are outlined. As a consumer of psychological information, teachers need to know how to use diagnostic information. The author lists problems of information overload: too much data and too little attention to treatment issues; different disciplines with different role obligations and thus a focus on different areas; too great an expectation from diagnosis; and most important, the need to have things explained "from the inside out," so that the person is brought to life, and empathy is generated.

Ysseldyke and Algozzine (1981) found that classifying pupils as SEI was significantly influenced by referral indications of a behavior problem before assessment data were available. Indication of a behavior problem is such a powerful influence in decision making that it overrides later data. The authors suggest that professionals should reject referral stereotypes and replace this with collecting actual data. In the next chapter I shall discuss the methodology for collecting information and processing it into a study of the individual self of the SEI pupil with direct implications for the teacher.

CONTRIBUTORS TO DIAGNOSIS

Although different states have different rules about who may legitimately contribute what to the assessment of a pupil, there are several professionals and lay persons who should play a part. We are speaking of what should be but is often not the case. Without multidisciplinary participation, the rights of the child may be in jeopardy, based on superficial or "test battery"-oriented programs. The fact that the representative member of any discipline may be talented or limited does not mean that the proper function of the discipline can be neglected, though some functions are interchangeable. Sometimes a teacher or psychologist may provide an understanding of the child's inner life as well as a psychiatrist. Roles and functions are not rigidly fixed. Verification from several sources should also improve the accuracy of information. Mutual respect among the major disciplines is essential. The goal is to solve a child's problem, not to play roles. Because the teacher will be reading reports and interacting with various disciplines, teachers need to be familiar with some of the language and methodology of their companions. Also, some disciplines provide consultation and it becomes important to the teacher to know how to utilize their special talents as well as how to explain the educational world to these colleagues.

The Child Psychiatrist

The child psychiatrist combines medical and psychiatric skills in diagnosis. The medical history is reviewed, which covers developmental accomplishments and anomalies. A physical and neurological examination should be included. Basically, a competent psychiatrist adds the following to the diagnosis: family dynamics, as seen in the child's inner life; fantasy and the significance of the manifest behavior (i.e., play, language) to the child's total personality organization. A primary ability of the psychiatrist should be an ability to engender trust of both parents and the child so that the interview will be as open as possible. Particularly in the area of differential diagnosis, such as distinguishing the part of the behavior related to retardation and psychosis in a child's behavior or to separate the defenses from the substrata, a child psychiatrist will be of significant help. There is perhaps more mystique about what the psychiatrist does than any other discipline. A major component is in a highly sensitive human radar that enables the catching of elusive cues and the ability to follow these up to get at the significance. Subsequently, psychiatrists may also provide therapy and ongoing consultation.

The overall relationships between special education and pediatricians is important and at the present still generally leaves much to be desired. But cooperation of the pediatrician is often critical, especially in helping the young child. The current condition is presented in detail in *Exceptional Children* (vol. 48).

The School Psychologist

The school psychologist's major contribution is usually in systematic assessment based on normative tests. For example, in assessing intellectual capabilities an individual test such as the Weschler Intelligence Scale for Children (WISC) is to be preferred because of the subtests that include scores on particular functions, including information, comprehension, memory, vocabulary, arithmetic, and reasoning. This test has both a verbal and performance scale and the discrepancies in the V-P are useful in diagnosis of learning problems. For primary and preschool, the related form is the WPPSI. The Stanford-Binet and the Peabody Picture Vocabulary tests are also often employed. For children with language expressive problems or who use other languages (when there is no available tests or form in the native language) the Lieter can be used. A new scale called the Kaufman Assessment Battery for Children (K-ABC) is designed to measure intelligence and achievement for preschool and elementary students in a new way. A special set of tests to detect learning disability in frequent use is the Woodcock-Johnson Psycho-Educational Battery.

An effort to assess not just what the pupil is able to do at this time, but his "teachability" has been gaining ground. This is the Learning Potential Assessment Device, which examines how learning could be improved. Feuerstein (1979) calls this "dynamic testing." After finding out the performance level, the effort is made to teach the pupil how to solve the problem by use of a rule or strategy applied to a similar test item. Then the pupil is reassessed on a parallel item to see if he has learned and can utilize the strategy. The major assessment is how much teaching is necessary to accomplish the new learning, which gives a learning quotient, so to speak, rather than a what has been "learned" index. Learning potential is of course a major concern of the special teacher.

In addition to cognitive functioning, the psychologist should provide information on the affective life of the child from interviews or projective tests. Psychologists are most likely to give intelligence tests and projective tests and less so to administer paper-and-pencil personality tests. A "projective" is a device that provides an unstructured condition with no right or wrong response and that is designed to get at aspects of basic emotional life. The common drawing ones are Draw a Person, Draw a Family (Family Drawing/Kinetic Family drawing where the family is doing "something"), the House Tree Person, (HTP) and sometimes Draw a School or Classroom. A story response may be made to a set of ambiguous pictures (the TAT-Thematic Apperception Test, or the form for children, the CAT-Children's Apperception Test). There are several forms of sentence stems which call for completion (such as I was afraid . . . , or Dad is . . .). The Rorschach test presents ambiguous ink blots that are to be described by the youngster. A common question to begin understanding inner life is "tell me your three wishes." Early memories are valuable as well as discussion of where the person expects to be in future.

There have been many efforts to provide codes for scoring responses to projectives. In some cases this has been verified, but in most instances the production has to be clinically evaluated and there is considerable leeway for interpretation. But, as one source of information, paticularly when the child's problem is obscure, these data are important. Some children neither know nor will reveal their feelings directly.

Interview questions also may be included. Achievement tests may be given (here or by the special teacher), and an effort is made to indicate the presence of possible learning difficulties. The psychological report also includes information on how the child reacts in the testing. The psychologist should be able to test in such a way as to eliminate cultural artifacts and distinguish the culturally different from the retarded child. The final case write-up should cover the overall personality style and especially school motivation as well as underlying forces, fit to the local categorization system with suggestions for planning.

Sometimes psychologists provide individual and/or group therapy for pupils and families. Dyer (1974) has written on the specifics of the psychologist's role in helping the SEI.

It is recognized from a study by Matuszek and Oakland (1979) that teachers and psychologists do not necessarily agree on the importance of various attributes. IQ, achievement, and anxiety about home are of common concern. Psychologists are more concerned with SES and adaptive behavior; self-concept is of greater importance to teachers. Surprisingly, ethnicity, language, home values, school anxiety, classroom manageability, and interpersonal relationships did not influence recommendations by either professional.

There is always a question of the validity and interpretation of a given test score, especially a projective. It is well for teachers to refer to such sources as Buros' *Mental Measurements Yearbook,* or references such as Sattler (1982) for questions in regard to test validity and reliability.

An analytical review of many scales for assessing behavior can be found in a chapter by Walls and colleagues (1977). Walls evaluates scales on objectivity, clarity and completeness. This source, along with Johnson and Bommarito (1971) and Walker (1973) for young children will help a teacher select the relevant scales for given purposes. An inexpensive and comprehensive source is the *Handbook of Psychiatric Rating Scales* (1981). Anderson's *Assessing Affective Characteristics in Schools* (1981) is a thorough text on all matters of this topic with especial attention to reliability and validity for those selecting such devices. Spivack and Swift (1973) have looked at instruments for teacher use and provided the key to the type of dimensions covered. The four basic areas covered in such scales are acting-out control problems, recessive behavior (withdrawn, anxious, unhappy), classroom adaptiveness (school adjustment, relationship to teacher), and cognitive reasoning. Spivack and Swift indicate that there is often a lack of validity, norms, or educational focus in the instruments and that few devices are available assessing adolescent behavior. Teacher ratings have predictive value, especially regarding peer behavior, because of the opportunity for observation in the broad social context of school. In a follow-up study of adult adjustment of teacher-rated problem children, it was found that the most useful index was in peer relationships: the children with inability to get along with other children were most vulnerable to poor adult adjustment (Janes and Hesselbrock 1978).

The School Social Worker

The social worker characteristically collects the family history and provides information on current conditions that may exacerbate the child's behavior, the possibilities for change and the family resources that can be utilized or generated. Frequently the ongoing contact or individual pupil and family therapy may be done by the social worker. It is well to recognize that in reality family contact usually means mother contact.

An astute social worker does not collect family histories as abstract documents. It is possible to get a two-generation case-family history without throwing much light on how the factors influence the condition at hand. What we hope to learn, in addition to the problem etiology as recalled, are the family dynamics, child's role, strengths and resources of the family, accessibility, and possible interventions. Social workers also function to generate other necessary community support for a needing family, such as welfare, medical and special services. The social worker may provide consultation to the teacher and therapy for the child or parents.

Other Special Professional Contributors

There are times when other specialists and/or a complete clinical workup is needed. There are area and regional resources which have the personnel for extensive multidiscipline assessment. Speech clinicians (both school personnel and external) are more and more a part of both the diagnostic and treatment teams. The League School has prepared a teacher's handbook for this area (McMillan 1978). A child neurologist may need to do extensive studies because there may be biological anomalies that do not appear at the start or are disguised when given behavior shows up later. Possible seizures, toxic conditions, tumors, dietary deficiencies, and allergies are examples of diagnostic aspects that need attention. Geneticists also play important roles. In fact the geneticist is the first stage in prevention. In some instances principals, special-education personnel, school guidance workers, or nurses will have a significant role in producing data on the child. Because some SEI children and youth also violate legal statutes, there may be court workers involved as well. At the present time, because of the widespread discouragement with the juvenile court system and the rights of children, there is a movement to reduce the power of the courts over children, which will mean increased complications for interventions in schools.

The Parents

Parents are of course primary contributors of information and should be partners from the start. The problem is that few professionals have the skill to work with parents as team members. Our methods are frequently demeaning and insulting, with a tendency to blame parents. We do not know how to explain painful material to them openly and honestly. We are inclined to tell rather than listen, to interpret rather than ask. Most parents have already tried a variety of remedial efforts. Many are hard-pressed by failure and a good many are overcome by life events. Yet most are involved and it will be difficult to provide restoration without their whole-hearted cooperation and participation. PL 94-142 mandated the new parental participant role; it will take us a long time to reorient our efforts to meet the condition. There is a tendency for school personnel to overemphasize noncooperation, a condition that is found with only a few parents. Most parents need help, which is not to say they need or will accept formal therapy as it is usually defined. Families with their own problems often see only the child's problems: it is an expression of helplessness and a defense against the true condition (Foster and Flomos 1978).

It is not the abstract family event but the psychological importance of the event to the child that we need to know. Religious affiliation may mean nothing significant on one hand or be the nucleus of the child's problem on the other. How many siblings is of less importance than what the siblings mean to each other. Family mobility at given times may have profound social effects, but one wishes to discover whether moving traumatized the child's social relationships or facilitated skills in making new friends.

The SEI Pupils

We already have acknowledged that adults and children see things in different lights, so obviously if we are to understand the child, we had best spend a great deal of effort obtaining a view of his or her phenomenological world or view of life. This ranges from their "history" of a condition, or when it started, to how it is now in their eyes. In fact the earliest memories of a child are often very revealing about his life-style. He can describe his view of his problem as well as the what and how of helping him (Levine, Clark, and Simon 1981).

Parents and youngsters disagree as to the cause of the child's problems (Compas et al. 1981). To the parents the attributions are more internal ("He could change if he tried harder"), while children see a balance of internal and external causality. Incongruity of the parent's and the adolescent's perceptions of problem behavior is chronic. A friend of mine who is a teacher sent this lament of a pupil who had written it in preparation for a meeting between his teacher and his parents (Figure 1).

Perhaps the most critical aspect of prevalent diagnostic procedures is the outcome in terms of the person to be helped by the process. Because of how we conduct our assessment, to many youngsters it is a kind of magic where they answer but only adults get to know what it all means. To humanize the procedure, it is important to include the child "in" to the greatest possible extent. We share goals and results. We ask what he thinks of what we believe we have found. A relationship rather than alienation should develop through the diagnosis. It has been found that self-judgments are at least as predictive as formal assessments (Shrauger and Osberg 1981). Pupils can usually make the significant contribution to the understanding of themselves. They may thus also be led to better self-understanding. Frequently the test data or other ideas about a child are not shared. We ask but we do not give. The perceptions of a pupil about his life is the richest source of useful information we have. Children range from the overly open, spilling out their insides, to the nonverbal or resistant ("I want to tell you but I can't. It's about my family"). There are techniques such as story telling for dealing with children who are reluctant to talk. It should be noted that the exchange of personal information tends to bond the child to the one who listens. This relationship formation based upon primary life sharing is often necessary for a teacher in order to work with the youngster. That is why, again, regardless of information in the file, the teacher has to be effective in talking with children and in the skill of interviewing, to be discussed later.

It is important to note that children and parents are not always in agreement regarding behavior problems. Pierce and Klein (1982) found significant agreement on only seven of fifty-two items of behavioral description. The highest agreement was on easily observable items and those expected of normal children; least agreement was on adult-child interactions and the child's feelings. They caution about taking parent perceptions for planning without substantiation. Their review of previ-

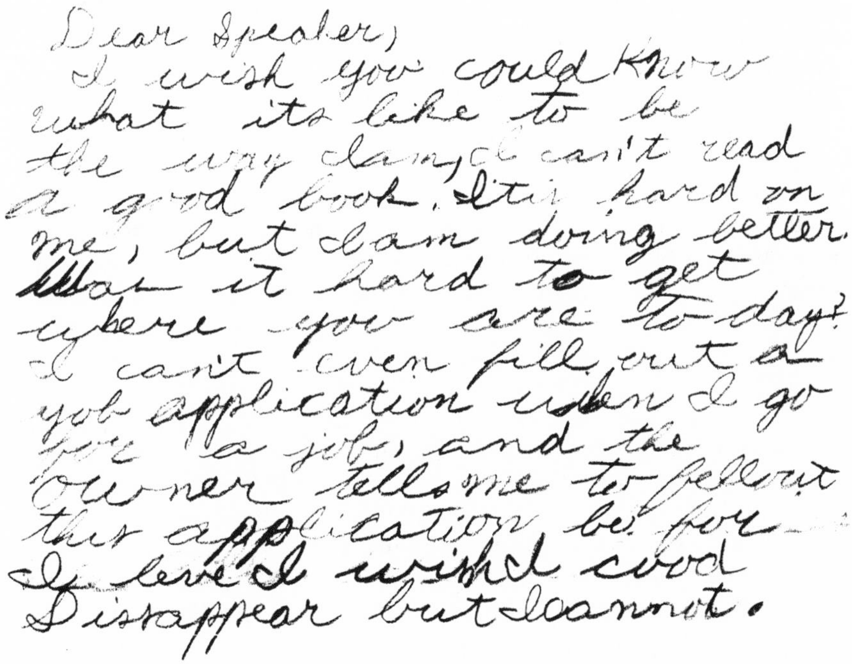

FIGURE 1. An SEI pupil's lament.

ous studies indicates that the agreement-disagreement issue is a complex one indeed, probably best understood in the conditions of each set of persons. Such discrepancy is in fact an excellent "objective" way to deal with family problems in the school setting. Moos (1982) describes having an adolescent girl and both parents fill out his family descriptor scale, and the differences in what they saw and what their ideal families would be became the basis for intervention plans.

Peers as Information Sources

There are two ways we obtain useful information concerning a particular child from peers. One is by observation and the other is by asking questions such as sociometric or role analysis. Usually one does not have to ask; rejection of a peer, fear, and avoidance or liking are obvious every day in a classroom.

The peer society exists in another layer than the pupil-teacher society and is often hidden from the adult. "You don't know how he is when you're not around," a group member will explain to the teacher. Children early develop attributions regarding the reasons for SEI behavior. They also see the teacher as the one who should take care of behavior problems. It is understandable that what bothers peers most is acting-out behavior that they judge to be more serious than hallucinations (Roberts, Berdleman, and Wurtele 1981). They have pragmatic judgments: "He takes your ball but you don't try to get it back." Sometimes they are perplexed concerning a pupil whom they have tried to help but won't play when invited. The behavior of peers is a vast reservoir of information as well as a potential for assistance.

Teacher Contributions

Obviously teachers have many many contributions to make in the study of SEI youngsters. They will have both normative information on achievement from the tests they administer in basic skills (reading, writing, math), as well as knowledge about various general areas (social studies, science). But they can also contribute actual examples of the pupils' performance not only in academic work but in areas such as arts and crafts. They know about interests and talents and specific levels of competency in given skills. What is more important, teachers are aware of the youngster's learning style and how he can best be taught.

The school personnel are usually the source of referrals and are the only professionals who have spent long hours with the child. They can offer evidence on a wide range of behavior, and this against normal development for an age. Because teachers see the pupil in work settings, play settings, relating to authority and to peers, they can sense assets as well as the pervasiveness of problems. Further, because the child is seen over a time span, minor problems can be worked out. No one says that teachers are always objective: they are biased as well as astute, as are observers from the other mental health professions.

To encourage objectivity, teachers can employ scales previously discussed under screening. The difference in teacher and parent perceptions is illustrated by a study of Graybill and Gabel (1978). Special-education teachers nominated parents for counseling whose children had conduct problems, but these were unrelated to parents' perceptions of their children's behavior.

Teachers along with others who see children professionally have a legal responsibility for citing abused and neglected children to the proper authorities. The matter is a difficult one to assess in most instances, although some blatant cases may be obvious. There are several reasons for difficulty: children may hide, deny, or explain away evidence; body marks may be hidden under clothing; and there are those children who invent abuse. Sexual abuse, much more common than was generally assumed, may be blanketed in fear and may be reflected in emotional disturbance. It is important to note that special children are more vulnerable to abuse. Overall the figure is estimated at minimum of 2 million abused children per year, the majority of the abusers being parents. With economic stress, violence in the family tends to increase. False accusation is of course a most serious matter: the teacher would do well to learn the procedures used in a given work setting. In addition, one must recognize the personal emotional dilemma in acknowledging that there are adults who batter helpless children, which most of us find horrifying to the extreme, even to the point of wanting to ignore the consequences.

Teachers as Observers

The behaviorists have stressed direct observation of individual behavior. The plague of subjective bias, made erudite by calling it clinical judgment, without external verification data, still dominates in many places. At the other extreme is the fixation on the minutia of time/incident graphs recording how many times a pupil gets out of his seat regardless of the condition, as if knowing this meant knowing the child. Wearing a helmet with a wiggle circuit recorder may give fascinating data to the researcher and may even be fun for a youngster; a classroom of helmeted pupils would be a sight.

There are contrasting types of information that are collected in the process of understanding an SEI pupil and his/her behavior. We collect *perceptions* of various persons, including sometimes the target person. These perceptions may have woven in various *interpretations* or *explanations* of what is perceived. Sometimes the perception is a *judgment* based upon explicit or implicit values having to do with good or bad, right or wrong.

It is equally necessary to collect data on actual *behavior,* what is done, how often, what preceded and followed a behavioral sequence, etc. The behavior needs to be interpreted to give it meaning in relation to the individual. Observational data have value in planning an intervention and evaluating results as well as in understanding the child. By using particular recording methods, it is possible to vary the type of information secured. For example, in *One Little Boy* (Baruch 1964), all of the ecological interchanges of a child and what he did are followed for a total day. Or we may wish to record frequency of specific behaviors (fighting, daydreaming, refusals) as well as indicate the intensity and duration of the episodes. We may expand this to include what preceded and what followed, that is, rewards or punishments. We decide the time sample to be included, which is always a difficult judgment relative to a reliable sample of given behavior. An excellent resource for observations is part 1 of *Child Behavior Problem* (McAuley and McAuley 1977). One should record both positive and negative valued behavior to give a balance. Another method is to record *critical incidents,* outstanding events as they take place over time.

First is the matter of selecting what to observe. If we observe "nervous mannerisms," we need to have norms for this behavior from nondisturbed youngsters. How long a time sample is necessary? How reliable is the observer? Is the schema for observation valid for the criterion assumed? The best way to get involved in the difficulties is to do some direct observation alone and in pairs, to set up categories, and to try to use the information, as is often done in child experimental psychology. We can observe a given behavior in a group of children or multiple behavior in a given youngster.

Not only can we observe children, we can observe teachers and code their acts as environmental stimuli. Even without precision, it is obvious that some teachers give little praise, much criticism, and poor directions; but just how much of what makes an excellent basis for discussion and consultation. Coding film tapes of teacher behavior is an excellent data source. The total "climate" can be "observed." The Fink interaction system has been used for this, and there is an extensive literature on the whole problem (Fink, 1970). One of the most helpful publications for teachers is by Walker (1978), which also appears in his textbook *How to Manage the Acting Out Child* (1979). Because we are obligated to evaluate treatment effects, the use of behavior time samples before and after, in the special setting, and in other settings, including the home, all add to our knowledge.

It should be pointed out that observation techniques do not remove judgments. There is judgment in what to observe, in how to observe, and in interpreting the meaning of data obtained. While there is still judgment, there is shared awareness of the data base. The great advantage is to remove vague impressions where the assumptions are produced out of minimal selective cues and maximal personalized contribution, which can be very biased.

Often by looking at what happens just before the targeted behavior, we learn of antecedent conditions that need attention. In fact, the behaviorist attention to the single case in detail results in a focus on the individual that is the essence of our goal in assessment. Behavioristic methodology encourages moving from vague to specific content. Baker and Thomas (1980) have analyzed in detail the assets and limitations of observation as a methodology, as has Hartman (1982).

THE DECISION-MAKING PROCESS: THE IEPC

The data collected on the individual pupil eventually are summarized and presented at a case conference of the Individual Educational Planning Committee.

Case conferences are the meetings where the experts and the parents convene (sometimes with the pupil) to discuss the nature of the findings and evolve a plan. Case conferences are as good as the "team" dynamics or as fouled up as the "team" dynamics. Often there are power struggles, dominance of a discipline, and role dances that confuse the real issue. Knoff (1983) has found that in final placement decisions there is a disproportionate influence, not matching the intent of the law. The school psychologist and special-education teacher rate highest and next the central administrator. The parent and principal are about equal and the other specialists and regular teacher still lower. If conferences are done well, as a mutual problem solving exercise, the conclusions can lead to appropriate interventions. Usually too much energy is spent on evaluating the past and deciding the label and too little on the current critical behavior and what can be done about it.

Clinical judgments have been found to be limited by the lack of recognition of parallel factors that may account for behavior, preconceived notions, and judgment processes of which the clinician is unaware; overconfidence and biases come into play after the fact. Arkes (1981) suggests three strategies to minimize this: active consideration of alternatives, attention to usually ignored data, and less dependency on memory relative to data.

Research (Beebe 1978) on team-planning meetings suggests that the participants themselves are usually quite satisfied with what goes on. It is also evident that, at this stage, there can be a relationship between the data collected and the general decisions, but the linkage is often lost in later stages. The study of the decision group's dynamics would reveal simplified planning is belied by what usually really takes place. There are a myriad reality conditions that enter in subtly or overtly. "There is a place for the pupil in a current program"; "It will be too expensive to set up what he really needs"; "The parents will never go for that"; "The designated teacher is not up to managing this one." So goes reality. The interplay of personalities and roles becomes activated in these meetings, which are first to decide the categorical issue: Is the pupil a candidate for special education and if so on what label or assessment basis? If not, there is an obligation to set up alternative strategies but often little or nothing is done.

Bagnato (1980) advocates "translated reports," which include particular developmental targets incorporated in the psychoeducational report. Clear goals are stated that predicate curricular planning. He found reports much more useful when cast in functional terms. Rather than give only test results, describe areas of strength and deficits clearly; emphasize features of the child's learning style, reward preferences, etc.; indicate developmental ceilings; and detail behavioral and instructional strategies. These suggestions are obviously getting at the essential problems that teachers have with current diagnostic procedures.

Although the meetings consume much staff time we should remember their purpose. In the past, schools and clinics have been too casual when it came to decisions, and parents were left out or had no recourse for either understanding the information or redressing what seemed to be unreasonable plans. There was a loss of trust in the institution of special education.

A 1982 study of the process of group decision in special education works in the IEPC meetings is revealing (Cruickshank, Morse, and Grant, unpublished manuscript). An average of five persons attended at a cost of $77 in professional time, not including costs to parents or the time for professional preparation. Parents attended almost 95 percent of all the IEPC meetings; the percent is somewhat lower for the SEI meetings. For SEI there were usually five to seven persons involved. PL 94-142 states that a person from the diagnostic team, one from building administration, and a special education teacher must attend every meeting: administrators attended 97 percent of the meetings, school psychologists 92 percent and special teachers 71 percent. The school psychologist usually has the responsibility for bringing the diagnostic information, regardless of source, and blending it with educational input. It is no wonder there are process problems.

To provide meaning, whatever is found by interview, tests, observations, or reactions from others has to be "processed." It has to be put together. Both the information source and the processing differ depending on one's theories of the child self. The position in this book is that all behavior makes sense if we could but understand the meaning to the person performing it. The hope is that common understanding and acceptance of the meaning of the diagnostic information can be achieved. We often forget that the most important persons to come to agreement are not the professionals. Parents have the need to understand and they have the legal right to reject the results. Their offspring cannot be candidates for special education unless they have been properly and adequately diagnosed with culture-free evaluation. Decisions cannot be arbitrary. Parents must be given written notice and every effort made to involve them in the processes: they have the final say.

Parents' councils keep the professionals honest by monitoring activities, participating in decisions, and lobbying for the needed resources for quality solutions. The *Advocate* (1979) contains a parent check list in dealing with the IEP. It covers such things as the actual instruction time, curriculum needs, degree of integration, and transportation. *Closer Look* and *Exceptional Parent,* which are regular publications, also contain help for parents participating in the IEP and special education in general. Because of the publicity, pain, and expense of a few court cases, it is all too easy to forget the fact that the vast majority of parents do care about getting the very best for their children and do work out reasonable plans with special education. They are often desperate to get correct and reasonable care. Sharing child raising does not come easily to some parents and some teachers (Lightfoot 1978). Information must be made available and explained to parents. They have the right to independent assessment, to legal counsel, and to appeal (Abeson and Zettel 1977; Ballard and Zettel 1977). The plan of assistance evolving from the diagnosis must utilize the *most normal setting* that is appropriate, starting with mainstream education, any extrusion requiring proof of necessity to accomplish the called-for goals. The Individual Education Plan must be specific and include academic, social, and vocational provisions. The goals must be put in such a way that progress can be evaluated—indeed the evaluation must take place at stated intervals. Forness (1979) has reviewed the situation and finds the parent role far from what is needed or even legislated.

The last person to understand the problem, that is the pupil, should be the first. Often these children have been "diagnosed" by parents, peers, and teachers, and many messages given to them on their condition, their poor prognosis, their "badness" or whatever. These have become part of the self-concept. In our experience with children and adolescents, often the hardest part is helping the youngster to assimilate new information about himself into his self-concept. Abilities, limitations, unrecognized feelings, possible strategies—for whom it is more critical to know about these than the target of all the activity? We will return to this aspect subsequently.

CONCLUSION

We have described a data base and process that fits the legal expectation for dealing with SEI problems. It is a multidiscipline and multifaceted procedure.

The fact is, a limited number of school-only personnel are often given the total responsibility for diagnosis, consultation, and treatment. The school psychologist in many states has the responsibility for diagnostic studies ranging from infancy to adulthood, and school social workers the responsibility for the family study. Decisions are frequently made on a paucity of information and superficial conferences.

Whatever the outcome of the information collected on a child, the teacher will have to assemble a working profile for planning strategies. Teachers teach pupils, not labels. Their unique responsibilities and the educational setting require a particular use of case data. Many teachers have reported to the author that they filed the reports from other professionals (when they did get them) and wrote up their own analyses.

The alternative to labels is individualization of the self through knowing the nuances of the youngster's nature and environment. This requires an ecological approach, concerned equally with the person and the place, because this is the only way to understand the meaning of behavior, which is a consequence of so many internal and external forces. While the knowledge of another human being is always partial, to the degree that we comprehend, we understand the *why* as well as the *what* of behavior. Sometimes, when we assemble what we already know, the picture is obvious and adequate without extensive tests and data collection. At other times we are faced with a quandary, especially concerning which interventions are required. Diagnosis is often progressive, starting with what *appears* to provide a basis for plans and then finding that there is much more to be known before we can have the proper judgments about what to do.

The next chapter discusses in some detail the type of information teachers have said they wanted to know about their SEI pupils and the resolution of these data into an appreciation of the individual self-concept.

3

Information Integration

TRANSITION

W E HAVE REVIEWED sources of information concerning the SEI pupil, although schools seldom have contributions from all the persons indicated. Two central questions remain: What specific information is essential and how can this information be synthesized to provide the most useful understanding for the teacher?

Over the years the author has discussed this issue with special teachers. The first chapter developed from their thoughts about pupils, in terms of self-concept and self-esteem. This chapter deals with the type of information that these teachers wanted to have available concerning a youngster and how such information made sense to them in terms of the typical self-concept patterns they found in their classes. The results of these discussions with teachers resulted in the information and planning grid in figure 2. There are several differences between this method of child study and categorization efforts to determine certification of a pupil as SEI. The grid is contemporary, concerned primarily with the here and now and the future rather than with etiology. Teachers are less interested in the past than clinicians. Second, information must be stated in nonpejorative terms, because parents now have access to records. Third, the teachers wanted to consider both the pupil and environmental conditions in their thinking. Thus the grid evolved.

THE INFORMATION AND PLANNING GRID

The information and planning grid organizes the flow of information for the teacher. Across the top is the sequence of exploration over time, A to G. On the left hand are the reminders of the areas of information to

72

Information Areas for Consideration	A — Nature and source of referral problem	B — Ecological: past and present	C — Past interventions tried/results	D — Individual self-synthesis assets, limitations, needs	E — Overall behavioral style	F — Interventions planned short-term long-term	G — Reassessment Replanning
Individual Child							
1. Cognitive-Academic							
2. Affective-intrapersonal							
3. Social-interpersonal							
4. Biophysical							
School							
Family							
Community							

Sequence (A–G)

FIGURE 2. Information and planning grid.

73

consider. As the teachers indicated, they wanted to have the whole picture before them as they worked out plans for a pupil. Because obviously not all cues will be relevant to any one pupil, a comprehensive scan is necessary. Thus, to think in these terms the team members recognize the progression of steps starting with a definition of the problem as stated in the referral; an ecologically oriented brief of the child's life, past and present; who has tried what to correct the problem; what do we know of the individual self, including assets and limitations; possible overall behavioral style, which suggests long- and short-term interventions; and finally, eventual reassessment and possible replanning. The teachers saw a value in thinking of the whole scope even to the eventual prognosis and possibilities for life stream as well as mainstream. They felt that attention to the whole prevented the myopia of reacting only to surface classroom behavior. The determining content that filters in at the various steps comes from information on the child, school performance, family situation, and community conditions.

Nature and Source of Referral Problem

The referral problem is what must be addressed in schools, although the underlying difficulty may turn out to be more complicated than the referral statement. What are the behavior foci that *someone* asserts as problematic? "Someone" is usually a teacher, parent, or mental health expert. Sometimes the youngster will state a problem. Who is bothered by what? The points of contention, the crises, or unsatisfactory functioning areas are pinpointed. Where is the system feeling pain? Who owns this problem? This does not mean that the judgments are legitimate, for adults or children may see problems that do not stand the scrutiny of "objectified examination." It is necessary to examine the basis and validity of the various perceptions of the problem. The ideal outcome is consensus on the problem by all parties involved.

From the pupil's side, it must be remembered that growing up is having problems—always being asked to do something new and struggling to cope. Some children are overconcerned and see minor developmental events as major; we saw that adolescence is characterized as a "problem" time of life. Other youngsters may hide their problem although they know they have troubles. And there are youngsters who will own up to no problem and, in due time, will have to be confronted with the denied reality.

Most problems have multiple ownership. Relevant adults have

their part. Always it is necessary to play the behavior in question back against the child's developmental level: Are we expecting something which is not within the ability of the age level or the developmental capability of the child? Is the behavior reasonable from the point of view of subgroup norms, although irritating to the teacher?

When we examine so-called problem behavior we find several different levels. Some behavior has significance only in the style of conduct. We want children to behave in a certain way because we adults like it that way—line up, sit in one's seat at the proper times, don't speak out at certain times, speak out at other times, and so on. These are traffic court items of behavior unless they are symptomatic of broader refusal to accept reasonable rules for social behavior. Normal pupils resist unexplained and arbitrary conformity demands that they sense are really for the convenience of the authority. At the other extreme are behaviors that violate the fundamental rights of others. Further, certain behavior is self-constricting, such as that of the individual who has no apparent motivation or who fails to make even minimal social exchanges. We anticipate that the persistence of such behavior will be self-defeating in the long term. The sad, alone, defeated child is a legitimate concern. It may be a hostile environment that precipitates given deviant behavior, such as too high demands or a nonrelevant school environment that induces considerable "behavior" that is seen by educators as a "problem." Always the first question is How significant is the problem? Although it may appear to be a simple matter to check off areas of concern such as lack of motivation, hostility to peers, etc., there are complications. A pupil fights but no child can fight 100 percent of the time, day and night. How often, under what conditions? With whom? What takes place before a fight breaks out? Generalized statements need anchorage in clearly defined quantitative observations whenever possible. More than one observer may be required. However, unless we give attention to the referral problem, further data collection and assessment may turn out to be unrelated to what has precipitated the referral.

Ecological Assessment, the Milieu Scan, Past and Present, Stress and Support

The second step is the milieu scan. No self functions out of an environmental context. The problem behavior of concern under the first step must be matched by an objective examination of the setting in which the behavior took place.

The reason for breaking up the ecological condition into past and present is to differentiate current effects of past stress from contemporary conditions. What was negative and positive in the past? What is happening now and what are the stress points and support points the youngster lives with each day? Do these conditions explain his choice of survival tactics? Does he behave in school "as if" he were at home? It should be pointed out that the same family system may offer support to a child at one age and be devastating at another, or the same constellation that confounds one youngster may not overwhelm another.

One important family scan is for abuse and violence. Teachers are obligated to report evidence of physical abuse, although it becomes a very difficult situation even when the evidence is obvious and there are referral sources. One looks for possible generating conditions in parents who may themselves have experienced abuse, or are now involved in a stressful situation that encourages abuse as an outlet. There may be inviting behavior on part of a child. Usually several factors congeal to produce abuse (Belsky 1980).

Ecological study is based upon the balance of two sets of forces: the proactive and reactive components of the child and the proactive and reactive components of the environment. Thus column B includes the child's life space as seen by the pupil and by external observations. The past ecological condition is important to study because the *residue* of that condition usually exists in the current self-concept of the pupil. Some pupils behave *as if* they were still in the past situation. The present teacher is not the belittling teacher of last year, but the pupil is still fearful. Mistrust is transferred from one setting to another.

The transactions between the individual and the present external conditions (whatever they may be) may signify whether the intervention of choice should be directed to the pupil, the setting, or both. We usually direct almost exclusive attention to the pupil, whether legitimately or not, because the pupil is "available." Families, teachers, school systems, and community activities are difficult to get at in the first place, and even if they are accessible they are hard to change while the pupil is available for intervention effort, logical or not. Apter (1982) has synthesized the issues around ecological assessment and interventions.

The milieu network is important because frequently we end up having to work with what exists rather than the ideal we would like. For this reason great attention is given to any potential support one may get from persons in the setting. Even in inadequate settings there may be certain resources in school, home, peers, and neighborhood, although sometimes it takes searching to find. The problem will be to activate positive potentials.

The impact of the family, the school, and the community are studied. Care must be taken to evaluate these conditions from a neutral rather than class-conscious basis. A time line of significant family events (births, deaths, divorce, geographical moves, economic status) is charted and a parallel line is made for problem behaviors to explore possible relationships. What is the child's role in the family? Parental and sibling roles and relationships are explored. Are caring and warmth, reasonable and consistent discipline, a behavior code, desirable roles for children, and models for behavior present? How do the family and classroom function as dynamic units?

The child or adolescent, being creatures of the family matrix, cannot be properly evaluated apart from the family genesis. It is only in the family interaction that we become aware of what behavior has been taught and is being sustained. This is a two-way street: the child is subject to family pressures and the child produces certain pressures on the family. It is of particular concern to educators when they must deal *in school* with behavior generated outside of school where there is no real access to intervention. This is a major difficulty in SEI special education.

The school and the family are two separate institutions, yet they both influence the pupil. The loss of primary power of the family in this society is well described by Keniston (1977) and Segal (1978). Shared power is difficult to manage. Influence from one sphere has an impact on the other through the youngster. Some children live separate lives in home and school, though such is not the usual situation, because children bring home problems to school and school problems home. When such is the case there are two choices. If one agency is the generator of the child's problem, interventions should start there. At worst, when there is no access to the home, the choice is to split off the school experience and provide a balancing hygienic environment. A compensatory school life may enable the child to cope more effectively with negative parts of the environment, or at least have a conflict-free sphere. Usually it is necessary to intervene in both home and school settings in concert.

Eric Bermann (1973), in his book on children as family scapegoats, illustrates how the child's negative role may be maintained as one link in a pathological family situation. The need to have a child "dumb," "bad," or playing some other role is all too frequent. Sibling relationships may be supportive or eroding. Most of us have seen families who have a child that can do no wrong and another who can do no right. The child's self-concept formulation may be a direct result of the sibling role the child has in a family.

The differing level of values in families is described by Johnson

(1949): a superficial overt conventional morality often reflects covert unfinished parental development in fundamental areas such as sex, aggression, or noncompliance to accepted norms. The child thus grows up identifying with the unconscious value system that is denied by the parent, even though that is the way the parent actually behaves. A common example is where the father admonishes the offspring to "study" and "do your work" and yet gives off cues as to his own essential disregard for school learning. Delinquent parents can transmit defective values even while they practice an external ritualistic correctness.

Without being aware of what is actually happening, a teacher or therapist can have unwarranted expectations for change through the child alone. Work with parents through the school or family counseling may be the keystone. We have found that family created and exacerbated SEI conditions are the least responsive to typical interventions in contrast to more tractable SEI conditions coming from school mismanagement. Families are usually more amenable to help when the situation is cast in a problem-solving context than when parents are made into "clients" for formal therapy. While schools can refer families for help to private or public services, schools are seldom in a position to require family therapy. Parent groups and parent counseling are useful for many families and can be done through school social workers or psychologists. Freidman (1973) and Love (1974) approach the family more in keeping with the educator's needs.

No matter how weak the family is, unless the youngster is removed, that family is still the primary milieu. A mother who is ineffective in discipline may at the same time be a loving mother with a real concern. A rejecting father may still have some resources to offer. Siblings sometimes become therapeutic assets. The assessment of possible assets of the family and the extended family (a significant grandparent or relative) is important.

There are other influence settings to be examined, the most obvious being the school. What has been the pupil's school history? Has it been a sequence of failures in school learning, peer relationships, or with authority? Are there signs of improvement or increasing failure? Were there traumatic years or transitions to less structured schools that precipitated the problem?

There are neighborhood activities and peer groups to consider. Some children have no friends and are the butt of the block. We read once in a while how such a youngster goes beserk and retaliates. The neighborhood models may be the source of delinquent ideology. We scan, too, possible community agency resources for particular needs such as sports and group activity clubs. For older youth the need for vocational plans, training, and jobs may be the community asset we must tap. When we finish the scan and consider what is needed, it may not be usual "therapy" at all, or even tutoring, but a Big Brother or Big Sister to foster a positive identification. Sometimes needed resources have to be created.

There are now formal ways to study the milieu. The work reported by McReynolds (1964) deals with the role of social climate and naturalistic observation in assessment. Prieto and Rutherford (1977) have presented a model that maps the community, graphically representing areas of function and dysfunction: for their purposes the schoolchild components are expanded to include peer, teacher, and subject-matter spheres. Each area is then checked for positive and negative interaction, and an ecological baseline card is filled out with attention to antecedents and consequences in a given environment. Jessor and Jessor (1977) have shown how critical the peer social reference group is in normal and deviant behavior. At adolescence, the child who gains independence often does so at the cost of closeness to parents, with dependency on certain peers for values and solutions— delinquent or otherwise.

Moos (1979) has scales that can be applied to family life, schools, and institutions. These provide some idea of how much the problem is internalized and how clean or polluted the setting. Chandler (1981) has personalized the assessment of the child's environment in his *Stress Inventory* designed to be used in schools. The survey covers thirty-seven life events that produce stress. Dickinson (1978) points out that covert as well as overt environmental conditions must be assessed.

For special education the most useful classroom ecological assessment was developed by Fink (1970) and later extended in Project Prime (Semmel n.d.). This device focuses on affective teacher and pupil behavior. Both are observed for on-task behavior. Teacher categories include making demands, appealing to values or legal sanctions, conditioned stimulus, use of criticizing or punishment, empathic expression, interpretation, humor, pointing out the consequences, redirecting the action, and probing. Pupil participation includes self-involvement, noise, verbal interaction/aggression, physical interaction/ aggression, verbal resistance and physical resistance. Data are collected on teacher-pupil dyads as well as the overall climate.

Swap (1974) has done a series of studies on the interactive nature of behavior in preschool and elementary classrooms and reveals chains of behavior sequences. Rezmierski (1973) recognized the subtle body language of nonverbal communication in her analysis of actual classroom tapes of teachers interacting with problem children. It well may be that such "almost-impossible"-to-measure conditions are more potent than the more visible elements. Kounin (1970) spent a great deal of his professional lifetime in classroom ecological data collection and has conceptualized classes as a system of signals. To him, the total ecological system provides sets of signals that induce certain behavior. The teacher who responds in terms of the simultaneous multiple stimuli and who can monitor individual patterns of child response without losing the group has that teaching sense he has termed "withitness." Such analyses may reveal why it is a pupil is a problem in one group and not another.

Long (1979) conceptualized "the conflict cycle." A situation develops that produces stress on the given pupil, based upon the child's self concept and coping inadequacies for the given situation. Stresses are of many types, fortuitous conditions, physical conditions, and psychological threats. These in turn produce feelings in pupils that they must learn to acknowledge and distinguish from their automatic behavior responses. If they do not distinguish, the ensuing behavior is expressed in some exacerbating fashion as aggression, withdrawal, or a myriad defensive acts. These in turn generate "natural" but unuseful teacher responses. Such inappropriate teacher or peer response accentuate the unfortunate pupil behavior, thus increasing the stress. A powerful struggle results. Person and environment are entwined. The conflict cycle requires process diagnosis in contrast to status diagnosis. It involves not only the study of the person but the study of the triggering and sequence phenomenon.

There are two purposes in assessing a climate. One is to have some gauge of the stress or support that may be generated by the setting. The second is to take measures to rectify climate pathology just as one expects to take steps to change the person behavior (Moos, Snowden, and Kelly 1979).

All children are in a life milieu—some planned and some not, some helpful and some provocative. Moos feels that feedback of data from his scales is a profitable method to induce change. When the opportunity is available, environmental change may offer the best promise, matching the person and the proper setting.

Past Interventions Tried and Results

It is often said that in education, when something we do doesn't work, we then intensify doing that which didn't work. By the time a youngster is categorized as SEI, we can know there have already been a series of efforts to bring about change. There may be resignation, frustration, or omnipresent efforts—even resorting to child beating with remedial expectations. We must be sure we know what was done—the actual acts—and the underlying feelings of the perpetrator and subject. What were the attitudes and hopes of those who applied treatments to the youngster? If no change takes place, is this considered a personal failure of the child or of the adult? There are children and parents who have tried and now have simply given up and have no hope. The complete story then is, what were the manifold results of failure? Perhaps nothing was done except to allocate blame as in the case of an unrecognized LD pupil, in whose case the message was: Why don't you try harder? You could do it if you tried.

The reason why we have such a mixture of success and failure to review is compounded by several conditions: (1) inappropriate evaluation of the potential of a child resulting in expectations that are out of phase; (2) improper interventions in type, extensiveness, and intensiveness (expected miracles from bargain-basement interventions); and (3) failure to recognize ecological seduction, putting a youngster back in stressful conditions with which he cannot cope.

The Individual Self Synthesis: Assets, Limitations and Needs

We turn now to look at the substantive items that will be integrated into a picture of the pupil's self-concept–self-esteem system. In addition to various data from sources discussed in chapter 2, for specific scales, for virtually all areas see Sabatino and Miller (1979). The "factual" data for each item must be aligned with the meaning of the fact to the individual self. An IQ has both objective significance and subjective meaning. The motivational behavior can be described, but again, where it fits in the self-structure becomes the important issue. As the categories are reviewed, we are interested in how we may obtain information and particularly what the implications are for future interventions.

The major information areas are indicated on the grid under the heading *individual child,* under which are the major headings *cognitive-academic, affective-intrapersonal, social-interpersonal* and *biophysical.* The goal is to avoid describing half a person, only the problem side. Although there may be only a few assets, there are usually some, and it will be these positive resources that we must call forth to produce change. There may be significant problem-free areas. The implication of the SEI pupil's sex is the first point to consider. Generally speaking, special education deals more extensively with the high-risk male sex and is less adept at understanding female self-development with the unique stresses that this society induces. This is so evident in the consequences of unplanned pregnancy, which affects both the young mother and the young father, but no one holds that the impact is, on average, equal. Special education may well prepare for more female referrals as we "equalize" sex roles. This is already apparent in increased female delinquency. Just as the female role is changing, the mirror-image male role changes as well; tenderness, love, and sharing are supposedly replacing aloofness, authority, and macho dominance in the possibility for males.

1. Cognitive-Academic Attributes and Behavior

Cognitive Ability

Obviously, the school being a place for systematic learning, teachers are particularly interested in the cognitive potential, talents and special attributes or limitations that contribute to the rate and depth of learning. The essential question is What is the pupil's quantitative and qualitative ability to learn? What performances should we expect? The psychologist's role and common tests used in cognitive assessment were discussed on pages 57–58.

It is generally accepted that an environment limited in stimulation or rewards for cognitive performance will result in false underestimations of potential. Mercer (1977) and her colleagues have provided procedures called SOMPA, the system of multicultural pluralistic assessment. Although it has not had universal acceptance, this and other methods reduce the impact of cultural differences on appraisal of cognitive ability.

Because any academic performance is compounded of ability, previous experience, motivational aspects, and certainly the appropriateness of the specific teaching processes for the particular child, the teacher cannot set expectancies from an intelligence score alone. In addition to giving specific subpart scores, an individual intelligence test can provide a verbal IQ, which is dependent upon the use of symbolic language and a performance score, which is more independent of verbal language. Clinics report much higher performance vs. verbal scores for serious learning problem cases. The psychologist may also discuss matters of test score scatter or pattern. General information may be low and ability to reason higher for example.

The pupil's use of language can be a critical indicator: concreteness, proper use of pronouns, leaving out words, syntax and flow of spoken language are cues for a thorough analysis by a speech therapist. There are autistic children who do not talk, and elective mutes who will not talk in certain places or to certain people, but not because they cannot speak. They have "decided" not to communicate under certain conditions (Kratochwill 1981).

A teacher may observe that the youngster can work when he really tries or he is up one day and down the next or is sad when he works so hard and can't keep up. Particular talents or at least areas of relatively better achievement may also be evident in the many activities of the classroom. A seasoned psychologist will use the teacher's data to evaluate whether or not the particular test performance is accurate.

Achievement

Assessing achievement is usually the responsibility of the special educator. Achievement testing has been plagued by norm referenced testing. While we may need to know the rate of achievement relative to the average pupil, Duffey and Fedner (1978) make the point that we should always use criterion-referenced achievement assessment. What specific tasks can the pupil do in each of the three r's? What the child knows and does not know provides objectives for the EIP. SEI pupils are often uneven in skills and knowledge: it is as if there were huge holes in what has been accumulated.

Dependence on concrete language tells us not to deal in highly abstract terms with the youngster. Some aphasic children have been misdiagnosed because no one recognized the specific nature of their speech limitation. A teacher ascertains a child's general state of knowledge from what the pupil says. Language is a gauge of both cognitive functioning and socialization.

Basic achievement areas include reading, spelling, and arithmetic and the subject matter areas at the secondary level. There are many stages of these skills, and the teacher frequently is the best assessor through informal tutorial sessions, stating the pupil reads words of a given difficulty in or out of context, etc. Oral reading is an essential method to find out exactly how the pupil performs. Reading for meaning brings in the most sophisticated reading competencies. The teacher keeps exploring until it is clear where the cutting edge of ability is, in order to direct effort at that point. The Gray Oral Reading Tests, with several forms, are a useful device for individual work, and the Peabody Individual Achievement Test (PIAT) has reading subtests for grades kindergarten through twelve. Individual diagnostic tests include the Durrell Analyses of Reading Difficulty and the Gates-McKillop Reading Diagnostic Tests. There are many others discussed in Sabatino and Miller (1979). The Wide Range Achievement Test (WRAT) is a very popular device for testing basic school achievement. Since it is brief, it serves only as a gross screening agent. A criterion referenced test, the Basic Educational Skills Inventory (BESI), provides early elementary skills and prerequisite precursor assessment.

Before giving a test, samples of the youngster's school performance should be scrutinized. Often the needed data are already in the pupil's classroom folder. It is interesting how often we depend upon test samples in contrast to using the collection of materials any teacher will have to demonstrate how a pupil actually functions. Exercises, workbook pages, and creative materials are usually available if we ask. In fact, in many instances certain testing is unnecessary. The evidence is in. As one child said, "Why do I have to do this goddamned test again? I know I can't do it. You know I can't do it. Why do we have to prove it again?"

Diagnostic spelling assessment is included in the previously mentioned Durrell test. Writing is a very difficult task for many SEI youngsters. One of the useful devices is to dictate a sentence, which will enable the teacher to see where the youngster falters. The LD-writing of afflicted SEI children often deteriorates during the writing of a single sentence.

Discrepancies between ability and achievement are of concern. A child who performs much lower than the indicated potential may have been subject to inadequate instruction, as well as personal conflict. It is also of interest how some children achieve at about the same level in all skills or knowledge areas while others are highly uneven.

There are conflicting data on the academic retardation of SEI pupils; there is no doubt that there will be many with significant academic retardation and/or learning disability. For some children internal distractions or behavioral resistance reduces concentration and motivation. For others schoolwork becomes an area of positive compensation for an otherwise discouraging life.

Englemann, Granzon, and Severson (1979) point out that we assess learner achievement but do not assess the prior instruction. We do not examine whether the state of academic progress is caused by inappropriate instruction. Since there are frequent cases of language disability, some schools use the Slingerland Screening Tests to identify children who need more intensive examination.

Learning Disability

Since LD-SEI combinations are frequent, evidence of learning disability should be checked. One device that deals with cognitive abilities (twelve scales), scholastic achievement (ten scales), and interest (five including scholastic and nonscholastic) is the individually administered Woodcock-Johnson Psychoeducational Battery. One would not use all of this in addition to a regular IQ test and achievement test. The problem is to ascertain the specific functions for which measures are indicated and give the pupil the fewest tests needed to gain the maximum information.

Often the best information again comes from the person who has been teaching the pupil. The specific errors made in reading or spelling, visual or auditory recall, and the inability to synthesize sight and sound cues may be noted. Difficulties may occur in perception and noting the proper dominance of certain elements. Others have conceptual difficulties in putting together appropriate elements, connecting a new idea with a previous memory or synthesizing a whole from parts. A youngster may have expressive problems, being unable to speak or write correctly. Some children have problems in all areas. The ITPA or Bender-Gestalt are considered revealing of LD limitations.

Study Skills

Ability is one thing; capacity to use one's ability is another. How to approach a new word with phonetics, how to look up a word, ability to concentrate, attend, read to answer questions—the list is endless. Some pupils lack study skills: they do not know how to go at a given task without constant supervision. The question is, how well has the pupil learned how to learn? For the LD-SEI youngster very specific compensatory, multisensory methods will be necessary along with work on the affective sphere.

If the child needs continual support, the task may be too difficult, or perhaps motivational factors are involved. Some pupils use a tutorial to obtain the human relationships. Many special educators feel they are really helping if they are immersed in task specifics and may unwittingly foster dependency. With the IEPs and accountability, there is the pressure to get the pupil up to grade level as fast as possible, and usually faster.

School Motivation

Academic motivation has to be added to ability to make sense of performance. Of course all pupils are motivated in some manner for some goal. Motivation to educators usually means school motivation. The youngster may be highly motivated, but the motivation may be to have fun, escape work, be noticed, or confront the teacher. Teaching is a different process with pupils who consciously acknowledge that they want to learn, conform, or adjust. This is not to gainsay that there are many who take an unmotivated stance to ward off conscious or unconscious fears of potential failure. If you don't try you can't fail (Lichter et al. 1962). The first action is to help a pupil see this condition and provide a quota of immediate success. However, when the youngster is only able to do that which is so far below the age level, even success can be self-interpreted as comparative failure. One such group of seriously SEI-LD adolescents reacted to the teacher's praise of their learning with, "So what? That's all baby stuff." Reading at the third-grade level gave them no satisfaction.

Many children develop a condition called "learned helplessness" (Thomas 1979), which is a conviction that they cannot control what they learn by their efforts. Effort does not (in the person's view) influence the situation; fate controls. Pupils who feel this way reduce their effort, become lethargic, and feel negative about their competence. Extensive failure encourages this condition. "I can't read" is a common response. Rewards have little effect. Discussion of the problem, a positive relationship with the teacher, and long-term instructional programs with carefully controlled successes and both internal and external rewards are keys.

Cognitive Mediation Ability

Special teachers know that children and youth show great discrepancy in how they can use language and symbolic thought to deal with their problems. Some youngsters are essentially nonverbal. They are not given to language for communication. In interviews a yes, no, or even a grunt may be all. Gesture and action are preferred modes. They tend to function at a concrete Piagetian level. Other children use language a great deal. They think a lot, cognate, are subject to fantasy and ideation. They use language to mediate their impulses and organize their behavior (Mischel 1979). Adults, especially teachers, are great verbalizers. Cognitive mediation is using thinking to control frustration, handle demands for immediate gratification, or make plans and structure life. Several self-control training programs will be discussed subsequently. Other children use talk as avoidance or have disassociated verbalisms that we have taught them. An "I be good" may carry no expectation of appropriate actions.

Reality Testing

There are two basic types of reality distortion. One is the neglect of external cues and the dominance of internal concepts, such as the schizophrenic child demonstrates in thinking others are after him or dangers lurk in safe places or that others make him do what he does. The autistic child attends to selective bits of the external world that have come to be important to him, say a special toy. External dangers may be ignored, as when a youngster, delighted by the pleasant sensation of the water, keeps right on going in deeper and would drown. The lack of logic is in the child's internal system.

Much more common is the youngster who has poor judgment, fails to learn by experience, and distorts as a defense. A child may even deny any act while doing it: "It's not my fault." "It wasn't me." Adolescent risk taking contains some inaccurate reality perception. Delinquents will say it is worth taking the chance believing (perhaps correctly) that few get caught. There is a magical component of luck or power that makes high-risk behavior reasonable. "It can't happen to me" has resulted in more than one pregnancy. To some, what looks like distortion is really a preferred gratification. A teenager tells the teacher or boss off, ignoring the punishment to come. The main goal is to feel momentary power. At the moment of taking a risk, one feels daring. We challenge fate and feel powerful. Adults who tell these youngsters not to do a given thing because of the possible consequences may actually be baiting them.

2. Affective-Intrapersonal Components

In the examination of socio-emotional impairment, the affective domain is of central importance. Here lies the emotional life, the values, social development, and the core of the self-concept. Some areas can be observed and some lie deep under the surface to be revealed by projective tests and in-depth interviews. Yet it is surprising how much is revealed during the social interaction of the regular or special classroom.

A masterful review and analysis of the social interaction dimension has been produced by Greenwood, Walker, and Hops (1977). They point out that withdrawn children have a lower chance of being identified than aggressive children. The methods used to ascertain the social dimension include observation, sociometrics, and teachers' reports. Rather than asking a sociometric question, such as Who is your best friend? it is well to explore how each pupil feels about all the peers as friends. There are classes where most of the social liking is bestowed on 10 percent of the class. It is well to remember there are some children who keep to themselves but are happy.

Self-Concept–Self-Esteem Identity

These are the summary core areas discussed extensively in chapter 1. How does the individual see himself? What is his essential self-characterization? While our use of the self is as the synthesis of the whole child, there are many specific self-concept scales that can be used (Wylie 1974). The Piers-Harris and Coopersmith are common and include school dimensions. Rosenberg (1979) has developed a very useful self-esteem scale.

One important aspect of the self is self-control, a subject of specific intervention programs (page 138). Kendall and Wilcox (1979) have a scale to objectify adult judgment in this matter: The Self-Control Rating Scale (SCRS) contains thirty-three items.

Identification Targets

If one had a single question to ask, it might well be Who would you like to be? Consciously and unconsciously, youngsters imitate, model, and incorporate aspects of adults, peers, literary characters, and television heroes and fantasied as well as actual parents. They may build an identity as a reaction *against* parental models they decry. A total style of life of another may be taken over, including the way the other person solves problems and the values that orient actions. Thus a class leader or gang leader has power in the character formulation. Teachers, as parent surrogates, have powerful influence on most young pupils and on particular adolescents. Who is the youngster's idol? When the figure is inadequate, remedial work will include substitutes. The worship of pop-cult heroes encapsulates some adolescents. Then again, many youngsters do not confuse these fantasy targets with more stable models. Sometimes peer tutors or "real world" characters who have a clear social role become models in place of paid professionals. One hopes the model will be a respectable citizen and not a drug pusher. It may be a club leader, a Big Brother/Sister, a relative, neighbor, or a coach. Volunteer grandparent figures may help. One does not become a figure for identification by wanting to be one but by exemplifying solutions to life problems. It is not uncommon for a therapist or teacher to be an all-powerful adult role model (Morse and Lockett 1973). Unfortunately, many teachers and other professionals appear to the youngster to have little to offer as models.

Level of Trust

The range of trust of SEI pupils ranges from gullible through average to nonexistent. Some are actually indiscriminately trusting, much to their woe. For the most part, present pupil trust is based on past treatment, though there may be exaggerations or denials of what we could expect. Trust is one of the attributes we would hope to cultivate by early family experience. As Erikson indicates, it is stage one to learn that most persons can be depended upon, are consistent and caring.

At each life stage trust must be extended or reactivated by appropriate conditions. When you trust, you are no longer alone. There should be a balance of self-independence and social relatedness. Trust diminishes alienation and is the essential ingredient for building relationships. The child who has not clarified the matter of trust may give up or make a career of testing. Such persistent testing (teasing, challenging, thwarting) is perplexing, especially to the adult who senses positive feeling on both sides of the relationship and is so eager to be trusted. But the effort of the pupil to get assurance and proof of trustworthiness persists. When the adult gives way and caves in with primitive counterreactions under testing, the hostility generated in the youngster stems from dismay and anxiety.

Trust may be too naive: "He never seems to learn." Or it may be specific—trust for peers or a special adult but not for others. Open discussion of trust problems is often the start of effective intervention. One can ask a pupil about whom he trusts. It need not be a mystery.

Value Incorporation

Most of us spend our lifetime trying to achieve and maintain moral behavior, often with differential success. In a society of mul- tivalues ranging from the "anticodes" of socially amoral rip-off to rigid socioreligious codes, it is no wonder incorporation of acceptable values has become a central issue. Kohlberg (1969) is one leading theoretician: he has scaled values in stages from amoral to the consci- entious-rational. We are interested in *what* code has been incorporated.

The sociopathic self lacks concern for others and behaves on narcissistic impulse with no regard for others' rights or welfare. There are many children who have grown up without being taught to care or have been brutalized out of caring.

Moral sophistication must be considered on a developmental basis, appropriate to the age. Also we differentiate values that may be appropriate to a given subculture from broad human values essential in a democratic society—equal rights for all regardless of race, sex, or origin. We recognize everyone's right to safety of person (physically and psychologically) and the right to one's space and possessions. One should not have to live in fear or jeopardy at home, in the neighbor- hood, in school halls, the restrooms, or the principal's office. Differ- ences of tastes and interests, such as in the clothes one wears, should hardly be confused with basic moral issues, although the school fre- quently tries to legislate about such matters.

We differentiate between the empty child with relatively few so- cial values and the child who has values but lacks the ability to follow them.

Self-Responsibility

A critical dimension in dealing with children is how responsible they feel for their own actions and for changing. The question to ask is Does the pupil feel he or she is responsible to do something about a situation or must help come from without? Does the pupil want help? Need it? What kind? Attribution theory should be applied at this junc- ture. The adolescent may blame fate, some circumstance, or himself. Attribution and sense of efficacy will be discussed in detail in paradigms for helping in chapter 4. Some pupils blame parents or exter- nal conditions. There are those who say "everybody does it." The feeling that one has no power of self-control is frightening.

Another critical aspect concerning the self, which Bandura

(1982a) calls the central condition, is one's sense of self-efficacy, or coping capacity. A scale has been developed for children that covers the sense of self-competency in cognitive, social, and physical domains. It is discussed in detail by Susan Harter (1982).

One must be wary of glib statements that children learn to make to satisfy adults, such as "I won't fight anymore because it's bad to fight," which is said to get out of talking more about behavior.

Empathic Potential

Empathy is the ability to take the role of another, to feel as another feels. There is usually an additional implication, which is to care for the welfare of the other. There are youngsters who are empathic but deny it ("I don't care how he feels"). Children who make a scapegoating of a particular peer excuse themselves by saying, "He doesn't care, so it's all right to call names or hit." We all find ways to dull our empathic feelings in war and social violence (Bandura 1974).

Empathy is an essential component for socialization. We see even young children who are sensitive to hurts in others and try to help. The Staubs (1978; 1979) discuss the enhancement of prosocial behavior.

Affective States

We search for the pupil's affective disposition, the dominant primary feeling tone. Some youngsters vary, while others have a more stable emotional state. The areas for scanning run the gamut of the emotions. Anger, love, hostility, anxiety, fear, hope—these are examples of the emotional states.

Of late, depression in children has been receiving more attention. Depression is usually accompanied by low self-esteem and a feeling that one is helpless to change conditions. It is believed that the depression may at times be masked, even by clowning activity. French and Berlin (1971) have discussed both childhood and adolescent depression. Kashani et al. (1981) find no single etiological condition, because biochemical, genetic, learned helplessness, life stress, and cognitive distortion are factors. Suicidal behavior is a significant problem at adolescence, but suicidal threats or attempts are a concern at all ages. Pfeffer (1981) has studied over 100 cases of preadolescents. Young children may think of death as pleasant or even temporary. Risk factors include depression, a need to escape an intolerable situation, school problems, a desire to punish parents, and a wish to be reunited with a deceased friend. Possible parental suicidal behavior should be checked.

View of the World

When all is said and done, how does the pupil see his world? This is in effect a distillation of items we have reviewed. Is the world a friendly or threatening place? Can one cope, or is retreat the best solution? Is it dull and mundane or are exciting new experiences likely? If life is bad, what is the use of trying?

The life events are processed by the self of the child. One adopted child feels favored by being wanted while another will focus his resentment on presumed rejection by natural parents. We are surprised both by youngsters who overcome tremendous difficulties and by other children who are so vulnerable.

The life viewpoint includes the hope index: What will the future bring? Since most helping adults have "made it" as we say, they usually see the world as a just place, where you get what you deserve. Reward follows effort, in spite of the confusing evidence about us, since it is very threatening to think otherwise (Lerner 1980). Many children do not see the world as just. No matter what you do you lose. Their time frame is often existential. Or they may concentrate only on the times things did not work out. The answer for the teacher of the SEI is not to argue their perception of life but to build a sub-milieu that is just and explain and demonstrate how it operates. It may be necessary to advocate for the pupil in the unfortunate school or community milieu. Most disturbed children come to understand a just milieu, and this can be a powerful tool for instigating change.

3. Social-Interpersonal

The next set of dimensions deal with social interactions as a complement to the intrapersonal conditions. Keating (1978) used the following three measures of social intelligence: the Defining Social Issues Test, which relates to the Kohlberg moral stages; the Social Insight Test, which presents a series of social dilemmas and alternative solutions; and the Social Maturity Index, which predicts effective social functioning. His results indicate that the domain of social intelligence is more difficult to assess than "academic intelligence," and he cautions against generalizing about this capacity. Greenwood, Walker, and Hops (1978) assess social adjustment related to treatment plans, pinpointing specific deficiencies.

Peer Role

Most children develop a particular role with peers; a leader or a scapegoat, a follower, a provoker, a moralizer, or a lawyer. There are those who can catalyze a group in no time at all. Others are observers who are isolated and left out of group activities.

For teachers a major concern is the role a pupil will play in a class and what it will do to the group. IEPs should include plans to deal with negative roles.

One major diagnostic channel is through play. SEI children are usually developmentally delayed in the level of their play. Often they cannot take a proper play role, follow the rules, or utilize symbolic opportunities in play. Since play is one of the most significant employments of children, as well as a therapeutic avenue, the child needs to be helped to use play.

Authority Relationships

How does the youngster react to various authority figures? Perhaps more than any single condition, this dimension describes the abrasive confrontations that so often characterize "problem youngsters." Is the reaction to one teacher common to all or an isolated phenomenon? We look for career *limit testers,* the defiant ones as well as their overly dependent opposites. Some youngsters will deal only with the top boss. Often the anti-authority character is highly authoritarian in the peer culture.

Attention/Relationship Seeker

A most prevalent descriptor used by teachers to characterize SEI pupils is "attention seeker." So much appears to reflect the child's bid to encourage others, especially the teacher, to "see" him. But this dimension often reveals a far more essential condition. For the normal child, to be recognized fosters growth. Being attended to provides the stimulus for gaining independence and moving up the developmental ladder. Pupils who are starved for relationships soak up attention but continue to need as much as before. Because of early (and usually persistent) lack of basic relationships in the family, some pupils are uncertain about their personal validity and worthwhileness. They need constant proof. But the "attention" they get from their behavior does not satisfy; their need is for deep and sustained primary relationships. Because of the social implications of "attention"-seeking behavior in school, such behavior should be explored for possible underlying needs for deeper relationships.

Likeability/Winsomeness

Of course teachers as well as other professionals differ in their capacity to like various pupils. We want most to help those we like. We tolerate more and reach out to them in spite of their behavior. On the other hand, there are obnoxious youngsters who are hard for anyone to like: although their needs may be greater than those of the likable ones, they get less of a positive response. What is it about a pupil that turns us on or off? The winsome pupil can frequently get away with more than is good for his future.

Out-of-School Activities

There are some children who do well in areas other than school: Once free of the school's confines, they have an exciting peer and activity life, with a set of buddies for better or for worse. Alternatively there are youngsters who have no friends once they are outside of school. The major "educator" may be TV. We ask about viewing time and favorite programs. Some disturbed youngsters are already neighborhood "bad characters" and are forbidden to play or interact with peers. Creative use of free time is a significant sign of healthy development.

4. Biophysical Factors

School puts so much emphasis on the cognitive and affective that the physical side may be virtually ignored in considering the state of a youngster.

Biological conditions may be related to academic performance, physical appearance, personality, and behavior characteristics. Prescriptions are written for the SEI pupil without any physical examination. Before a child is described as lazy, we might know if he is in a state of fatigue. One should check out physical conditions before making psychogenic explanations. Sabatino and Miller (1979) provide ways to screen for physical conditions, hearing, sight, and motor functioning. "A Screening Device for Classroom Teachers" is found in the Videotape Training Packages (Morse and Smith 1980). Items are related to sensory impairment, nutrition, epilepsy, minor brain damage, and learning disability. *However, these are screening checklists; diagnosis is a medical province.*

Some biologists assert that physical determinants are behind all pathology, even specific affective behaviors. For example, Lambert and Windmiller (1977) present evidence that hyperactivity is a biological phenomenon that in turn adds stress to the subject's interpersonal relationships with peers, parents, and teachers.

Physical State/Health

Knapczyk (1982) has described the importance to the teacher of identifying physical problems, such as chronic anemia, of SEI pupils that interfere with instruction. Pupils sometimes come hungry to school. There is television watcher's fatigue. In contrast are the vigorous, energetic pupils who have energy to burn and never slow down, thus overtaxing adult caretakers. To call a hypothyroid child lazy is obvious malpractice. Children's reactions to illness or limitations range from denial to malingering.

Allergy treatment and special diets may be helpful in particular cases. Children with critical lead levels are said to be at risk for SEI behavior (Marlow and Erreva 1982). Sight, hearing, and other senses must be ascertained. SEI education should include the blind-disturbed or deaf-disturbed where the treatment requires sophisticated knowledge of both categories.

Neurological Integration

A teacher can often discern the fine and gross motor performance through classroom observation and examination of classroom products. We can hope for a neurological examination, although competent child neurologists are in undersupply. Perception is more than visual acuity: it is the ability to operate on what is seen to make useful judgments, such as figure and ground or patterns. A clumsy youngster should be checked out. The Bender-Gestalt Test is one source of data reflecting neurological integration. Gait and body control are visible. There are children who are unable to control physical movement and others who are driven to motoric outlets for tension and still others who are bored into restlessness.

There are conditions that require expert medical studies and neurological scans: encephalopathy, epilepsy, and brain tumors are not within the teachers' or general psychologists' province to assess. Toxic conditions and drug-induced behavior happen too frequently not to be checked out, especially with adolescents.

Appearance and Body Image

The body conveys an omnipresent message. How does the "physical youngster" look to others? Pleasant, well put together, with a sexually appropriate physique? Or is the total impact one of an ill-arranged set of physical characteristics. Are there disfigurements? Is he/she well or ill kept, thin or heavy, strong or weak?

This is not to suggest that all children should be of a pleasing appearance: it is to say there are unfortunate social standards applied, and whatever the body makeup, the youngster has to live with the implications. The body-image models for boys and girls at adolescence dominate the developmental period, body weight being the most obvious item. But a boy's perception of muscular appearance or a girl's comparison of her breast development may become a central attribute in the self-concept. It is not just the physical reality, it is how you feel about your endowment, the registry of private judgment. Before we can give our name, we already have given the signature of our physical habitus and body language. There may be physical stigmata in facial features or other parts of the body, such as misaligned teeth, a harelip, or simply grossly atypical features. What do these conditions cause others to do in interaction and what is the child's conscious and unconscious response? How is what one thinks about one's body incorporated into the self?

Birth Conditions and Postnatal Trauma

The researchers' focus on this area is expanding. The mother's diet, use of drugs, and state of health during gestation are now considered of diagnostic importance. In addition, there is the question of brain damage at or after birth. The history of such conditions may clarify certain behavior but must be evaluated by medical experts. A history of high fevers is noted. A serious accident may turn out to be a turning point in the developmental history of a SEI child.

Medication/Drugs

There are listless children who are reflecting a condition from prescribed medications. Not only may past and current administrations of medication give cues to physical states, they may describe concerns and leave an impact on the child's sense of control.

Developmental Rate

The *rate* of growth varies significantly among children and youth. Developmental lags create adjustment stress. A child may be developmentally young for his chronological age. Adolescence may be delayed. A child out of phase, either because of a lag or acceleration, encounters difficulty with set expectations, especially at adolescence.

The Denver Developmental Screening Test (DDST) for young children from zero to six years of age is used in developmental assessment. The items cover four areas: person-social, fine-motor adaptive, use of language (response and product), and gross motor ability.

Temperament

The leading work done on the biology of temperament suggests that, rather than specific predetermination of particular traits, temperaments are reflected in styles of behavior, or by *how* rather than *what* they do. Thomas and Chess (1977) speak of easy- and hard-to-raise children. The characteristic style of a youngster may be in conflict with the temperamental style of particular caretakers. Elements of temperament can be assessed in infancy; a twenty-three-item teacher questionnaire on temperament is available.

PERSON SYNTHESIS: SELF-CONCEPT PATTERNS IN SEI PUPILS

Our emphasis has been on the data concerning the individual self of SEI pupils. Why then turn to general patterns? First, we are not speaking of categorization or certification. What we are addressing is differential diagnosis. The overall category of SEI includes several subsets or syndromes with particular dominant characteristics. These characteristics provide a cognitive map for intervention. This does not belie the fact that, within each pattern, we still concentrate on the idiosyncratic nature of each self. The symptoms that we have been discussing are meaningful only as understood through the self that produces that behavior. Each individual is unique, but the uniqueness also usually embodies a general overall pattern. Sometimes the pattern may be clear and representative of a recognized syndrome. Often an individual is a mixture. The various syndromes provide a matrix around which individual data are integrated and thereby give meaning to that data. What is a common thread that integrates the behaviors?

There are four major syndromes that clarify self-concept differences of the population called SEI pupils. These are (1) the reactive (about 25 percent), (2) the neurotic (some 25 percent), (3) the value defective (approaching 30 percent), and (4) the "psychotic" (8 percent). Other referrals as SEI are found to be primarily retarded or organic. Of course there are combinations and sometimes no single dominant syndrome. The task of differential diagnosis is to sort out what behaviors give clues to the core style of the self. This in turn makes sense of manifest behavior. For example, many SEI children act out, but their reasons are so different that the modes of helping such youngsters vary.

The Reactive

Potentially normal selves *react* to extreme stress. Many of the 3 percent of children with very disturbed behavior are not really SEI at all. It is estimated that one-fourth turn out to be SEI look-alikes, children who are under severe contemporary stress. Histories indicate that they demonstrated the skills expected, had adequate self-esteem, and appeared to be on the way to a workable self-concept. Then something happened that exacerbated their relationships, produced stress, and precipitated a crises or downturn in their lives. It may have been a growth deviation, such as atypical adolescence, or slow biological unfolding so that the demands of the first grade are too much. Such children are not "disturbed" children and youth, although they may become so. They express normal responses to what is for them an unbearable and frustrating condition. Some are traumatized by a crisis or plagued by pressure. Although their manifest behavior may be just as unacceptable as the true SEI clientele, there are perceptible differences. Since they are *reactive,* they are behaving normally to an excruciating condition. Sometimes the result is depression and despair, and other times aggressive acting out. For no apparent reason a peer group may turn on a pupil, a given teacher may reject him, a family may become punitive, or the family may disintegrate. Usually, in reactive disturbance, the condition can be traced to one or more traumatic life events or to a chronic pressure that finally can no longer be handled. Unemployment, divorce, remarriage, death of a parent or favorite relative, and frequent migrations present quandaries to children and adolescents. We all need support systems and react to their disappearance.

Under such stress the *previously normal self-development* breaks down with an appearance of profound maladjustment. The work with children of divorce makes it evident that crisis intervention is needed, and that even the previously stable child usually takes a year to return to the normal pattern. Because divorce has become so common, it is often nowadays downplayed as a traumatic event in a child's life. There is usually a struggle in the family before the event. There is shock. Sometimes there is a time lag of the impact of an earlier divorce. With little children there is lack of comprehension of what divorce means in their lives. With preadolescents their denial often covers up anger and guilt, as if it were their fault. With adolescents, embarking on their own cross-sex exploration, it is often even more devastating, a fact overlooked because they are supposedly old enough to understand it. The parental narcissism, search for identity, custody battles, and loss of a loved one can undermine the youngster's self-esteem. The aftermath may bring unexpected anxiety and trauma or being cast in the role of an adult confidant. Reactive conditions should be separated from a life event that precipitates an already marginal or disturbed self-concept. In such cases the event just breaks down a marginal adjustment of the self that has already been flawed by chronic negative life experiences. For the "reactive" child, previous self-development will be normal with an absence of severe problems, which is not to say an absence of typical problems of growing up. Although there is a certain reactive aspect to most disturbance, the true SEI child has internalized learned responses to the negative environment: a mere reduction of the external stress does not produce change. Learning new replacement responses is required.

Sometimes it is not the overt condition but the covert perception that changes, as when a child with a happy preadolescent peer relationship feels keenly that she/he is rejected at adolescence. "Objectively" the rejection may not be acute; "subjectively" the youngster starts a dehabilitating sequence that does not go away with commonsense guidance. One looks with care for telling effects of economic stress on the family, birth and death of family members, family disruption, peer conditions, and certainly academic and social conditions at school, including relationships with teachers. Given that we have differing levels of vulnerability, for any of us there is a stress point that sends us into "reactions," but unless the stress is chronic we bounce back.

Treatment for the reactive syndrome is dual. First is crisis intervention with the youngster. Such help should be available without the need to categorize the pupil as SEI. The help must be just as sophisticated and as penetrating as will be required for the special pupil, but the delivery process should be simplified. If help is given so that the youngster copes and/or environmental changes can be worked out, the probability of success is high even with a relatively low investment. The stress-producing circumstances will need to be eliminated or reduced. The changes in the environment may not need to be huge to provide the relief, but getting any change may be very difficult. If the father has decided to leave the family, that may not be reversible, but the impact of the decision may be altered by work with the child as well as effecting minor changes in the father's behavior. Death has to be accepted as a fact and the whole matter of grief, grieving, and facing such a traumatic condition constitute cause for intervention. "Treatment" for an abused child (who may actually blame himself, instead of the parent) should deal with the abuser as well as with the child.

While situational conditions are every bit as difficult to alter as personal ones, they constitute a major intervention course for the reactive syndrome. Sometimes only a specific interactive system will be contaminated, but frequently the intensity, say of a jealousy over a new sibling, will result in problem transference to other situations, and peers in general as well. Mistrust of a parent who lied about an impending divorce may spread to teachers.

Special education in its present form has moved away from meeting the needs of children until they become chronic. Thus regular education and mental health are obligated to provide prevention and crisis help, but little is done in the average school.

True SEI children and youth also have reactive responses because of their already acquired vulnerability. We often forget that an added traumatic event may also produce exaggerated or different behavior in a child who has already been chronically disturbed through past experiences or biological proclivities. Most SEI children continue to live in environments that accentuate problems. A child who is already poorly socialized is disciplined with severity and reacts to this reality as well as to his underlying condition. An autistic child is rejected by a frustrated, screaming parent. SEI children so often have these life events added to their acquired limitations. So many times, in looking at the lives of our charges, we say, "Who needs that to happen on top of it all?" Interventions for crisis are the birthright of all SEI children, not just the pure reactive group. Crisis intervention can be useful in warding off more impairment for the already impaired or it can be the best way of getting at the fundamental problem. For true reactive patterns, the solution is a change of the ecology so that the healthy processes of the self can take over again, but many times the youngster must be taught new coping skills to deal with unfortunate circumstances that cannot be rectified.

The Neurotic Self-Concept Syndrome

The nosology for a prevalent pattern of SEI pupils is childhood and adolescent neuroses. The neurotic self-concept is a self incapacitated because of acute internal conflict. These youngsters have incorporated standards for behavior, but they are unable to match their behavior to the standards. For example, a youngster may acknowledge he shouldn't fight, but he still does and then repents and promises to be "good." He believes he should sit in his seat but wanders. He shouldn't steal but still does. He does not have the ego skills to manage his impulsive behavior. There is guilt, anxiety, and subjective distress although it may be unrecognized or denied by the individual. However, there is the capacity to relate, feel for, and empathize with others, even though this does not mean the expected behavior will follow. The ability to care is there but often shows up in obtuse ways such as testing and provoking. There is usually more impulsivity and acting out than can be tolerated. Fear of failure and inadequacy may result in not even trying. Some feel cheated out of their rightful due. Resentment against those who depreciate the youngster is often acute.

When we examine the self for value internalization we find it reasonably intact, though often immature for the age. It is in ego skills where the lack is prominent. We tell them to "try harder," but many of them have already tried, with no success.

Neurotic children suffer from low self-esteem at some level. Some suffer depression (though even this may be covered up by clowning). Children may be driven to self-despair, believe they are bad, and do things to get punishment. A few reflect a complete loss of all hope and resort to self-destructive behavior and suicide attempts.

Defensive behavior is common in the neurotic self. The defense against an intolerable sense of self-inadequacy can be denial ("I don't care," "I can't"). Projection is common ("It's their fault, they made me. I didn't do anything"). Offense may be the best defense, as shown by temper tantrums and aggression. For others, fantasy and daydreaming allow the escape from too severe a reality.

There are several common subpatterns to the neurotic self syndrome: (a) acting out and destructiveness of various types practiced on persons and property to get back at perceived unfairness; (b) the passive turning in on the self with withdrawal and depression; (c) psychosomatic symptoms; (d) alternative passive-aggressive behavior. Symptoms include poor social relationships, school failure, hostility toward adults, tics, outbursts followed by contriteness, self-defeating efforts to relate to others, and even at times an escape into overintensive preoccupation with achievement. The psychosomatic reactions include hypochondria, soiling, enuresis, colitis, skin reactions, eating problems, and some asthmatic reactions. Indigestion, sleep abnormalities, and food aversions may be present. There can be fears, phobic reactions, and compulsions. One specific school reaction is school phobia—fear of going to school or of leaving home (Kahn, Nursten, and Carroll 1981). The range of reactions range from defiance to boredom and withdrawal.

Anorexia nervosa is one alarming pattern that affects particularly adolescent girls who refuse to eat. In some cases this may be related to sexual fears, in others to defiance, the desire to be attractively thin, or as an outcropping of severe personal depreciation. Crisp (1980) holds that the therapy requires hospitalization until the patient can be committed to "grow up" and change. Garfinkel and Garner (1982) emphasize the family role, the overwhelming low self-esteem and low personal efficacy.

There are children who do not speak, usually in selective situations; hence the name *selective mutes*. Obviously, while this may be tolerated for a time with young children, it comprises a most difficult manifestation for the schools as time goes on. Usually psychotherapy and ecological pressure are combined in treatment (Kratochwill 1981). Typically, the families are incompetent in consistently enforcing rules for behavior.

Child depression in elementary school children is characterized by low self-esteem, reduced capacity for fun, and excessive guilt, often with suicidal ruminations. These children tend to be socially withdrawn, unzestful, and do poorly in school (Poznanski 1982).

Gisela Konopka, an esteemed professional of many years' standing, addresses adolescent suicide (1983). She finds that the suicidal youth feels totally unworthy, abandoned, and neglected and harbors underlying anger. His future seems hopeless and he is depressed. Indeed for many youngsters this is a statistical probability. There is not yet the balancing effect from a history of having conquered difficult situations. As Konopka points out, these are, for much of society, "doomsdays." We have not helped people learn that living embodies some pain in our search for utopia. Her advice is a double prescription of love, caring, and respect, share our own pain, communicate honestly, accept their strong emotions and work toward creative outlets for feelings. A teacher must never ignore suicidal threats, and consultation about them is essential.

The cognitive map for treatment of those with a neurotic self-concept has two basics: teaching specific skills to handle the overwhelming frustrations and the substantiation of the worth of self through relationship. There is often a need for controlled expression in therapy through play, activity and talking modes. Distorted ecological interactions that sustain the pupil's behavior have to be analyzed, interpreted, and changed. Individual or group counseling is usually indicated, but at the same time a therapeutic milieu is a corollary. Since the family matrix may have produced and/or is sustaining the condition, alteration of the family's interactive patterns may be necessary. The teacher can resolve many school situations through Life Space Interviews (to be discussed subsequently). Preaching, moralizing, and admonitions are not appropriate, though clarification of values and the nature of what is really going on may help. The specific learning task is clarified and teaching is directed to provide the necessary academic or social skill leading to better adaptation. Success is reflected in improved self-esteem and a reduction of defenses.

Since these children and youth have the capacity to relate, albeit often in their own self-defeating ways, the maintenance of stable adult relationships of caring is essential. The teacher recognizes the efforts to provoke and discusses these behaviors with the pupil. The pupil tries to make the adult behave like those who originally caused the self-distortion. It is interesting how many of these pupils, when they improve, will wonder how the teacher could have stood them in the "old days" when they were then condemning the teacher! Adults sense the capacity of neurotic children for human relationships. Some of them are delightful for a time; they do care and want to be reasonable. This may induce in adults frequent requests for instant improvement and anger when such change is not forthcoming. Time, consistent proper handling, and overall progress mixed with regressions is the outlook.

There is fear of failure, which means providing easy step success opportunities. We can expect the child to put on us that which he has experienced elsewhere, and we must guard against falling into this psychological trap. Anxiety is present in oversupply. Desensitization and neutralization will have a place. Fears must be faced.

If there is individual psychotherapy that is producing material and insights, these need to be related to classroom activities. Socialization training will help some. Above all a stable, nonflappable, trustworthy adult-teacher relationship and interesting do-able tasks will be required to replace past experience.

What can be expected in improvement for the neurotic pupil? While overall the prognosis is favorable, the severity and extensive time of the condition are qualifications. Some improve without organized intervention. There might be fortuitous events or biological growth with increased mental age that improve coping capacity. If the precipitating factors continue, minimal change can be expected, as seen by youth who put themselves together only when they can leave a pathological home. Shepherd, Oppenheim, and Mitchell (1971) did a follow-up study of English children where it is noted that the chronic behavior was usually a response to a disturbed family.

Cass and Thomas (1979) conducted a longitudinal study of 200 children treated in a child guidance clinic for a variety of emotional and social problems. They found that 53.5 percent of these subjects retained their same relative mental health position, while 46.5 percent changed positively as they matured. Their untreated group obtained healthier adult ratings than the treated group! Overall the neurotic childhood did not portend severe adult adjustment. The younger the age of referral, the poorer the adult adjustment, probably because of more serious behavior. Withdrawn behavior in girls and aggressive behavior in boys are related to poor later adjustment.

Both Saul (1979) and Antonovsky (1979) emphasize the importance of positive traits as well as negative ones for prognosis. From Saul's study, on the positive side, are strong superego, independence and adaptability; low self-concept, aggressive or escape reactions and egotism are negative.

Gersten et al. (1976) followed over 700 children for five years. They concluded that neurotic behaviors (regressive anxiety and isolation) declined with age. However, those with high peer aggressive behavior and conflict with parents showed high continuance.

Selves with a Significant Deficiency in Appropriate Value Internalization

Many children and youth grow up under conditions that fail to facilitate the internalization of adequate, age-appropriate values. Their deficiency is in socialization, not just in social behavior. The labels associated with these youngsters include omnipotent narcissistic, sociopathic, psychopathic, and sometimes, in error, delinquent, though certain delinquents do fit this syndrome. While value deficiencies are characterized by impulsiveness, they should be differentiated from the brain-injured or neurotically impulsive youngsters.

The self-concept problems of these unfortunate children are revealed by several dimensions. They grow up without adequate empathic nurturing resulting in a lack of ability to feel for others or to envision or care how other people feel. In the past and present environmental scan one usually sees extensive deprivation of mothering, love, and care that establishes human bonding. Sometimes there is simple neglect of the child's behavior, a kind of permissiveness that allows the child to follow his own impulses with only irregular parental explosions. Teachers see this in the extremely narcissistic or omnipotent pupil. Low empathy is combined with an absence of a proper internalized standard for behavior. The youngsters reflect the part of our culture that says and acts on the basis of do what you can get away with. Many of these pupils have high ego skills to manipulate in the real world, though often school skills are low. The youngster with this self-pattern usually knows how to exploit the environment to serve personal gratification, since one lives for immediate pleasure. There is little time perspective in their existentialist view. Their ability to mediate behavior for long-term self or moral values is very limited. Rights of others are held in low regard, which causes havoc in schools. They get away with what they can (Erikson 1977).

There is reality anxiety in the place of an internal anxiety. Smith (1977) points out how chronically disruptive these children are who have no or very little capacity for guilt. They fear getting caught, not as a moral matter but because of the restrictions that might be imposed, although in reality they often are not.

Some of these youngsters have a restricted circle of socialization that includes only their family or their gang. But many, when the chips are down, care only for themselves. There are the con artists who have developed considerable social skills for exploiting others and are given to self-serving manipulations. Some are interesting to have around until they exploit us. The primary narcissism of some omnipotent children is based on the idea that the world owes them a living or whatever part of it they want at the instant. Unfortunately, there is a secret admiration in many of us for those who do in the system, which results in a covert permissiveness on the part of some adults. With regard to rewards, it is what rewards, and rewards now.

These are times of crises in values, which is why this syndrome is so important. We live in a confused moral climate of conflicting values on every side. While we see today a broad accentuation of social concern we also see a cracking of moral values and a do-your-own-thing attitude of by certain parents regardless of what it does to children. Many adults carry individual rights to the point of exploitation of others. This condition is discussed by Harrington (1972), who thinks that the pressures of our society are producing a new generation of value-deficient individuals.

It is common to label less severe value defects as sociopaths and the most severe as the psychopaths. In the case of the latter, aggression is often random and craving for excitement is dominant as indicated by King's child murderers (1975). They feel powerful and "exist" when doing a dangerous thing, but they risk their lives as little as possible, preferring a condition where the gun gives them control. There is a deep recognition of power and a demand to have the odds in their favor. Many are in a continual conflict with the external world, though not troubled internally.

The chapter by Helen Morrison in Reid's book, *The Psychopath* (1978), deals extensively with the concept of the asocial child and sociopathy based on a review of the research. However, the mixture of dynamics (sociopathy) and syndrome (asocial behavior) should be separated because we know other syndromes also produce antisocial behavior. Morrison indicates that a child does not grow out of this pattern but decries the pessimism regarding treatment, pessimism that is born of the difficulty of working with these children. Morrison plans a new volume on treatment. Many "empty" individuals play the con artist role with charm and engaging ways discussed by Smith (1978).

The failure to differentially diagnose these relatively empty individuals causes great difficulties. Society has a right to be protected from them as well as an obligation to provide them the best help possible. It is not always easy to tell to what degree a child has no appropriate values; almost all have rudimentary slivers of a code.

The adult relationship needed is of quite a different order here than with the neurotic. Keeping one's cool is important. Being realistic and not romantic about life is crucial. Demonstrating that one can be law-abiding and survive is essential. Interventions include a type of modeling along with a supervised, planned milieu where rewards come only for acceptable behavior. Unfortunately, many adults become as manipulative as the clients. Schools have their greatest problem with this self-concept syndrome, and vastly altered designs will be needed to help them.

The treatment for value-deficient selves is obvious to describe but most difficult to achieve. They need—if possible—to have values instilled and to develop empathy. In a word they need socialization. This requires living in a universally supervised and monitored environment where it pays to behave. They need figures for identification. Willie Hoffer in "Deceiving the Deceiver" (Eissler 1949) demonstrates that the helper must be one up in ability and be in command, though not in the authoritarian sense. One does not argue against their value differences as many try to do. In a society like ours the sociopath has too many successful case examples evident in prominent positions.

Again, classical psychotherapy is not the general recommendation. Some use of confrontation and direct reality awareness is applicable. Using work as therapy usually falls short of the manifold life circumstances and personality needs of these youth (Ahlstrom and Havighurst 1971). A controlled milieu, very difficult to achieve in school during school hours let alone for the total life space, is desired. Many will require institutional treatment but there are to date very few institutional programs with the proper design. The first need is for benign and savvy adults who know the nature of this impairment but do not counterreact. It is very hard for most of us not to hope for trust that isn't there, or love and empathy that aren't there either. In defeat, we turn hostile as a defense against our own ignorance and reject the youngster. Adults who are knowledgeable, strong, and not sadistic are hard to find. The youngsters need modeling and internalization *as well as* external surveillance as we all do at all stages in our lives. Complete surveillance and specific tasks with immediate gratifications for compliance are necessary to help them learn to conform or at least to be patterned. Correct behavior must pay off in real terms. Though they may never achieve what we would like in caring, some find ways to get returns for reasonable behavior. But others ask why work when I can get my dope money or car parts by stealing so much easier? This is true even if there are jobs.

Often there is severe neglect and abuse in the home. Violence is common, along with brutality. The mother tries but is ineffective, while father, as a figure of identification, models a life of crime. The youngster has had to work out his own self-protection for survival. It is not uncommon for the violence of these youngsters to lead to their own self-destruction. They may well be ego intact and a match for most healthy adult personalities.

Value absence or value deviancy is the core aspect and governs the teacher response. Without being hopeless, one recognizes this condition. One explains rather than "value clarifies." Teacher counteraggressive tendencies are kept under control. Limit setting through direct rules is a big part of the curriculum. The search for a relevant (to the narcissistic self) curriculum is constant. Direct values of school learning are emphasized. The hedonism means that external rewards loom large. Times of excitement and fun are included lest the school be one long boring battle. Most of all, satisfactory social and academic behavior is to be rewarded, and as immediately as possible. Fortunately all but very few pupils have at least some residue of concern that one can utilize. Alternative school programs are essential. You are likely to get only the specific changes you teach for during the program with minimum spillover to other environments (Minuchin, Chamberlain, and Graubard 1967).

A recent study reports the eighteen-year follow-up of aggressive and disturbed adolescents from a mental hospital into adulthood (Fareta 1981). Fareta finds a high degree of antisocial and criminal behavior persisting in childhood though psychiatric involvement lessened. While the majority were no longer known to an agency, as a total group they still accounted for a great deal of the criminal and psychiatric problems. One-fourth continue to need intensive treatment. He found that environmental deprivation and family disorganization factors were of greater predictive relevance than the psychiatric diagnosis.

Robins (1966) has perhaps the most telling studies in this field. The most certain prediction was ascertained from highly antisocial behavior, its variation, intensity, and extensiveness. Signs of antisocial behavior included early onset of discipline problems and poor peer relationships. The number of symptoms is a better predictor than any special one. Sixty-one percent of the sociopaths remained seriously antisocial as adults.

Though these children do not fit many accepted definitions of SEI, they are a special-education responsibility. At present, since they constitute the major school and societal problems, they are bootlegged into special education, but special education has no right to ignore this syndrome. Teachers need assistance with these youngsters, not all of whom are beyond help by any means.

The Staubs (1979) reviewed the psychology of prosocial behavior in its many facets. While there is a developmental aspect, there is nothing automatic in progression to more sophisticated prosocial levels. They list three underlying motives for prosocial behavior: to obtain social approval, adherence to internalized values or norms, and empathic feeling for certain persons or classes of situations. When it comes to value-defective youngsters, the huge task we have becomes apparent: we cultivate the advantage of social approval by rewards, we pattern values, and we do all that is possible to generate empathic recognition.

Delinquency and Violent Behavior

There are two additional specific behaviors that confuse the self-concept organization under discussion: delinquency and violent behavior. The difficulty comes when we take the *symptom* of delinquent behavior or violent behavior and imply that either is generated by a particular self-concept structure. This refusal to look beyond the symptom has been the cause of poor program design, especially in delinquency treatment.

All delinquents who violate norms of the large society are not of the same self-concept genesis. Delinquent behavior is a legal definition and not a psychological syndrome. If a minor child breaks a law (runs away, steals, destroys, robs, threatens, or harms another), he is delinquent. As a consequence, he is subject to juvenile court action, should the behavior be discovered and should legal action be taken. Law breaking does not define a particular personality profile (Coffer, Mayahn, and Ostrov 1978). A child may run away to join a peer culture, to escape sadistic treatment, or to avoid reasonable discipline. A youngster may steal because this is the code of behavior of his particular social environment, because he has no regard for the rights of others, because he feels rejected and deprived or because society offers no way to earn money or he wants money fast and easy to support a drug habit. A teenager may kill out of panic, in fear, or because at the time of ultimate destruction of another human being he feels exhilarated and powerful. The long and short of it is, neurotics can be delinquent, psychotics can be delinquent, and sociopaths can be delinquent. Some steal alone, some in gangs. Some are anxious about doing wrong and others are only anxious lest they be caught. A comprehensive study of the delinquent classification has been undertaken by Smiley (1977). The results emphasize the multiple personality conditions involved.

It is interesting that 42 percent of the population in juvenile correctional institutions are defined as handicapped: the prevalent categories were EMR, ED, and LD (Morgan 1979). Offer, Marohn, and

Ostrov (1979) indicate four psychodynamic patterns of delinquents: impulsive, narcissistic, empty, and depressed. As one would anticipate, the proportion of learning disabilities in a delinquent population is higher than in a normal population; the same could be said of other disabilities. But the idea that LD causes delinquency or some special types of delinquency is not borne out. The deficiencies in academic achievement that many delinquents have are from multiple causes (Kulitz, Zaremba, and Broder 1979).

The implication of multiple causation is clear: any one type of treatment for all delinquents will be inappropriate. Interventions, regardless of the delinquent label, should follow in logical order from the differential underlying self-concepts, not the symptom alone (Stumphauzer 1979).

Doing a delinquent act does not necessarily mean becoming a career delinquent. Loeber (1982) surveyed the studies to discover the continuity factors. He found that children who initially show high rates, varieties, and settings for their delinquent behavior are more likely to be the persisters. Overt delinquency declines in preadolescence, while covert increases.

The overall lack of our professional ability to predict how a given youngster will behave in the future makes the decision all the more difficult. If each of us were to have made a career of our own most delinquent act, the percentage of delinquency would be much higher than the annual 5 percent that it now is.

Gold (1978; Mann and Gold 1984) sees the schools as central in society's reaction to delinquency. He defines delinquent behavior as a deliberate, knowing perpetration of an act that is subject to legal sanctions and finds juvenile delinquencies thirty times the volume of the recorded delinquent behavior. Delinquency occurs in all social classes and, to Gold, as an ego defense against depreciation of self-esteem. A major cause is failure to be successful in the student role, peer socialization, and in extracurricular activities. Then disruptive behavior "leads fairly easily to self-aggrandizement." There is additional focus on revolt and an aim to damage the source of hurt, which the subject views as the school. Thus the remedy is to create alternative schools that provide a high quota of successful experience and warm adult relationships with evaluation based on individual progress rather than norms. There are questions as to whether programs should be part of or isolated from regular school, volunteer or assigned, and how long given recalcitrance can be tolerated.

The educational difficulties of delinquents have been reviewed by Gagne (1977). Frequent language disabilities lead to low reading achievement: behavior modification remedial programs have been useful. Communication skills are deficient. The youth are preoccupied with a search for power and masculinity. Truckenmiller (1982) finds little *average* impact of education, vocational training, and opportunity, and the problems of intervening successfully in friendship or family generators are unsurmountable. On the other hand, John Mesinger (1982), long an advocate for special education helping delinquents, has concluded that if we applied our current knowledge, we could build effective alternative educational programs.

It should not be forgotten that delinquency can be a self-destructive solution to problems as well as an antisocial category. A million children a year run away to escape parental supervision, strictness, and abuse; and sometimes they are pushed out by parents or stepparents; or it may be school problems. There are depressed delinquents with low self-esteem who attempt and sometimes succeed at suicide. These are more likely to be girls than boys (Miller, Chiles, and Barnes 1982).

Violence and Extreme Aggression. Because of the current alarm over the amount of violence and extreme aggression of children and youth, this matter needs clarification. There are the shootouts in schoolyards, murders in classrooms, assaults upon teachers, and rape in the daily news. School has become a most unsafe place for youngsters. Vandalism in schools, parks, and public buildings is epidemic. The old and feeble are preyed upon. It used to be considered a center city phenomenon, but it now happens in various locales, which frightens the middle class more. We feel unsafe and we don't like it. Schools are unsafe and that is very disturbing. Even in some small cities pupils are afraid to use the restrooms because of threats. Teachers find tires slashed. The mass media creates an obsession with what is already a sordid condition. While some institutions and people bring aggression upon themselves, innocence of victims is more typical. Training courses in how to avoid rape or mugging are a necessary but hardly a sufficient social intervention.

These should be concerns of special education. In tracing severe aggression, Moore (1982) makes an important distinction. There are children who act out from families, which though caring, are incompetent in socializing the youngster. The more serious are youngsters who grow up in families of rejection and abuse. Addiction to a steady diet of television violence is one serious sign. We do know that both punishment and catharsis are seldom effective to reduce aggression of this type (Baron 1977).

We have already indicated that violent behavior is possible from the neurotic child and the sociopathic as well. Violence is no respector of syndrome. When a girl is bored on a Monday morning and shoots up a playground with a gun given to her by her father, one has more than a youngster with which to deal. The calm, even ideal student who snipes at neighborhood targets may be a paranoid psychotic. The untargeted aggression of the psychopath knows no prediction: it is just a matter of happenstance. There is episodic anger and violence between both strangers and friends. Suicide and drugs can be seen as violence against the self.

The young have good reason to take up with violence as a solution, given our society. We have so many examples from the KKK to confrontations with every authority. We murder public figures. After the fact we explain why; before the fact we can't predict who, except statistically. Violence as a social method is practiced by terrorist groups to enhance their cause, which they deem the "right." Intolerable center city frustration and unjust treatment perpetrates a riot. We fight our periodic wars that kill haphazardly and we poison the environment.

In dealing with these problems there is no simple clinical solution and no quick way of social reform. Agee (1979) believes that these youth, though very aversive to treatment, can be helped. She deals with limits, changing peer influence and overall design of milieu and reports research on the methodology. She also indicates when to persist and when to give up. Every possible approach should be used, including milieu as well as individualized counseling. Above all, we cannot excuse ourselves by scapegoating the victims any more than we can go sentimental in the presence of a career of violence.

Psychotic and Autistic Self-Development

The categorization of childhood psychoses is complex: at least one set of authors sees infantile autism, childhood schizophrenia, and developmental psychoses as three categories (Noll and Benedict 1981) with proposed differential treatment. Here only the two categories, autism and childhood schizophrenia, will be discussed.

There are many children called autistic who represent a combination of brain damage, severe retardation, and sometimes even aphasia. Differential diagnosis is very difficult. Autistic children are no longer SEI but are classified as other health impaired, although SEI training is still common for their teachers. Childhood autism is a developmental disability of biological origin. Menolascino and Eyde (1979) indicate the following biophysical causes: congenital malformations of the central nervous system; residuals of pre- and postnatal infections; metabolic errors; chromosomal disorders; cerebral anoxia; or a cluster of language and auditory limitations and seizures. If the educational process is geared to the uniqueness of the biological limitations, these authors do not despair.

The self-concept of the autistic child remains rudimentary and very seriously atrophied even when early consistent and appropriate help is provided. This is because of the child's limitations in integrating useful patterns of behavior consequent to interaction with the environment. Figures differ on incidence, partly because of the similarity of certain behavior to seriously retarded and brain-damaged children. Estimations are in the neighborhood of 1 in 2,000 to 3,000 of the total child population with boys outnumbering girls 5 to 1. Biological limitations are usually combined with learned behavior aberrations. Often the layer of completely discordant behavior can be peeled off by thorough low-key but strongly persistent adult handling. The underlying biological limitation will still be evident but less self-defeating behaviors can then be taught.

There are several processes that can be used for preliminary screening such as those by TEACCH, Rimland, Wing, and Wood. There is an inability to develop normal relationships to persons or objects in the environment. The condition will have been evident before the age of three. There is language dysfunction ranging from no language at all to rudimentary expression that lacks external meaningfulness. Ornitz and Ritvo (1976) have presented a most thorough review of the syndrome, tracing it from the now disregarded Kanner concept of the "refrigerator mother" cause to the present, under many labels. They list that onset is probably at birth and includes failure of adequate modulation of sensory input with hypo- or hyperalternatives. The youngsters are often highly involved with touch, smell, and taste in contrast to hearing and sight. They may persist in destructive self stimulation, such as scratching or head banging. Developmental rates are uneven and delayed. Eye contact and affective responses are minimal, which results in relationship difficulties. There may be bizarre mannerisms and body movements, which are often repetitive. Speech may be delayed, echoic, or completely absent. These authors indicate that 75 percent of the autistic children are misclassified as mentally retarded throughout life. Some later develop seizures. Failure to develop any usable language by the age of five is indicative of poor prognosis. A minority will be able to become self-sustaining, and those who are relatively the most normal in development constitute the best potential. Ornitz and Ritvo's view is that there is no rational or specific treatment for autism, but early intervention, work with parents, behavior and speech therapy, and special education are among the treatments recommended. Their general discussion covers the definitions espoused by the National Society for Autistic Children (Schopler 1978). McDonald and Sheperd (1976) indicate that diagnosis and etiology do not necessarily provide cues for the educator. Everything from custodial treatment to electroshock has been tried. The most promising evidence is for benign behavior modification, parent involvement, and training in specific tasks. Teachers concentrate on direct instruction related to the specific life survival tasks the child needs.

One of the most prolific writers for educators has been Lora Wing (1976). Paluszny (1979) writes of both the pathology and treatment in a very readable volume. Balow and Reid (1978) have developed a source book for both parents and professionals. Schopler, Brehu, and Kinsbourne (1971) found that autistic children reacted more favorably to structure than to nonstructure and have produced considerable teaching material (1983). The overall cue is, programs should have a great deal of specific structure (Rutter and Schopler 1978). The role of parents in dealing with specific autistic behaviors has been emphasized and parent training programs are favored. Teachers have found the series of books by Mary Wood and her associates particularly useful in setting up programs for young autistic children. Cases and methods are given in sufficient detail to be directly applicable (Wood 1975; Purvis and Somet 1976; Wood and Williams 1977; Bachrach, Mosley, Swindle, and Wood 1978). The developmental therapy group at the University of Georgia, in addition to publishing materials, conducts training institutes and produces a newsletter for a teacher-support network.

Particular autistic children may show specific talents such as artistic ability as the case of Nadia (Selfe 1978). Her particular artistic ability astonished the workers and stood in juxtaposition to her relationship and language handicap. But in contrast to Nadia there are the majority of autistic children who are limited overall. Less than a quarter can be expected to fall in the normal range of intelligence and the level of intelligence is predictive of eventual status. While some of these children have speech, often its echoic and dissociated nature provides no real communication. This is one reason why speech therapists and sign language have become part of some treatment programs. The effort is to replace the direct action—screaming and demanding for communication—with more reasonable interaction, even though typical language may never be achieved.

Children of this nature are not to begin by being mainstreamed. They require special classes or day school support along with complete assistance to parents. The preferred teacher and aide to pupil ratio is 1 to 1; certainly the diligence needed in teaching them basic life routines requires such investment. There are programs that propose depersonalized behavior modification. In contrast there are also those who believe relationship is the key and that the child must be brought through the basic humanizing-socializing sequence. More to the point is infusion of behavior modification with a very warm relationship. Because of the small number in the population and the difficulty of treatment, programs lagged until parents organized and made demands. The strong national organization, the National Society for Autistic Children in Albany, New York, is augmented by state organizations.

While the general prognosis is limited, certain children do respond and special education must maximize individual capabilities.

The adolescent autistic child continues to need highly specialized education (Oppenheim 1974). The adolescent age merges into the need for group homes where living and community involvement in sheltered workshops and all possible normal activities with protective oversight are preferred. The highly idiosyncratic planning necessary for each child is illustrated by parents' reports in the *NSAC Communicator,* which is published by the National Society for Autistic Children. Finding what particular things a particular adolescent can do and matching ability with opportunity is most painstaking. Teachers use high gratification experiences (such as going to the ice cream store) to teach adequate public behavior. The teacher must recognize the great fears parents have for their youngsters' future when they will no longer be able to provide for them.

Most authorities hold that there is no effective treatment without parental involvement; Schopler and Rerchler (1976) have described their TEACCH program, probably the foremost in the country, which was first established in North Carolina. In the TEACCH program, parents are cotherapists and are given extensive training and support as well as primary status. The problem is seen as biological in genesis. Children are evaluated in a center, parents are consulted and observed interacting with their children, and all impressions are shared with parents. Families are offered a trial experience in one of the "modified" self-contained special-education classrooms available. Parents participate in the classrooms and in home programs.

PEP (Psychoeducational Profile) is an instrument used to center on the task items to be taught and covers the functioning level in sense modalities, motor, cognitive, and language. Abnormal affect and social patterns are also scaled. Parents watch the therapists and converse with them regarding their efforts to teach to the problems revealed in the diagnosis. The design is essentially pragmatic, not bound by any single theory. *Focus on Prevention* (Schopler 1978) is a useful source for program description.

The expectations for the teacher will differ with degree of impairment, of course. But painstaking steps toward a goal, focusing attention, much repetition, and many rewards will be in order. Areas where the pupil seems to be able to do reasonably well are emphasized. The teacher lends an adult ego. The combination of gentle but persistent pressure on unacceptable behavior and rewards (that the child cares about) for acceptable behavior constitute the continual routine. Learning how to learn may be half the effort; getting attention, defining the task, recognizing progress, and rewarding success are all important. A rich curriculum based on the arts, music, and story telling is the birthright of every special pupil. A report of a recent Minnesota conference on preparing to teach autistic children covers these areas in detail (Conference on Preparing Teachers for Severely Emotionally Disturbed Children with Autistic Characteristics 1977).

Knoblock (1982) takes a humanistic approach, emphasizing peer and teacher relationships in small classrooms that contain both regular and autistic children. The program has been worked out over the years in his school called the Learning Place. Teaching the child to play, affective education, communication, music, and the arts are central in an informal setting with normal children. While the children described have serious problems, the data here as elsewhere make it difficult to know the exact nature of the pupils. There is an optimistic outlook from this tightly knit program and team of workers. They take full advantage of the social interaction potentials of peers. Koegel, Egel, and Rincover (1981) stress the need for comprehensive diagnosis and the psychology of their learning characteristics as well as education and maintenance of gains.

The difficulties in assessing the results of the follow-up studies reside in the diagnosis, particularly in combination with brain damage, lack of common criterion and a wide variety of uncontrolled elements. Nonetheless, prognosis can be charted in a general way.

Ornitz and Ritvo (1976) provide a critical review of the field. They report that two-thirds to three-fourths are destined to be limited throughout life, those with seizures and brain dysfunction the most retarded and overall impaired. Failure to develop language, inappropriate use of toys, and cognitive deficits by five indicate poor prognosis.

The minority without these conditions are mostly shy and passive in later life while others seem to make a transition to childhood schizophrenia. A small minority will be able to live independent lives, but with lacks in social judgment and empathy. The positive impact of behavior therapy, special education, parental and residential care is subject to the level of impairment.

Lotter (1974) followed thirty-two autistic children (eight to ten years of age) for eight years. One was employed and some 60 percent required "extensive care and supervision." The case for education is made on humanitarian grounds and the lack of predictability rather than on explicit results. Employability and amount of schooling were not related. Sheltered workshop and protected living situations may be a possible goal for some of the more adaptable. Their findings parallel the follow-up reports of Rutter at Maudsley Hospital in London.

In 1972 Wing reported on sixty-three adolescents and young adults who had been diagnosed as childhood autistics. Fourteen percent were doing well, functioning on a good level. Twenty-five percent made progress although they were "markedly abnormal." Most of the remainder had become less difficult and a few (mostly those in institutions) had regressed still further. They note that none of these cases had special-education intervention.

Ward (1976) has the most optimistic view based upon structural therapy, which is a high stimulation of individual and milieu treatment focused on development of body images and cognitive development following Piaget. Emotional stimulation is also included. While they admonish all to have realistic goals based upon actual capacities, they see their results as evidence against pessimism. Of thirteen cases, ten were found to be maintained in home and community programs as long as six years after discharge. All thirteen had shown some positive results of special-education programs originally developed for the retarded. Eleven continued in special education. The original diagnosis of autism included only one classified early infantile autistic. McDonald and Sheperd (1976) criticized Ward's psychogenic approach and in their review of the studies report that in general 1 to 2 percent recover to normality; perhaps as many as another 5 to 15 percent were borderline; and another 16 to 25 percent fair. This means that the majority are poor to very poor.

The criteria of intellectual function and especially speech are central for prognosis. There will be the rare remarkable complete recovery. The energy, skill, and time to maximize the performance at any level will be extensive. There will be significant changes for about a third, leading to far more reasonable lives; for the others, basic self-care and habit formation—very important in themselves—can lead to a more congenial existence.

Childhood Psychosis

While of low incidence, childhood schizophrenic relations do occur often enough to be of general educational concern, and puberty is often the time of recognition. The basic condition is a distortion in reality perception in thought processes and a change in interaction with people and other aspects of the environment. While the schizophrenic may have normal intelligence, "tested" intelligence is usually impaired in some areas and there may be a combination of schizophrenia and retardation (Baker 1979). Thinking tends to become perseverative, penetrating in some areas, shallow in others, and unconnected with integrated thought. The cognitive processes necessary for normal self-concept development are distorted. Drive may be obsessive or extremely passive. Behavior is socially inappropriate and often regressive. Bizzare motions may replace outwardly purposeful ones. Believed fantasy may replace reality. Obsessive questions about conditions reflects an essential unsureness about life. The self may become depersonalized and referred to in the third person. Delusions, phobic reactions, and hallucinations may be present. Pervasive anxiety underlies the schizophrenic self.

There is considerable difference of opinion concerning the nature and genesis of childhood schizophrenia. Bettelheim (1950) in the treatment program at the Orthogenic School, considered the development psychogenic and that the behaviors were symbolic manifestations of psychological problems. Henry, in *Pathways to Madness* (1965), described the behavior as normal reaction to a pathological family condition, the child responding to covert double-bind family demands. The contrary view is a biological, chemical, or neurological causation, based on the higher frequency of hereditary factors in the histories and twin similarities. It is probable that persons with higher biological vulnerability are also responding to what is, for that individual, overwhelming stress. It is also evident that some children were "different" from infancy while others appeared within the normal range until a given time, such as adolescence, when atypical behavior ensued.

Rabinovitch (1980) sees an integrated phenomenon in autism and schizophrenia. He distinguishes between this impairment and other autistic groups with neurologic abnormalities, seizures, and deterioration. If the onset is early (within three years), the core problem is dysidentity—a failure to develop a sense of self with autism and language idiosyncrasies. The reactive symptoms are fears and diffuse motor behavior. The survival provision is a simplistic environment where sameness and routine activities are required and a concrete orientation is used regarding time, numbers, local geography, and other necessary living conditions. When the onset is at adolescence, the dysidentity is the *loss* of the previous sense of self with general uncertainty and impaired reality testing. Anxiety and panic may result in excessive motor behavior or inertia. Substitute identities can become a way to restore the self and fantasies are used for compensation. Their 200 cases followed later as adults were still evidencing "inordinate immaturity," monotonous speech, language peculiarities, perplexity, impaired reality testing, and generally passive or docile behavior. While, in their view, etiology is unknown, it is thought to be developmental, either neurological or neurochemical, with a likely genetic component. Treatment includes help for the family, particular individual supportive psychotherapy, natural behavior modification (praise/relationships/pleasurable activities) and special education as an absolute. Pharmacology will not change the core dysidentity but may be helpful in dealing with anxiety. Teachers who are not familiar with schizophrenic children and youth will find the filmed histories of these patients (available from Hawthorn Center, Northville, Michigan) a sober but positive survey of the problem.

For the teacher, the important aspects of interaction are two: expression of caring and concern for the child even when there is no response; a reality orientation to educational and life experiences. The uncertainty, questions, and anxiety are responded to with clarification and reassurance. The same questions asked a thousand times must not produce short-tempered adult responses. The schizophrenic's struggle to organize life means that there is a dependency on patterns and that changes have to be explained. As they come to trust the teacher, the query Is it time to go now? becomes also a clock exercise. Reassurance is given. But the teacher seeks to engage the child in worthwhile activities at whatever level possible, whenever possible, and recognizes each achievement. Rather than remaining with repetitive responses, activities are constructive and involve learning reasonable social interactions with a sequence of concrete examples. Teaching methods to deal with environmental realities are important. Life should contain satisfactions and times of joyful experiences. Some schizophrenic children show overall general arrested development and then life survival skills become important and a sheltered workshop and protected environment the goal. Others have particular intensive interests and talents—mathematics for example or art—that can be encouraged and make for a societal role, though blunting and distortion of affect may never be altered.

Early school indications of later schizophrenic processes have been noted (John, Mednick and Schulsinger 1982). Inappropriate school behavior, disciplinary difficulties, anxiety, loneliness, and inhibition were noted in the cases of males. The first sign in adolescent development of schizophrenia is the inability to respond to the primary stimuli in a pattern; other signs are easy distraction by trivia, ambivalence, thought disorders, and fragmentation. The value of early identification is to prevent the development of a psychotic identity (Bauer and Bauer 1982).

Educators help schizophrenic children achieve four things: trust in adults, social skills, academic and vocational skills, and pleasant personal experiences. Effective teachers become deeply involved with the life of these youngsters, being reassuring and ready to support their need for environmental certainty. At the same time teachers lead the child to feel more adequate by leading them through painstaking steps of increased coping ability. They search out special talents a youngster may have in academics or art and hope for some eventual articulation of ability and occupation, though work will usually be in a protected life environment. Interaction skills often start as lessons in formal manners and speech phrases. Enjoyment is provided through music, dance, the arts, and games. The teacher serves as insurance during trips, camping, and exploring the world. Little by little the self evolves. In teaching the schizophrenic self, though each child is singular, one knows that reassurance and support will be general needs. Reality is explained and re-explained. Concepts are made concrete. When the pupil drifts away or starts a compulsive ritual, the teacher intervenes with suggestions of more appropriate behavior. The curriculum is made to fit potential whether it be learning self-care or calculus. A uniform and stable classroom environment is maintained with explanations of changes.

Children and adolescents are subject to psychotic reactions apart from childhood schizophrenia. Drug reactions and eventual burnout from sustained drug use and overdose have been romanticized. The uncertainty of drug consequences, the introduction of new drugs and individualized psychobiological responses indicate detoxification and stabilization before assigning diagnoses. Again, expert medical diagnosis is needed to rule out toxic states due to lead ingestion, delayed disease sequelae, or tumors.

Childhood depression is believed to be on the increase. Whether or not severe depression represents a psychotic state, neurotic reaction, or both may be argued, but its many manifestations and different intensities are often overlooked (Arieti and Bemporad 1978; French and Berlin 1979).

Much has already been implied concerning the prognosis of childhood psychosis: some make a complete recovery, function adequately enough to take care of themselves, while others require a protected environment. Periodic regressions may take place. Eggers (1978) has presented a thorough follow-up of fifty-two child psychotic patients (ages seven to thirteen) followed on an average of fifteen years. Twenty percent recovered completely, 30 percent reached relatively good social adjustment, and 50 percent had moderate or no improvement. Family psychiatric disorders or poor family environment were not prognostic. Most studies give an overall general poor prognosis, with a 50 percent "recovery." Usually prognosis was more favorable for children who grew up without indications of psychosis until rapid personality changes took place (loss of contact with reality, reduced activity, inappropriate and strange pursuits, speech disturbances, anxiety, diffuse fears, distrust, coldness, and sometimes brutality). Delusions and hallucinations are rare but fear of death and loss of identity was common. Acute precipitation was found in forty-two cases while fifteen were considered chronic. Those who become psychotic before the age of ten had poorer outcomes. Higher intelligence is a positive indicator. Twenty-six of their cases had subsequent cyclothymic phases.

Goldfarb et al. (1978) point out that the many previous studies are difficult to evaluate because of inadequate descriptions of the children studied. Their first data on seventy-eight young psychotic children were collected at intake to residential treatment when the mean age was 7.2 years. All "began life as highly deviant children with massive irregularities and deficits in the emergent latticework of their personalities" (p. 163). The treatment period (which was cooperative with parents) covered four years. The children were followed subsequently for an average of 8.7 years to adolescence or early adulthood, to an average age of 19.9 years. The original diagnostic criteria were gross and sustained impairment of emotional relationship; unawareness of own personal identity (appropriate to age); pathological preoccupation with particular objects; sustained resistance to environmental change, abnormal perceptual experience, and acute, seemingly illogical anxiety. Communicative speech had not developed and mobility was distorted.

The authors' central concept is embodied in a five-point global ego integration scale on which scores ranged from very severely impaired to normal on social maturity, self-care, and educational response. Even with the most severely impaired there *may* be islets of normal or exceptional accomplishment. These splinters of talent do not provide a general resource for self-development however; they exist in isolation. All of the children were from intact families to start with and about 77 percent of the children were able to go home to their families at discharge. Virtually all of the children showed at least some specific areas of improvement. Twenty-eight percent were able to adjust to school, community and family living. Eight years later in the continuing follow-up, 72 percent were still able to live at home, almost 49 percent being now classified as mildly impaired, which was a considerable improvement over the 28 percent originally making a relatively satisfactory adjustment. Thus there was a continued improvement in self-adequacy for some very disturbed children after intensive treatment. Additional children with continuing serious problems were still able to live with their families and function in the community. Of the fifty-one individual and combination variables under analysis in this study, twenty-five were significant positive predictors: IQ and ego status at the initial period were central (ego status includes attachment, cognition, language, self-awareness, and educational response). The higher the ego organization, the more favorable the prognosis. Those at the lowest levels remained grossly impaired at follow-up. In their view, if comprehensive impatient care is provided (optimistic intention, therapy, education and milieu support), some progress may be expected as children grow into early adulthood. In most cases requiring eventual institutionalization, the children were initially the most limited.

Eisenberg (see Goldfarb 1978) comments that this study gives grounds for optimism. He sees infantile psychosis (autism) as having its onset within the first thirty months and holds that this condition does not develop into schizophrenia. In contrast is the schizophrenic disintegrative psychosis where normal development for the first years is followed by cognitive, affective, and behavioral deterioration, rarely before age six or seven. He points out that previous studies had an improvement rate from 14 percent to 40 percent, except for Bettelheim's Orthogenic School, which was higher.

It seems that the more the child had going for him or her to start with, and the more appropriate psychoeducational and family intervention, the more favorable the prognosis. Wing (1976) says that appropriate education or therapeutic education is the essential ingredient.

CONCLUSION

There are of course other diagnostic systems and categorizations than the simplified syndrome categories presented above.

The American Psychiatric Association has a new diagnostic manual, *DSM-III: Diagnostic and Statistical Manual of Mental Disorders* (American Psychiatric Association 1980). Clinical entities have been expanded through the use of multiple axes around the primary diagnostic axis. These include five individual dimensions producing specific developmental disorders for children and adolescents. Environmental and physical causes are included. For example, *conduct disorder* in the old schema is now undersocialized aggressive, undersocialized nonaggressive, socialized aggressive, socialized nonaggressive, and atypical. The American Psychological Association has withheld acceptance of *DSM-III* and has a task force developing another nosology where the preliminary categories are descriptive and do not delineate descrete personality patterns.

For statistical and research purposes these systems may standardize some of the variance in this cumbersome field. For teachers the procedures are of little value. Forness and Cantwell (1982) compare DSM-III and special-education systems; they make the case that SEI teachers should all understand DSM-III terms because the terms will appear in reports and will be used in interdisciplinary communication. There are considerable difficulties in coordinating the educational and clinical systems. Handbooks are of considerable value to a teacher because they cover common problems of an age (Wolman 1978; Woody 1981).

In addition to the orientation proposed around the major syndromes discussed above there are sources that focus on common behaviors found within syndromes.

A fascinating series of interventions based on specific symptomatic problems fits well with using the problem behavior focus of the chart in figure 4, pages 174–76 (Schaefer and Millman 1977; Stein and Davis 1982; Schaefer, Johnson, and Wherry 1982; Schaefer, Millman, and Levine 1979; Schaefer, Briesmeister, and Fitton 1984; Millman, Schaefer, and Cohen 1980; Schaefer, Briesmeister, and Fitton 1984). These books cover therapies for school behavior problems, general behavior problems, adolescent problems, psychosomatic disorders, family interventions, and group processes. One can look up a case dealing with encopresis, aggression, school refusal, mutism, or virtually any problem that children are heir to. Treatment plan or plans are described with explanations. The symptom is put where it belongs, in the context of the individual who has the problem.

Quay and Peterson (1979; 1983) have developed a behavior problem checklist that consistently produces four personality types: the child with conduct problems, the neurotic, the inadequate and immature, and the socialized delinquent each with instructional counterparts. Von Isser, Quay, and Love (1980) found three primary dimensions that Quay had previously identified as conduct, anxiety-withdrawal, and immaturity.

It should be noted that the search for self-patterns for predicting differential interventions is a circular process. On one hand, one's theory sets up expectations of what one should include in an assessment process. On the other hand, by factoring a set of questions we can arrive at a given set of patterns whether the questions cover all of the behavior we should examine or not. Then we can apply theory to explain the computor output. While recent work reveals that various differential student profiles are found (Elitov 1984), there are still the individual child differences *within* any given cluster, just as in the case of the syndromes described above. To reiterate, teachers teach *individual pupils* with idiosyncratic nuances. They do not teach syndromes, general profiles, or symptomatic behavior. They teach children.

4

The Helping Process

S O FAR OUR STUDY has been leading to this crucial chapter and the question How can we conceptualize helping SEI pupils? The positions about helping, often unfortunately borrowed from adult practice, are varied and contrasting in nature. Since individual psychology is a process approach, not a position, our task is how to utilize various theories in change efforts. Characteristically in training, two solutions to helping are offered. Proposal One is to select a theory as adequate and pit it against all others. The other solution is to be eclectic, picking pieces from here and there on an ad hoc basis. Based upon individual psychology, with a focus on the child self, once we are clear about the various methods and complications of helping, we can be selective on the basis of what is appropriate for the particular pupil. This requires an understanding of various approaches. It also requires a dispassionate attitude so that we are open to what can be relevant for a particular situation. The difference between what we propose and eclecticism is that selection from the various ways to help is oriented by the core of the process of individual psychology, the nature of the individual child.

THE LAND OF HELPING

Those who teach SEI children are members of a significant proportion of the professional population dedicated to helping others in distress. The motivations of this group vary and their ideas of how to help vary even more. Many professions are included in human helping full or part time, lay or professional. Helping in America is a major industry. There is a constant proliferation of literature on how one human being can assist another. Almost anything you can name is considered "therapeutic" by some group whether it is screaming, meditation, problem solving, dancing, physical punishment, hypnosis, drugs, or conditioning, to name a few. Helping is a field that is susceptible to gurus and ritual. Our purpose is to cut through this confusion and come to a conceptual understanding of the underlying essence of helping disturbed youngsters.

An excellent orientation is to examine our own experiences and the experiences of others we have known well when change has resulted from giving help. Every one of us has changed certain of our behavior—or at least we have tried. There may also be changes that happen and we do not understand why. It may be feelings, behavior, or ideas we would alter. Periodically there will be some habit that we would eliminate from our repertoire. It may be just a specific change of a speech mannerism or the place we keep the car keys, or it may be a more significant segment of self-management, such as eliminating late snacks. Sometimes our goal is to have a complete alteration—more or less a new self and life-style. Every bookstore has a table of self-help books. No one has computed the amount of effort that goes into trying to foster positive changes in human behavior. In reviewing our own efforts and those who worked with or on us to produce change, we see mixed results. Some changes work out and some do not. We may have found no way to change certain aspects of our behavior, regardless of our effort.

If one could just change 10 percent, it might make a significantly different person. For some children small change suffices. Others need a larger percentage of change. Normal children, to say nothing of SEI youngsters, live in a constant milieu of change efforts. The goals, expectations, processes, and hopefully the responsibility for changes are the substance of the IEP, to be discussed subsequently.

The Helper and the Helpee

Many major problems in helping stem from the differences in the helping configuration seen by the helper and helpee. In the case of a youngster, there are usually several sets of assumptions concerning what should take place. Since few children refer themselves, they are captives, selected for help by teachers, parents, or others. The forced nature of the association is one reason why there is so much resistance directed toward teachers and therapists—those very folk who see themselves as the rescuers. We know that all children do not come to the "mandated" helping condition with the same attitudes. They are not adults who contract and pay for assistance. Schools, prisons, and many mental health institutions are expected to provide help whether or not the client wishes to cooperate. The forced nature in the "contract" with a child is one source of conflict. Helpers see themselves as useful and critically important in creating a desired change in youngsters' behavior, often ignoring the implications of the child being in a no-choice situation.

Adults are often oblivious to the subtleties of giving help. After all, we are engaged in virtuous work. But the effect on the youngster may be quite other. Not to be able to successfully cope on your own increases one's feeling of impotence and learned helplessness. Even the young child reminds us often that he can do it himself. Helping can create dependency. This produces ambivalence, thanks for the help but no thanks for the self depreciation of my not being capable of self-management. This ambivalence becomes shrill at adolescence when being an independent person is the major theme. Those who help must expect to be a target for resistance. We should be up front about this dilemma.

Taylor (1983) has outlined the path of events of a person who is caught in a serious problem and does not typically seek out professional help. First one tries to explain why the difficulty happened and how serious it is, what the implications are. The second stage is how can one master the condition, to get personal control so that this will not happen again. The third phase is the search for self-enhancement in spite of the event to maintain self-esteem. These steps are useful in thinking about children's responses.

It is difficult to describe the delicate balances of forces that have to be generated and maintained by the helper. Janis (1983) has enunciated control phases. Through enhancing the helpee's self-esteem, the helper develops power as a significant reference person. Recommendations must be made in such a way as not to impair this supportive relationship and at the same time provide judicious independence from the helper. When there is a sharing of confidence, and the confidence is not betrayed, trust develops.

Brickman et al. (1982) coded the various perceptions of helping and coping. When one looks at IEP meetings and evaluation sessions, the echoes of Brickman's analyses are there influencing how help is given, received, and judged. There are two central issues about which helpers have conflict: Who is responsible for the child's problem predicament and who is responsible for the needed changes in behavior? First Brickman describes the *moral model.* Here the person with the problem is considered highly responsible for his fate because he made errors; he is also highly responsible for solutions to his dilemma. One must help one's self, since the condition is attributed to a lack of correct effort on the part of the person. Helpers cannot make change; they only attack distortions in the situation and exhort the person who must change. In this model, when the desired change does ensue, the person will feel more competent with resultant higher self-esteem. When there is failure to change, the individual loses a sense of competency and self-esteem; resignation is the outcome. In the moral model, the world is a just place and you get what you deserve.

The second model Brickman terms *compensatory.* In this model a person is not responsible for his plight and thus should not be blamed. Physical or environmental deprivation is at fault. But he is still held responsible for solutions. He will have to compensate for handicaps by special efforts and is responsible for using the help the helper provides. Energy is directed not to seeking the causes of the situation but to solutions. The person gets the credit for solving the problem and learning how to cope. There may be hostility if a person is called upon to solve problems not considered his fault. In this model, the world is not just, and those who fail can blame prior circumstances, parents, teachers, fate, or poor advice from the helper.

The third model is the *medical-behavioral,* where the person is also not responsible for his condition: it is beyond his control, a consequence of biological or environmental conditions. It is interesting that both the medical and Skinnerian determinism fit this explanation. Also, the victim is not responsible for the solutions since they are produced externally. One should follow the advice of experts who know what must be done. The person is seen as ill or with faulty learning experiences and in need of help. Because cause and change are external, no guilt or personal weakness is implied. However the power of change lies with the helpers. This model fosters dependency and lowers the sense of competency.

The final model is *enlightenment.* Here the person is responsible for his condition and should feel guilty, done in by his own works and not by others. This encourages a negative self-image and a low sense of competence. But the person is not responsible for the cure. An external helper is essential. Solutions come as the helpers indicate the true nature of the problem and how to deal with it. The victim is to submit to the discipline of the helper and adhere to the rules of authority. Brickman finds this model used in treatment programs and in schools.

The present author has found that teachers have a wide variation in the way they use the four models with the SEI pupils. In general, the younger the child the more the compensatory model is used; with adolescents, the moral model is assigned. Delinquent behavior in school settings is often responded to by the moral model or the enlightenment model. It is important to recognize that the helper-helpee roles differ with each design, as does the power assigned to the helper.

A great many implications flow from Brickman's paradigm. Many case conferences and IEP meetings are fraught with mixed assumptions by the various participating members, consequently plans do not match. Often the assumptions are implied but not overtly recognized. At other times they are overt: "I can't do anything with him." "He won't do what I tell him to do." "He should try harder." "It's his fault. He keeps getting into trouble he should avoid." Pupil assumptions about change often differ from the teacher or parent. Parents, for example, give significantly more child attributions (it is the child's fault) than external causes. Children attribute their problems to both themselves and outside causes about evenly (Compas, et al. 1981). Children have given the present author a wide variety of ideas on how they could be helped, from lickings and hypnosis to "tell me what to do" and "I have to try harder." The first adage for helping is to clarify the ideas of various parties of responsibility for the situation and change. Of course the Brickman system is oversimplified. In reality most helpers change their stance with different children and for different behaviors. Nonetheless, one should be aware of what one is doing. Admonishments of "you can change" imply different things than "we can do it" or "these medications will take care of it." Also, the different ways we intervene have implications for the self-efficacy of the person being helped. We are teaching certain attitudes about the self by our approach. Bandura (1982a) proposes that the central characteristic to ensure change is a sense of self-efficacy. This is because one's judgment about the possibility of change mediates the one's motivation and thus the investment in the effort to change.

Helping and Systems

So far, the focus of helping has been on the individual with the problem and this does not satisfy the ecological approach of this book. Persons are not islands. Individual behavior is partly a product of a system. We all respond as part of the system we live in as well as by individual inclination. How much individuals act alone or in response to group forces depends partly on whether our locus of control is internal or external for a particular situation. Do we listen to our inner voice or go with the social tide? Achieving a functional internal-external balance of locus of control is a matter that plagues children, adolescents, and adults. At any rate, since we are social creatures we do not stand alone. We function in a web of social forces. We operate out of a support system. Looked at in this way, helping theory needs to be conceptualized beyond the individual focus.

Nicholas Hobbs, the father of the Re-Ed programs for disturbed children, has been a seminal thinker with regard to helping, searching for the irreducible essence. He rejects the sequence of trauma → repression (UnC) → behavior symptoms → therapist's interpretation → patient insight → mitigation of symptoms. Insight and interpretation are far too limited to produce change (Hobbs 1968). Hobbs sees the first source of gain through the therapeutic relationship itself, the person experiencing engagement and commitment with another human being without getting hurt. The person learns to share his feelings. A second source of change is getting one's verbal cues straight and free of their anxiety-producing potential. Personalized verbal and situation symbols of the past must be rid of negative messages. Third, he credits transference, which is to say the client acts out his problem with the therapist as a child will act out his hostility to a teacher who has done nothing to provoke such behavior. This irrational behavior is interpreted. A fourth source of change comes from putting the locus of control in the client rather than the therapist, so that he practices responsibility for his decisions. This leads to a fifth aspect of helping, specific and concrete ways to learn new behavior. In a recent brief but poignant paper, Hobbs (1981) carries his ideas to a broader context for SEI education. He asks "What is it that causes substantial and predictive changes in human behavior?" He looks at psychotherapy, meditation, the born-again Christian movement, Unification Church, traditional religions, Alcoholics Anonymous, and many other efforts and asks What is this power to transform people? We can ask Do these elements have a counterpart in the SEI classroom and total special educational enterprise? The first Hobbs' common element is a *belief system* that imposes "order on experience to reduce its absurdity." We ask Does the special class or program exude a set of beliefs about people, their potentials, and a way of life that has meaning to children and youth? Do we explain what we are doing and why? Is there a clear code that makes sense? Do we scrutinize our micro school society for the value system? Second, Hobbs points out that there must be an *interpreter* of the belief system, a therapist, guru, or teacher-counselor. We ask Does the teacher live the system and provide a figure for identification, interpreting and helping the pupil to fit into the system? The third aspect is *communication.* The movements he studied make use of confession, discussion, and exchange of experiences. There is a public effort to verbalize problems and solutions. In Re-Ed there are pupil powwows. Life Space Interview sessions, group classroom meetings, or group therapy are other examples. The fourth element is *action:* One *does* good work, missionary efforts, helping others as is done in Alcoholics Anonymous and the Unification Church. In special education this would be constructive behavior and work on prosocial projects—doing something for others. Finally, Hobbs sees the importance of *community,* a solid support group that cares about its members. Change and survival of change take place most effectively in a caring community. There are common experiences, beliefs, and commitments. This is the support group concept, and a support group is also necessary to maintain the change. This operates in a few special-education programs. Therapy should involve the support system, yet much therapy is still directed toward a child who is then expected to survive without a caring support group. Delinquents are often returned to a negative support group. These propositions explain a great deal of why our special-education efforts have been less than astounding in producing change: we have not grasped either the individual or the ecological necessities of our endeavor.

Generalizations Concerning Change

There remains a considerable mystique about creating significant change in a child's behavior, but there are some general principles that help a teacher in selecting appropriate processes.

1. The most useful procedures evolve from assessment and are individualized to fit the unique self. Methods are relevant to the case and not to helping in general. We start where the child sees the problem. A youngster may see school failure as *the* issue, while a clinician might see school failure as one consequence of a total neurosis. We respect the pupil and what he senses, even if it is second or third choice for us. Some pupils like to talk, some hate it, and there are nontalking children and youth. Traditional psychotherapy is a strange process to many children. Others like having a private adult for an hour but avoid doing any business. Some children continually exhibit their problem, always acting straight out of their impairment. With other children the problem lies buried, surfacing only at times and not directly accessible.

2. Children are to be told about legal rights regarding therapeutic

efforts and what choices they have including the right to refuse a given treatment. Even "the good offices of special education" may be subject to the child or youth's decision. We already know that to violate the pupil's psychological nature by "giving" what he doesn't accept will bring problems, yet we impose over and over again, of course always for his own good. The aim is to develop a mutual agreement about the method to be utilized and the fit with the child's perceptions of what is needed. We want to be allies and not adversaries.

3. Prescriptions such as the child needs "psychotherapy" or "behavior modification" signify very little since there are many connotations and nuances to such terms. The focus starts on the changes needed rather than universal remedies. There are many different ways to increase a self-esteem, for example, some direct and some indirect. The child's conscious and unconscious responses may be different than perceived by the helper. The pupil may see the reading teacher as a kindly, caring person who also happens to be preoccupied with reading. The behavior modifier's provision of a chart and rigid controls may be seen primarily as demonstrating caring and demonstrating that someone who really knows can guide him to success. Some youngsters see behavior modification as being very helpful and others as a superficial manipulation device to make it easy for the adults.

4. Adults tend to overprescribe what and how to help a child. In effect, they operate on the assumption of their wisdom versus the child's. A later elementary-age student once told her helping teacher that she knew what that teacher was going to say to her, namely how hard it is with parents like hers not to get into trouble. Asked what the adult should say, the reply was, "You should tell me it's my life and I can either mess it up or not. I know what I'm doing. It's up to me." Of course not all youngsters feel responsible, but those who do should be given assistance to help themselves as they see fit. Too often our helping encourages unnecessary dependency. Being classified SEI already indicates you cannot help yourself as normal children can. Brickman's paradigm is a good way to approach the situation.

5. Often fortuitous events are more significant than planned events. An adolescent finds a person and falls in love: the world changes regardless of or in spite of therapy, tutoring, or what have you. A preadolescent finally gets a buddy who makes him feel accepted in real life, thus altering his behavior; but the change is attributed to the intervention procedure stated in the IEP. The recognition that highly significant effects are constantly being produced by factors unknown or unrecognized by the helpers makes for difficulty in verifying the power of interventions. Because of their behavior, many SEI young-

sters are prone to incidental or fate events that add to their difficulties and counter our good offices. We teach a child to come and talk rather than hit. Another teacher is on the playground and responds that the pupil should take care of himself and not come crying to adults to bail him out all the time. A pupil begins to feel he can achieve and gets assigned a belittling teacher who rules with ridicule. Finally the family seems to be able to support the needs of the youngster until the father loses his job and with it his sense of adequacy. There are multiple causes of problem behavior and of changes.

The Psychology of Interventions

Special SEI teachers study the psychology of intervention not only to design their own efforts but to understand what and how other professionals and laypersons can contribute to change. To this end, we present a model that considers (1) the underlying psychological processes that bring about changes, (2) settings and designs where the planned interventions take place, and (3) ties between the psychological processes and helping experiences in the classroom.

The discussion of the various psychological channels for change is based upon a nontraditional concept of therapy. The term has achieved a broadened context. We used to hear that teachers did therapeutic things, but of course they were not therapists. The magic of that term was reserved for the one-to-one psychotherapy done by the psychiatrists, psychiatric social worker, or clinical psychologist who were anointed by training and held the rights of practice. Others were handmaidens, second- or third-class change agents, so to speak. Somehow a major "therapy" hour could create more change than all of the other twenty-three hours of living during the day! Hersh puts the situation very well (Hersh 1968). The nature of the mental health business used to be clear. There was certainty about normality and pathology and all fitted into a narrow band of conformity based upon WASP ideology. This is no longer acceptable. The very concept of deviance has been challenged. Hersh continues that we used to know the legitimate professional mental health helpers, the clinical trinity mentioned above. Now everyone is a potential mental health worker! This especially includes teachers, ministers, parents, and aids. Many splinter therapies have developed. Trade secrets are no longer held by the guilds. People are helping people without the blessings of recognized training. There has always been a back-fence therapy going on and we know how friends and associates can be therapeutic or the reverse. Jones (1977) lists twenty-nine organized anonymous groups including Delinquents Anonymous, Disturbed Children Anonymous, Sexual Child Abusers Anonymous, Neurotics Anonymous, Parents of Youth in Trouble Anonymous, and Psychotics Anonymous. There are organized parent groups in all areas of special education. The content of therapy has also changed. Teachers do reading or learning therapy as private practice. States legislate who can legitimately, independently, and with professional title engage in psychotherapy as a gainful occupation with a view of protecting the public. Guilds are notorious for not policing practice: currently the most crucial issue is who can get paid by health insurance. Redl (1959) pointed out that "pressurized cabin therapy" (traditional psychotherapy) is but one method, albeit a crucial and in some cases the major process. He also describes milieu therapy through corrective living experiences that have therapeutic potential. We conclude that restorative interventions are no longer restricted to formal therapy.

Interventions have to do with the psychology of how a pupil learns new behavior, how he or she changes. What are the psychological processes that enable any of us to alter our immediate and long-term responses? With children and youth such learning is compounded with growth phenomenon. Five channels for effecting change are listed in figure 3. All have validity under certain conditions just as they can be inappropriate in others. Bandura (1974) has put the issue very aptly. He says we are limited in our search for ways to help by our concepts of human nature: we find what we expect, ignoring whatever else might be there. Individuals who take any single channel for interventions will be forcing all children into one mold. The child remains the same individual regardless of helper preference or distortion. Only the perception of him changes if one looks through psychoanalytic glasses or behavioristic glasses. Bandura says that the human race would never have survived were it as limited as some psychologists' vision. We see only what we look for. But the varying orientations persist and commonalities or underlying principles are ignored (Goldfried 1980).

THE MULTIMODAL MODEL OF INTERVENTION

Just as assessment is focused on knowing the individual pupil, the intervention processes must be individualized. While the subcategories

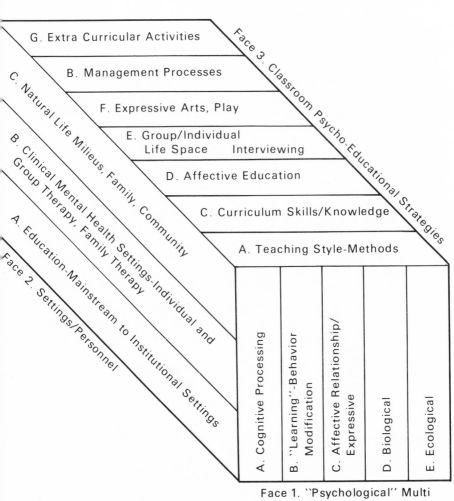

FIGURE 3. Intervention model. This paradigm interrelates three aspects of interventions for emotionally disturbed children. It is not self-explanatory and is to be used with the text discussion.

discussed in the last chapter suggest broad approaches that undergird the direction of remedial effort, the IEP must be specific in what is to be done.

Schools and families operate on a symptomatic approach: certain behaviors are to be changed and the sooner the better. Unless the specific target is attended to, there is discouragement. In fact the early school mental health movement, based upon a dynamic approach, often said to the teacher that the pupil would get worse before he got better. This is not the way one works in schools. At the other extreme is the fixation on symptoms: if the pupil can be made to stop a given problem behavior, all is solved. What we know now is that we must work at both levels, the specific symptom and the self of the pupil with the specific behavior as well. There is obvious interaction between the two levels of operation because behaving more appropriately usually enhances the self-concept.

The goal of this section and several subsequent chapters is to see the relationships between the psychological modes of intervening, the programmatic place where the intervention takes place and the specific operations that take place in the special classroom. Figure 3 presents the model. Face 1 represents the "psychological" modes for interventions, the underlying channels that are utilized to produce change. Face 2 indicates the settings where interventions take place. There will be extensive discussion of educational settings in chapter 5. Face 3 contains the hands-on psychoeducational strategies that are the educational reflection of the psychological channels. A lesson plan or an educational strategy very seldom exploits only a single psychological channel. Strategies overlap, but for conceptual clarity the channels and strategies will be discussed individually. In any teaching act or learning module there are a variety of processes operating simultaneously.

Cognitive Processing

While cognitive and affective processes are intertwined in all of a person's behavior, present theory emphasizes a more or less unique role for cognitive interventions. Certainly self-awareness implies a cognitive process "knowing." The power of mental processing pervades adjustment. Of all assets, a clearly functioning intellect is to be coveted. Human beings live in the world of concepts. There is no end of talking—in fact some of our children are swamped with verbiage! We are distressed because so many of our SEI pupils have confused concepts and appear not to think logically. We speak of dissociation between words and actions. Recognizing the way children think as they develop has been the central thrust of Piaget's work. Adult helpers must recognize these stages in children. The "preoperational" child from two to six is egocentric in cognitive-language development with a limited ability to consider the viewpoints of others. The drive is to master the necessary symbols. Personal hedonism gives way to a desire to please others if they are reasonably treated, which is not the condition of many of our SEI youngsters. This should be the "good boy-girl" stage where the need to be accepted is strong. From six to twelve Piaget describes the concrete operational stage where rote learning, imagery, and concrete memory take over. Concepts are assimilated to stable structures. Children are now able to use their concrete operations in thinking and problem solving. Moral development is parallel, a preoccupation with rules and laws for behavior, a reflection of concrete structuring. The final stage of formal operations, coming with adolescence, is a conceptual stage with logical systems containing abstract and symbolic thinking. Imagination enables better future prediction and hypotheses. This is the period of moral philosophy, based on abstract ideas of right and wrong. The stages are not precise and not inevitable. Disturbed children may not reach the levels as expected and may think with distortions. It is easy to see, even in this brief discussion, how thinking and adjustment coalesce. The teacher must relate to the thinking level, dealing on a concrete level when the child is at that stage and so on.

Wilson (1981) maintains that a Piagetian orientation of moderate depth interpretations that allow for the most effective cognitive restructuring of either past or present experience will be cognitively appropriate. Chappel (1977) presents exercises in problem solving and consequential thinking for this purpose. Metacognition trains pupils to use cognitive strategies and sharpen their knowledge about strategies to approach an academic or social task.

The cognitive processes embody perception, short- and long-term memory, integration of relevant past knowledge, manipulation of symbolic elements (language especially), thinking abstraction, generalization, insight, and problem solving. The main difficulty adults have in the use of the cognitive mode is that we go on as if our level of cognition is theirs. Thus we use words or concepts that are not understood. The result is empty verbalism and children learn to imitate our words. We tell them to say "I'm sorry. I won't do it again," and they repeat the words sans an appreciation of what the word sorry implies or any connection between their statements and their behavior.

In an astute examination of self-control through cognitive interventions, Pressley (1979) finds much divergency in the strategies used from simple instruction to modeling and motor participation in sequences of responses. The pupil must recognize when he is in a self-control situation, analyze the aspects and formulate a plan to prevent misbehavior. The plan may alter external or internal factors and the plan must be actualized. He raises serious questions about the generalization of strategies and a need to test out our practices in classroom settings.

One seeks to encourage new and appropriate perceptions, not only in the world of things but in the world of people through social cognition. Delinquents were paid to talk about themselves on a tape recording and to take some psychological tests (Schwikgebel and Kolb 1964). At first they expressed only anger and frustration, then they became depressed, and finally they began to search for solutions through problem solving. At the final stage, real help—such as a job—had to be offered. Insight about one's dilemma sometimes leads to further depression rather than solutions. Reality factors are still there after we cogitate about them.

Bandura (1971) includes the ability of a person to perceive vicariously what happens to others and benefit by this understanding. Making explicit the desired role for a pupil often enables him to "see" what it is he should do, so the function of a model can be facilitative. There is some evidence that role playing not only solves a particular problem but can be used to encourage a generalized pattern. Lebsock and Salzberg (1981) first trained role behavior in a special setting, then in the classroom for generalization. They used contingencies to enhance the effect and found positive continuance and transfer at follow-up. Bibliotherapy is reading about how others deal with problems, a vicarious experience (Russell and Russell 1979). Children may identify with various characters and how they solve problems. Bettelheim (1976) finds universal problems of children in the content of the fairy tales, which explains their interest in so many retellings. In these folk tales perennial problems reoccur and are resolved: the weak become strong, the evil are punished, the ugly become beautiful, there is the magic of wish fulfillment. Unexpected things happen—the frog becomes the prince. Indulging in the fantasy of this magical world makes real life less painful and reduces the feeling of futility.

The common combination in the same child of SEI and LD characteristics presents special problems in using with cognitive interventions. Minskoff (1980a; 1980b) deals specifically with deficits in social perception, a condition that she holds is the most serious of learning disabilities. She proposes training through step-by-step analysis of nonverbal communication including body movement and posture language, people's use of space, and affective components of speech. Her curriculum includes specific teaching regarding facial expression and gesture.

Wallbrown et al. (1979) propose that many "behavior problem" children are children with social misperceptions. These pupils with social misperceptions "are unaware and insensitive" to the effects of their behavior on other people. They do not know how to behave. They miss reading both verbal and nonverbal cues. Their behavior is not antisocial, based upon intention, but results from misinterpretation of certain behavior.

This channel includes the world of fantasy, projection, and dreams, partly conscious and partly unconscious. The child in play, stories, and drama fantasizes himself in another role or sees a solution to a difficulty. Here we remember that certain children have to be taught what is "real," separated from their fantasy, while other children use fantasy to define aspirations.

It is not easy to be precise about cognitive functioning and how various aspects work, though we describe mental functions such as insight and comprehension. The interplay with unconscious mental activity is even less clear. We wake up with a problem solved during sleep!

It is interesting how often cognitive "admonitions" are made to children. We tell a child to "reason out" why he should do a certain thing. We say "think it over." Adults generally deal in word symbols.

Increasing attention has been paid to specific cognitive therapeutic procedures in recent years. Beck (1976) holds that this presages a new school of therapy. In a general volume called *New Directions in Cognitive Therapy* there are two chapters that are especially focused on SEI pupils, one on cognitive therapy with children and the other with adolescents (Emery, Hollon, and Bedrosian 1981). Spivack, Platt and Shure (1976) see adjustment revolving around interpersonal problem solving and social cognition. It is their view that there are many ways to help children and adults improve their interpersonal cognitive problem solving (ICPS). Hallahan (1980) edited an issue of *Exceptional Education Quarterly,* which deals with all phases of cognitive training and has published work on self-monitoring (1982).

When it comes to applying cognitive processes in work with children, one should remain aware of the Piagetian stages of development mentioned above.

Because a person's problems are often the result of erroneous assumptions and distortions in thinking, unraveling faulty reasoning processes should lead to better adjustment. Pupils who can introspect are good candidates for cognitive mediation. We hope to bring the unrecognized into awareness to provide insight. Mahoney (1977) sees the move to cognitive procedures as revolutionary and advocates a combination with learning theory. He states four general propositions:

1. The human organism responds primarily to cognitive representations of its environments rather than to those environments per se.
2. The cognitive representations are functionally related to the processes and parameters of learning.
3. Most human learning is cognitively mediated.
4. Thoughts, feelings, and behaviors are causally interactive.

Mischel (1979), in questioning youngsters, found that even preschool children have methods of dealing with social situations that they may recite to themselves. Zevin (1979) sees talking to one's self as the child's way of learning self-control. Russell and Roberts (1979) have experimented with problem-solving training for elementary children: the steps were identifying the problem, generating alternative solutions, assessing the consequences of each alternative, collecting information, relating to personal values, and making the decision, later reevaluating the consequences. The presumption is that these children would then have the ego skills to carry out their plan. Munger (1979) used social cognition dealing with problem-solving techniques adaptable in the normal elementary classroom. Problem-solving skill and internal locus of control increased. But this did not necessarily result in more satisfactory classroom behavior.

One of the specific cognitive process programs is that by Fagen, Long, and Stevens (1975, 1979). Here the skill clusters include the selection of incoming information, storage (memory), sequencing, ordering of information, plans, anticipation of consequences, and the inhibition and delay of immediate impulses. Evaluation indicated significant improvement in self-control.

Concepts and methods specific to self-control have been reviewed by Polsgrove in Wood, ed., 1975. To him the methods include self-management (self-monitoring, contingency contracting), cognitive methods (self-instruction, problem solving, modeling), and rehearsal. The basic premise is to have the youngster understand the goal (and accept it) and then set up learning processes by self-reward contracts. Modeling and rehearsing the new behavior are important.

Workman and Hector (1978) have reviewed behavioral self-control studies in three areas: on-task behavior, academic production, and disruptive behavior. For the first two it appears to be promising, but it seems to be inconclusive for the disruptive behavior. Overall, they conclude that self-control training is as effective as external contingencies but caution that long-term effectiveness is yet to be evaluated.

One of the most perspicacious discussions of self-control of SEI students is by Fick (1979). He points out that in most behavior management, external control is the major mechanism either in the form of external contingencies or a teacher. Often there is no transfer to other settings. To him, self-control is the self-capability of creating procedures to change one's behavior by altering either the external or internal environment. His procedures start with the pupil's motivation to change, asking if the pupil believes he has the power of control. This involves self-assessment, observation, and a planned strategy to solve the problem. The teacher's function is to help with the plan. Further the teacher models and openly describes his or her own self-control sequence. Basically the teacher thinks in terms of the pupils' capacity to change their own behavior. Fick advocates videotaping or recording by the child of all events for a period of time. Various contingencies are made available for self-selection. One must not only learn to give self-directives but must be able to analyze the environment for conditions that encourage undesired behavior.

There are other skills as well, such as appreciating others' feelings (empathy), managing frustration (coping skills), and the ability to relax. A thorough examination of this topic can be found in the issue of *Behavioral Disorders* (1979) where Long, Fagen, Morse, Haring and others discuss this complicated procedure. Mahoney and Thoresen (1972) present a different analysis of the acquisition of self-control skills. The first strategy is self-observation, which will result in awareness. Simply recording often leads to change, particularly if antecedent events are recognized. The second process is ecological, altering the antecedent in the environment. The third method is alteration of the consequences, external and internal. Often the cognitive labeling of a process that has previously been vague enables a change in control.

A somewhat different approach to self-control is advocated by

Kurtz and Neisworth (1976). The elements include cue regulation, which includes "talking to the self" to regulate the cue—giving one the needed cues by cognating, as it were. A second aspect has to do with moving from other to self-administered rewards—planning, if you will. They also employed self-observation to clarify what was actually going on. This involves accurate self-perceptions.

Albion (1983) analyzed twenty-six classroom investigations of self-control and he found methodological problems with many of the studies. Half involved the pupil giving self-directive statements, commands, intention statements, and the like to regulate behavior. Self-goal setting, evaluation, and selection of rewards are frequently incorporated. Albion raises cogent issues regarding transfer of self-control skills and how to obtain internal rather than external reenforcement. He concludes that the research evidence indicates "self control procedures are learnable and useful techniques which can supplement classroom academic and behavioral management programs." In fact, cognitive interaction with affect can be through the mediation of self-insight, knowing about the self and its vicissitudes (Guidano and Liotti 1983).

Learning new information about behavior, why given things happen and other relevant information, can help the troubled child. This had been called *psychodidactics* (Selby and Calhoun 1980). The big danger in cognitive process is the danger of teaching rote words. There are many times a youngster can respond with the correct hollow verbal catechism without doing anything to foster the proper accompanying behavior.

There is one final, highly significant aspect to the cognitive channel; that is the direct and indirect impact on the SEI pupil of the curriculum itself. The old saying that knowledge is power suggests the value of curricular content that enables the child or adolescent to understand the world, internal and external to the self. Knowing how things work is one step in control of one's destiny. It is difficult to imagine a person negotiating even a protected environment without basic skills. We know that getting a driver's license is a major preoccupation for the adolescent LD nonreader, for example. Thus the challenge to the cognitive processes latent in a relevant curriculum has significance for the SEI pupil and is one way to prevent losing out. When the curriculum for a group of delinquents included the study of the juvenile code and rights, the result was directly empowering. Knowledge that leads to a job is direct.

But there is also an instrumental benefit to school learning. Many

SEI pupils are very low in achievement; they know it and they defend the self against the implications by denial and avoidance. The important secondary gain from achievement is in self-esteem. Even small children delight in demonstrating what they know. Thus academic learning is a powerful intervention for the direct benefits and has a therapeutic potential as well.

There are many interventions and classroom processes that fit the cognitive processing channel, as we shall see in discussing classroom interventions. Life Space Interviewing is one. Many of the affective education programs are academic in nature, which is to say they depend upon cognitive learning. Cognitive experiences are the mainstay of formal education, the natural course of events for school.

"Learning"—Behavior Modification

All of the intervention channels involve change—the pupil learns something new. However, here we restrict learning to classical and operant conditioning.

Behavior modification is the most written about and currently the most utilized of the channels in SEI education. One arresting thought for teachers and parents is to recognize how often we are already trying to use behavior modification techniques but in reverse order of our intention, unwittingly rewarding the wrong behavior. As we examine this channel, it will be evident again that in actuality it functions in synergy with other channels.

Learning paradigms examine in detail the exact nature of the given learning process, describing precisely how it can be used. Teaching the desired new behaviors requires very careful organization of the learning conditions, to the point of how often we reward the desired behaviors when they first occur and subsequently.

Classical association theory was first used with substantive paired associative learning such as the words in a foreign vocabulary and to fix new connections between a given stimulus and a particular response. It represents one explanation of the way we learn new behavior through associations in rote learning. The cognitive processes in the first channel are represented as combinations of these sample associations. Emotional life is seen as associations as well, such as learned fears of social situations. In desensitization training the goal is to eliminate fear or anxiety associated with a given condition such as talking in a social situation or anxiety over test taking. The popular therapy for fear of flying follows this paradigm. The basic premise is to pair the negative association with a positive one, making certain that the actual outcome behavior resulting is the desired one. First the individual is taught how to relax so that this capability is in the repertoire of possible response. Then the individual pairs a low provocative, imagined situation (speaking to one friendly person or taking a simple quiz for which the youngster is well prepared) while at the same time remaining relaxed. One must make certain that relaxation is the dominant response. The stimulus for producing anxiety is gradually increased and made more real. The pupil takes a very simple test in a friendly atmosphere, maintaining a relaxed state and eventually learns to take an actual exam without panic. We all use similar learning to overcome debilitating responses.

Operant behavior modification is also familiar to all of us. We reward ourselves on Friday with something pleasurable after working hard all week at tasks that are less than pleasurable. According to the Premack principle, activity that is more sought after or pleasurable can become a reward for doing things less pleasurable. The contingency is the reward one gets on performing the required behavior and is seen as a stimulus for encouraging the desired behavior in the future. There are extensive applications of this type of learning, from the single M & M for sitting in one's seat for a given time to a whole milieu that operates as a token economy. Obviously the society operates as a token economy, with money the contingency. Rewards can be external (points for prizes, opportunity to use a computer, learning games, free time, teacher approval, even grades under certain conditions) that must have value to the learner. Rewards can also be internal (a sense of achievement, new understanding, curiosity satisfied, pride in a product, self-esteem with mastery). The fact is that teachers and parents have fostered learning this way since schools began. What the behavior modification experts have done is to help teachers see how they can be more effective in fostering such learning and the importance of immediate and highly gratifying rewards, especially with SEI pupils. In particular, behavior modifiers have shown how, by unknowingly rewarding the very behavior we wish to extinguish (acting out, non-task-oriented activity, etc.) with teacher responses (attention, even if negative) we may give the pupil an unintended reward and thus reinforce behavior we would wish to eliminate.

The teacher or therapist has a conscious awareness of what specifically is to happen and doesn't fall into the trap of "teaching" the wrong thing. For example, the pupil seeks attention. The teacher attends negatively (assuming this will be received as punishment) "Be

quiet," "Get in your seat," "Do your work." To the real attention-
needing pupil these are positive contingencies. To be negatively
noticed is better than nothing. When such behavior is not rewarded it
may die out but there are children where the internal need is for relationship at any price. Then a positive response in depth should be
provided in other situations rather than relying on a simple denial of
any teacher response. Internal guilt may drive some pupils to get punishment. There are pupils whose self-concept is being a bad person,
which makes punishment have a different meaning. Again, there are
times when a teacher's positive response may produce the opposite of
what has been expected, as when the peer code condemns the teacher
to enemy status. Praise can be embarrassing and the punishment rewarding. A significant contribution of the behaviorist movement has
been to alert child-raising persons—teachers, the clients, parents, and
various professionals—that one must examine with care what contingencies are actually being induced in a given situation.

Of course neither classical nor operant conditioning is as simple
as this because pupils are not uncomplicated. Rewards are idiosyncratic, a matter of the particular youngster's makeup. Teacher praise is
desired by one and alienates another. Nonetheless, along with other
channels, the learning channel is crucial for educational practice.

The process starts with charting the frequency of the behavior to
be changed. Careful records are kept of the number of incidents over a
given time span. These records may be compiled by a teacher, but
often another observer is needed. Sometimes the child and the teacher
keep the tally and compare figures. The reward schedule for mitigation
of the behavior is decided, at best with pupil participation. Rewards
may be given immediately to keep the sequence in focus; later there
may be a longer time span. Checklists, token boxes on pupils' desks, or
visible records may be used. When the pupil produces the given quota
of desired responses, the agreed-upon reward is presented. Some children otherwise unable to delay gratification have learned to wait for a
highly coveted reward. The hope is to finally wean the pupil from
special added extrinsic rewards to the reward of less conflict with the
system. Pupils differ greatly in capacity for self-sustaining internal rewarding, even if there are many gratifications in the classroom overall.
One major difficulty in using contingencies is the knowledge by the
teacher of what are effective reinforcers for a given pupil. In a study of
this problem it was found (Raschke and Stainback 1982) that though
teachers' and parents' rankings of consequences agreed, these were
different from the child's rankings and only the child's rankings correlated with student performance on an academic task. Raschke (1981)

has devised a questionnaire to ask students to indicate what they most like to do, equipment they prefer to use, and social contacts they value, as well as other individual advice from the pupil to the teacher. This enables a teacher to take advantage of the Premack principle. There is a vast research on scheduling, rewards, and other facets of behavior modification.

Use of the learning channel for change contributes to individualization because the intervention is planned for a specific child and specific behavior. Since the method is task specific, the pupil and teacher know what is to be learned and progress can be assessed toward the terminal behavior. Some argue substitution of other symptoms will take place on the elimination of the given symptom, but this is not usually the case. While there will be behavior not amendable to this learning channel, it offers a way to deal with many vexing classroom behaviors. If we are able to change the presenting behavior that brought the SEI pupil to special education (see figure 2, column A), we will have started a reversal worth a great deal to the child and teacher.

Early behavior modification was done with very difficult children, autistic and very retarded. Leitenberg (1976) has published excellent material on the use of behavior modification with hard-to-help children populations, including psychotic, delinquent, and preschool.

The caution concerning this movement stated by Mahoney should be applied to *all movements:* "I might add that I have seen very few clinical cases as simple or straight-forward as those traditionally portrayed by the behavioral journals. The awesome and intimate complexities of real-life human problems are often humbling reminders of our relative ignorance and impotence in the field of clinical psychology irrespective of one's orientation" (Leitenberg 1976, 6).

In a somewhat similar vein, Farkas (1980) reviews the history, criticisms, and promise of behavior therapy. While he sees the label as a rallying point for persons of this belief, he suggests there should be a blending with the larger therapeutic community, all with common ethical imperatives.

Alan Ross's volume *Child Behavior Therapy: Coming of Age* (1981) brings practice up to date with practical attention to school situations and is notable for the inclusion of a broadened set of concepts. Among the specific targets are such recurring problems as aggression training in a protected environment of a classroom and later transferred to an easy and then more challenging real-life situation. Gardner (1977) keeps the individual child and his needs in the central position and emphasizes self-regulation. He deals extensively with the complex nature of reinforcers for special pupils. When learning theory moved out of the laboratory into natural settings, its value for teachers was greatly enhanced. Hops (1983) discusses three major approaches to social skills training: reinforcement, modeling, and coaching. No particular treatment plan appears more powerful for producing long-term change in problematic pupils and Hops advocates a combination of procedures specific to each child.

A particular laudatory statement of the value of behavior modification as the channel for all aspects of programming with SEI children at all ages, can be found in Haring and Phillips (1972). Applicable to both teachers and parents, this work covers application for both academic and discipline conditions. The authors start with procedures for very careful observation of the actual academic and/or social behavior. Very precise goals and schedules of reinforcement are set up. Behavior modification is also extended to programmed instruction, teaching machines, and cybernetics as well. Special education is cast in feedback loops, specific behavior, and reinforcement. Another leading theorist, Stuart, advocates that the person be in control of the process (1977). Of course the self is actually involved, recognized or not.

Before leaving this learning channel, *some clarification of the concept of punishment* is necessary. Punishment is associated with behavior modification probably because of the use of shock prods in the early work with autistic children. Time out, isolation booths, and other similar techniques are used extensively. As a rule Skinner and his followers *do not* advocate punishment. Positive rewards are considered much more effective.

Unfortunately physical punishment continues to be a very active issue in some special-education programs, behavior modification oriented or not. Punishment has been used since time immemorial in schools, families, and institutions. Psychological punishment is also meted out as therapeutic, derogatory messages, shaming, and efforts to instill fear, for examples. The idea persists that one builds character by such techniques, learning by negative contingencies. Many adults will say that it worked with them, forgetting how complicated the total conditions were where a dramatic episode changed their behavior forevermore. It is not always evident what the child actually learns by a punishing event. For every success story, there are the others where punishment is added to punishment with no change except for resentment and hatred generated, for which someone pays a price later. Punishment absolves the "crime" for some pupils, leaving them free to commit another. They paid and accounts are now even. For others the humiliation is as powerful as physical punishment. For a few the physical pain may be what registers. But we are teaching brutality by administering brutality, which has no place in the educational regime.

Some punish because they think it works, some view it as God's will, but most punish out of the desperation of failure to get the child to change. Sometimes punishment is a result of an adult temper tantrum. Heron (1978) reviews the many meanings of punishment and points out the danger to low-self-concept pupils. Redl has done likewise (Redl 1966). The basic problem is that punishment may suppress certain behavior, but, as Heron says, it does not teach new behavior as replacement. He also is concerned with the modeling that a punishing teacher depicts for pupils. Behavior modification puts the emphasis on producing proper replacement behavior.

When negative contingencies are employed, self-determination of the punishment works as well as teacher decisions (Pease and Tyler 1979). A teacher may let the pupil set the time out ("Come back when you are ready," or, "Bring me a new contract"). While this works well with some pupils, it would be nonsense with others. There are pupils who will load it on themselves and others who will give a once over very lightly. Some pupils have no idea of what to do or why.

A central problem with severe discipline is that there is no symbiotic adult-pupil interaction in trying to work out a feasible plan to learn proper behavior: it is the pupil's fault. One institution has the opposite approach. In their view a "discipline" situation is a result of inadequate adult planning and interaction as well as the child's problem. Hence, the adult and child go to a third party to discuss what should be done as a restorative act. In joint effort, both adult and child pay back to make a positive contribution to the total welfare. Perhaps both the teacher and pupil should go together to the quiet room, or take time out! Smith, Polloway, and West (1979) review the Supreme Court's decision that gives permission to implement corporal punishment in schools. Since proof of efficacy even when used as a last resort is not forthcoming, they declare the need for a moratorium on such methods and put the responsibility on special educators for finding alternatives.

Wood and Lakin (1978) have written a comprehensive review of the problem. It is reported that all but a few states permit corporal punishment, though its actual use is often covered by legislation and discipline codes. Under these conditions it is permitted in more states now than it was ten years ago! In no state is exclusion or time out forbidden in schools. According to Wood, professional organizations often hedge on the issue while there are an increasing number of cases brought by parents against its use.

In another paper, Wood (1973) expresses concern over the strong focus of isolation and punishment in special education. In place of such interventions, he suggests a sequence from diagnosis to planning with a great deal of flexibility through negotiation to prevent stringent punishments.

Time out is nondegrading negative reinforcement, that is if there is positive attraction to the classroom situation. This is really not new; historically isolation has been used as punishment. Hewett (1968) lists the conditions for time out. He says it must not be a consequence of teacher exasperation, not as punishment but as a way to help the pupil gain control and for a specific time. No lecturing should accompany the return. Social ostracism is used as a powerful contingency in certain military and religious settings.

Gast and Nelson (1977) have explored the time out concept in detail. It may mean removal of material, of attention, or of the subject from the situation entirely. Time out is "out" of positive reinforcement and can be highly aversive if improperly used. There should be prior explanation and alternatives proposed for control. Documentation of use is required, and even the size and nature of time out rooms for seclusion is a matter of definite legal concern.

If the pupil does not begin to respond after a few time out trials, one should turn to other procedures. The current author's experience is that, especially after a blowup, one does not want to depersonalize the situation. While being with a child and being useful may not be easy at such a time, it does humanize the situation and does not leave a child alone at a time of personal turmoil.

One does not resort to external rewards willy nilly, especially when there is an available internal gratification for encouraging desired behavior. Unneeded extrinsic rewards teach the child to expect something other than satisfaction from the behavior itself. However, the reverse can also be true. Some adolescents were berating their helping teacher at the close of the year for having "bribed us with cokes." Then they decided that cokes had been necessary, otherwise they would not have discussed their problems. But, they added, they didn't need cokes any longer.

Dickson (1976) made an interesting analysis of the use of token versus teacher verbal reinforcement with disturbed pupils. He found praise to be as effective as tokens or effective in combination with tokens. He concludes that it depends upon the attitude toward the teacher, and one should not take for granted a negative attitude. Teachers would do well to emphasize warm, positive attitudes. So we are back where we started except that in practice, teachers have not realized how important positive rather than negative feedback is.

While most behavior modification has been done on an individual basis, Graubard and Rosenberg (1974) have shown how the whole group can be rewarded if all are on task when a given signal occurs. Rewards need not be a competitive affair between members in classes. One cannot automatically assume it, but self-concept improvement often accompanies changes in specific behavior improvement (Ryan, Krall, and Hodges 1976). Barth (1979) has reviewed some twenty-four studies related to home reinforcement of school behavior, and concludes that this is a very promising procedure for special pupils that is not adequately recognized by special education.

The Affective Psychological Channel

The affective mode of intervention includes direct efforts to arouse or channel feeling components. There are many processes invoked to deal with emotions, some of which we have already dealt with under cognitive and learning headings. In this channel we are speaking of conditions of trust, of well-being, efficacy, and hope, as well as modulation of fears, anger, and alienation.

A central condition is the extension of caring by the teacher, sometimes called relationship therapy. The class can sometimes serve as social support system where the pupil has a sense of belonging. There are also the expressive therapies of play, art, music, drama, and the dance, all of which have become hyphenated words, art-therapy and so on. There are cathartic experiences when feelings are expressed sometimes directly and sometimes in sublimated ways. Happy experiences can be programmed for distraught children. This channel is directly related to SEI children since by definition they are in special education because of affective aberrations. Behavior change depends upon replacing the impact of past sorry experiences with healthy, restorative ones.

One submode is through so-called *discharge therapies.* For the most part, adults do not feel comfortable with direct emotional expression. When a child says he hates his brother, he is likely to be told that he really doesn't or he shouldn't or that such feelings are terrible and he is "bad." Adults are inclined to stem a child's crying, thereby teaching that crying is undesirable behavior, when it may be best to let it run its course. Basically the value of expression of affect (in the presence of an accepting adult) seems to be freeing the energy that was devoted to holding in so that it can now be devoted to alternative strategies. But it is also true that venting of anger alone does not provide new ways to deal with this feeling the next time. Following discharge should be the teaching of alternative strategies.

Affective arousal may be encouraged. There are many ways in which latent or submerged feelings can be surfaced. Confrontation procedures are one way. Group activities and group therapy may encourage a youngster to socialize if his efforts to relate are responded to. Bibliotherapy presents opportunities to empathize with other human beings and their dilemmas. Creative writing has recognized therapeutic potential (Brand 1980). Drama may be useful and role playing can be employed. The creative arts such as crafts, art, music, and dance often give muted and symbolic expression to feelings. In ways such as these affective states are mediated. Obviously these techniques are parallel to normal school curriculum areas (Robbins 1980). The concept of action-oriented therapies (Nickerson and O'Laughlin 1982) will be discussed in chapter 6.

One approach is through fantasy, which allows temporary freedom from one's self, gravity, time, and space. You can be magic. Properly used, play can be helpful in fostering affective and social gains.

Games are another direct approach to affect. Obviously some games have many other cognitive and social components as well. A prominent authority, Eli Bower (Shelars and Bower 1974), uses games to induce given emotional states, positive and negative, following this with discussion. Games can incorporate structured social interactions. Family games are used to help families bring out their feelings.

Human interactions that demonstrate caring and love foster identification and are in the affective psychological channel. The continuum of basic human relationships start with those human behaviors merely observed by the youngster and adopted from the model. The model might be in the media (stories, movies) or in a person, such as a slightly older peer functioning as a producer of usable patterns for behavior. Gang leaders and older siblings may demonstrate how one handles a given situation: modeling can work for or against school goals.

From the point of view of dynamic psychology the more profound process is identification. This requires an affective bond with the person, who is frequently an adult. The impact of love and the adult parent surrogate function is often stated as important but hardly explained. Why does love, caring, and providing for a person become a facilitator of change? When one is loved, one experiences an unconditional regard for one's self from the loving one, though this does not necessarily include approval of given behavior. One is loved in spite of undesirable behavior, as mothers are supposed to do. The result of being so loved is to free one from the need for pretense or defensive behavior. Carl Rogers calls this unconditional positive regard. One feels secure as well as being of value to another human being. One is listened to. One is responded to. One "owns" a portion of another. This is essential in parenting and surrogate parenting which is teaching. The adult accepts the child even when he or she is misbehaving and at the same time the adult models appropriate behavior. Through the process of being so accepted, one comes to care about and love one's own self. There are many SEI children who have been severely damaged by the nature of their past "caring" relationships. Unless the capacity to relate has been killed off, as in the case of the extreme psychopath, the child will eventually respond with trust when the new relationship is trustworthy. But it takes a long, long time and is fraught with weeks of testing to make certain this adult will not give up and go primitive as the adults did before. This being loved is not because of what you produce or because of your good deeds, but because you are a human being. The pupil tries to become like the person loved and identification is facilitated. We incorporate elements of the other's nature, how they behave, their values, their style of coping, and the like. It is no wonder that parents who provide so much caring are the prime figures for identification, especially when they enjoy and give to their offspring. Parents provide shelter, food, and protection. Schools have a difficult time in giving such essentials to the pupil; it is interesting how often children prize even tokens of regard from teachers. Some schools do provide meals, clothes, and even things to play with. The function of institutional care is to blend material and relationship giving as a surrogate family. The teacher, even in regular schools, looks for ways to add to relationships and is concerned that the pupil's material needs are met. Making fieldtrips, giving little social events, and writing a postcard to pupils are all done in recognition of the fact that in a material culture, psychological caring without concrete evidence is not enough.

One does not simply love, one cares for and does things for the youngster, Bettelheim (1976) said it for all of us: *love is not enough.* The child gives up primitive behavior as he identifies with someone who is not primitive and who meets his needs. Parenting is at the same time giving and setting up expectations and limits. Those who make demands on the pupil must obviously also be the ones who provide.

Sexual identification patterns become incorporated into the self through this channel. Sanders (1975) advocates the training of parents in ways of expressing warmth through role playing so that modeling can be facilitated. It was particularly interesting in her work that the disturbed children took over their parent models by *talking* about their problems in place of acting out.

But we cannot leave the topic without recognizing that fear as well as love can produce identifications. One incorporates the fear-producing person to ward off potential demage to the self. Thus the feared gang leader's behavior or a sadistic adult can set up such anxiety that becoming like that person seems the only solution and the adapted behavior becomes the pattern used to deal with others. Anna Freud described this identification with the aggressor even in small children (1946). They play being the dentist (who hurts you) on their fellows. The teacher relationship will be expanded in the chapter on teaching.

In individual therapy there is a significant emotional involvement between the child and the adult. Directly (verbally) or indirectly (play therapy, drawings, etc.) the child begins to reveal the problem. Because of the security of a protected therapeutic situation, feelings and behavior can be admitted that were denied or repressed. The classroom should also be such a safe place. The child may transfer his distorted relationships with previous adults to the therapist (or teacher) and act out the problems in their exchanges. Since these problems are a consequence of unfortunate prior relationships, a healthy replay provides the pupil a chance to learn new and healthy relationships. Sometimes the material is left for the child to digest as he will, and sometimes it is explained so that there is insight concerning the causes for behavior.

When the teacher relates to a value-defective pupil, there is still the need to relate, but the pupil will be less likely to identify. There is more explaining, more didactic discussion and emphasis on acceptable patterns of behavior. There may be a low-key confrontation approach with a great deal of reality enforcement. Unfortunately most of us regress to nagging and moralizing. The empty child still has needs. With the schizophrenic child, the fears and questions have to be explained and reassurance given along with directions and modeling of reasonable behavior to meet given situations. This becomes more like one-to-one teaching with explication and direction to give structure that the child cannot provide from his own resources.

With the advent of adolescence, relationships become vastly more complex because of the growth stages described in chapter 1. Now therapy may confuse attachment because of sexual and independence striving as well as anxiety. There may be more risk attached to the behavior of the adolescent and the power of the peer group must be recognized.

It is evident that children and adolescents are no intrinsic respectors of given adult roles. When there is no individual therapy, teachers are often cast in the therapeutic role regardless of the intent. Because they accept pupils and deal with so many issues, there will be transferences, recognized or not. For teachers, the use of life space interviewing (pp. 213–19) is advocated rather than an imitation of traditional therapy.

What the special teacher can learn from the affective process is equal in importance to that learned from the behaviorists and cognitive theorists. Do not neglect the motivations and feelings. The emotions of normal and deviant children can include love as well as hate, prosocial responses as well as aggression, and satisfaction as well as depression. When these emotions become fouled up by experiences, there will be aberrant responses. SEI children and adolescents need to be made secure, be responded to with kindness and love, and to be cared about as we teach them the way of life. Man does not live by mind alone. There is attention to the unconscious and to the expression of feelings. However, all manifest behavior does not represent outward evidence of deep internalized conflict. Seeing all behavior only as a repetition of early life experience can be misleading.

Ekstein and Motto (1969) see many so-called academic learning problems of psychogenic origin. Lichter, Rapien, Seibert, and Sklansky (1962) demonstrate how adolescents often displace personal problems onto school such as anxiety about masturbation, fear of competition, or a general sense of inadequacy, which are acted out around academics.

The affective modification channel is used in a somewhat different context in Strain and Cooke (1976), where the focus is on development of affective responses, particularly altruistic behavior through modeling.

In using any channel one can become overly involved in the process itself, forgetting that the goal is the end product—a happier, more adequately functioning youngster—and that there are usually many means to that end.

Biological Interventions

In our society the major mental health intervention is biological—pills and pills. Biofeedback is direct control of the body organism (Fuller 1978). Food allergies have been indicated as a cause of violence in some children where allergy reactions affect the neurological network (Moyer 1975). Many hold that all SEI impairments will someday have demonstrated physical counterparts. Twin studies of schizophrenia demonstrate the degree of biological linkage. Toxic conditions and drug-related behavior abnormalities are part of the biological story as are the results of minimal brain damage.

The biological intervention channel will be discussed under the headings growth phenomenon, specific motor interventions, biofeedback, and medication and psychosurgery. (Those who wish a primer, see Morse and Smith 1980). A thorough discussion which includes genetic, neurological and biochemical implications can be found in Rhodes and Tracy (1972).

Growth Phenomenon

Significant changes in behavior sometimes appear from maturity, as we saw in the discussion of Piaget. An autistic twelve-year-old has different behavior manifestations than the four-year-old autistic. For most children, growth is involved in increased cognitive power, ability to reason, level of insight, and motor ability, which affect behavior. Because of the wide variability in normal development of very young children, parents are sometimes advised to wait and see what happens with growth. Adolescent behavior is to some extent precipitated by physical change.

With age there comes increased physical strength, which makes certain behavior more lethal, and thus may be more frightening to the child as well as the adult. Sexual drives are an example of growth activitation, though with a wide spectrum of social input as well.

There is also the therapeutic impact resulting from rectifying some of nature's abnormalities, such as harelip, poor alignment of teeth, and even eye position. This is particularly true of the face, the focus of interaction. The implications of differences such as those who grow slowly, late, or to a restricted height (as well as the reverse) are growth phenomena.

Specific Motor Intervention

Motor-based manipulation and training is a part of the biophysical approach. We teach motor coordination: catching a ball may be critical for self-esteem. Body touching is part of a language system. We can do damage by how we restrain the child in a tantrum. The overuse of adult power and the denial of movement can panic some youngsters as a final insult to their being. Back rubs and body caress, as parents know, have for most children a soothing effect. We hold and we rock.

(Of course, for those autistic who already rock this would be counterindicated.) The body sensation of a back rub is also combined with the relationship the child has to the adult as well. When a particular child gets erotic stimulation from such intervention, obviously this would be counterindicated. Movement education as well as physical education are useful interventions.

Biofeedback is a special case of organ control. A very impulsive SEI brain-injured boy once described his problem: "I just get cited. When I get cited I go wild." Can we help him recognize excitement coming on before it overwhelms him? Biofeedback requires the youngster to recognize a given physical body state and learn to use self-monitoring for control. Lynch et al., and Kamiya et al. (1976–77) described results of biofeedback with children. Biofeedback use with children and youth is increasing (Strider and Strider 1979). Closely allied with biofeedback though not with external instrumentation are techniques fostering relaxation (Cautela and Groden 1978). The Striders discuss relaxation for stress management. Relaxation decreases anxiety, hyperactivity, and irritability in school-age youngsters. In the old days, teachers would tell pupils to put their heads down on their desks to rest and relax for a few moments with highly differential results. Now, to counteract tension, children are taught progressive relaxation. They can imagine a relaxing condition or perhaps "feel" their toes relax, finger, relax, and finally their whole body relax. Pupils are highly motivated by the hand-held devices used in biofeedback. Schultz and Walton (1979) see biofeedback for stress control as natural curriculum content in physical education, health, or biology units. They suggest self-regulating language coupled with the appropriate emotional state and provide various classroom demonstrations.

Direct influence on the organism of a different order is through hypnosis. Overall, hypnosis has had minor application but is increasing for inducing behavior changes (Kaufmann 1970; Lawlor 1976; Gardner and Olness 1981).

While medication and psychosurgery are practiced only by the medical profession, educators need to be aware of the conditions. Often a pupil in the class is being medicated. The recommendation of diets for autistic children and the concern about particular food allergies or toxic effects of red dye are much in the news. Research on these matters is inadequate.

Fortunately there is practically no use of operative physical intrusion today. In the past limited lobotomy and shock therapy were practiced even with children. Drugs are another matter, with new experimental medications continually on the market, especially for so-called hyperactive pupils. Medications may directly affect certain cognitive abilities as well as produce side effects such as lethargy. There can be idiosyncratic responses in reverse of what was anticipated (i.e., becoming more active rather than sedated). There should be no use of drugs without continual medical monitoring. A main function of medication is to enable the child to make use of educational and therapeutic programs and to be more generally manageable so that other methods of help can be applied.

Hormone treatment in the case of the boy with undescended testicles can create significant alteration in psychological behavior. There is no specific drug for a specific category and children respond differently than adults. A detailed current analysis of these matters is found in Weiner (1977) and Werry (1978). As professionals, teachers should be informed of medication efforts and should regularly report behavior observations to the physician, especially in cases where the monitoring is left to chance. Some children are medicated to a degree where they actually fall asleep in class.

Axelrod and Bailey (1979) point out that teachers should have a copy of the medical prescription, purpose, and parent's request; accept only drugs from a responsible agent (not the child); keep the drugs labeled with child's name and dosage; and maintain a precise record of dosages as minimal for legal protection.

A most useful publication for teachers is Gadow's *Children on Medication: A Primer for School Personnel* (1979). This is a research-based, clearly written, authoritative reference. Gadow points out that the lack of information results in uncertainties, unrealistic expectations, and sensationalism. Of the possible 110,000 drugs, he discusses psychotropic drugs that effect affective and cognitive process and antiepileptic drugs used in convulsive disorders. Some drugs are used for both. Since many drugs have a generic name used in scientific discussions and a trade name, teachers can be further confounded. Gadow further states individual factors enter in variances, intolerances, side effects, and addiction. He separates hyperactivity (persistent, excessive restlessness) as a developmental disorder from anxiety-produced tension states. His hyperactivity includes inattentiveness, impulsiveness, and often low school achievement and behavior problems. Adjustment goes downhill: a reasonable prevalence is 5 percent of the elementary school population. The common stimulants now used are Ritalin, Dexedrine, and Cylert. Some children react favorably to these medications, but it is estimated that between 10 and 20 percent will not respond. He states that the evidence from well-controlled studies for megavitamin and the Feingold diets do not at this point support the claims.

For various seizures (grand mal and petit mal; idiopathic if cause is unknown and secondary or organic due to known brain damage) different drugs are utilized: most common are Phenobarbital, Mysoline and Dilantin for grand mal and Zarontin for petit mal. Drowsiness and irritability are possible side effects. Various cognitive abilities may be diminished.

Gadow also discusses the treatment of a particularly embarrassing problem to the child, enuresis, which affects 15 percent of normal six-year-olds. Tofranil, an antidepressant, is helpful to something over 50 percent of the cases. Psychotherapy first, then combined medication (Trofanil) are indicated for anxiety attacks and school phobias. Various medications have been tried for childhood psychosis. Sometimes they can make the symptoms worse; at best tranquilizers may suppress symptoms. Involuntary movements (tics) have been treated with Haldol. From Gadow's review, the role of drugs in the treatment of childhood depression is unclear. Again, the reader is urged to purchase this informative, inexpensive resource.

Temperament is another biological condition, previously discussed. Here the role is to recognize the biological nature of temperamentally generated behavior and not attribute psychogenic causation to biology. For example, temperamental impulsivity requires external adjustment; impulsivity as a product of high personal anxiety level suggests therapy. The treatment fits the next channel, the ecological.

The Ecological Channel of Intervention

We recognize that most individuals behave differently in various situations. We do not lose our "personalities" but we respond differentially to different settings. Certain persons or certain behaviors may remain quite constant regardless of the setting. For example, the extremely anxious child is driven by anxiety wherever he or she is. Most of us are differentially anxious; in certain settings we are free of debilitation. Another aspect of the ecological position is the recognition that we are not islands. We operate in systems and relationships. We have support systems that may undermine us. The systems include families, peer and neighborhood groups, and school groups. Because it is easier to victimize the child than to change the teacher or parent systems, there is a reluctance to use ecological approaches.

Special education is in part an ecological intervention, expecting the child to respond in a different way if we provide the most appropriate setting, and that more efficient learning will take place in the appropriate setting whether this be a special class or institution. Children who produce problematic behavior in one setting with one teacher may function quite well in another. Settings contain inductive forces that may be supportive for desired behavior or seductive for unwanted behavior. But there is always a person interactive with a given environment. While some environments may be very powerful, we can usually predict there will still be individual differences in response.

The significant contribution of ecological intervention is to balance efforts directed to the attributes of the child with interventions directed to the attributes of the social setting. The child is not to be blamed or scapegoated as the single cause of the problem. Moos (1979) reports the case of an adolescent girl being personally counseled concerning school problems when the real provocation came from family behavior. Moos has been a leader in devising ecological assessments. While the ecological position offers much opportunity for the classroom teacher or the family therapist, it may at times be even harder to change elements of such systems than the child. Ecological theory implies one of two things: (1) All children have a reactive aspect even when they have already habitualized considerable impaired behavior; (2) If we adequately reduce the external stress and restore balance, children will often recover on their own. This emphasizes the strength of the organism and the drive for normality, given half a chance and an uninsulting environment. In fact special services may have a major function as respite from overwhelming pressures in order to allow self-recovery.

One can be ecologically oriented and hold a wide variety of theoretical psychological positions, but there should be an analysis of the *balance* of interaction—what is produced by the individual and what is produced by external forces. A combination of the ecological and other channels is usually required for change. The child needs a positive, nurturing milieu that not only minimizes calling forth undesired behavior but fosters normal growth. In special education the first consideration should be ecological. Try another teacher, classroom group, or school setting. It is easy to expect too much from the environmental change alone. After a honeymoon of surface change, internalized behavior reasserts itself, and other interventions are needed.

Milieu purification can be thought of as a greenhouse condition. With the right chemical ingredients in the soil, temperature, sunlight, and moisture the plant grows strong enough to later survive in a less maximized growing place. With normal good care and no special therapies added, a child can sometimes recover, become adequate, and develop strength to cope with the real world. But we must watch that we do not put that child back in the very environment that first produced the difficulty.

Some SEI children, the schizophrenic and autistic for example, will have to spend their lives in a protected milieu. They need a favorable ecological environment to compensate for the nonremedial conditions of their impairment. A halfway house or aftercare facility, which is as "normal" living as possible, are examples. Sheltered workshops provide employment. They may have all the special education and therapy needed to get them to their maximum potential, but this is not enough to survive alone in this society. Yet they need not stay in a closed institution.

The danger of not giving adequate total support during and after special-treatment support is probably the number one cause of "treatment" failures. Neuhaus, Mowrey, and Glenwick (1982) discuss the need to engage community resources through a youth services delivery system in implementing the ecological approach. The recent effort to empty adult hospitals and send the patients back to their cities to live without an adequately protected environment has been the major tragedy of mental health in this decade. A protected environment of a halfway house will not be cheap. Applied to children, one does not put them back in a polluted mainstream educational setting when they can't be expected to survive there on their own or even with marginal help. Ecological support is provided in the form of professional personnel, personal networks, and whatever is needed. Apter (1982) has brought together a comprehensive ecological stance for SEI programming, for not only the school but other community systems including the family, welfare, and mental health and legal agents. He covers the theoretical concepts, diagnosis and intervention based on the ecological model.

All children are in milieu "treatment" twenty-four hours a day—only the "treatment" may not be therapeutic. Redl (1959) has discussed the nature of a treatment milieu and emphasizes that a good milieu is related to individual needs. The milieu factors include the social structure, implicit values, regulations, group life, activities, and physical conditions.

The ecological scan on figure 2 indicates the need to search out the areas of negative interaction. Could we change the family, the tasks in school, or infuse the neighborhood with a group worker or find a Big Brother/Big Sister and thus alter negative environmental components? This does not mean a stressless environment. Specialized ecological intervention must have a finely tuned balance between relief and expectation, providing an environment with which the child can cope. The possible overprotective nature of special education services has been criticized.

The ecological approach portends individualization of interventions *both* for the individual and the environment. A good example of this is found in Strain and Shores' (1977) article where the behavior at issue is social withdrawal. Strategies to increase positive social interaction must be attentive to both the child's output and the adult and peer response. The nature of these elements is revealed only from the careful observations of the interactions.

There is a two-faced quandary in the ecological stance. On one hand, SEI pupils, especially at adolescence, can find school difficult because the school lacks relevant experiences and flexibility, a condition that fosters frustration and thus deviancy. On the other hand, given the variance in behavior, there are also children for whom an approriately accommodating school with a wide range for difference cannot provide the intensive help a particular youngster needs. Not every setting can be shaped to fit every possible pupil. An unusual ecological intervention called positive reframing was developed by Jessee et al. (1982). Essentially it consists of reframing the problem behavior so that the positive ramifications are evident. The result is that the same ecological situation has a new and reasonable interpretation. For example, withdrawing behavior is recast as an effort to get in touch with one's sad feelings. Limit testing is interpreted as an effort to get close to the adult. In peer conflict "you don't fight with people you don't care about" (p. 316). Basically they see this reframing as taking out the secondary gain in power over staff. Children's behavior certainly has an impact on the setting just as the setting influences the child. Emery et al. (1983) suggest that children can change the ecological adult interactions by changing their output behavior. The ecology is not a fixed condition.

Summary of Intervention Channels

The central psychological components embedded in the vast array of procedures used to alter behavior have been reviewed. Except for a few devotees of a given channel, most professionals rely on a variety of channels. It is virtually impossible to react on the basis of one channel only even if we try. While the various components are combined in active practice, they were abstracted for theoretical examination.

That the field is adapting many channels is exemplified by two recent publications. Halleck (1978) calls for integrating psychopharmacology with dynamic and behavior modification using individual, group, and family settings. Rich (1978) first reviews the channel or theories of causality and relates each to an intervention system with goals ranging from specific to global and cognitive to affective. There are two associated authors who have been pressing the multimodal approach, Lazarus (1981) and Keat (1979). In the first instance, the concentration is on the many facets of affective life, methods of diagnosis and related interventions. The Keat presentation is organized around the following modes: behavior, affect, sensation, imagery, cognition, interpersonal relationships, and drugs-diet. He includes a classroom assessment schedule as well as specific devices and interventions built on this model.

EVALUATION OF INTERVENTIONS

Chapter 3 included information on the differential prognosis for various syndromes. Here we are considering success of various intervention modes. Unfortunately much evaluation of various intervention channels is explicitly or implicitly designed to "prove" the efficacy of one mode or setting for treatment over another. The rigor of the particular treatment is seldom included. We know little of the nature of the cases treated (which from our previous review of syndromes is essential) or criteria for success, and the follow-up conditions are seldom assayed. Still the "what works best" query goes on and on. All modes of intervention report success and, if they are honest, failures too. But the treatment X the client variables get lost. Whatever the greenhouse effect—individual therapy, group therapy, and special education are all specially controlled subenvironments—we know it is not enough to expect changes there. The question is Does the change maintain outside the greenhouse? If aggressive behavior toward classmates decreases, will it also decrease toward other peers? There is the matter of transfer and generalization. Is the change sustained? The caveat is that the subsequent situations should be reasonable ones, yet often we put the child back into a pathological environment. Often the longer the delay for assessment, the less gain, but there are also many instances of improvement continuing after the intervention has ceased.

In general, improvement is found for about two-thirds of clinic populations and nearly the same for control groups, regardless of setting or professional orientation of the therapist. This is to be expected since any one style of intervention will fit some and miss others. Smith and Glass (1977) examined several hundred therapy outcome studies, though these were not primarily of children. They found outcomes not related to therapists' experience and that paraprofessionals were as effective or better than professionals. The paraprofessionals' lack of ritual and self-disclosure made them more attractive to clients. Garfield (1983) has reviewed "reviews" of psychotherapy effectiveness and indicates the influence by the personal views of the researchers, ill-defined treatment methods, the nature of the patients, and the outcome measures.

There has been considerable attention to new therapies and particularly brief therapy. Leventhal and Weinberger (1975) claim brief therapy highly effective, equal to long-term, and report other studies in agreement: "Cases rated initially as being most disturbed are most likely to require further treatment" (p. 132), which is not to say they do not benefit from brief therapy. Children who are acting out fall into this group. Eighty-six percent of the cases were rated improved by brief therapy.

Teachers will be interested in Ashcraft's report (1970) on therapy and educational achievement. There was no significant difference in achievement by those who had therapy. If parents were also in treatment, greater gains were made. Other studies have found that improvement of cognitive and affective domains tend to be related.

Lewis (1965) did a most perceptive analysis oriented to the educational consumer. As a generalization he finds the studies do not suggest treatment groups as having significant improvement over nontreated, though control is most difficult. Lewis finds even less support for therapeutic intervention enhancing adjustment. The studies suggest two-thirds to three-fourths improvement regardless of treatment. He feels the evidence for reconstruction of personality does not mean that more specific symptomatic behavior cannot be changed: he sees evidence for specific rather than global changes.

Shore and Massimo (1979) followed a group of disturbed adolescent delinquents fifteen years after a community-based program including psychotherapy, remedial education, and a job placement, with multiple channels being used. There is evidence of high success in vocational and life adjustment compared to the control group.

Shearn and Randolph (1978) examined the results of previous studies of the impact of reality therapy and find them inconclusive, the methodology inadequate, and frequently yielding no positive results. In their four-group design they found no significant differences for on-task behavior or self-concept resulting from the process.

In a recent summary of the results of psychotherapy in general, Epstein and Vlok (1981) conclude that psychotherapy is more effective when focused on realistic, relevant issues such as teaching social skills. Most effective seems to be family therapy, which is another way of saying the ecological system.

Using global ratings of outcome, the impact of various interventions on school maladjustment were studied in an English study by Kolvin et al. (1981). The strategies were a mixture of modalities, some of which related to the channels. Play therapy, counseling, work with parents and teachers, behavior modification, and group therapy were among the methodologies. All interventions proved superior to no treatment, effectiveness increased with time, group therapy and behavior modification were the best in general. Independent of the intervention strategies, the ecology of the school had an important impact.

A critical review of thirty-three studies of individual, group, and family therapy outcomes for adolescents points toward a positive outcome for psychotherapy (75 percent) over no therapy (39 percent). However the author says that methodological deficiences abound (Traumontana 1980).

CONCLUSION

The differential evaluation of various interventions is confounded at best. Usually some clients improve, some do not by any treatment modality. There is little attention to the appropriateness of a match of the intervention and the needs of those to be helped. The fantasy of one correct intervention for everything results in futile efforts to compare methods. Even more dubious is the conduct of the actual treatment. We hear about individuals being in treatment of some type, but they may not be present at half of the sessions. And then, what actually takes place in the helping process is often a far cry from what is proposed. Also, in some cases there is considerable change in extraneous conditions that are seldom if ever put in the equation. Some problems are of reasonably easy access for individually focused change while others are embedded in a resistant individual and support systems. The technology for evaluation should be based on the individual case, or N of 1 goal attainment methodology where the variables both in and around the particular person are taken into account and related to the child's IEP.

5

Settings for Interventions

TRANSITION

WE HAVE DISCUSSED the nature of SEI pupils and the psychological modes underlying the helping process. This chapter constitutes a bridge from these matters to the particulars. The chapter is an overview of the places and substance of interventions, face 2 of figure 3. By all odds, the most extensive time is spent by the child in the natural life milieu (labeled C on the cube). The home and living routines, the neighborhoods and after-school activities consume the largest segment of exchanges. For the most part these are least purposefully organized. For the teacher the liaison with this biggest slice of life is essential but difficult as is evident in our efforts to join hands with parents. Next to the life milieu, A, formal education, absorbs the largest segment of time and energy. For any school-aged child this is equated with adult time at work and constitutes a vast investment. With such significant times comes both obligation and opportunity for helping. The third area, B on face 2, constitutes more specialized clinical settings, ranging from individual and group therapy to the actual replacement of the natural life milieu with an institutional program. There is no clear separation of the educational and clinical, for some institutions are extended schools and all institutions include some fusion of education and the clinical.

Confusion in Setting and Function

There are myths that are perpetuated by professions and settings that should be examined by every teacher lest expectations become

166

remote from reality. Three issues will be examined: the places problem, the professional problem, and the team problem.

1. The myth is that, given the place, we will know the process. Territorial jurisdictions have divided the places into educational and mental health, splitting up the youngster into pieces. When a child is referred to a mental health agency for therapy, we have an idea of what might go on, but without checking we may be in error. The same problem exists with the ideas about the "school place" where certain assumptions are made about what happens there. Different schools are psychologically different places in what is taught and how teaching is done. The great euphemism is "working with," which covers a multitude of variations and a few sins. In a later detail of the educational places, it will be evident how little we can tell by knowing the place where the youngster sits. There will be less cross-agency recrimination if we are more explicit about what specific program comes with the place.

2. There is a professional uniqueness problem. Who is licensed to do what to whom? Professional guilds have much invested in protecting turf. Psychiatrists, social workers, and psychologists may all practice individual and group therapy under various legal statutes, perhaps with differentially assumed social prestige. There are restrictions on who will be paid by health insurance as well. The unique medical rite is in dealing with the physical aspects of illness and prescribing medications. Teachers are licensed to teach certain children, ages, and subject matter, not to give therapy. In truth, as Hersh (1968) reminds us, while the guilds do battle over the prerogatives, in actuality neat definitions of role no longer maintain. What is "therapy" no longer has a set image; who actually performs such activity is no longer defined as simply as it was, and activities called therapeutic are no longer circumscribed. As we all know we have received help in other than neat packages. We may have been changed by a chance event or by something we read or by conversation with a friend. The reason that professional uniqueness is helping is not what the professions maintain is evidenced in chapter 4, fact 1 of figure 3. When one or more of the psychological channels are active, restorative potential is established. It is not who does it or where, it is what is taking place. Of course some settings and some professionals will have unique resources for encouraging particular changes through the use of the channels.

Help may or may not take place in the designated places or by the designated persons. Just as teachers "teach" and sometimes little learning takes place, therapists have pupils "in therapy" and no change takes place. Children are more complex beings than fit the rubrics we set up. We remember too that parents are the generic teachers and helpers, unlicensed though they are.

3. Teaming is another assumption to examine. The choice is to have one profession conduct several functions with the youngster or to have several persons conduct single functions, except for the educateur residential program when multifunctions are vested in one new type of professional, the teacher-educateur who participates in all activities from getting the child up until bedtime. We have opted to have many different professionals each doing his or her own practice, except when, by default, the teacher is expected to do everything. There may be one or several teachers, a therapist (plus others for various family members), a recreational therapist, social worker, administrator, psychologist, and perhaps others. It is no mean task to mold the persons into a concerted effort. When we do, teachers are high in time with the child but low in influence on the team. Much has been written on teaming, even the team of teacher and parent, to say nothing of interagency mental health and education cooperation. In residential work when all of the team are in one administrative milieu, it is hard to get cohesive effort. There are more meetings to share and cooperate than there is actual sharing. Generally schools provide little time for team meetings.

All who work with the pupil are part of the milieu, restorative or provocative, as the case may be. In many instances we work at cross-purposes, much as some fathers and mothers do.

There are problematic relationships between the individual or group therapist and the teacher just as there are with parents and therapists. Teachers often expect too much—a kind of magic cure that is encouraged by the mystic rituals some therapists wrap themselves in. Privacy means a limited sharing of information. Therapists who deal with individuals often expect impossible things of a teacher with multi-obligations in a classroom setting. There may be no communication at all. Even jealousy can be present. There is need for face-to-face meetings to develop trust. Failure to make progress with a pupil may not be due to the teacher's effort. It may be a consequence of cross-purposes within the milieu system.

Children seldom recognize our hierarchy. They share griefs, joys, and problems when and where they occur and not by the clock or the place. So all helpers with SEI children are overlapping generalists to a degree. At times they "misuse" the teacher as a parent surrogate or therapist. On the converse side, the "therapist" may be asked about arithmetic and for help with homework. Whoever is available when they have a particular need is expected to give a response, which is why the processes of helping get so mixed up. In some places the territorial rights and role prerogatives are such a problem to the adults that children are continually reminded to take this to your therapist, that to your teacher, and something else to the reading specialist for an answer. There are times when this would be done with good reason since particular skills are the province of various professionals. Professionals are not interchangeable even though some functions overlap.

EDUCATIONAL SETTINGS

There was a time when school was a holding company for the SEI pupil while the mental health experts straightened out the pupil's inner life. When the pupil was "cured," then energy would be available for school learning. Fortunately, this is no longer a tenable view. Schooling has significant potential for activating the various remedial channels on face 1, figure 3.

A teacher with a rich educational program sees the child in many types of situations, in group life and in adult relationships over an expanse of time. There are times of grief, frustration, joy, and thoughtfulness. It is for this reason that so many of the psychological intervention channels are activated in the school setting, as we briefly reviewed when the channels in figure 3 were discussed.

Cognitive experiences of a wide variety are the mainstay of education. The use of this channel is both directly applied to the pupil's problems and indirectly used through the effect that skills accomplishment and new information has on self-esteem. The learning channel offers untold opportunity for the teacher to engage students in appropriate activity. In all teaching but especially with SEI youngsters the power of relationships is an ever-present intervention. Relationships are both individual and group, as will be described. The biological intervention channel is less obvious. While teachers do not prescribe medications, they often administer them. In addition, teachers are responsible to report back to parents and doctors adverse effects of drugs. For adolescents with drug abuse, educational programs become part of the curriculum. Teachers are expected to do screening of physical conditions as recommended in the grid in figure 2. Furthermore, biological development is a major consideration of an SEI teacher. There are evidences of developmental delays to be scrutinized. Always the school experience is tuned to the biology of ability and age, as is most evident at adolescence.

Ecologically the teacher intervenes in negative conditions in the home and neighborhood whenever possible. In the classroom ecological conditions are employed in arrangement of the chairs, desks, dividers, and equipment; there are "centers" for various activities, a quiet place, a time-out space, and sometimes study booths.

Therapeutic potential through the psychological channels are already part of the educational experience and regular curriculum. It is a question of *how* the media are used: reading versus reading therapy, drawing class versus expressive art, and so on. Teachers make up stories with children, which Gardner (1971) considers a therapeutic communication. Photography has been advocated as a medium for therapy for SEI children. Camping is often included in normal school and has been reviewed as a therapeutic tool by Tavormina (N.D.). Filmstrips used in guidance can be related to work on adolescent aggression (McDonald 1973) and reading can deal with tensions (Spoerl 1959).

The impact of a school experience on a child can go in many directions. The child folk dances with others (a social experience), is involved with a teacher and peers (a relationship experience), becomes more body aware and controlled (an identity experience), may become skilled enough to perform (an ego building, legitimate self-display experience), may invent or create particular forms (an expressive experience), may learn things about dance as a form (a cognitive experience). Or it may be just another required exercise.

Unfortunately, special-education classes are often even more restricted than classes in regular education: the reverse should be true. There are elementary programs that are highly affective, spontaneous, and child centered. Body activities are used to develop "body awakening," and there is, in addition to "headtripping" (academics), physical touching, and a great deal of sharing. SEI teachers need freedom— O'Rourke (1977) says unlimited freedom to innovate using the various psychological channels. In brief, when one looks at the five modes for encouraging change in behavior, there is an educational parallel to each one.

Of course there are times when education can provide all the help a SEI pupil needs, or even a single teacher can be enough. But more often the teacher knows that special therapies are needed as well.

The Cascade of Educational Services

Educational Interventions (face 2, figure 3), take place in a variety of settings. A great deal of educational energy goes into the decision of where the special pupil should be placed, with the underlying implication that the mainstream is somehow best because it is least special and least extruded. The more essential question is Where can a given youngster be best helped? Peterson et al. (1983) suggest that the levels of the cascade or intensity of service are probably overstated: overlap is considerable and variability in sevices within the same name, the needs of children being served and the lack of any finite criteria for differential placement are all involved. This does not make a case for the lack of a spectrum of services. These preoccupations on *where* interventions take place—mainstream to institutional settings— presuming this to be the crucial matter. The truth is, the determining factor is not *where* but *what* takes place (wherever) related to crucial pupil needs. The psychological interventions discussed in chapter 4 are the essential processes, wherever they are applied. True, it may be easier to evoke given processes in one setting over another, but there is less uniqueness to the impact of a setting than we assume. To paraphrase Leinhardt and Pallay (1982), the setting itself is not the primary variable. Their research suggests the following: (a) intensification— small class size permitting more one-to-one contact by an able teacher; (b) clear goals and mastery learning, new material presented at a regular rate; (c) increased time spent in cognitive activity, (d) a management system to encourage task orientation; (e) positive, encouraging teacher affect; (f) facilitating positive self-concepts. The true issue then is, where can these conditions best be developed for a particular pupil, and no placement is an assured setting.

All the same, many educational programs do not have a complement of services and use whatever they have for any problem regardless of goodness of fit. The concept of a sequence of service is laudable. Beare and Lynch (1983) point out that programming is much more difficult in the two-thirds of public school districts classified as rural.

Deno (1970) developed a study that has come to be known and accepted as the cascade of services, starting with the mainstream for most pupils, moving to the resource room, special class, and institution, each with a smaller proportion of pupils, the last being the placement for very few.

The problem with any hierarchy of services is in equating any given administrative format with a presumed intervention potential, since *mainstream* really defines nothing, nor does a *special class*. The variation within each format is great. We need a cascade of services, it is just that the settings are diffuse entities and define little of the actual psychological input.

There is also an assumption that severity of the problem automatically defines the needed level for service. This is both true and untrue. For example, there are schizophrenic children who may be helped adequately in the mainstream with ancillary support and therapy. On the other hand, an ego-intact sociopathic youngster may be impossible to monitor or provide with necessary control even in a special class. Or one might decide a child could be helped very adequately in a *healthy* mainstream class but there are none of quality available.

Figure 4 is a joint effort of several disciplines and parents working on the development of a comprehensive state plan for SEI children. It will be noted that it is based upon an LEP (see index) rather than the IEP, though the IEP is implicit within the broader context.

Column 1 is the mainstream, which frequently requires services from column 2 as well. Column 2 includes consultation, resource rooms and special classes. In column 3 the balance may be tipped toward an educational format in alternative day schools, or the schooling may be part of a mental health day school program under community mental health. Column 4 indicates that many children who are in group living settings may use any of the sequence of educational programming or have in-house special education. SEI children and adolescents in need of total milieu care also have integrated special education. Such institutions may be educational or psychiatric in orientation. Column 5 provides for those children who will not be moving back up toward the mainstream.

The importance of an *integrated* cascade of services was revealed in a state study. There was the ever-present scarcity of enough service at all levels, especially for the most seriously disturbed psychotic and sociopathic. The greatest shortage was in help for adolescents. There was no way out (column 5), which resulted in SEI children being kept in state institutions who could have been released if there were a sheltered living provision, since they had no viable home or alternative placement. Every level of service felt they were dealing with children who needed more than their particular service could provide. Thus all services were operating in a somewhat zombie fashion, feeling depressed and frustrated in trying to help youngsters who really needed more complete and astute interventions than they could provide. Whenever there is a lack of the complement of services, what is available is utilized and overloaded to the detriment of children and staff.

Educational intervention strategies, curriculum, and method follow the child regardless of the setting. If a child needs a particular educational design to best learn, he will need it wherever he is placed. Placement is the location where a program can be made functional. Some settings are more feasible for given adaptations than are others. If the need is for a high degree of individual support, this will hardly be possible in the regular classroom. The more the educational design moves toward the highly specialized children, the more intensified should be the two essentials of special education: (1) more teacher time available per child and (2) more specialized teaching and related services. What can be done in a twenty-four-hour-day structure is more intense than what can be done in a school resource room.

Our subsequent interest in the cascade concept will be in the role of the special teacher in various settings, chapter 8. Consulting with regular teachers utilizes a different profile of skills from the special teacher's abilities than teaching a group of retarded schizophrenics in a clinical setting. A resource teacher seldom has the group conditions to deal with, which is the lot of the special-class teacher.

CLINICAL SERVICES

There are examples where special-education classrooms, resource rooms, or even mainstreaming is sufficient to maximize pupil potential. Just as not all disturbed children need therapy, conversely some *only* need therapy and not special education, for they may have no problem with schooling.

There are naive educators, or educators with poor experience with mental health personnel who are proud to go it alone and avoid the contamination of what they consider a "medical model," as if all therapists were of that persuasion. Often, in the cases where the going gets tough and exclusion is not possible, or with severe cases, the same eduators will try to pass the cases over to mental health. In other programs, the educators recognize the SEI pupils need mental health services but have not been able to get them. Generally speaking, the requests for such therapeutic help from teachers is far greater than the help available.

Currently we are faced more with a financial as well as an ideological battle. If the school IEP says the child must have therapy or institutional care, education can be forced to pay the bill. Considering that good institutional treatment costs more than going to a university,

FIGURE 4. Educating emotionally disturbed children

	CHILDREN AT HOME			CHILDREN AWAY FROM HOME		AT HOME OR AWAY
	1 Children Who Can Utilize Regular Educational Services.	**2** Children Who Need Intensified Special Education.	**3** Children Who Need Special Education and Intensified Mental Health Services.	**4** Children Living in Group Care Programs.	**5** Children in Psychiatric Hospitals.	**6** Young Adults Who Need Continuing Educational Support.
DEVELOPMENTAL NEEDS						
ACADEMIC	The vast majority of children can learn and develop in a modern school program of high quality. Some will develop transitory problems requiring academic support and remediation.	These children have difficulties related to: specific learning impairments; interpersonal relationships; and/or, psychological stress.	These children manifest impaired social, motoric and cognitive abilities. They are often nonproductive and rejecting of school tasks.	These children can participate in regular school, special education, day treatment, or small on-grounds school programs.	These children require a highly controlled, therapeutic setting in which to learn. Their educational problems are usually secondary to their emotional problems.	These young people have a limited capacity to pursue normal work roles. Some have had limited educational opportunities.
HEALTH Physical and/or Psychological	All may need counseling or clinical services for normal growth problems. This becomes especially important during such periods of stress as third grade transition, adolescence, and career decision time.	They often have emotional and/or physical problems. These are, however, manageable within the school setting.	They exhibit serious psychological and/or neurological problems characterized by profound personality disturbances.	They often have adjustment problems due to separation from their families.	Many suffer from psychosomatic or physical illnesses, or have demonstrated life-threatening behavior. All exhibit severe emotional problems.	They suffer from chronic medical and psychiatric problems that are not easily ameliorated.
FAMILY LIFE		Their families have sufficient strengths to participate cooperatively with the school to meet the needs of their children.	These families often require therapeutic assistance because of the impact of a profoundly disturbed child on family relationships.	These children do not have intact families, or they come from homes experiencing severe health, social or economic problems.	These families cannot be expected to cope with the complex needs of their children. They will need supportive clinical services and counseling and guidance.	Some may be able to live with their families. Others may not, depending on the nature of their difficulties and the capacity of their families to meet their needs.

	Regular Education	Special Education	Day Treatment	Group Care	Psychiatric Hospital	Continuing Care
COMMUNITY LIFE	All need recreational and social experiences of high quality, wide variety and easy access.	They often require help in utilizing community resources. Some will need special programming to meet their social and recreational needs.	Such children require planned, therapeutic, individualized help to meet their social and recreational needs.	They need a full range of normal experiences in the community with adult support, supervision and assistance.	Though separated from normal community activities, their needs for stimulating peer relationships, gratifying social experiences, and recreation must be met.	All require support and assistance in initiating and sustaining adequate relationships and social experiences.
The Setting Designed to Maintain the Student is as Normal a Program as is Compatible with His Needs	A Regular Education Program with Emphasis on Affective Life Experiences and Enriched Curriculum.	A Special Education Program which Provides Continuing, Intensified Special Services.	A Day Treatment Program which Provides Educational Services in a Planned Therapeutic Milieu.	A Group Care Program that Supervises the Educational Needs of Its Residents.	A Multiply-Designed Educational Program in a Psychiatric Hospital for Children.	A Continuing Care Program which Provides Supervised Educational and Life Experiences.
P R O G R A M — ACADEMIC	A flexible format with an enriched, diversified curriculum is needed to enhance social and academic skills on an individualized basis.	Integrated, supportive, remedial and special class programming are necessary. Curricular alternatives and innovative programming are essential. Emphasis must be placed on the student's academic, social, and emotional growth.	The school component is the core service and must provide a highly flexible program with a wide range of curricular alternatives. Remedial services and other special arrangements should be available for adolescents.	Tutorial, remedial and special education services are necessary for those children not placed in public school or day treatment programs. Such on-grounds programs must be highly specialized and individualized.	The hospital must have a comprehensive and enriched educational program. Special education for those with learning impairments must be provided. Coordination with all disciplines is necessary to create a therapeutic milieu.	Job training, sheltered workshop programs and other protected work experiences are essential. Continuing programs that stimulate learning and offer personal enjoyment must be available.

FIGURE 4. Educating emotionally disturbed children (*continued*)

	E L E M E N T S						
A planned mental health support program must be provided. Adequate self-esteem, useful interpersonal skills, and positive social attitudes and values must be developed.	E L E	HEALTH Physical and/or Psychological	Adequate diagnostic and clinical services are essential. These must include psychologists, social workers, health personnel and other specialists.	A full range of diagnostic, treatment and supportive services are necessary. Clinical staff must work closely with the school program.	These children need a planned, supportive, therapeutic environment. Many will need casework services for behavioral difficulties because of separation from their families.	Individual treatment, psychiatric nursing, and social work and medical services are essential. The living situation must be planned, benign, and therapeutic.	Dietary and health standards must be guaranteed. Many will require medical supervision and social work services.
Emphasis must be given to the affective lives of all pupils and to the development of a healthy school milieu.	M E N	FAMILY LIFE	The school must interpret the child's needs to his parents. A continuing working relationship with the family is essential.	Guidance and counseling for the family must be provided. The clinical staff will help parents in their utilization of other community resources.	The setting becomes a substitute family and must provide opportunities for healthy relationships with peers and adult identification figures.	All families will benefit from supportive services, direct treatment, or counseling and guidance in planning for their children.	For those in substitute family settings a supportive, healthy and stimulating environment is essential. Such settings must be well-supervised, comfortable and pleasant.
The school must serve as an advocate for the development and utilization of adequate community resources.	T S	COMMUNITY LIFE	Schools must collaborate in the development and provision of adequate social and leisure time experiences for these children.	A liaison program to mobilize other community resources is needed. Planned weekend and evening activities may be necessary.	Social, recreational and work opportunities must be provided. Participation in appropriate community activities is essential.	Gratifying social and personal experiences must be provided in the hospital setting. Integration into community activities, when therapeutically indicated, is essential.	Programs that offer opportunities for social activities, peer relationships and enjoyment must be available. These must be benign and supportive.

what special education program is able to assume the costs? This may be changed by a recent court ruling against New York City and New York State, *Roe v. Ambach et al.* If the full range of services cannot be supplied by the school, the school must contract with an outside agency. The definition of therapeutic psychological services given in this case is one in which use of "methods of interpersonal relationships with the intent of assisting a person to modify attitudes and behaviors which are intellectually, socially or emotionally maladaptive."

The legal issue of psychotherapy for SEI pupils is complex, as Grosenick and her colleagues indicate (1982). The basic question is Are public schools obligated to pay for psychotherapy as a "related" service? The concern is not whether the pupil needs psychotherapy, but a more restricted concept, Is psychotherapy needed in order that the child can benefit from special education? and if so, Is the school obligated to pay? While there are some interagency agreements for such services, it is well to remember that the school is mandated to provide special education while mental health agencies as yet have no such legal requirement to provide therapy. Can the schools require therapy for individuals or families even if they were to provide the costs? With budget stringencies there is a great reluctance by the school to extension of services. For children or families with family health insurance it is often possible to get prepaid therapy from public or private mental health personnel. When the funds run out, the case may be dropped.

Finally, the vast variety of types of treatment mean that saying a pupil should have therapy does not define what will take place in any given referral. The variations in therapy match the diversity in education. Communication problems were mentioned above under teaming.

Not all therapists or services are able to accept children. Child and adult therapy are significantly different. Children are more limited in experience, concepts, and vocabulary. Depending upon the developmental level, they may not deal in abstractions that therapists often use. They are dependent and seldom come willingly for help. Parent involvement is usually a necessary corollary to child treatment. Adolescents present special problems because of their struggle for independence and conflict with authority.

Crisis Clinics

Many communities have walk-in and phone-in services for persons in crisis. These may be manned by trained volunteers (adults and teenagers) backed up by mental health experts or by the experts themselves. These are not for long-term treatment but for immediate assistance in times of personal crisis—such as drugs, suicide, fear, urge to run away, immobilization, etc. Such service is of considerable help to a teacher confronted with a catastrophic condition, usually after school hours, which demands more than the school resources. It is illegal for teachers to take in a child on their own even in an emergency.

Individual Psychotherapy

Individual psychotherapy may take place within the school, administered by legitimate school personnel, including counselors, but more likely the child will be taken to a public agency (child guidance clinic, a community mental health service, or even the juvenile court) or to a private social worker, psychologist, or psychiatrist if the parents have means. Children and adolescents seldom elect therapy; they are a captive group, a condition that is often ignored but should be worked through.

Psychological treatment implies a direct exchange between a trained therapist and the youngster, under conditions where the youngster knows he is safe and free to explore problems and solutions. There is confidentiality, and, one hopes, trust. Sessions may be a time-limited series or extended. Neurotic and psychotic youngsters are better candidates than the sociopathic. Talking therapy, the typical procedure, may not work with young children, and play therapy, puppet drama, or art therapy (drawing, painting, clay) may be employed along with work with the parent. What goes on in therapeutic sessions depends to a considerable extent on the persuasion of the therapist.

To say that the child is in therapy conveys very little to the teacher. It is not the purpose here to present an exegesis on child therapy: a most highly recommended book on this topic is *Counseling and Psychotherapy with Children and Adolescents* by Prout and Brown (1983), which contains a lucid, detailed exposition. Rather than emphasizing the generic psychological channels of our chart, therapists usually define themselves as belonging to a particular school. As a matter of fact, most are eclectic nonetheless, following our advocated multimodal model, with selection of methodology appropriate to the situation rather than the fitting of a child to a system. The common schools of child therapy discussed by Prout and Brown may be familiar to the teacher; certainly behavior modification and dynamic approaches, Freudian and derivations are in the common domain. RET, or rational-emotive therapy, emphasizes discovering and giving up irrational beliefs that cause malfunctioning. Glasser's reality therapy focuses on basic goals and one's identity through confrontation with real-life problems. Rogerian person-centered therapy depends upon a trusting relationship, is nondirective and attentive to the self-concept. Many school counselors have been trained in this school. Adlerian therapists are concerned with the reorientation of purposes and goals leading to more adequate social relationships. All of these methods depend upon activation of the psychological channels in various combinations, and they contain many ideas that teachers can use. One caution: if a therapist claims to be of a given school, adherence to the tenets should not be taken for granted. Other sources include Harrison (1979) and Corsini (1979).

The research on efficacy of psychotherapy is not definitive and is a matter of heated debate. The comparative results with children are outlined in Prout and Brown (1983). In addition to ambiguity of what is actually done and the suitability of the method for the child and time lapse, there is the difficulty of assessing change and assigning causes. What we do know is that the right help for the given child can make a vast difference in the adjustment of a considerable number of children.

It may be a family member who needs therapy rather than the pupil. It is frequently the mother who is targeted because, overall, mothers are more available and responsive. However it may be the father or a sibling who should be getting help. Highly stressed parents such as those going through a divorce should have help available. Often a single mother may be seen as the culprit when in reality the problem is basically a financial problem that will not be relieved by psychotherapy.

Group Therapy

Group therapy follows the variant procedures found in individual therapy and may be done in schools or external agencies. We will see the classroom counterparts in chapter 6. Since many children have social problems, group therapy seems a realistic medium. The function of the group is to provide support and solutions to problems and to help children realize they are not alone in having difficulties. The child-adult relationship is diffused because of the numbers. Typical group work depends on verbal exchange. All of the schools discussed before are represented. The clientele may have a predominant common problem—delinquency or shyness, for example. The building of the group is a complex operation discussed by Rose (1974) and Redl (1966), among others. Usually there are two adult leaders; it is not an easy intervention to direct, especially when anxiety gets high and acting out results.

The group may focus on actual social crises in their living space or on an individual's problems. Outward Bound uses the challenge of nature and survival. Activity group therapy (Slavson and Schiffer 1975) is an example of the affective expressive psychological channel where the youngsters do crafts. Games or drama and camping are other examples of content. Again, when one reflects on the channels on face 1, figure 3, it is evident that there will be a mixture employed with cognitive, learning, and affective channels usually interwoven. The possibility of parent groups (or more often mother's groups) is to be considered. These may take the form of group therapy, of counseling, of parent training, or of special classroom meetings.

A particular therapeutic group is the *family:* So many times a teacher sees a problem embedded in the family matrix. Until this part of the child's ecology is changed, corrective efforts in school are continually undermined at home. While family therapy intervention is currently the fastest growing practice, it is easier to advocate than to accomplish. Some parents will accept this help willingly if it is available, while others (especially the fathers) are highly resistant. Special training is required over and above being an individual therapist. Again, the methods used cross various channels, and there are developing "schools" of practice as we saw in individual therapy. It is no mean feat to get a family of five together consistently and on a sustained basis to deal with their problems and produce change. Usually our SEI child's place in the family is but the tip of the iceberg, and there may be generations of family contention. Teachers do not refer a family for therapy but rather suggest the possibility of parents seeing a proper professional for a consultation on what might be done about the situation. Most family therapy also provides members individual time as well.

Milieu Therapy

Every child is in a milieu, therapeutic or not. Mental health agencies provide residential care ranging from day schools to small group homes and children's psychiatric hospitals. Such programs will be discussed in detail subsequently. Again, there are wide differences in design and quality of institutional care. Some operate only on the learning channel with token economies. Others may depend upon relationship and specific therapies indicated above. In effect residential therapy should represent a special milieu with various therapeutic ingredients. We are again back to the use of all the channels to provide a rich experience for children. Powers (1980) sets the goal of such a milieu as helping the youngster understand as much as possible about himself, why he behaves as he does, and the consequences of given behaviors. The setting must model other methods of behaving that are productive and gratifying. How well this is done is dependent upon the actions of those who live with the child in the many activities as much as by specific therapies.

Natural Life

We recognize the positive or negative impact of the milieu as a treatment medium, amorphous though it is. Given the fact that most children are in their own natural life milieu, we see the importance of interventions introduced where the action is. Primarily this is the ecological channel, changing the environment. Family or parent therapy and training also serve to change the pupil's life space. If we believe the milieu shapes, then our goal will be to shape the milieu in as many ways as possible.

One activates community services. For example, Family Protection Services may need to explore financial needs and housing conditions. The concept of after-school programs and night "hospitals" have been recognized as the way to protect some youngsters. What are the community resources for activities? Community centers, scouts, boys' and girls' clubs, and organized recreation programs may be important to control peer influences. One of the most significant programs is the Big Brother/Big Sister movement, which provides identification figures and relationships as well as activities. Churches are often overlooked assets. When there are not services to augment the school program, teachers can appeal to certain service clubs whose members are concerned about youth to get things started. A number of SEI pupils get into trouble not in school or even at home; they can't manage the negative seduction in their community life. Since SEI children are not always easy members of community activities, the agencies who accept them need consultative support to make it work out.

New programs for young children include both early intervention programs where mothers bring their children and work jointly with mental health personnel or the mental health worker goes to the home to teach the parent how to respond to various situations. A home consultation program is more prevalent with autistic children but has been adopted for other types of disturbance as well.

In many areas active parent groups have taken on professional stature for providing help. They are informed, go to conferences, and read what other professionals read. Feelings of guilt, anger, and frustration can be acknowledged to each other. The impaired child's impact on the family structure and siblings is always a matter of concern. Discussions of many facets of parent involvement can be found in *Exceptional Children* (1975, Vol. 41). One of the most helpful resources for the teacher is edited by L. Eugene Arnold, *Helping Parents Help Their Children* (1978). Among the chapters is one on filial therapy, showing that siblings can sometimes provide significant aid. While it is not always feasible and certainly siblings should not be exploited, they have the value of seeing life more as the SEI child sees it. An exhaustive review of studies of children as therapeutic change agents has been done by McGee, Kauffman, and Nussen (1977).

It is evident that too many teachers are trying to go it alone without external mental health and agency help. There are a wide variety of possible services from the traditional to quasimental health programs that our pupils need. Life is more than school. Taking care of the pupil in school is not enough; the goal is to care for the youngster wherever his life reaches and to maximize the positive resources for his mental health.

FROM THE INFORMATION TO THE PLAN: THE IEP AND THE LEP

The crux of PL 94–142 is the individual educational plan, the IEP, which states the goals and accountability of the program for the SEI pupil. Although there are many difficulties with this and current efforts to erode it, after all is said and done the essence of IEP must be retained and expanded. All of our insights about children, their self-concept, and how to help that we have discussed up to this point come to focus in what we are to do for this individual pupil, the last column in figure 2.

The plan for the IEP is grand and has great potential. One difficulty is, for the most part, that the responsibility is left to the individual special teacher and of course has become the bone of contention in the teacher's life. The teacher often is made the scapegoat. As one teacher put it, "With all of the student rights, parents' rights, regulations, and paperwork you can't win. You are either neglecting a pupil or abusing a pupil. Your goal becomes keeping out of litigation."

The IEP is to contain present levels of educational performance; annual goals, including short- and long-term instructional objectives; specific educational services to be provided and, if relevant, the extent of mainstream experience; date of initiation and anticipated duration; and finally objective evaluation procedures for periodic reassessment to ascertain whether or not instructional objectives are being met.

Considering the comprehensive nature of restorative interventions for SEI children we have reviewed, this is a myopic statement; it is cast in educational terms, levels of educational performance, instructional objectives, and educational services. While some interpret *education* in the generic sense, the press of budget limitations and the prejudices against mental health, a schooling definition is most common. Even here it is too often a constricted meaning of schooling, sometimes covering just academics. Certain special educators may believe that through commonly accepted educational tactics, especially academics, we provide all that is needed for SEI children and youth. For others this restricted view is a legal cop-out to avoid the complications of reaching beyond the typical school curriculum. The national policy mistake is making the school the lone responsible community service.

Nothing could be more accurate than the statement by Kaye and Aserlind: "In truth, much of the success (or failure) of PL 94–142 in achieving its main goal of providing quality education for all handicapped children lies in the effectiveness of the IEP—how it is perceived, conceived and carried out" (1979, 138). Consequent to a federally funded study, these authors see the need for the IEP being considered both a product (the statement) and a process with many activities, stimulating all participants to interact. It is not supposed to detail the teacher's everyday activity. While there is the IEPC meeting, it is also anticipated that meetings will continue in the working relationship with parents and other professionals.

These authors have identified seven dimensions essential to evaluating an effective IEP process:

1. Team behavior—why a team and how developed
2. Communication—who talks about what
3. Decision making—who and how about decisions

4. Conflict resolution—what is done about them
5. Trust—how to build it
6. Organization and responsibility—who is responsible for what
7. Time—how to get the time needed to make it work

They conclude that there should not be state standardization of the IEP because of the need for local flexibility.

In a 1979 BEH government policy paper draft, *Individualized Education Programs* (IEPs), the twofold intent is clarified: (1) the holding of the IEPC meeting where parents and school personnel jointly make decisions about the pupil's program; and (2) the document, which is a record of decisions made. Thus it is a parent protection, a management tool to ensure appropriate special education, and a compliance-monitoring document. The IEP is not intended to be a specific instructional plan. Short-term instructional objectives are steps of progress toward the goals on a quarterly or semester basis. The specifics "in daily, weekly or monthly instructional plan" do not need to be included. The related services necessary to assist the child to benefit from special education are to be included, a contentious matter as we have seen. All resource commitments are to be clearly stated. Significant changes in services cannot take place without a formal meeting. It is *not* a performance contract that can be held against a teacher or agency if the achievement of the child does not equal the projected growth on the written statement.

The IEP is the result of evaluation and placement and is to be accepted *before* placement or services. Not all service personnel need attend the meetings. The intent was that the meetings be small and confined to those with an intense interest in the particular child. In a Michigan study the actual attendance ranged from two (less than the legal quorum) to as many as twenty-eight, with an average of four. The state and local agencies have discretion over the child participation "where appropriate." We found the expected zero attended at preschool, 13 percent between ages thirteen and fifteen and 25 percent at the sixteen to twenty-one age level.

The essential action is to put together the data from diagnosis and intervention procedures and activate this in a concrete plan for the individual SEI pupil (Kaye & Aserlind 1979). Sometimes there is so much red tape and reporting that it becomes difficult to recognize the real child behind it all. Yoshida et al. (1978) analyzed the contributions, interpretations, proposals and evaluations of alternatives, and final decisions of the team. School psychologists were most involved along with other appraisal personnel, the social worker, and counselors. Administrators participate more then medical personnel or teachers—special or regular. The fact is that the teachers, the very ones who must do the work, are lower in satisfaction and participation. They should be at the center of the process. Gilliam (1979) studied status and participation. He found parents often need training to be effective participants in the IEPC (as do the professionals). There is a special parents' workshop that can be utilized by school systems and organizations for this purpose prepared by Nazzaro (1978).

Goldstein et al. (1980) examined the IEP process through naturalistic observation. The resource teacher was found to be the most generally involved of the average 3.7 participants and the heaviest participant. Parents were the major *recipients,* not the producers, of information. The majority of the meetings did not have the legal representation for PL 94–142. Parents who attended were usually the mothers. However, satisfaction was high and spread equally over the participants. Most frequent topics were curriculum, behavior, and performance. It was also concluded that parents need training to fulfill their roles and responsibility. Price and Goodman (1980) found the average teacher time for an IEP was 6.5 hours, about one-third of which was beyond the workday, (a considerable investment).

It is often found that IEPs for SEI children concentrate on academic goals based upon extensive testing of psychological attributes. As Arter and Jenkins (1979) report, the dominant instructional model in special education involves assessment of psycholinguistic and perceptual motor abilities. Based upon the profile, individual prescriptions are made. The six assumptions they question are that such differential educationally relevant abilities actually exist and can be measured; that existing tests used are reliable; that they are valid; that prescriptions can be generated to remediate weak abilities; that remediation improves academic achievement; that best methodology can be generated from ability profiles. After an intensive examination of the evidence, they conclude these assumptions are not proven and have set a rigidity on methology to be used by teachers, which is not warranted. They call for a moratorium on the process.

There are handbooks and computer programs to assist in individualizing instructional goals. One is based upon individualized programs and also organizes small groups for instruction (Frankel, et al. 1979). Teachers evaluate the children in fifteen skill areas with items from a wide variety of tests. Each child is then programmed for instruction. The process is repeated every month. Turnbull, Strickland, and Brantley (1982) provide help for the individual teacher in composing IEPs.

Anderson, Barner, and Larson (1978) studied 400 IEP plans containing over 2,400 instructional objectives. Plans averaged five educational needs and four general educational goals, methods, and/or curriculum materials. There were six instructional objectives and five months estimated for achieving the goals. They observe that many educational plans did not provide enough support for classroom teachers. Seventy-five percent of the instructional objectives were directed to basic academic skill areas. Only 10 percent were social, emotional, or behavioral. One must remember these were not all SEI pupils. Who was to be responsible for the objectives? Special education teachers for 75 percent and regular teachers for 25 percent of the objectives. The major evaluation procedures were teacher made although there were standardized tests, observational procedures, and rating scales. Six percent of the plans did not have parent signatures.

In PL 94–482 we are moving toward a broader concept in the present mandate that vocational goals be included, although this was part of PL 94–142 as well (Razeghi and Davis 1979). Vocational aspects include industrial arts, homemaking, and consumer education as well as the full range of vocational opportunities. Sequential instruction is to be provided and on-the-job opportunities made available in cooperation with vocational rehabilitation. Access to vocational education is a right of the SEI student; this may be the most appropriate element around which to build the whole IEP for certain adolescents. The concept of career education as an integrating force for whole curriculum is advocated by career education specialists (Brolin and D'Alonzo 1979). A special publication for vocational considerations and limitations in SEI education has been published by the Council of the Behavioral Disorders (Fink and Kokaska 1983).

For the teacher there is another major objective in the IEP, which is learning tactics for survival—what to do and when to do it. Since appropriate classroom activities are a day-to-day if not a moment-by-moment process, management tactics need to be agreed upon and realistic to the predicted behavior.

Building the IEP

The basic strategy of the IEP should be a problem-solving one, assembling the materials from the diagnostic chart (fig. 2) to enter in short- and long-term goals evolved from specific needs and assets. The information on the chart is considered in light of the possible interventions from figure 3.

There should be understandings at the very start of what each is to do: the teacher, the child himself, the parents, the social worker, psychologist, administrator, and whoever else is to be involved. And as much as possible, the specific responsibilities should be indicated. For example, if the boy is desperate for identification, who is to find an appropriate "Big Brother"? If parents are to stop their pseudotutoring or certain punishments (or conversely use certain restrictions), this should be noted. A treatment plan is a social contract, not just an assignment given to a teacher.

If the committee sets a general goal of improving self-esteem, the logical question is What is the source of low self-esteem? Is it within the educational province? Suppose the self-esteem is dependent upon school achievement, and yet the pupil is satisfied with relatively low and slow progress. This may be a matter the teacher can deal with directly. Unless the teacher has the therapeutic skill to enable the combined SEI-LD youngster to absorb the meaning of the LD impairment and face his continual limitation, self-esteem continues to be low after modest but expected gains. In one class of institutionalized SEI pupils, the merciless scapegoating of one member with a fatal disease defied all efforts of mitigation until it was revealed that he symbolized the "death" they all saw for themselves. They never expected to get out of the institution, probably a reasonable guess for some of them since their functioning was limited and no halfway houses were available. Or to take another task: Is it always possible to compensate for family rejection by being a caring teacher and thus raise self-esteem and reduce the symptomatic behavior?

The need for support systems to aid teachers in carrying out the IEP has been generally ignored. A very clear statement by Safer et al. (1979) emphasizes the need to involve parents and have time to evaluate effectiveness. Their study revealed that teachers felt that the IEP process left less time for teaching. They had to reorganize the classrooms to meet the IEPs and felt others decided what should be done while they were left accountable.

Deno and Mirkin (1980) have practical advice for teachers on designing IEPs. Rather than the overattention to procedural compliance, they advocate concern for substantive compliance. This follows the general concepts embodied in the chart in figure 2, originating in the precipitating behavior. For each specified behavior they suggest progress, mastery, or performance graphs showing the rate of improvement for the objectives to provide information for communication. This system depends upon clear goals, frequent progress measurement, sustained programming to test the method effectiveness, and consideration of necessary program changes, which are all very time consuming.

A new dilemma has arisen in regard to IEPs from the competency movement and upgrading the quality of general education. Some districts have legislated that graduation means having met minimum competency in a given set of criteria. Many of our pupils will not be able to do this. Even if they have knowledge, they seldom do well on the tests. Safer (1980) points out what is likely to happen, especially in mainstreaming, if special children are held to the same competencies for graduation as the nonhandicapped. In Florida 56 percent of the emotionally disturbed, 49 percent of the socially maladjusted, and 49 percent of the learning disabled passed the communications subtest, and 17 percent, 25 percent and 17 percent respectively the math subtest of the minimal competency. The alternative of individualized minimal standards for special pupils is proposed, but there is a question of legality (see the whole issue of *Exceptional Children,* 1980; vol. 47).

Evaluation of Progress

The law mandates periodic evaluation of pupil progress. In fact, evaluation lies at the heart of accountability. As Column G depicts in figure 2, the assessment of progress toward the objectives of the IEP also provides the data necessary for any revisions in the IEP. It is well to remember that the current push for accountability is a reaction against the previous behavior of special educators and mental health professionals where there was often no reevaluation. Fatalistic low expectations resulted in perfunctory treatment that frequently offered no promise. Time was when the restricted availability of special education in institutions and schools led to custodial life plans with commensurate deterioration.

The purpose of IEP evaluation is diverse. First, have we done as intended? Was the plan really carried out? This is evaluation of the process. Second, is the expected change forthcoming? Third, are diagnostic revisions suggested and/or new interventions indicated? Assessment is also reassessment. A new set of goals may be in order. Just as often failure is due to inability of some agent to do as was expected. For example, when a subject blows up, the teacher could use a LSI technique to get at what provoked it, but the teacher cannot follow through because of group responsibilities and there is no standby help. Many an excellent intervention goes awry because of feasibility.

The reassessment phase is an evaluation of the plan and educational resources, not simply one of the IEP statements or the teacher. Are there better ideas we now can envision? Is it that the time span we anticipated was too brief? Have we uncovered deeper layers of conflict than we originally discovered? Has behavior modification ceased to be appropriate? Perhaps the liaison with the therapist does not allow for enough symbiotic classroom-clinic cohesion. Some children show remarkable ability—hidden ego resources come into play—to control themselves when it is clear they must do so or pay consequences. Others plateau almost immediately and little more positive happens. In fact, they may regress. Resistance, testing the teacher, social stimulation from peers, and fear of failing can all produce acting out: early and continual reevaluation is necessary. While the teacher is evaluating every moment and altering immediate strategy on the basis of the interactions taking place, there is not only legal sanction but considerable value in standing back from time to time to get a perspective.

Positive changes are most likely to be seen by the direct worker. Thus the special teacher or therapist sees more change, on the average, than parents and the other workers. The pupils themselves often announce quick improvement to prove they are "cured," but then some children saw no problem in the first place. The importance of improvement to the person making the judgment and differences in settings serve to confound the evaluation process. Changes in a protected classroom environment are not always an adequate base for evaluating changes for the normal, nontherapeutic environment.

Evaluation is the Study of the Single Case—the N of 1 Study.

The direction of assessment is toward an N of 1 analysis. There are two distinct emphases to N of 1. The first is the single case examples in behaviorist reports: the person is his own control. Behavior of the pupil before treatment, the baseline, is compared with behavior during and after treatment. Treatment can be suspended or reactivated to see the effect on the given behavior. The attention is to individual cases (Kratochwill 1977).

The other style of N of 1 derives from the total study of the individual case. There is a long history of N of 1 theory (Chassan 1961). In order to predict what interventions are in order, many attributes of the individual pupil are assessed as is shown on the grid. Then predictions are made on the basis of the nature of the individual. If an SEI pupil has high anxiety, low self-coping skill, and an active personal wish to change, then a high degree of external classroom structure will be stabilizing and productive. If there is no desire to change, contingencies have to be added. Of course we have not eliminated measurement problems. The aim is to make sense for individuals who have *overall syndrome* patterns indicated in chapter 2 but also have *individual nuances* of the self-concept, seen from the diagnostic grid, that also are important in assigning and assessing interventions. We set up criteria for success prior to evaluation and do goal attainment scaling. A specific procedure that embodies N of 1 has been developed by Haskill (1979). He feels that one of the big problems in evaluating change is the lack of instruments that cover all of the potential change areas. Tests or rating devices are often inadequate. Frequent samples of naturally occurring behaviors are converted into quantitative scores by the Q technique. By charting the child's behavior to use as the control, it is possible to evaluate change, reflecting the uniqueness of individual behavior.

One approach that can be applied to both individuals and programs is called the Intervention Efficiency Index (Bagnato and Neisworth 1980). Essentially what is used is the developmental gain with separate skill scales for motor, language, cognitive, and personal-social behavior and the length of participation. There are several cautions mentioned by the authors, including the measures themselves and gain scores as criteria. Also, one should be aware of the individual differences in potential for any of the growth areas, "greenhouse effects" of special settings, and long-term maintenance of gains.

There are other proposals that will relieve us of simple test-retest evaluations. Scott (1980) proposes more attention to examining natural phenomena, using the chronolog method, which is a running narrative of an individual's behavior including the context. These naturally occurring observations are then categorized. Murphy and Bryan (1980) propose the use of single-case methodology but across a variety of behaviors of the same individual in a variety of settings. Assessment of progress remains a prominent problem.

From IEP to LEP

Someone should be doing a comprehensive plan, and it would bring reason into the system if the school began it. It is quite clear that for SEI pupils what we need is not an Individual Educational Plan but a

Life Educational Plan that considers prognosis and the ramifications of the child's ecology. The relevant community agencies should be accountable with the school to look beyond the school to the life-future prognosis. Admittedly, school is a huge chunk of time, but it is supposed to be preparation for the span of living years after school, not just preparation for more years of schooling. Also, as reviewed in this chapter, many therapeutic and other nonschool experiences must be blended in to make a reasonable future for the SEI pupil. The milieu aspects must be included along with assigned responsibilities.

However it is easy to underestimate the power of special education. The resources of a caring teacher, school achievements of the widest variety, and planned group life embody extremely important therapeutic potentials. The extended time available is a resource. Further, much work with the parents can be done through schools. The plea is for the special teacher not to be naive or unwittingly be put in the catbird seat as the agent for creating improbable changes. The iconoclastic, flexible teacher who has a program that is often least like regular school, will stretch education to make the maximum possible impact. A teacher who goes to court when the student's case comes up may be doing more that way for the youth than hours of classroom will do. Helping a pupil find a job may be the most therapeutic thing for an adolescent. A weekend camping trip with a group of preadolescents may provide more basic human interaction than a month of regular school or group times. Providing the opportunity for a parent's group can sometimes accomplish indirectly what a frontal push for traditional family therapy cannot. The ways of usefulness are many and varied.

Our examination of assessment and the interventions is complete. We have considered planning. Now we shall concentrate on the multifaceted roles of the teacher of SEI children and youth.

6

Teaching Dilemmas and Resolutions

TRANSITION

WE HAVE STUDIED the nature of SEI pupils, their problems and the psychology of interventions. In psychoeducation, the psychological processes are blended with educational processes to fit individual and group needs. While the setting is usually a classroom with a combination of individual IEPs, there are other arrangements as well, such as special tutoring, resource room teaching, consulting, and planning mainstreaming. There are unique demands in the various teaching roles and even in the classroom role in various settings such as public school or an institution. Nonetheless, wherever the SEI pupil is, the helping concepts remain the same.

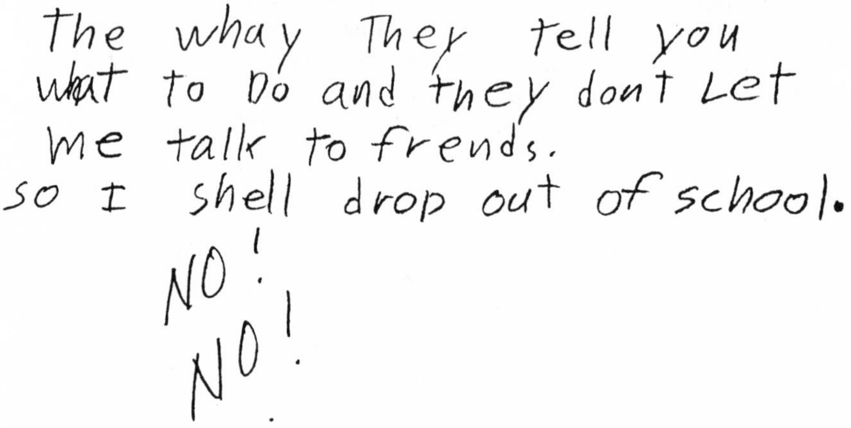

The whay They tell you what to Do and they dont Let me talk to frends.
So I shell drop out of school.
NO!
NO!

FIGURE 5. Try as every teacher does, it is not always possible to make school a pleasant place for children. One youngster expressed his views as shown here.

Just as the teacher needs to understand the nature of the work of mental health colleagues, so must these colleagues appreciate the complexity and the limitations of special education. This is particularly relevant for the various disciplines in collecting data, consultation, and participation in formulation of IEPs.

THE TEACHER'S ROLE IN THE OVERALL SCHEMA

Psychoeducation includes aspects of all three faces of Figure 3. The basic psychological processes embodied in the channels on face 1 underlie what is done. Face 2 includes the various special educational formats to be discussed in chapters 8 and 9. Face 3 is the focus of this chapter, the actual activities that take place in teaching situations, classroom activities one "sees" going on in classrooms. These classroom happenings can be viewed as just a series of events or as an integrated set of phenomenon. Arguments over whether SEI education is subject matter or relationship, therapy or schooling, behavioristic or dynamic, structured or open should be long behind us. The combination of procedures is a consequence of the diagnostic data and the derived interventions as indicated through the IEPs. Strategies will be manifold and individualized. Various emphases on the given psychological channels melt together to comprise an effective classroom. When one observes a good teacher, one sees a kaleidoscope of individual and group work, formal and informal operations, academic and activity tasks permeated with interpersonal relationships. To integrate the elements of face 3 and to infuse elements of the prior chapters requires a conceptualization of the teaching-learning process.

The Major Classroom Functions

What goes on in this process can be subsumed under three headings: personal teaching style, relationship phenomena, and the substance of curricula and method. The logic of this tripartite division comes from a functional grouping of operations teachers conduct revealed in studies starting with Barr (1948; 1955). Some researchers and theoreticians focus only on a limited phenomenon or a particular dominant aspect such as how the teacher asks questions. The result is a penetrating discussion of a limited aspect in isolation, leaving out more

FIGURE 6. Plot of teaching functions. Axis 1 is orthagonal, making a three-dimensional space.

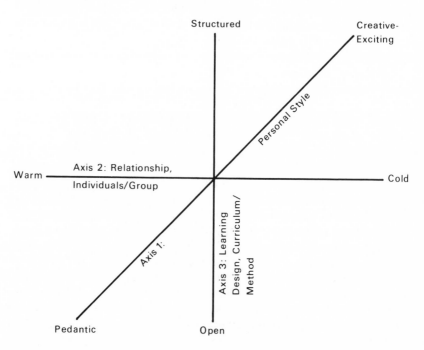

than is covered and ignoring the meaning of the specific process in the totality of what is taking place. Figure 6 sums up the specifics in three axes: Learning Design, Relationship, and Style. Though these are separated for examination, it is obvious that none function in isolation. The quality of any single classroom activity in any one segment reflects what is going on in the others at the same time. The teacher's style is a significant aspect of relationships with individuals and groups. Relationship quality is in interaction with the learning design found in curriculum and method. The specific curricular elements such as the teaching of reading have endless articles and books devoted to practice. These special methodological and subject matter aspects comprise subparts of the curriculum content area of axis 3.

It is very important for anyone who is going to undergo a supervised student teaching experience to sort these matters out. Our studies (Swan 1983) have shown that compatibility of the student teacher with the supervising teacher is crucial in learning (to say nothing of survival!) through such tutelage. Ratings are higher if the student identifies and adopts the mode of the supervisor. There are of course supervisors who know how to teach through this process but education, psychology, and psychiatry have all too many supervisors who are oblivious to the press they create to "be like me" and ignore the need of the new professional to develop his or her own variant of performance, of course within legitimate perimeters. The two most significant experiences in the molding of a teacher's performance are what happens in student teaching and the first year on the job.

Axis 1

Axis 1 comprises personal style, the idiosyncratic way each teacher goes about the business of teaching. This personal flavor has been the subject of many studies searching for the one and true teacher personality, which does not exist. What has been discovered is that there are many ways to project a surgent, creative personal presence. At the other end of this axis is the pedantic, dull, anxious, and defensive personal projection—a boring and rigid attitude are common examples. One can plot his or her personal teaching presence some place along this scale. There are many positive constellations that are useful in classrooms, and they are not identical.

A classic study of this matter (LaVietes 1962) in special education demonstrated the vast difference in styles of two teachers who were both judged to be equally effective. One was very outgoing and engaged in all possible exchanges with pupils. The other maintained a low profile, quietly penetrating the setting though with minimal overt interchanges. It is very possible that such differences in teachers as people would also explain some of the particular consonance and dissonance that occurs from time to time between even a good teacher and given pupil. Few of us have flexibility to equally meet all needs of the gamut of SEI pupils.

Teaching style is seen as an outgrowth of the particular personal assets one has. It is also clear that life conditions and frustrations tend to constrict personal effectiveness, and thus the teacher's contemporary mental health state must be acknowledged as well as basic personality attributes.

Axis 2

Axis 2 comprises the relationship quality, ranging from warm and positive to cold and even hostile. The two components of this dimension are relationships with individuals and with groups. Skill in one does not ensure equal capability in the other.

Axis 3

Axis 3 contains the core of the teaching process, curriculum, and method. The organization of the learning experience ranges from highly formal and structured to open and informal. This dimension includes both affective and cognitive components of curricular and extracurricular activities.

Various situations and curricular goals may cause a teacher to move from one position to another on these axes' dimensions; typically the teacher's performance tends toward an underlying consistency. Valid migrations are related to variance in individual and classroom conditions. Inconsistent teachers are often sized up each morning by pupils to see what class is going to be like today.

One can plot his/her position in teaching space depicted in figure 6 by recording a place or range on the three axes. One has phenomenological judgments: "This is where I put myself and this is where I would like to be on the axes." Observations by colleagues are another source of information. Supervisors make judgments, often with evaluative bias of what they consider the "right" position.

It should be evident that there is no one "right" position implied in teaching space that meets all classroom demands. However, differences can be clarified and suggestions can be made for changes most appropriate for the particular class at a state in development. An effective stance for one class, or one time of any class, or one task may not be suited to other classes, times, or tasks. There may be an overall goal of where one hopes to end up over time. Because of the various need structures indicated in the IEPs, to a degree each pupil attends his own individualized classroom based upon his needs. The miracle is how some teachers accommodate to such a wide range of individual differences. Certain popular models for teaching stress quite specific parts of the three-axis complex but the fact that they ignore various dimensions does not mean these dimensions are inactive. Something is always going on in each of the axes whatever theorists recognize or ignore. For example, one stance may pay great attention to the relationships axis, with little attention to organized academics, while another may emphasize learning exclusively. Such differential attention does not obliterate the fact that teachers are always functioning somewhere in teaching space on all three axes. When there is the pretense of machinelike, nonpersonal teaching (in fact one system likens teacher behavior to a computer), such actions convey to the pupil certain affective messages and priorities. Research on nonverbal communication has amply demonstrated how much goes on in gesture and body signals. A teacher may give an order to sit down but express anxiety and indecision and then wonder why pupils challenge him, or he may say "We are now going to learn so and so," when he has no conviction that these children can learn it or even that it is worth learning.

What Determines Professional Stance in the Teaching Space?

Rather than what a teacher would prefer to do, pupil needs determine the position to take. One does not design the same regime for a sociopathic child as one would for a depressed child. Age influences are also important; adolescents must feel more in charge, making decisions. A dependent child will seek more external support. What we know from the diagnosis sets the pattern for individualized assistance. A teacher may wish to be open but the group requires structure. A teacher may feel warm toward the pupils but a warm expression frightens a particular child. Creativity for curricular innovation may have to wait on getting the group organized.

Interviews with pupils suggest considerable tolerance for a range of teacher behavior on the three axes, but limits as well. For example, the point on the relationship axis between "impersonally distant" and "hostile" is significant. Or, when open becomes loose, chaos results. Structure may be reassuring while rigidity can be frustrating. Changes in position may be called for by group conditions, almost of the moment. It can also be seen how high fixation in a given style may be very difficult for certain pupils to utilize. A pupil who is convinced he cannot learn may have difficulty with a very warm teacher in a very open setting who overpraises. His combined caring for the teacher leads to wanting to please while his inability to cope gets him upset. A teacher who organizes appropriate learning experiences but is cold and distant interpersonally may be meeting half of his pupils' needs.

Tutoring a single child is a complex task but there is usually time to work out the procedures. Dealing with a group adds layer upon layer of complexity, different levels of task, different relationships, and different use of personal attributes, all the time recognizing that the IEP "plan of assistance" for each pupil differs. Thus, too rigid a position on the axes would be unresponsive to both the diagnostic differences and the states generated by temporary conditions. Even the most disinterested student may find a spot of self-motivation and external pressure can be temporarily reduced. Equally, even a child with reasonable self-esteem has days of discouragement. Group contagion turns a student who desires to learn into an escape artist for the time being. Thus, adequate teaching of the disturbed is based upon conceptualizing the functions represented in the three axes combined with a continuous reading of the individual pupils and the group, then moving appropriately in teaching space. If there were not so many excellent teachers who can balance these factors well (granted, with times of stress) one may well believe this task to be impossible. The accommodations necessary to fit SEI pupils are much more extensive than for normal pupils. The flexibility has to come from the teacher.

Does SEI Teaching Really Differ from Regular Teaching?

Before we examine the elements of the three axes in detail, the relationship of special teaching of SEI pupils to regular teaching needs clarification.

Unless one considers SEI children and youth as a different branch of the species, teaching them is highly related to teaching normal children. Disturbed pupils do not produce disturbed behavior 100 percent of the time though some may appear to do so. They usually have some normal interests, some time periods, and some involvements that are typical for their age. SEI pupils are at once so different and yet so like other children it is important that we see the similarities as well as the differences.

Special teaching is a particular case of regular education, an extension of the individualization found in good regular education. But at the same time most SEI pupils bring to the classroom outcroppings of behavior different from the normal, sometimes in kind but often in degree. Unfortunately, in many instances special classes become only narrowed-down regular school classes trying to subsist on bone-dry fundamentals and repetitive drill. The educational thesis seems to be, if they haven't learned then intensify that same effort over and over again. The reverse should be true: the most relevant curriculum and the most inviting methods should be used in SEI teaching. Thus the special teacher practices both as a regular teacher and special teacher. For example, developmental reading is combined with remedial reading. Sometimes the difference extends to reading therapy where the teacher's skill supports a broad regenerative experience for the pupil beyond the skill itself.

The SEI teacher does not start teaching a grade level or a given subject but at the point where the youngster is depicted in the IEP and moves ahead from that point by a variety of methods. Bauer (1974) stated the case succinctly under the concept of educational therapy. The goal is development of skills and cognitive functioning and the promotion of ego functioning. Ruth LaVietes (1962) saw the common goals of regular and special education as achievement of an organized body of useful knowledge, group discipline, stimulation of creativity, imparting of social and ethical standards, and at the same time increasing the pleasure of learning and the child's ability to meet frustrations. With disturbed children she adds the goals of making the child feel adequate and hopeful by undoing distorted interpersonal relationships, reducing anxiety by having only appropriate expectations and overcoming resistance to learning through stress on nonpainful, pleasurable aspects of learning. This takes place in a benign social reality. There is more emphasis on feelings and more tolerance.

In Swift and Spivack's comprehensive review of literature on specific SEI teaching methodology (1974) what comes out in bold relief is the need for relating what the teacher does to the specific problems of given pupils, the IEP prescriptions if they are accurate. Tasks must be made clear, specific, and of an acceptable length. Many games are employed. Rules are made explicit. Role playing is employed in dealing with anxiety. Many behavior modification techniques are included with considerable attention to praise. One of the most interesting aspects of their analysis is the variety of procedures used for a given problem. Sometimes methodologies that appear to be in contrast are found in different studies aimed at the same purpose, as, for example, speaking in low tones to get attention against alerting the entire class by random questions. What this illustrates is that a particular method does not solve the problem for the teacher except where that teacher has a sense of when a given procedure in the method smorgasbord is appropriate. They conclude that SEI pupils lack a minimal capacity for independent learning. They need all types of support. Active pupil participation should be stimulated. The teacher relationship is a central factor.

We can summarize the essential differences between regular and special-education teaching with the following points.

1. There is a significant extension of the concept of individual differences, through the IEP and accountability. The range for SEI pupils is represented by the needs in the diverse syndromes from autistic to psychopathic. It is well to remember that wherever they are, pupils still learn as individuals. Learning is a private affair and very singular. Classes or other groups do not learn, each member learns. This is why each pupil goes to his own school regardless of our percep-

tion. At the same time that all learning is individual, there may be a significant parallel learning in the group or subgroups by various class members. Social learning requires interaction with others.

2. Normal pupils have somewhat uneven profiles of skills and knowledge, while SEI pupils typically have higher variation in what they know and can do in various areas. Starting where the deficiencies appear may put the teacher back to rudimentary processes—getting attention in the first place, or establishing the most basic rules of behavior.

3. Prognostic studies indicate that the typical SEI student learns at a lower rate than the average student. Thus even when making gains, the pupil may continue to fall behind. Those making astounding gains are the exception. Teachers cannot expect to find gratification through seeing the progress that is typical for regular teachers.

4. Equal attention is given to both cognitive and affective learning. With SEI pupils, social learning is a more overt teacher task. So many act out that discipline, management, or better still, socialization becomes a major teacher preoccupation. True, regular teachers are involved in discipline and seek to foster social growth. In fact some regular teachers spend more time on discipline (true social learning?) than anything else. The difference here is that SEI pupils will frequently lag far behind the appropriate social behavior for their age. Not only do they need new skills, they also have to eradicate their store of unacceptable social behavior. The same can be said about the maturation of self-concept and the enhancement of self-esteem, which are tasks for all teachers but an omnipresent concern with SEI teachers. It takes more innovative and persistent effort to help SEI pupils stabilize a reasonable level of self-esteem.

An intense interlock of academics and affective components in learning is characteristic of disturbed children. Jones (1968) demonstrated how entwined these spheres are in normal children. In SEI pupils, related achievement difficulties (namely reading) and attitude defections (namely hostility to authority) have been long recognized. One teaches a particular self as well as a subject or skill.

5. For the SEI teacher more effort is devoted to motivation and finding ways to make the learning experience nonthreatening and even enticing. When one asks regular pupils why they do the work, it is usually because they have to "to go to the next grade" or because "you gotta" and quite often because "it's fun." Special pupils lack this general faith as a propellant. They have too many blocks, such as fear of failure, learned helplessness, and more pressing personal priorities.

It is usually more difficult to find personally relevant experiences for these children, caught up as they frequently are in problems of their own person, far from ordinary school curricula. Not only is it difficult to find curriculum relevance, but there is also the matter of method relevance. A class of SEI pupils were showing high anxiety and resistance to reading—they were very far behind. The teacher, building upon Bettelheim's work on fairy stories, was aware that the children were very involved in hearing these stories over and over again. The reason lay in the issues in the stories. For example, the underdog won out regardless. The powerful (adults) fell to schemes of children. Glovinsky (1979) has reported his use of this "relevance" in teaching reading. The reading activities, cognitive stimulation work, and crafts were made into a pervasive unit. Cardboard castles appeared in the classroom. Word lists and questions were developed for each story used. Also the dynamics of the stories were discussed; with only oblique reference, it was clear that the conditions in the stories had strong personal meanings.

6. Particular attention is directed to avoid failure in any learning. There is no way to absolutely prevent failures—if such were even desirable. However, the SEI teacher concentrates on designing tasks that minimize failure as much as possible. Small steps in new performance, specific accomplishments, and a great deal of support are built into the activities. The pupils come with histories of failure in school and outside. They have no risk capital in their self-esteem account. A pupil may feel failure relative to norm peer performance as a reflection of limited potential exaggerated by self-expectations. Expectations that can never be met may be set by parents or teachers.

7. SEI teachers find themselves engaged in support for their pupils in a wide variety of ways uncommon to the typical classroom teacher. There are intensive cooperative efforts with other disciplines. Often SEI teachers are privy to intimacies of the family and pupil. They may find themselves the support for a mother who is struggling with many problems. They may go to court on a case, plan excursions, and become an advocate for needed services. In short, the special SEI teacher is more involved with the total life of the pupil than is common in regular teaching.

8. SEI teaching requires particular attention to group dynamics. Regular classes can end up with a combination of youngsters whose behavior mitigates against educational goals. Most SEI pupils have manifold personal and social difficulties that make them supersensitive to group forces. It has been said that a special class is a group of ungroupables.

A classroom should not be automatically assembled by computer;

the group dynamics of a given group and the impact of each additional member are matters of great import. Certain classes never develop a reasonable balance. The addition of a new member to a class can be a disaster unless there are resources available to work out the resulting behavior. Teachers who have a "vacancy" often get a pupil whether or not this is in the interests of that pupil or the class. In the small, intense, problem-saturated special class, every member has a potent impact on the group, which is why this topic will be expanded later.

DETAILED EXAMINATION OF PERSONAL STYLE

The three axes are of equipotential for the special teacher. The order of presentation is from the most individual aspect, axis 1, to axis 2, use of the personal attributes in relationship and then to the most obvious axis 3 curriculum.

The Personal-Style Axis

It is difficult to see the specific psychological channels that are activated by personal style. Yet it is clear that this teacher attribute has an impact on both the affective tone in a classroom and some of the choices a teacher makes concerning method. Thus individual and group relationships will reflect to some degree the teacher's personality. On the method side, an anxious teacher will generally want a tighter curricular design. Certainly we can observe the differences in classes with creative, zestful teachers where there is an expectation of something exciting happening. Some teachers are comfortable only when teaching their "best" subjects, where they are authorities. Unraveling this axis will give an opportunity to reflect on personal assets and liabilities.

Personality studies of teachers are easy to do and fascinate trainers, but the results can be summed up in one generalization: There is no one successful constellation of characteristics for a special teacher. It is common to idealize the SEI teaching role, stipulating a combination of eighty-eight necessary competencies (Dorward, 1963) probably found in one of a thousand.

Characteristics said to be essential to the SEI teacher cover the

compendium of the good regular teacher only more so. Certain characteristics are counterindications, such as intellectual dullness, lack of
interest in disturbed children, lack of patience and perseverance, high
needs for gratification from pupils, and low ego strength to name a few.
The amazing resilence of our young professionals is evident by the
number who succeed in spite of the odds. The basic characteristics
needed are not that elusive: the ability to establish relationships,
creativity to create fresh and exciting conditions, self-insight to permit
objectivity, flexibility to meet the ever-changing scene and of course
the cognitive ability to acquire the special skills and make discriminations and evaluations.

Actually, most of the teacher failure or exhaustion is due to
(1) improper placement given the teacher's personal attributes and
training, or (2) lack of adequate support in the system. That is to say, it
is a program failure, not a personal teacher failure. To discover the
demands of a particular position, the person to interview is not the
administrator but the teacher who last had the position and can distinguish fantasy from the reality.

How does the teacher-to-be see the role of a special-class teacher,
both on conscious and unconscious levels? Self-insight facilitates the
separation of pupil reactions toward the teacher into those which are a
consequence of personal characteristics from pupil behavior
transferred to the classroom from elsewhere. Many SEI pupils not only
lack trust in adults but have had specific poor experience with teachers
and school. They come to the class with built-in negative bias and bring
this to the most noble of teachers. They may react with fear, hostility,
or negativism. Often they provoke and test to put the adult down. An
extreme case of the latter is found in the book *Ribbin, Jiven, and
playing the dozens* (Foster 1974), which depicts the particular games
that delinquent adolescents play at the expense of adults. Newman
(1974) describes the "you're not fair" game and "our other teacher let
us" game and many more. If a teacher does not understand pupil problem transference, he or she is most likely to respond with a countertransference stance of defensiveness to prove who is boss or who is fair
to avoid personal devaluation and feelings of inadequacy. Knowing
one's own limitations and nature helps gauge the meaning of a pupil's
behavior. Consultation may be needed to clarify what can be done to
prevent being the unwitting foil for the very problem that brought the
child to the special teacher.

Special teachers cannot expect to maintain self-esteem from what
they get from disturbed pupils' responses. We all want to be liked,
respected, and successful in our efforts. Sometimes even the most

disturbed pupils will give us encouraging indications that we are liked and are achieving what is intended. But they are far more likely to give little on the positive side. If the teacher's life outside of school is not sustaining, he or she must not expect to be sustained by the pupils. The tendency to be a buddy rather than an adult deprives the pupil of the authority he or she needs.

In interviews with SEI pupils, it is clear that they recognize how hard they are to live with. They don't see how the teacher stands them, though this may be the last thing they would admit to the teacher until long after. It is not uncommon for them to come back years later and express their appreciation and reminisce over prior escapades.

On the other hand, not every response of a child is transference out of his or her case history. Since we always operate at the cutting edge of the pupil's ability to function in a satisfactory manner, any helping person is bound to make mistakes at times. We can put a youngster down by unreasonable demands. Pupils continually present much behavior that provokes counteraction. This in turn touches off sensitive areas that all adults have. When the adult responds to behavior in a typical nonprofessional manner, this begets more pupil acting out. In learning theory terms, we have rewarded the wrong responses. Adult reactions must be under control and not at the beck and call of pupils who could otherwise induce anxiousness, anger, or overly solicitous responses from the adult and by so doing reestablish evidence that fits their distorted view of themselves and the world. There is no place for anger accompanying the necessary rule enforcement or dismay when assisting a pupil with low involvement. The classroom atmosphere can be attuned to pupil needs only when adult countertransference reactions are well under control. An SEI teacher must not feel required to save the pathological world. One encourages pupil growth without at the same time demanding it to appease one's own needs.

Even professional adults have certain types of children, sets of responses, or situations that are more comfortable than others. There are kids we like and kids we dislike, so to speak. A useful exercise is to analyze such reactions. We may lack skill to interact reasonably with a pupil because he or she arouses certain feelings of discomfiture. We get upset. This is particularly true of reactions to the psychopath. Even with a common diagnostic category (say, autistic), we find them not all equal. Through self-insight a teacher recognizes things that cause personal reactions, so that conscious efforts can be used to keep relationships in balance.

The teacher's personality also includes personal motivations, some of which are very relevant to teaching disturbed children. On the one hand a teacher must be interested in encouraging a child's academic achievement and his social and personal development. On the other hand this interest has to be modulated; any child is cared about because he is a human being and not because he learns well for us, feels better for us, or behaves more reasonably for us. If our gratifications come only if he pays us with achievement, a strain is put on the relationship. Adult satisfaction is best expressed as a reflection of the child's own gratifications from an experience. We must exude hope, but realistic hope. It is not that we should not care about pupil progress; it is that the caring must be under control and rewards not given only when the student meets our particular expectations. Caring is not a bonus for teacher satisfaction. Care is the pupils' birthright. Such educational tightrope walking is complex and difficult. For the most part there is no question in a student's mind but that we want and are pleased with any progress. The fear is of being cared about only in ratio to his achievement production when what he needs is to establish basic trust through the untaxed caring given by important adults.

Finally, there must be an assured, nonanxious manner as part of the teacher's personal style. Disturbed pupils, for their own survival, have learned to assess the adults' nonverbal communications. Anxiety will out. For example, fearful that the pupils will misbehave, a teacher lists twenty prohibitions. Pupils know just what to try after such an invitation. Anxious about fights, one can be so explicit about warning Joe and George not to fight again that they are called upon to fight to preserve their identities—the opposite of the teacher's intention. Anxious anticipation of disinterest in doing the assigned work is demonstrated when a teacher starts with threats that begin with "if we don't get our work done."

One way to reduce anticipatory anxiety is to plan for the worst that could possibly take place (and seldom does). If one is prepared, the uncertainty of on-the-spot decision is removed. Much anxiety in teaching is the fear of losing face with children or supervisors, since many teachers still live with an outmoded concept that they themselves should be able to help every child in all the ways stated in the IEP, taking problems in stride as the expected condition with disturbed pupils.

SEI teacher training seldom covers personal growth. There may be pieces of unfinished business that will not be obvious without considerable personal counseling. Coupled with self-awareness is what has been variously termed *ego strength* or self-efficacy—the ability to cope—which lies at the core of personal self-esteem and self-adequacy.

Some of us have histories of success, while others have met many defeats, are indecisive, and even after finally coming to a decision we may doubt its correctness. If adult stability is not demonstrated through the way one copes, a child will not see a figure for identification in the teacher. The certain and able teacher will not have it easy, for there is inevitable testing by SEI pupils regardless of the teacher's effectiveness.

Thus, while there is no single personality profile that is associated with the good teacher of disturbed children, there are characteristics that are important, still leaving a wide latitude for differing individual styles and room for being one's own self.

RELATIONSHIP: INDIVIDUAL AND GROUP

For the relationship axis we call upon the affective psychological channel in figure 3. There is always a relationship existing between pupils and the teacher, good or poor, intended or not. We communicate by what we say and how we act. Those who ignore or muffle this channel merely ignore that fact. A teacher who pretends not to respond to a pupil's satisfaction or frustration has already responded with the value statement that those particular child's feelings do not merit attention. There is seldom neutrality in the message world. What is verbalized constitutes a half-communication. The youngster reads our body talk, gestures, and expressions. What we feel will out and what we feel is a reflection of what we are like. One of the most devastating conditions exists when the adult verbalizes one thing—say concern—and then sends out opposing nonverbal messages of disinterest. Facing conflicting messages, children depend on the more primitive nonverbal language channel. A pupil may say he just knows the teacher doesn't really like him, although the teacher says he does. Actions speak so loudly that the pupil cannot hear the words.

There are systems of studying the characteristic pupil-teacher interaction style that can reveal both the general pattern and specific sequences (Fink 1972). Nonverbal responses can also be analyzed (Rezmierski 1973). Teachers maximize success by differential aiming of questions to individual students and by giving positive feedback (Dembo 1978). In a preschool study Pastor and Swap (1978) found pupils were more disruptive in regular classrooms than in special ones. Special teachers more frequently interpreted and explained. Ignoring was more common by regular teachers. Teacher presence (more feasible in the special-class pupil-teacher ratio) and structure resulted in fewer disruptions in special class. Lyon (1977) found that both special teachers and regular teachers responded to pupils rated low on social and personal attributes with more negative nonverbal communication.

A few programs make a fetish of teacher impersonality. One abjures the teacher to cast off all feeling because feeling for the pupil would destroy the rigidity needed to conduct the given program with absolute objectivity. Another advocates confrontation and outgaming difficult youngsters as the mode of control. Actually, teachers do not always follow such program formats. In one program advertised for a nonpersonal, mechanistic approach, the teachers were as warm and involved as one could expect to find anywhere. Of what use is praise in behavior modification if the pupil has no regard for the teacher? Teachers of the disturbed are expected to be warm, decent, concerned, and caring individuals regardless of the style of intervention advocated. Aspy (1972) lists as essential psychological factors composing relationship the building of trust, acceptance of children, and the capacity to care. He provides scales to assess these conditions in the classroom. The quality of the interpersonal relationship enables the teacher to serve as an identification figure for appropriate behavior. The way we manage our own feelings as adults becomes the image for the youngster. It is particularly important that disturbed children see adults handle frustration, anger, and affection in reasonable ways. There needs to be a basic attitude of hope. How can a child learn to believe in the future if he does not see this in his teacher? The child must have a chance to interact with persons who can model behavior that then can be integrated into his own self-concept.

There are several specific skills that a teacher uses to cultivate useful relationships with pupils. One does not relate in a vacuum. Eleanor Craig's book about the first year of experience, *P. S. You're Not Listening* (1972), demonstrates the power of a teacher's concern and human relationship to facilitate pupil growth in all areas.

Governing the Expression of Interpersonal Closeness

Not all children can respond positively to a teacher's expressions of interpersonal closeness. Some shrink as if they were to be hit; some find erotic stimulation even in the physical presence of certain adults. Others may feel interpersonal closeness and be able to respond positively only when the teacher is physically close. Sibling rivalry can also be stimulated at times by the observation of closeness shown by the teacher to a classmate. Thus, the teacher has to be observant and study the way pupils react to closeness. Most children also need some time away from peers and adults. Adults who are always hovering may simply be irritating to the pupil's wish for independence. Working through these reactions utilizing discussion means making it clear what is happening.

Developing Empathic Responsiveness

While teachers are not primarily engaged in direct interpretation of the underlying motivations for behavior, they must be sensitive to such possibilities. Rather than interpretation, the teacher's response is one of supportive behavior to help the pupil with the underlying emotion. For example, a youngster is frustrated by the difficulty of doing an assignment and begins to disintegrate. Commonly, teachers confront him with admonitions or even threats to get back to work. In contrast, the empathic response is to recognize how he feels, to talk with him about frustration, a common emotion that we all know, and then mutually work out a solution to the particular situation. The empathic teacher recognizes that even as with adults, behaviors of children are moved by deep underlying emotions such as fear of failure, rejection, loss of self-esteem or love, hate, and anger. Although the teacher may not directly expose the underlying feelings, the youngster is responded to in a manner that will help in efforts to deal with the inner state. The steps are as follows: The teacher comes to know the pupil through the diagnostic records and direct contact. It is not only knowing what the pupil does but understanding why, an appreciation of the inner dynamics. As one teacher put it, "I know what he is thinking and feeling before he shows it or even when he cannot put it into words." Now what does the teacher do with this empathic understanding? Then the teacher plans in a way that takes into account those basic emotional feelings. This means that the special teacher has a higher toleration for symptomatic behavior than would a regular teacher with a typical classroom. Realizing that the symptomatic behavior may well be a defense covering either conscious or unconscious feelings, the teacher responds to the underlying condition. When the pupil says, "I don't like this work," but the teacher knows he really is saying he doesn't want to fail and is afraid he will, the teacher responds to his unspoken condition by supporting him through his fear of failure. It may be by verbalizing how much we all feel like this at times, or it may be by moving in quietly without words and giving a little unobtrusive help so that he *can* do that which he fears he cannot. This is done through active intervention by direct assistance rather than through interpreting the behavior and its possible causes. Astute teacher planning helps the child to bridge over his block. Redl (1966) calls this hurdle help. Correct support reduces the underlying anxiety and makes it possible for the pupil to invest his energy in the learning task again rather than in acting out the inner conflict. This is the nature of teacher empathy and, because it gives the child what he needs at the time, he is the better for it. The pupil senses the teacher as the benign giver of help. This is the essence of the relationship-building process in therapeutic teaching. It is through doing things for pupils, not some abstract concept of relationship.

Morgan (1979) has a concretely grounded exposition of empathic response for SEI teachers. She interviewed the pupils who felt that they were understood by their teachers. She found empathy pervades all activities, including how well the instructional material and methods fit, how the teacher organizes the environment, responds to feelings (when you are about to be upset, stays close to you, verbalizes feeling for you), and personal qualities (sense of humor, warm, calm, relaxes, smiles a lot). Morgan puts the elusive concept of empathy to work in the classroom.

Psychological versus Humanistic Acceptance

There is a tendency for mental health personnel, including special teachers, to be overprotective. We should not replace any self-responsibility the youngster is able to exercise. Nor is acceptance provided through being nondemanding or even nonexpecting. Psychological acceptance means providing the particular support the child needs to develop to his maximum. What interventions are needed come from the diagnostic process. One does not accept the sociopath by reducing the reality he must face. One does not accept the manipulator by being manipulated, or a schizophrenic youngster by accepting his idiosyncratic world as external reality.

One expects academic effort and behavior to vary from child to child and day to day. Even in overall improvement there are times of regression. Teachers speak of good days or bad days, knowing that a disturbed child will have both. The flexibility of adult demands is a response to this variation and should be discussed with the pupil so that flexibility does not become perceived as permissiveness or unfairness. While there is a high tolerance for symptomatic behavior, confusion and bedlam have no place. The teacher is as ready to tighten as to tolerate. As Lavieties (1962) puts it, the teacher presents a benign social reality to children who have experienced distortions.

It is often said that the disturbed child needs a predictable environment. That begs the question of what in the environment should be predictable. Pupils should always be able to predict certain things such as that the adults will listen, care, work with him, and attend to his inner needs. Predictability is not interchangeable with arbitrariousness. The same unsatisfactory behavior resulting from ignorance, forgetfulness, deliberately baiting, and an overall loss of control does not deserve the same response. Identical behaviors are often not equal behaviors because their causes and intents are not equal. On a bad day toleration goes up; when the pupil is intact it goes down to maintain psychological consistency.

Relationship Starts in the Initial Interview with Each Pupil

As the program begins, the first step is to interview each pupil. It is amazing how different the child appears in real life as opposed to his records. It is a shock to see a plaintive case record turn into a wild and anxious enfant terrible or a fire setter who is warm and relating or a career delinquent who is depressed but eager to know his teacher.

Ten new pupils (the magic number in many schools) should not be brought together without prior individual contact, preferably with both parent and pupil. The purpose is dual: to get one's human radar in operation concerning the youngster and to set the tone of the relationship. One asks about the hopes and expectations of the pupil and past experiences in school and with teachers. It is well to write down what agreements have resulted and what tasks are foremost with both having a copy of the educational plan as the IEP is discussed.

In a most benign way, using pertinent information from the file, the teacher talks about how problems will be handled and what is expected for the class. The teacher can ask what she should do to be helpful should certain behavior occur. The pupil is asked if he knows any of the others who will be in the class. The purpose is to enable the first relationship to be between each single pupil and the teacher. One asks about school achievement, likes and dislikes, and the prides and pains of the youngster. It is much easier to begin a relationship through such an interview than it is to meet a group at one whack. The pupil should sense that the teacher "really knows him" but without prejudice or threat, and it becomes clear that she knows about kids with problems and how to help them. The reality of life is openly discussed. Sometimes these interviews result in a honeymoon with a class, where things are unbelievably pleasant for a period. If the pupils are really disturbed, even with the best start of a program, the problems will begin to out, but the best possible start is critical.

The pupil's two *personal IEPs* are explored since they determine pupil action even though they are not in the files. The *overt* personal pupil IEP is what the pupil consciously wishes to have happen, his goals as stated, which are sometimes only a parroting of what the adults have said. With young children they are simplified: "Stop fighting" or "Learn to read," which often becomes accomplished in their eyes with a most simplified surface change. They didn't fight for two days, so they are "cured." Adolescents are far more complicated, cautious, and usually guarded at first. The second *covert* pupil IEP is based upon personal needs that are too uncomfortable to talk about or are even unconscious. It may be to resist adults—or just teachers to prove he can't really learn, to avoid work if possible, to get by with little effort, or whatever the impairment dictates to the pupil. After a brief period of grace, the transference of the SEI problem will begin to show. *We can rest assured all pupils have their own conscious and unconscious IEP* with long- and short-term goals although they are often only vaguely formulated. The pupil's view of the wished-for and real future are reflected in the personal IEP. The more astute the teacher is at this stage, the more honest and real will be the interchanges. Brickman's ideas (p. 127) are important to review in planning interviews.

The Search for Assets

While the saying that every child is better than others at something is a snare and a delusion, most disturbed pupils do function relatively better in some areas than in others. Even with no outstanding talent, they have relative talents. In emphasizing the healthy part of the child (figure 2) we hope to capitalize on what he can do effectively. With one child this may be only a slight ability in drawing, but that is something. Another collects postcards. This one knows his numbers. Another can make realistic animal sounds. Whatever intact area the child has is exploited by the teacher. Any uniqueness offers the opportunity for honest praise and attention. Frequently overall achievement is low, but a special area of knowledge provides possibilities.

Teacher or Therapist: Roasting an Old Chestnut

Is a teacher a teacher or a therapist? In the past, teachers were said to do therapeutic things but they were not therapists. Of course the characteristic roles of teacher and therapist are different and of course the roles overlap. One can argue jurisdictional matters, professional turf, and training. When does play become play therapy? Or school activity become activity therapy? Naming a process "therapy" does not necessarily make it so. Is it music, or music therapy? Is it *who* does what that decides whether or not it is therapy?

All special teachers need skill in counseling and in effective talking with children. Life Space Interviewing (p. 214) can be used to work through personal problems, group situations, and to clarify the decisions a teacher has to make as well as to counsel the pupil. If there is a traditional therapist working with the child (usually true of less than one-third of all SEI pupils), perhaps intrapsychic problems can be worked out there. The teacher participates as a team member in the transfer of results to real life. The pupil believes in himself not only when others believe in him but particularly when he does something worth belief.

Teaching versus therapy is no longer worthy of debate because the concept of therapy has changed, as we have seen. The processes of restoration for many children and for many problems can be facilitated far easier in an active, attractive school milieu than in an office. Teachers do not imitate therapists to be therapeutic.

Summary

SEI pupils have social and emotional problems as their defined condition, and special education is the designated legal intervention. Ignoring the affective component would be impossible as well as absurd.

The more the classroom operates within an adequate milieu with all of the needed resources, the more the teacher can focus on academic aspects. The less the ancillary support the more critical will be what the teacher manages to incorporate in the classroom. For example, the teacher, through LSI, has been quite successful with John. Yet he wanders around aimlessly. Something seems to be on his mind, but he cannot communicate readily; there is even a question of whether or not the problem has any definite structure in his mind. He draws the same picture over and over, of a little house with flowers around the front. He is easily distracted and does little work even when the teacher works individually with him. The available diagnostic information is not too helpful, but it indicates he carries a considerable load of anxiety. What is behind the present plateau in his behavior? If there is no one else to work on the problem, the teacher will either have to give up or go behind the mask to uncover what is happening in order to make progress.

GROUPS AND THE RELATIONSHIP AXIS

In the course of a day of teaching disturbed children the teacher will play many roles both for individual pupils and for the group. In Fink's (1970) study some teachers expended half of their behavior giving feedback or direction; asking questions or purposefully ignoring were the most frequent behaviors. The control methods included surface behavior responses, applying authority, refocusing on the tasks, and appealing to values and interpretation. Pupils spent 60 percent of their behavior on tasks; the other 40 percent included many avoidance and diversionary tactics from refusals to general disturbance and aggression.

LSI, Mediating Skills, and Talking with Children

The major intervention with SEI children in schools remains teachers' talk—some of it productive and some considerably wasted and frustrating. There are two major reasons for talking to youngsters, whether by teachers or other mental health professionals: (1) to understand the pupil and (2) to foster desired change. Adults believe a lot in word magic to direct behavior. One generates cognitive process through the use of language. Another goal of talk is to generate trust and usefulness through the interaction. The formal interview is not the usual mode of a teacher. Managerial efforts are converted to understanding through talk. The significance and application of a rule in a given instance deserves clarification even though the decision is rigid application of the rule. Humanizing discipline is essential in a therapeutic classroom.

Life Space Interviewing

The basic methodology for teachers working either with individuals or groups is called Life Space Interviewing, introduced by Redl (1959a). It enables an on-the-line worker to deal hygienically with problem behavior, giving meaning to a particular event.

If one is not careful, talking with children takes on a confrontation stance. While LSI is reality based, it is interactive in nature. Essentially LSI is a planful conversation between pupil(s) and the responsible adult, the teacher. We want to know how the youngster sees and thinks about an event. We enter into his conceptual system. We neither talk *to* or *at* the child: we talk *with,* we interact. Once we are clear how the child perceives the problem (even if the pupil's view cannot be accepted as satisfactory) we are in a position to work out, hopefully with concurrence, a possible resolution. When one is in an action setting, it is not possible to deal with problems in the abstract. Teachers deal with concrete issues. Talking together is the process of sharing lives, an important teaching methodology. Relationship develops through mutual problem solving.

Useful teacher talk with children is alien to the stereotyped telling, admonishing, or threatening. The teacher's conversations with pupils about their classroom behavior do not follow the typical pattern of psychotherapeutic interviews with interpretation, depth probing, and concentration on the unconscious elements.

The SEI teacher needs a place to talk privately with pupils, preferably a glassed-in "office corner" of the classroom, though many events are group happenings with the whole or part of the class. The goal is to pick up on the vexing situations or crisis events, which are usually so evident or even omnipresent and cannot be ignored. These problems are, in fact, public in the teacher-pupil domain. Conversations are built around the events that have taken place. Because LSI deals with ongoing life events, Redl called it life space interviewing. He recognized the need for a mental health skill to use in mediating the life space apart from classical therapy, which he at one time termed "pressurized cabin interviewing" (1959a), although LSI can be effective in traditional therapy sessions.

There is a limit to how much behavior should or even can be planfully ignored, but there is nothing simple or easy about utilizing everyday behavior for insightful behavior gains. Faced with difficulties that must be handled in one way or another, the teacher develops some method. The typical response is a fishwife approach. All too often teachers report that they feel themselves resorting to nagging or even yelling and harsh commands or piling on threats and punishment. As the pupils build up tolerance to any given level of nagging, the teacher is driven to intensification in the struggle for control. Some teachers aspire to the "white coat" simulation and attempt to operate as traditional therapists. While most teachers have the capability for learning formal therapeutic skills, it is difficult if not impossible to combine a deep sustained private individual approach with teaching the class group. The real objective is to engage the pupil's own motivation toward goals that both he and the teacher accept as reasonable.

Detailed procedures for LSI, not as a fixed set of steps but as conceptual organizers, are presented in conflict in the classroom (Long, Morse, and Newman 1980). First is objective exploration of the instigating conditions of the event by getting the individual or group perception, then follows testing for depth and spread—Is this incident attached to some central issue or does it represent a common problem? Next one clarifies the content, the exploration of reality of the perceptions. To enhance the feeling of acceptance the adult operates with empathic responses, avoiding value judgments at this point. Following this, there is exploration of possible motivation for change with a consideration of possible alternatives. In the final resolution the adult view is included in working through to a resolution. This includes strategic planning against what should happen if there is a repetition and what can be done to avoid a repetition. The conclusion may be referral to a therapist, discussions with parents, restriction of freedom, a contingency design, or whatever appears relevant to modifying the behavior. Hopefully both adult and pupil agree. Of course there are times when freedom and times when restriction will have a teaching potential for a given child. Often the message soaks in even when the pupil will not give in verbalization. It may be that a pupil's value deviance becomes clear and yet conformity must be required. Seldom can one expect talk alone to produce change. It is the strategy planned for the future that counts, applying aspects of the various psychological channels. If behavior modification is pertinent, one uses it. If exploration of inner feelings is germane, then one goes in that direction in closure of an LSI episode.

There is a vast and critical difference between ending with arbitrary punishments or rewards against what Dreikurs and Grey (1968) call logical consequences. Natural consequences are those which, as perceived by the child, are "logical" results of behavior. While there is no illusion that all situations can be covered in this logical consequence way, it should be the prevailing mode. When such is possible there is an active role for the child in shaping his own destiny. The point is that the follow-up plan is evolved with the pupil participating but with adult clinical awareness as well, both focused on reality factors. Only when the teacher has an empathic relationship with the pupil will the process be more than mechanical.

The flexibility of LSI is in its open-ended problem-solving methodology. One follows a process rather than aiming at a specific conclusion. At closure it may be necessary to reinforce sanctions, refer for more work or specialized help, organize behavior modification, or limit freedom in conditions where it is misused. While certain crises have to be met with mandatory imposition of the adult's wishes, the more important incidents usually yield understanding for the child, and thus better his chances for recovery.

This type of discussion with children, conducted by teachers, usually focuses on behavior that has taken place in the preview of the teacher and are focused on manifest behavior. However, there are times when the teacher, by training and/or with proper supervision, does develop the significant counseling role for the child. Many children move directly to basic issues in their lives from crisis situations more easily than in traditional therapy. There are children the very nature of whose difficulty, lying as it does in the unconscious, will show only in crisis events. In tandem with psychotherapy, LSI counseling can also assist in transferring control and management to the classroom life situation even as underlying difficulties are still being worked through by a depth therapist when that is required.

The LSI is particularly advantageous in schools. It starts with actual experiences and deals with real problems on a conscious level. It comprises the central problem-solving process, which puts into operation many of the concepts discussed in this book. To learn to use it effectively requires a sensitive and empathic exchange, rather than confrontation. The quality of the relationship and the clarity of the exposition are what count. Once a teacher has been trained in the use of LSI, elements of more traditional therapy can be fused around the reality base. In fact, it lends itself well to the uncovering of the dynamic content and the planning of strategies. Often questions based on the three wishes or early memories around a given type of behavior can be woven into the exploitation of an incident to give perspective. LSI does not necessarily depend upon a crisis. A teacher can reflect on observations over time such as, "I've noticed you look unhappy when you come to school recently." There is virtually no research on the effectiveness of LSI. DeMagistris and Imber (1980) explored the effects of LSI on a small number of disturbed boys and found improvement in both academics and behavior; implications are included for other possible advantages. Articles in the Winter 1981 *Pointer* bring theory and practice of LSI up to date and relate current concepts to the history of the methodology. There are some similarities to Glasser's *Reality Therapy* (1965) but with more emphasis on the interpersonal relationship between the pupil and the helper.

The extent to which the teacher becomes involved in life space interviewing depends upon several conditions. With total milieu support, the time that has to be spent in converting life events into behavioral understanding may be minimal. Many therapists in institutions use some aspects of LSI to deal with crises whether they recognize the fact or not.

Not every potent individual or group life event can be thus exploited. Nor can every child be brought to an appreciation of his behavior through this means. It is difficult to see what a psychotic child who is obsessed with his fantasy could make of the usual problem solving discussion except to reinforce reality. Young children and the nonverbal child may not find verbal concepts easy to use, but adult concern is felt by the young child through nonverbal elements of communication. At times, a simple declarative setting of a limit may be more salutary.

There is also the problem of "overtalking" children, talking an event into the ground, or verbalizing in abstract concepts that overwhelm the average child. The learning disabled child cannot grasp certain abstract concepts and a schizophrenic child does not necessarily understand. But even with the autistic, verbalization of what we are about is important. We do not ask a youngster to be good or behave reasonably but provide specific concrete steps along a road to improvement. The application of life space interviewing for learning disability children is discussed in Cruickshank, Morse and Johns (1980).

With adolescents the need for independence frequently means an anti-authority stance. Adults are balancing on a tightwire. A low profile is essential and moralizing is seldom effective as we "consult" with them. We make points more by what we are than what we say to reduce resistance. There are of course wide variations in children's willingness to disclose themselves, and we should respect their reserve. For children who do not verbalize a great deal, language is not their primary mode and other tactics can be used to reduce resistance, such as putting ends on stories, or playing The Talking, Feeling, and Doing Game (Creative Therapeutics 1973) which is a therapeutic game for children. The dice and questions make a game of various topics about behavior. For example, a card may ask "What of all things would you most like to avoid?" The teacher and the pupil take turns in responding.

The variety of purposes of conversing with children include exchange of information, problem solving and planning, collecting new diagnostic information, and one-to-one learning situations. Little children wander across boundaries in their associative processes as they explain matters rather than make direct progression to a goal. One expects non sequiturs and idiosyncratic associations. Adults have to guard against using words and concepts that are not understood by children.

Rather than specific target questions, oblique techniques or projective questions may provide understanding: What would be good to change about school or home? When did you first know you had a problem? How would you finish this story (after a cue)? How do kids your age choose friends—what is important to you? Your favorite adult? Television show? Who would you like to be like when you grow up? What do you think will be happening to you in two years? Games you like? Things that are the most fun to do (or to avoid at all costs)? If we can get them to explain things as they see them, we will learn much more.

Della Piana's book *How to Talk with Children and Other People* (1973) is directed specifically at talking about children's problems. The flexibility of LSI allows one to go in many directions and offers an adaptable, nonmoralizing process.

LSI with Groups

It is not simple to delineate the use of LSI with groups. The dynamics of group life makes the conduct of a group discussion very difficult and at times impossible. Usually two adults are necessary because of surface management problems. The same goals and the same problem solving persist, and reality focus is used as with individual LSI. But the sequence of steps easily becomes lost in a welter of interpersonal flack. Morse and Small (1959) analyzed a series of such group interviews with very disturbed and acting out youngsters. In some cases the resistance was so strong that nothing could be done in a group session. Other groups gave surface compliance just to get out of the situation. But there were groups that congealed and began to work through problems, sometimes with amazing personal responses and intricate relationships revealed. Subsequent individual interviews would often be indicated to take up matters missed, avoided, or inappropriate in group sessions. A high percentage of classroom behavior is part and product of group life, not the single isolated outpouring of an individual. We live in groups, are substantiated and depreciated in groups. Groups have personalities and characteristic pathological behaviors.

Teacher and Group Relationships: Leadership Quandaries

Teaching is a group operation for the most part. Schools are group agencies. In fact we gather pupils into groups with the goals of homogeneity that accentuates certain group dynamics. Then we put one minority adult representative in charge, given the role of teacher, to deal with the peer forces.

When there was an implicit recognized authority role for adults, the pure authority role may have been workable. Today a teacher gets very little free influence by virtue of his role. Teacher efforts to counter the effects of group processes often fail. Many of the children and youth in SEI programs are there because they cannot get along with peers or adult authority figures; the solution is to put them together and call it a special class! If the pupil has a group-peer problem, then remedial procedures for this should be in the IEP, perhaps as a central aspect. In contrast with those who work with individuals, skill with group life is specific to teachers and group workers.

Obviously groups can have strong positive forces as well as negative. Strain, Cooke, and Apolloni (1976) found the following group strategies used: modeling, reinforcement strategies, and planned use of group behavior modification rewards. They raise an ethical question regarding responsibility for peers put on youngsters who are already burdened with their own problems as is done in positive peer culture programs. (See Vorrath and Brendtro [1974]. The second edition is now in press. Brendtro has suggested ways to prevent misuse of the concept in recent papers and in the second edition.)

Hunter and Meyers (1972) related special classroom climate to pupil attitude, behavior and achievement. Acceptance, low rejection, problem centeredness, and control were significantly related to favorable pupil attitude and productivity. It is no secret that some teachers even see the group as the enemy, observing that almost any pupil can be worked with on a one-to-one basis. In a classroom group, pupils learn parallel to peers, and "sibling" conditions may be reenacted. This may lead to competition, cooperation, or disaster. Competition for motivation may center on who will be finished first. You have free time when your work is done. For some this is a stimulant to achieving the task; for others it is the invitation to cheat, resist, mess up a peer's activity, or be humiliated by being last.

Obviously the group also is rich with peer "teachers," whether we like their curricula or not. Members demonstrate modes of behavior. Peer leaders may color the whole tone of a group. Groups are a social laboratory. Roles become assigned and the mores of the group sanction what activity is to be practiced. Can these group forces be turned to an asset rather than be a liability? Strain has edited a volume that emphasizes the function of normal peers as models and tutors and put the emphasis on positive interactions (1981). The peer group is seen as the largest source of reinforcing contingencies that can be utilized to foster cooperative behavior. SEI programs have utilized specialized group programs, a natural offshoot of group involvement. These range from problem discussion groups to activity groups where after school or during school time is set aside for crafts, plaster of paris, clay, wood, models, or what have you. The creation of the object is ego gratifying. Pupils have the opportunity for destructive cutting and pounding and constructive creation of objects.

Traditional classes have similarities and differences from groups designed expressly for therapeutic work. First is the selection of clientele. For group therapy, members can be selected to create an internal balance: no more acting out than can be cushioned by other members and the leader so that their impact is absorbed. Such internal group balance is difficult to accomplish in classes that serve the needs of schools with many more acting out pupils than passive ones.

A second issue in therapeutic group work is the type of leadership to be invoked. It is generally conceded that leadership is to be much less didactic or adult controlled than in regular teaching. There is the recognition of the confidentiality of the specific content discussed. This in itself induces freedom, and pupils (especially adolescents) "take off" on teachers, peers, or situations with abandon. Some school personnel get very uneasy at the thought of kids spouting off to a colleague. In group work done in schools, such cathartic expression must be closed off before the pupil returns to the regular setting. Other problems in group work conducted in the confines of a public school include the use of profanity, wasting materials, and treats. It is hard for the pupils to understand (and authorities to accept) a relatively passive adult leader.

A third issue is the use of group interaction. In some group-oriented counseling programs every social interaction is potential grist for the mill. Children and adolescents can be more open (which can often mean openly hostile to each other) than is easy for peers to digest. Peers have little hesitancy in saying devastating things to each other in classes or on the playground but anticipate adult censure; if this is not forthcoming in the group session it may appear permissive to pupils.

A fourth issue in school group work is the content of the group activity. Group discussion depends upon the verbal expression of difficulties, feelings, and solutions. With young children this is very difficult to maintain over any period of time even though it has been advocated for psychotic young children (Speers and Lansing 1965). Adolescents indulge in verbal talk as a pastime, but not all adolescents are talkers either. With the younger children, play activity or a crafts program is the usual content. The particular materials available are an object of importance, since some are too difficult, too stimulating, or too complicated for particular children.

Most groups, including special classes, go through phases. They have an initial status and role-establishment period that may result in areas of mutual chronic irritation and others of smooth operation. The group determines how they wish to use the adult leader, which may or may not be what the teacher intended. The hope is that there will be built-in gratifications in the group activity to use as a lever toward positive social relationships. As this happens, more of the feelings of the members are communicated and a certain supportive tone emerges. To be listened to, sympathized with, to lead, to follow, to be missed— all of these social potentials, feeble though they may seem, can be nurtured. The group method is oblique and does not anticipate rapid or clearly visible immediate changes of the pupil in the classroom unless the group work task is on the nature of self-control.

Redl (1966) has talked about the "invisible" group. Except for the autistic and a minority of SEI children still dominated by the narcissistic self-evolution, children are responsive to groups and their group image even when no group is around. Adults are often low powered compared to peers. One of the SEI professionals most sensitive to this is Paul S. Graubard (1976). He has shown that it is preferable to make any contingency benefit the whole group rather than resort to intragroup competitiveness. If all pupils are working at a given signal, the whole group gets so many points so that it pays to cooperate unless your personal motive is to foul things up. Social systems provide much planned and fortuitous feedback. One needs to know what the actual peer code is and what values are espoused in the peer culture. Youngsters clarify for their peers what is acceptable and what is not.

Formal Group Work in the SEI Classroom

One team of school and mental health experts, Anderson and Marrone (1979), have become convinced that a major emphasis should be placed on group therapy as part of the classroom curriculum and have produced tapes that portray the process. The psychiatrist or other mental health worker directly observes the classroom and together with the teacher maps out the plan. Teachers are given a short didactic course in concepts of child psychopathology and treatment. Then the psychiatrist demonstrates the group process with the teacher as a co-working learner. The teacher and a teacher's aide eventually conduct the daily sessions and the mental health professional continues to conduct a joint session once a week. There are extensive evaluation and planning sessions after the class meetings. The group has held several thousand such sessions with problems that have numbered less than the fingers on one hand related to family objection or breach of confidentiality. The tapes and booklets describing the program are available for professional training. Their ground rules are that the teacher is in charge; there should be "space limits," with chairs in a circle; and rules of operation, content and confidentiality are explained. Children and adolescents learn to use these media to deal with their everyday problems as well as their deeper life problems. Anderson and Marrone conclude, "In sum, after our experience with over 6,000 groups during the past 12 years we cannot imagine a program for emotionally handicapped students that would not fit the proven, cost effective methodology of therapeutic discussion groups in the classroom" (p. 15). This is a quality program, including a defined training program with a great deal of clinical input and the safeguards necessary to utilize this design in schools.

In the group process one starts by recognizing the importance of the *reason* for the group as perceived by the adults and the pupils. This may range from crises to a group brought together on its own initiative to discuss a common problem. The *substance* of the group experience also has many variations. There are simple talk groups, contact groups, play groups, activity groups, and specific therapeutic groups. Ground rules differ. Some use the group's intermember experience and anticipate insight. Others expect that the activity itself will carry the change. A third aspect is the leadership role of the adult. The range of leadership roles may be adult moralistic (planned or not) to neutral and facilitative or interpretive.

Sheldon Rose (1972) has a very clear, behavioral-oriented approach to treating children in groups. As he puts it, the goal is to get behavioral changes. Considerable use is made of contracts and assignments, but he goes much further with modeling and relaxation procedures to use with anxiety-ridden pupils. Attention is given to transfer of skills learned in the group to other settings. While the book is cast in behavioral terms, his sense of group life is far broader than this might suggest. The information is valuable for classrooms as well as therapy groups.

Zeeman and Martucci (1976) describe a special class for preadolescents using open-ended Glasser meetings as described in William Glasser's *Schools without Failure* (1969). Among the topics suggested are: "If you were principal, what would you do" (p. 176). If you had a million, "What would you do with your life?" (p. 166). "How do you make friends?" (p. 172). They found it very beneficial.

Leadership Roles

What do adults mean to pupils in a psychological sense? The roles may change moment by moment and differ for various pupils. Each role comes with certain social expectations and with distortions by pupils. One needs to appreciate one's personal relationship to the class—are we a peer, parent surrogate, or savior? At one time a teacher is assigning tasks, asking for hard work, and at another giving gratifications. He may be assisting the pupil at a self-chosen activity, giving requested help. He may be the judge of the "law" of the classroom or judge of a product a pupil makes in crafts, a recognizer of the personal accomplishment. He may be a policeman breaking up a ruckus, or a protector of a child who is afraid. Sometimes the teacher is the confidant or a parent–older sibling surrogate. Of course all of these roles are produced by the same teacher personality. In the analysis of adult role with groups in a therapy camp, when the campers were swimming, it was "watch me" and "protect me." In crafts it was "show me," "help me," "see what I made." On a cookout it was "give me now" and solve squabbles. In the study sessions it was "teach me."

Understanding Groups

Many classroom groups have a history and their own norms and relationships worked into a consolidated style of group life. They come to accept the behavior as the natural course of events even though there may be continual aggravation and pain for some members. A pupil's sense of being part of a group does not necessarily imply compatibility. If this is *your* group, *your* class, and *your* teacher, you feel you belong even if rejected. To be removed, even if scapegoated, is a psychological defeat for most children.

Some groups develop a style of internal scapegoating, called "playing the dozens." The mutual teasing and taunting of each other goes on with increasingly vindictive "mother" names, or what have you. When one member loses his cool and strikes back in anger, he becomes the legitimate target of all members who vent their spleen, hitting the hapless victim. Then the game starts all over again. Sometimes only those who "signify" (make clear their intention to play) are included in. A teacher may be surprised by the sudden outburst, not realizing that the game was in progress. Other groups gang up on the teacher where any weakness equals license to attack. Driving out a teacher gives one a feeling of power as well as anxiety; after all, adults are supposed to be able to manage such as I am.

New groups usually have a sequential development in relationships with the teacher as well as between members. At the start is a brief honeymoon, though the anxiety of certain members may be so high that this is very short-lived. Then there is the evolution of individual group roles. Often the peer culture values win out over the adult values. There may be overt struggles until a set of relationships is more or less accepted.

After the teacher has managed the more vigorous acting out behavior (often more than even some of the members can tolerate) the group often settles into a nagging, scapegoating, swearing, or name-calling period. They set each other off. The movement from such a plateau to more acceptable behavior is often very difficult to achieve, since the typical classroom contains children who are insecure, with low self-esteem and are easily defeated. The best escape from curriculum pressure may be disruption.

Redl (1966), a most prolific and profound writer in this area, has described twin phenomena of group life, "contagion" and "shock." Teachers recognize both in their classrooms. A youngster who defies the rules without any appearance of guilt and who has status in a group can start a contagion chain. When children act out, anxiety should result, leading to guilt, which generates a modicum of control. But in contagion, the opposite happens. When the peer leader acts out with the free abandon, the others are induced to follow suit. In the presence of the guilt-free leader, the anxiety of the group members is converted into heightened acting out rather than control; a junior riot can well take place. The usual adult control techniques have low power and it requires dramatic adult action to break the contagion chain. As the members keep getting higher and higher, each cycle of acting out produces more anxiety, which in turn is converted to more acting out rather than control.

Suddenly something may happen to break the spiraling cycle. Redl calls this shock. Perhaps the instigator goes too far. Perhaps a group member's guilt begins to act as a control damper and a counter trend starts. An adult may show such intense response that a reversal is set in motion. Suddenly the acter-outer loses command and in fact becomes the target of a "look-what-he-did" response from others. They relieve their guilt by pointing out his more extreme behavior. The whole tone changes and anxiety now leads to guilt, contriteness, and control.

The SEI teacher uses several tactics in such a situation. One is knowing the role of members in order to head off the provocateur before he really gets under way. A second is to insulate the group from contagion influence before it gets out of hand. Sometimes, at a proper moment, a teacher can induce shock. A show of teacher "anger" may bring the group back. The least one does is conduct a post mortem LSI.

A special problem is the introduction of new members to a group that has an established pecking order. The class may make the new member the temporary favored one or the scapegoat. New members upset tenuous power balances and friendship extensions. For this reason the teacher works through the feelings when the new pupil comes in and uses the manifestations for individual and group discussions to clarify feelings and build up possible understandings. Since entering a group usually produces anxiety, care has to be taken to help the new pupil without favoritism being shown. These phenomena take place when an SEI pupil is mainstreamed into a regular class as well.

Two other group phenomena are also common in SEI classroom

life. One is the segmentation of a total behavior episode into individually performed parts, with each segment relatively innocuous in itself and each suited to the role and inclination of the individual who takes the particular part in the group. But each piece fits in the jigsaw puzzle to comprise a total group act of an unacceptable nature. Yet no one really feels he has done anything himself since each behaves in a small segment within his own guilt toleration range. The group actions fit together so well that no one even recognizes how each plays his separate part. As the kids put it, "nobody did nothin' " even in the presence of the "nothin' " chaos. There are idea persons who act out nothing themselves but put the image of possible misbehavior before the group. There are those who are suggestible and ready to go along but not creative enough to have produced the idea originally. Another will flesh out a part of the action. This makes the next one do his part in completing it. No one feels guilty because no one "did nothin'." But the place can be in a shambles. Subsequent work with the group is necessary to unravel the event and determine how each part led to the next player. Children and youth must understand how they behave in a group and the influences of group members. The group life space interview is used to trace the development of an event and what each one did. The scenario is reenacted for insight. Plans for prevention are made. As each member learns his role (some discover they are the dupes of the others), individual sessions are needed for individual instruction. Peer leaders can be shown how to maintain leadership roles but in a useful direction. Taking away a negative role without replacing it with a useful role does not work well.

A final group process in special classes is the instant symbiotic subgroup. There is no buildup as there is in contagion. In symbiotic behavior, before a teacher can get a word in, the subgroup is at each other. There seems no way to prevent this instant interaction of the clique. Careful study of several of these interactive subgroups has provided a key to understanding. The members are children with similar or complementary underlying patterns. For example, a symbiotic subgroup of four boys were all found to have common instigating histories: rejecting mothers with negative responses to women; aggressive fathers whom they feared; mild learning disabilities, which made schoolwork difficult or impossible; and finally a deep sense of personal inadequacy and low self-esteem. Furthermore there was constant intrastimulation of the same dominant self-segments within each individual. When you touched off one area, you activated the individual pupil's other poor feelings as well. A common mechanism for improving self-esteem was to put down someone else. Since these pupils had so many areas of hurt, almost everything a teacher did (including being an adult) touched off a sensitive area, which when activated, aroused the other damaged areas. Being a woman, encouraging schoolwork, being directive—anything a teacher did aimed at one pupil would start the group cycle because it activated the hurts of all others with their similar problems. The situation produced instantaneous disturbances with no lead time for teacher intervention. Separation was tried, but they found ways to keep in contact. Intensive therapies with individuals and with the group were necessary to finally establish control. As they all learned about themselves and each other and knew why they were continually upset by each other, some control began to be possible.

The teacher spends considerable effort to induce positive elements in the peer culture. To improve the tone of the group life there are fun trips together (camping has been especially pertinent), good-time affairs, and parties for birthdays and other natural occasions, all of which produce happy memories to counteract unpleasant group history. Academic or extracurricular activities (such as producing a play), which require cooperative effort, aid in positive group life. Hobbs (1981) spoke of the importance of support groups. Much of the positive feeling in a classroom group is the consequence of how the individuals identify and feel about their teacher-leader.

The culmination of the relationships that come to characterize the human aspects of the special class constitute the tone. While this is a difficult matter to describe, when one walks into a classroom the tone is usually discernable. It may look like a battleground with the pupils viewing the teacher as the enemy and the teacher viewing the children as opponents. It may be a relaxed atmosphere with people working, or it may be a confused place with little coherence to what is going on. There are many unstimulating and perfunctory special classrooms. In another room, the atmosphere can be summed up as hostile. One class appears firm but friendly while another is aimless and wandering without apparent direction. The elements that constitute the tone of a psychoeducational program include trust. Pupils should know that the school environment will be responsive to their opinions and requests. It is a place to learn, and there are goals and activities with purposes and relevance. And it is an interesting and exciting place. The physical setting also contributes to the tone. Dilapidated surroundings, basement rooms, and sterile settings create an institutional blandness.

The way the adult responds is a basic element in creating tone. Take one specific example; some teachers have booths or cubicles. They are presumed to reduce the distractibility of both the anxious and the neurologically handicapped. One teacher calls these "cells" ("Go back to your cell and stay there until I tell you to come out"). Another teacher, with the identical physical situation, says, "Don't you think you should go back to your private office and work for a time until you get this finished?" In both cases the child knows he must comply and does comply, but certainly the respect for the pupil is vastly different.

Rotating Tutoring as a Group Phenomenon

Some classes are conducted by a teacher going from one pupil to another (or they come to the teacher's desk) in rotation. Perhaps the pupils are around a set of tables and the teacher goes from one to the next on a chair with rollers. Very clever? If you like the teacher, the sight of your teacher working with a pupil who is not you makes you want to keep her at your station as long as possible. It is upsetting when the teacher leaves to serve the "competition." One possibility is to play dumb to get more of the teacher's time and relationship.

Relationships and Discipline

Discipline is not a topic or a process of singular nature, though some have written using control as the basic core (Walker 1979). Discipline is a part of everything a teacher does. It includes the teacher's sense of authority and ability to set clear limits. Curriculum has to be relevant and within the capacity of the pupils. Teaching style is part of management. We expect many incidents of unacceptable behavior from disturbed youngsters but we do not want to induce such behavior by poor methods or curricula. Behavior modification contingencies, group and individual interviews (LSI) and counseling are involved. There may be temporary exclusion to quiet corners or quiet "rooms." There are external people to talk with the pupil. There is direct teaching of "self-control."

Handling of individual pupils must be differential, though group reaction to differential handling is hard to explain to youngsters. Pupils know how to play the even stephen game, meaning that given behavior should result in the same consequence to everyone. But children do know about individual differences in age, in problem behavior, size, strength, academic ability, and skills. Differential treatment can be accepted when that differential treatment is seen as relevant and in keeping with each individual's problems and prospects. This concept has to be discussed with the group. The teacher asks, "Is there any way I could better help you (meaning each one) with your problems? Since no two of us are alike I try to do the best I can for each one." What this suggests is a structure that is differential, not rigid, and infused with relationships. In contrast to legal consistency, psychological consistency is founded on the nature of individual children rather than absolute rules for a procrustean schoolroom. Equal treatment for unequal pathology is not equality at all.

We do everything we can to maximize the inner self-control (superego, conscience, values, socialization, etc.); at the same time a social order requires laws with social consequences for unacceptable behavior. Indeed, if our society were designed in this fashion, one assumes that most SEI children would have been prevented from learning their unacceptable repertoire. But there are many loopholes in real life.

To some, discipline equals punishment. The real function of discipline is to create conditions so that pupils learn improved self-control. Tactics necessary for securing order in an emergency are not to be confused with setting the stage for long-term learning of self-management.

1. *Teacher Personal Behavior.* Check out the possibility that the problem behavior may be, at least in part, a consequence of some improper teacher expectation. Or it may be something in the teacher's behavior that sets a child off.

2. *Limit Enforcement.* Limit enforcement depends upon support in the setting. A teacher cannot use methods in the classroom that will not be supported by those next in the line of command. It is uncanny how pupils sense any staff dissonance and exploit it.

Referral beyond the classroom teacher implies an overgroup person or persons and implies a working relationship—the "team." This team pattern may include such sequences as the teacher to principal to other specialist or the teacher to therapist. The sequence at certain junctures may include the parent and others. A supporting person should always be available or on call. The more immediately accessible the support, the less it is usually needed because the child finds no manipulative opportunity in the control chain.

The problem for the teacher is how to use the support referral process without at the same time losing more control than is gained. There are times when referral sets a limit and clears the air. All has been done which the teacher and pupil can seem to work out together and yet unacceptable behavior continues. The way in which the child is referred becomes critical. "We need some help with this behavior" differs from the implications of "I can't do anything with him—see if you can." Three-way conversations may be necessary. Pertinent others—both child peers and adults—may be needed. It may turn out that the teacher needs consultation relative to certain practices employed with the pupil. It may mean that the pupil needs more intensive interventions than can be given through the class setting.

The important persons in the child's milieu must share in the efforts to help. Some teachers see calling in help or contacting parents a sign of failure. If these things are done not as a threat or as hopelessness but as the logical next step after a real appraisal of the situation, referral should not represent teacher failure or a last-ditch attempt. Long (1979) has described the conflict cycle that often occurs in a discipline situation. A pupil acts out in response to a stressful school situation. The teacher observes the acting out and reacts, which elevates the problem situation. If the pupil is referred to an overgroup person (the principal), there is even more elevation. The principal supports the teacher and may well overreact. Now the pupil is in really big trouble, though the original issue was not that critical. Perhaps the escalation ends up with an exclusion and parent involvement. What Long points out is that the precipitating event itself is not that significant an issue, but vested interests make it so.

3. *Gratification.* The gratification level of the educational experience has a lot to do with the control potentials. If students like the class, control is available, which would not be true if the pupils wish to escape. Being sent out can be punishment or a reward depending upon the situation.

4. *Flexibility.* Limits and boundaries are, to a degree, permeable. There is unacceptable yet sometimes tolerated behavior, such as in language. Automatic reprisal systems are often not effective because they do not accommodate to the nuances of particular behavior.

5. *Unrealistic Expectations.* In general, we expect too much improvement too soon for most disturbed children. Change takes time, it takes the building of self-esteem and the generation of hope. Since our aim is maximized self-independence and self-management, we should not expect miracles.

The basic goal of discipline should never be lost. It is to facilitate a pupil's internalization of acceptable standards of behavior and development of strength to manage one's self. Self-control is the goal, but this is a long-term goal. Not all disturbed children have the capacity for incorporating the social values or the necessary performance capability. They will learn to approximate acceptable behavior because of external sanctions. Some will need special external support for a lifetime.

6. *Teacher Control of Emigration and Immigration.* The teacher is the major decision maker regarding both emigration from and immigration to the classroom. A pupil who is sent to someone else for problem solving should not be able to saunter back into the classroom after the session, using the send-out as a way to defy the very person to whom he must eventually comply. Send-outs, send-homes and temporary and permanent exclusions are not to be given a tone of punishment. They represent the fact that, at this time at least, the internal forces within the child and the constellation of control forces and support that can be put together are not enough to handle the situation. Sometimes a child will be able to gain adequate self-control through a time-out process or self-initiated seclusion in a special area of the room, an office, or in space outside the class. Other children would misuse such situations. There are children who never learn that we mean what we say until exclusion is actually practiced. They do not accept words as meaningful since their past experience indicated that adults did not match words and action. Painful and stressful though these lessons may be, the hope is that referrals and exclusions teach all parties something. (Brief emergency exclusion from the classroom or school is one thing. Cumulative suspension of over ten to fifteen days per school year constitutes a change of placement and requires an IEP review. For details see Grosenick, J. K. et al. [1981].) The child sees that his behavior will not be tolerated. This may lead to self-control with resources we did not know he had. Or it may be the opening to teach specific ways, short of exclusion, to cope with acting out. Here is where our counseling dialogues should be helpful. When there is persistent breaking through, more resources must be marshaled to help the child. Control and discipline actions are therapeutic interventions.

7. *Innovative Procedures.* Teachers continually search for new methods to teach proper behavior. For example a procedure to deal with very vexing symptoms has been described by Mandel et al. (1975) called reversing the problem behavior. Many maladaptive patterns are highly resistant to change, such as swearing, persistent stubbornness, and the like. Efforts to interfere make the adult a constant adversary. The proposal is to counter pathological fixations through their own strength. "Make your own rule" reverses the battering against requirements set by the adult. To illustrate, a girl who swore compulsively and continually had her language lesson in the analysis of the meaning of her profanity. The many meanings of a profane word were examined. The same word *shit* may have some sixteen meanings depending upon

inflections. Now these authors had considerable success in reversing the significance of the nonacceptable behaviors taking the problem and accepting it as a channel for teaching. Obviously, this will not always work.

Obscene language is a prominent issue with a fair number of SEI pupils. When the teacher gets involved, there is often much secondary gain to the pupils in contesting the teacher's limits. Rather than using punishment, positive reinforcement (bonus tokens) were given when the language responses during a given preset time period were within the limits set. The inappropriate behavior was satisfactorily reduced (Epstein, Repp, and Cullinan 1978).

8. *Maintain a Reasonable Degree of Structure.* The teacher needs the ego strength to set and maintain a reasonable degree of structure. Since certain children fight any set of requirements, the clear delineation of the limits can actually generate opposition. Such pupils will need serious, careful, and long-term discussion around this problem, for it may be an outcropping of their core pathology. But for most children, a set of limits that are reasonable and can be defended as appropriate to a school setting are a vast help to stabilize the environment. Taking sides for or against structure is superficial. All lives need order and structure. All environments need clear overt and covert structure. There are those who hold structure or rigidity as a value in itself. "Structure is good and permissiveness is bad" is spoken like the first commandment of special teaching. Used this way it is really a crutch or avoidance mechanism. If there is a rigid structure with no leeway, a rule for everything and the rule always expressed in an absolute form, the teacher does not have to interact. One calls on the ready rule to deal with every situation. As one teacher put it, "I have a rule for everything. If a new situation comes up I make another rule." This legalistic approach offers escape to those fearful of looking at the psychological meaning of an issue. The degree to which the group can participate in rule making differs at different points in group development, but possible participation is maximized. There can be tyranny when a group makes impossible rules. Rules should rest upon basic human rights and essential school requirements, they are not petty processes solely to make things easier for the teacher.

One of the longtime experienced special teachers stated his view of classroom management thus:

The children participate in setting up rules, regulations, and duties for the classroom. Their idea of how a classroom should operate correlates surprisingly closely with that of a regular classroom. They agree that not much can be produced in a noisy, disorganized classroom. They also found agreement on such ideas as lining up for recess and lunch, one person at a time in the bathroom, no chewing gum, classroom cleanup duties delegated to everyone, etc. Most all of the boys at one time or another violated the rules unthinkingly or else consciously to test to see whether or not the rules would be enforced to include them. Two isolation areas are set up in the classroom where the students can go to settle when they are overstimulated or upset. Some students request to be isolated because they can't work well unless they are in a low-stimulus setting, which the "isolation booth" affords. The student having some disturbing situation, be it hyperactivity, depression, instigation of upsetting behavior, name-calling, swearing, etc., is taken aside from the group where he and the teacher can talk privately. The incident will be discussed and then the teacher will aid the student in interpreting what the situation means to him and possibly the people around him.

The teacher needs a good sense of humor because humor is a most helpful device in helping the children accept situations, and of course the teacher is sometimes the victim of a joke, which is best accepted as such rather than an occasion to pass moral judgment on such an incident. Seemingly serious problems can be made to appear less serious and something they can cope with when they are able to laugh about the problems. Quick tempers are cooled when the humorous side of the situation is made evident. The students often discuss their problems together while working on art projects or when a behavioral problem affects everyone in the class. Their treatment of the problem is usually serious and candid and they are able to show good insight and empathy for one another. The group has become more solidified and group pressure is most beneficial in helping classmates adjust and conform to acceptable behavior.

If the students are unable to settle in the classroom isolation area, they are removed to the school clinic, which gives them a chance to talk to the teacher and/or the principal more freely and they can release their feelings verbally without bothering anyone. During these times they often pour out many of their problems and demonstate how much they want support and help from adults. If the student is unable to settle after being isolated in the class and clinic, and if he still refuses to cooperate, he is then sent home. Either the parent picks up the child or the principal intervenes because this introduces objectivity into the situation, which sometimes is loaded with emotional involvement between the student and teacher. For example, a child may feel that he is being treated unfairly by a decision made by the teacher; he can talk this over with the principal, ask for his/her opinion and receive an "official" decision.

Life space interviewing is frequently used to discuss problems, alter provocative behavior, promote motivation, and to increase the student's self-understanding and insight. Each child is apprised of the bounds of acceptable behavior in which he must operate; these bounds varied for each child depending on their problems and needs. Some boys needed more structuring than others because of their lack of inner controls. The boys who lack inner controls rely on the teacher; it is like an "ego lending agreement—having the teacher stand close to them, a hand on a child's shoulder, their touching the teacher's coat or keeping their eyes focused on the teacher for a look of acceptance or disapproval are commonplace." (This example is from the experience of Charles Heuchert, then with the Livonia Schools, Michigan. Currently Dr. Heuchert is a professor of Special Education, University of Virginia. He graciously permitted its use.)

No one expects instant change or quick personality reversals. After all if there were not deep-seated difficulties, the pupil would not be in the SEI class in the first place. Severe management problems of a continuing nature are legitimate reasons for complete restudy of a case and replanning procedures. When it is obvious that the management measures being used are not producing any real change, a new approach is necessary before resorting to futile efforts at repression. Possible models range from dynamic to behavioristic (Charles 1980).

7

Curriculum and Method

S AY *teaching,* and the image is pupils in a classroom doing academic
lessons. The last chapter demonstrated the critical role of style and
relationships in SEI teaching, but this is not in lieu of curriculum and
method. Here we concentrate on the third axis of figure 6. What do we
teach (the curriculum) and how do we teach (the methods)?

THE DESIGN OF THE LEARNING EXPERIENCE

Point of View

The psychoeducational model proposes equivalent attention to the
academic and social curriculum. SEI pupils are usually in need of both
affective and cognitive experiences, each with intensified and circumspect presentation. The psychoeducation position is that academics
alone are not enough but without substantive formal learning, school is
not school. The affective and cognitive are not separate endeavors with
periods for each. Together they compose one blend of experience.
Essential learning takes place in many settings—formal and structured
classrooms, free and choice periods, on the playground, at lunchtime,
in the whole school environment including extracurricular aspects and
through mass media and community living experiences. The average
youngster spends more time with the television set than the school
desk. The school is but a part of the social matrix where learning takes

place. Sometimes the power of the school to teach is overrated because of the time consumed in formal school arrangements. Unique restorative potentials reside in the total educational process.

Many SEI children (over half in our studies) are significantly behind in a variety of skills, some to the point of having virtually no competency at all. Other youngsters are functioning academically at their level of ability but not so behaviorally. Most SEI pupils will show deficits in both areas.

Academics are important not only in the skills and knowledge they contribute. School learning has direct therapeutic potential. To be behind, not to read, and to find the others mastering what you cannot leads to depression, low self-esteem, or rejection of formal education. Learning what normal children learn is one excellent—even necessary—way of counteracting emotional and social problems. For an autistic child the learning of life-survival skills is vital to increased independence. It is also true that children who have their major failure area around schooling respond more readily to special-education programs than a child where the central problem is in the family or some other nonschool condition.

A Brief Look at a Few Diverse SEI Models

It is instructive to examine a few models used in SEI classrooms. One is impressed by the variety of practice found in what are generally accepted as successful programs. At the same time, one is moved to ask How can it be that sometimes what appear to be oppositional designs work? Leaving aside the recognition that descriptions tend to emphasize successes more than dwell upon or even admit failures, there are several considerations worth having in mind in examining models. Our purpose is to find concepts to use in organizing a classroom and not to expect to find a ready-made pattern.

For one thing, pupils are flexible and have to adapt to reality. Pupils are also influenced by the belief of the teacher in what is going to work, just as the teacher is influenced by the certainty of the model's advocate. Then too, for reasons we have seen, a design will no doubt fit a segment of the divergent SEI population even though not all. It behooves us to be particularly aware of the types of pupils and severity of their problems. Age is another critical variable, most programs being oriented to the elementary pupil. We also know from previous chapters that there is more than one path to a given goal. The models do not always describe the degree of individualization that goes on. Teachers may not subscribe to the model one hundred percent of the time. During visitations this author has never failed to see a wide variety of practice and enrichment going on (as well as sometimes unfavorable teacher behavior) that had not been included in the scripture written up on the program. Settings also differ in the degree and nature of support for the classroom as described, a condition that is often ignored.

One looks at models for the substrata that are implicit. Every teacher is an educational philosopher selecting experiences that are deemed to be of value; the models represent a philosophy. Every teacher is an educational psychologist, selecting effective methods. Many special educators are not grounded in the philosophies of education and are thus subject to the fads of the moment. Kauffman (1980) points out we do not always know where we are going or why. (To explore these matters, see chapters five and six in Wingo [1974].) As to the psychology, the models may or may not be obvious, but they are based on one or more of the psychological channels we have indicated.

As the models are presented we do not intend a comparative evaluation. It is not a matter of right or wrong but a search for significant classroom organizing concepts. These are operating programs. The interesting thing about many of the designs is that there are integrated teacher-education programs incorporated with the ongoing pupil program (Morse, Bruno, and Morgan 1973).

One of the most rigorous designers of special classroom programs over the years has been Hewett. Starting with *The Emotionally Disturbed Child in the Classroom* (1968), he has continued to explore new formats and new possibilities (Hewett, Taylor, and Artruso 1969). Few have described the practical workings of the classroom for elementary SEI pupils as well as Hewett has. He has listed five levels of skills: (1) preacademic (sensory-perceptual, body coordination); (2) basic living (self-care, health, hygiene, safety); (3) communication skills (oral or verbal); (4) school skills (rules, three Rs, etc.); and (5) community skills (out-of-school adjustment, vocational, career). In their new work, Hewett and Taylor (1980) are less concerned with definitions and categories of SEI children than with their readiness for a given response level. What can the pupil do? To this end they have elaborated their six developmental stages. For each stage they have a series of curricular tasks. The first is *attention,* which has to do with perceiving the environment through a sensory modality. The *response* level has to do with motor and verbal response skills. These then must be *ordered,* put into form for school routines. The *exploratory* is investigating the environment, knowledge about it, and active participation in its ongoing activities. The *social level* includes both relationships with others and with the self. Finally there is *mastery* of core academic and vocational skills. For each of these levels the authors end up with a curriculum.

The engineered classroom plan is a generic approach since, in place of special education categories, the basis is the lack of readiness for regular classroom functioning. The organizing concept is to provide the pupil with an educational task that is at the cutting edge of ability, wherever it may be, considering current deficits. Never should a pupil be subjected to extended failure; one moves down the complexity level or the task difficulty to the level where the pupil can perform successfully. The special classroom has various centers: the order center with simple games to foster attention, response, and following directions; the exploratory center with arts, crafts, and science activities; the communication center where the activities require social interactions of a cooperative nature; and the mastery center with individual tables for academic work. Assignments are made to keep failure at the very minimum and a rich variety of materials are utilized. The classroom is highly structured and a check mark system is used with attendant rewards, but the organization pattern is developmental. His is essentially an educationally oriented program intended to get the pupil able to function in a regular classroom. Educational rather than dynamic diagnostic aspects are emphasized. Hewett was one of the first to produce special reading materials of high interest to adolescents with very low reading ability.

One remembers that each day contains many many minutes to be filled with useful experiences for each pupil. Children are great consumers of materials: Hackneyed workbooks and perfunctory worksheets will be used if a teacher has no other ideas. Creating units is a time-consuming task. While Hewett's program is highly structured, skill oriented, and uses behavior modification rather than the diagnostic approach advocated in the present text, the total school experience is broad. Some "double" classrooms contain a teacher and teaching assistant with a shop, crafts, and even a little "zoo" for a child to utilize during earned free time. He sees the need for a wide range of activities that are interesting to children.

Haring has been the leading exponent of precision teaching over the years. White and he developed a six-step program at the Experimental Education Unit, University of Washington (1976). First, general plans are made for the class as a whole, long range and immediate. This includes materials and instructional strategies. The second step is comprehensive assessment of each pupil's abilities and deficits. A noteworthy innovation is the utilization of materials for assessment from the actual proposed curriculum. From this, a precise analysis is made of the learning pattern and instructional procedures. One gets the impression of a rigidly organized system with specific behaviors pinpointed and item-counting each day with measurement the king. The pinpointing reaches even to the number of words to be copied or whatever on each task, charting the results on a graph, and then making changes in the teaching to increase the performance up to a predetermined level. Keeping the books on progress is no small matter. While it is true that the child is subservient to the system in these periods of specific academic training, the total program contains many activities such as crafts and dance and is not as confining as described. Albeit, the way pupils are viewed and the goals that are set are based upon the achievement graphs on the tasks, which provides a mechanism for specific individualized student curricula with careful evaluation. One of the important contributions of Haring's position is the breaking down of tasks into parts and giving immediate feedback so that the pupil knows results, even at times doing the charting himself. The specific task is made clear to these frequently muddled students. Because the units are at a level the pupil can do, success and immediate feedback are coherent. This is a very motivating condition for special pupils who cannot wait for delayed gratification.

Gallagher (1970; 1978) provides an overall plan starting with the job interview, then dealing with educational diagnosis and curricula, with an emphasis on behavior modification. To her mind, scheduling for each day is of prime importance. She advocates individual office work areas and starts the day with fixed work periods and teacher-planned activities that flow into more flexible periods and pupil planning. Her eventual aim is for teacher supervision of the pupil to be replaced with self-control and for extrinsic rewards to be replaced with natural reinforcement as the children become more self-sustaining and increased integration with regular classes becomes feasible.

There are literally hundreds of programs based on a behavior modification-educational tactics combination. Quay's work deserves special mention. He has a long history of theoretical and practical concern for special education of the behaviorally disordered. His diagnostic system is based upon a behavioral model developed from the screening device described on page 49. Behavior modification is applied to both social and academic behaviors. Quay and Galvin (1970) have developed a sequence for modeling social behavior with given steps from demonstration to role playing and trial application. This model is largely educational-remedial in content and method, concentrating on what the teacher can do in the classroom with educational procedures, again to get the pupil ready for the mainstream.

On what might be considered as the opposite role, A. S. Neill (1960) has spawned a number of applications to SEI special education. Three programs will be examined briefly in the pattern of the humanistic open classroom approach. It should be noted in each case that the teacher is very involved and unusually dedicated.

Grossman (1972) deals with work with very difficult delinquent youngsters. Here the belief is that kids can best be helped through caring and having a primary respect for them as human beings. The pupils described represent our most distraught center city youth. The central characteristic of this model is dealing with the continual crises that occur in the lives of the pupils. The youth are always living just on the edge of disaster. Thus the center of the program is dealing with the youngsters as human beings who are under great pressure. Schedules are completely flexible. Major decisions are made on the basis of staff discussion, each evaluated with great concern. The effort is to create a place, a program, and a staff attractive to these youngsters. The classroom included a combination recreation center-regular classroom. There was the gym, art studio, and shop in one section and blackboards, desks, and maps in another. One staff member was almost continually working out crisis problem situations on an individual basis. Things the boys needed so much, material things from clothes to allowances, were provided. Snacks and coffee as well as lunch were provided. Therapists and teachers were both totally involved. The curriculum had its skill learning, its geometry (and remedial work), but far more central were the life problems of the students, the discussion of personal difficulties, delinquency, and social jams they were in. A great deal of work was done with families whenever possible. Even the tutoring sessions were mixtures of task and personal issues. There were many trips and excursions. In this model the lives of teachers and pupils became very deeply involved and there were many relationship problems, which were sometimes explosive, as a youngster began to try to "get his head on straight." Gratifications are given on the basis of need, not earned for achievements. The pupil as a person is the center of everything; what he feels, his whole life, and any aspect of it comes into this school.

Dennison's (1969) is another in-depth approach based on a studied awareness of the life history of the pupils with an approach more humanistic than clinical. Dennison is philosophical in his orientation and discusses the application of both current humanists and Dewey. He worked from the inside out, waiting for cues from the children as he tried to help them master personal and academic skills. In many instances he is more permissive and goes as far as he can to allow pupils to work out their problems without interference. But he has a very sophisticated concept of adult authority. It rests upon the fact that children need adult help and they will respond to an adult who can really assist them. He sees the teacher relationship as a natural facet of human relationships and sees no reason to be an authoritarian adult.

Another example, and somewhat different, is the position of Knoblock (1982) who describes a school for very disturbed and autistic pupils. Playing down diagnostic conditions, he advocates a deep personal relationship and emphasizes process variables. His aim is to respond to the feelings and behavior of children, since true learning takes place only in the context of the relationships, and when the learner feels good about himself as a learner and person. The teacher role includes that of advocate in contacts with home and agencies. Considerable emphasis is put on group processes with the small classrooms comprising of both normal and disturbed pupils. Each person is to define himself and his own goals. And helpers (teachers) must respect pupil rights, view the learning situation as a community, and guarantee equal opportunity for the goals of each learner. The central force is the child, his self-direction, his expressed needs, and his own self-evaluation. Goal setting is crucial. Teachers are catalysts for the child's learning experience, which is to bring about personal growth whether through academics or other types of learning.

The interpersonal relationship aspect of teaching is a major component. There is an acceptance of emotional expression. Social and academic goals are indicated. The school is flexible and fluid with scheduling and structured routines of lower priority. The child is a self with goals and purposes and he finds that these include traditional skills. There is a mixture of both normal and special children in Knoblock's classrooms.

Close to this position and yet significantly different are classrooms that employ an in-depth approach rather than the existential position in the humanistic design. The product is a blend called educational therapy. The plan for the child begins with diagnosis of the youngster as related to normal developmental processes, as has been elaborated in this volume. The child's needs, drives, and defenses are a significant part of the picture. The teacher could be considered an educational therapist, using the school for all phases of corrective influence. There is a willingness to go into the affective life, but this is balanced by a clear image of trying to provide the best possible educational experience and a broad one. Work in the affective areas is not seen as digression or intrusion, but the cognitive experience is stressed for the cultivation of skills and knowledge.

There are several who have developed the current view of this position including Rothman (1971), Fenichel in the League School (1976) and the educateur program (Linton 1969). One of the characteristics of these programs is the team nature of the enterprise. It is multidisciplinary. Many pupils are inhibited in their learning not because of intellectual limits but because of unconscious motives. The combination of education and therapy leads to several premises: it is true that sometimes learning cannot take place without reduction of anxiety and fears, but it is also true that learning itself can be therapeutic and gratifying and lead to higher self-esteem. The most important element in these models is the teacher. These are not permissive classrooms, and rules are developed but not for arbitrary application. Rothman has listed basic concepts in this position: acceptance of all the child's feelings and attitudes without moral judgment; the teacher must help the child accept his feelings without guilt; all behavior is meaningful; alternatives to destructive behavior must be presented; the child, through self-insight and the teacher's help, makes decisions; and finally the teacher must uphold reality.

The educateur group developed an unusual design under the leadership of Guindon (in Morse, Bruno, and Morgan 1973). Her influence has expanded from the inpatient programs for disturbed and delinquent to the public school. Success with delinquents is especially noteworthy. The reeducation process takes place in a milieu with emphasis on the ego strengths of the children and youth—this in spite of their internal conflicts. The strengths are revealed by multidisciplinary team studies. Group roles and interaction receive equal attention, which gives the work a psychosocial orientation. The teacher's theoretical orientation is based upon the concepts of Erikson and Piaget. The four-year training for the educateurs is preceded by careful selection since this work depends on the individual's interpersonal capacities as well as skill in activity leadership and typical teaching. Supervision is intensive. The educational emphasis is around the discovery method but is unique in its evolution of understanding. One of the innovative curricula focuses on the historical development of man around basic themes such as religion, art, music, and work in each cultural epoch. The younger children work at their level on an integrated program of the various skill areas to understand these matters through stories, crafts, art, music, and dramatic representation. There are concrete products for a given historical age such as making clay dishes, preparing food, and making models as well as the analysis of how man evolved his life-styles in each period. They sing the music, do the dances, and write television scripts as well as do spontaneous drama. Skill subjects are worked through these themes, although special discovery curricula in skills (i.e., math) have also been evolved as well. In subsequent years, the older student rerun the cycle at much more sophisticated levels. The belief is that disturbed children must have help in putting their world together and this is one way, along with individual therapy, to help it happen. The school would make both the Harvard psychologist Brunner and the philosopher Dewey happy. This approach represents a very high level of psychoeducational synthesis. Here the teacher sees the combination of a concern for the special problems of a disturbed child and the educational process. After all, these are children with special needs because they are disturbed. We are reminded that even with the problems, teachers must seek the strengths to build upon and be creative in thinking through the presentation of curricula. The teacher plays multiple roles to integrate the child's life. Re-Ed, which has been discussed on prior pages, evolved from the educateur format. Western Michigan University has an SEI teacher-training program that follows this design.

There are other schools that operate specifically on the psychoeducational model, such as the Mark Twain School described by Laneve (in Long, Morse, and Newman 1980), which has as the heart a teacher/advisor who is the advocate, helper, confidant, and counselor as well as teacher for some ten students. They conduct small group discussions on in- and out-of-school problems almost every day with their groups. They also are trained to work with parents. While natural consequences are used, there is no punishment. The time, energy, and sophistication of the staff is the core of this program for adolescents.

The Rose School for elementary age children, operated in Washington, D.C., by Nick Long, is dedicated to the psychoeducational approach with very difficult center city youngsters. Long uses individual and group LSI and his concept of the conflict cycle to deal with the stream of behavior problems presented by these children. The crisis manager works through issues for therapeutic gain and social learning. There is an organized academic skill curriculum and socialization curriculum based on learning self-control. The pupils are seen dynamically as having severe school and life stress. Recognizing one's feelings is an essential part of the program. The relationship with teachers is stressed at an in-depth level. The Rose School comes to have a very generalized group meaning to staff and pupils. All areas of the curriculum are examined for innovative possibilities. (For examples of specific curricula see Long, Morse, and Newman 1980.)

Another interesting program for young disturbed children is the nurture class mother's knee approach for young schoolchildren in London, England. Following the ideas of Piaget, growth is seen as evolving from the child's interaction with the environment, which takes place through play with materials and objects, somewhat akin to a kind of spontaneous play therapy. When the play gets out of bounds in destructiveness, the teacher intervenes and sets limits in no uncertain terms until acceptable play resumes. The teachers do not push academics; they read to the children and as soon as there is any show of interest follow it up with skill teaching. Activities such as baking cupcakes are converted into a mother's knee activity. They all decide what they are to make, go to the store and purchase materials needed, and continue the process as one might in a home. There is no "cooking period," for the activity may cover more than a day. Natural arithmetic is involved in the measuring, counting, paying, and weighing procedures. The teacher's aides may bring their ironing to class. The children ask questions about what she is doing, what her children are like, and so on. Pupils may go to visit to see where she lives and see what her home and family is like. In this way they are straightening out their concepts of life, learning from the mother surrogate. Then they will have interest and energy free to work on the less personal tasks. It is also believed that parents must be involved, almost like a cooperative nursery. The equipment and program is tried by parents on parent nights. Parents also sometimes make equipment. Many mothers are overwhelmed by their problems, and a helping group for them works out assistance in the course of group meetings. The groups have professional leadership but are in no way typical therapy groups. They are informal clublike associations, which have as their goal working the mothers into natural community support groups.

In examining models one remembers that differences may reflect differences in clientele, age, or setting as well as differences in theory. Whelan's cycle (1977) starts with moving from unrealistic to realistic behavior expectations. He examines school conditions leading to failure and relates these to potentials. In a later phase, a plan is made in the hierarchy of skill learnings for teaching specific lessons. Then specific minimum progress aims are set, which are applied to the individual performance chart made for each learning experience. Progress is charted daily so that strategy changes can be made as necessary. The final stage is a review of the performance and child's reactions to plans for efficient new programs.

Since the hope is that many SEI pupils will return to the mainstream, teaching school survival skills is a consideration. In examining the successes and failures of pupils returning to the mainstream it is evident that returnees are often expected to perform even better than some of those who are already in the class. Certain skills stand out as reducing the risks. One is of course academically functioning well within the range of the classroom, so that the youngster does not stand out as needing a separate teacher preparation and is not seen as a "retardate" by the peers. There is also the need for independent functioning. The pupil has to be able to function with the minimum teacher support in the regular classroom. Anticipation of failure and "I can't do it" responses, disinterest in the tasks, and avoidance tend to bring on nagging responses from the regular teacher. Regular teachers anticipate that the pupil will be classroom conforming, and when not, an agreement with the pupil on what is to be done is needed. This is why some programs concentrate on "sit in seatism" to get them ready. At any rate, responding to the routines is a big thing in most classrooms if one is to survive. Following social conventions regarding peers and authority figures is expected. School survival skills are an essential curriculum strand.

Familiarity with the particular receiving educational system's curriculum guides and basic textbook series is essential for the SEI teacher. Sometimes these are adequate and appropriate. For those returning to the mainstream or already partially mainstreamed, careful attention is paid to the content to be mastered. Most often adjustments must be made. First, one teaches at the pupil's current level of achievement, which will usually involve remedial methods; second, special procedures will be needed for those with limitations in learning abilities; third, because of the confounding of past learning, much care has to be taken to counter expectations of failure and the defenses that have been built up. The rate, level, and expectations are in keeping with the individual pupils. Often continual informal assessment is needed to pinpoint skill deficiencies.

Skill Programs

The vast literature on teaching the basic academic skills presents no simple solution to the teacher in this essential area. Since many SEI students present deficiencies, even the teacher of adolescents must be prepared to start remediation at beginning levels. Methods are not unique to our students; teachers are expected to know the general methods as adopted to our clientele through their training course work. For example, there are schemas embodied in the various reading programs. Some build up from letters to words usually with drill. Others are more naturalistic, building skills around experiences such as telling or writing about a trip.

The essential sequence is to assess the level at which the pupil performs through direct diagnostic testing, by looking at the pupil's productions, or through diagnostic interviews. There are children still at the readiness level, for which Hewett has procedures. Learning the skills of how to learn (meta skills) is a developing area. Attending, listening, and remembering can be enhanced by specific training.

Once we know where the youngster can perform in any skill area, teaching can begin using one of the many sequential programs. Most school systems have materials, either through a text series or specialized methodologies. It is helpful if the skills are broken down into substeps and arranged to be as self-directive as possible. Already the movement is toward the use of the computer as better software becomes available. These sequences worked out with feedback loops. For most children the process is fun and corrections less painful than by a tutorial.

In an overall way, multisensory approaches are advocated especially for reading. Fernald (1943) and Gillingham (1960) combine seeing, hearing, motor tracing, and sometimes add touch. The pupil hears the teacher and himself say the word while he looks at it and traces it at the same time. With SEI pupils it is important that progress can be recognized, so active response on the part of the child is followed by active feedback.

While special attention is usually given to reading, reading is part of total language development, speaking, writing, and spelling. Few adults recognize the painful process that writing is for SEI-LD youngsters. It must have considerable utility to be worth the effort. The necessity of knowing numbers is increasing in this society. It is not only a matter of simple calculations: to get a drivers license it will be necessary to read, write (spell), and understand numbers expressed as distance.

Sequential programs for skill training are put out by almost every publisher of special-education materials. Science Research Associates publish the popular *Distar* series for language and reading. The American Guidance Service also has series, as do most major publishing firms.

It is interesting that basic literacy stops with the skills mentioned. Science and other informational areas such as social studies are far less explicitly organized.

There are now social skills curricula added to the other common skills. *Marathon* is one such social skills curriculum for adolescents, put out by Abt Associates after much research (Stanfield Film Assoc., Santa Monica, California, 1984). Filmstrips, games, and activities for individual pupils are incorporated in this lesson-by-lesson skill build-up. A somewhat different affective curriculum has been published for secondary SEI students by the Orange County, Florida, Public Schools (1983). Skills are specific: self-control, communication, problem solving, and behavioral interaction. Included are staff training materials and ways to engage parental cooperation.

The expectation is that there will be increasing skill teaching resources from readiness to job-getting skills, all adapted for computer teaching. At the present time there are already more computer programs than meritorious programs. But the revolution is about upon us and wealthy districts are already active. This means that SEI teachers will need computer competency and connections with the growing educational computer networks. There are programs that can save a teacher time in composing skill lessons. Pupils can generally be motivated by computer interaction in learning as well as finding educational games a reward.

Curriculum as Action-Oriented Therapy

It is recognized that SEI classes are often dominated by basic skill learning and knowledge acquisition. No one denies the necessity of these experiences, but a steady diet can be deadly. Because of their behavior, SEI pupils have often been denied their birthright to engage in the arts and in extracurricular activities. The curriculum should include all that we wish for regular pupils. Furthermore, the arts have particular therapeutic possibilities. The fascinating observation is that so many generally accepted curricular areas have therapeutic counterparts. There is art and art therapy (The American Art Therapy Association, Inc., 5999 Stevenson Ave., Alexandria, Virginia); play and play therapy; drama and drama therapy (McCaslin 1980); music and music therapy (Benezon 1982); and dance and dance therapy. Activity (games/crafts) becomes activity therapy. There is sometimes a certain cultishness around some of these special therapies and especially the training. The suggestion is not that every SEI teacher become certified in a dozen "therapies," but to recognize the special way these media can be incorporated to enrich and heal in the SEI classroom. If there are special therapists available to provide such programs, all well and good, or they can be consulted for ideas. But the goal is to incorporate these pleasurable experiences in the classroom and for the SEI teacher to have times of fun with the youngsters.

This is the use of channel "C" on the Intervention Model chart (figure 3). Perhaps the most astute expression of this concept is in a volume edited by Nickerson and O'Laughlin (1982) entitled *Action Oriented Therapies*. They include articles on expressive therapies including art, play, story telling and writing, drama, and music. Games and dance are discussed in terms of the physical challenge they embody. It is interesting that Piaget described the development of rules in games as part of moral development. There is no magic in these media per se; it is how we use them. To write a class play, produce the scenery and television tape requires creativity, language, social interaction, responding to the "director," and a myriad of exchanges, including role taking. Acceptance of social obligations may come easier in such a setting than from lectures on behavior. Sometimes a major project of this type can make the term. The Institute for Theater-Learning (173 Croyden Road, Jamaica Estates, New York) uses drama to build ego strength and then the "show" is taken on the road to "give" to others.

Dehouske (1979) discusses the adolescent who needs to talk but resists when given the opportunity. She uses original writing tasks, involving a writing workshop atmosphere with typewriters, tape recorders, art supplies, and notebooks. Many stories, with visual effects, are slightly disguised autobiographical works. She illustrates how it works with stories written about a "deformed" line amongst the straight lines and the Iron Man. Many pupils keep journals. Her final statement is an excellent summary: "However, the teacher must be willing to put forth a great deal of time, energy, and thought in order to listen to the students, decode their messages, and weigh teacher responses therapeutically" (p. 70).

One of the teaching methodologies that evolved from sociodrama and role playing is role reversal. We all behave differently in different situations, such as when given a leadership responsibility in contrast to being a group member. Sometimes this situational induction is humorous when we see a pupil play being "teacher" and imitating our ways.

The role of being an SEI person in our society has little to recommend it. The behaviors are anything but those denoting good mental health. They are consumers of service, always on the receiving end. They have to be "managed." They are "bad." There is very little natural practice of what we want them to be. Not surprisingly, if we reverse roles we can often reverse behavior, and they get to practice something new and desirable. This is why the privileges of being crossing guard, message carrier, or whatever are so useful. The major procedure has been cross-age tutoring where older youngsters help younger ones, or the older teach what they know to someone who is not informed on a topic they know. They become helpers—even of disturbed as described by Duggan (1978) where adolescents who did this were observed to develop empathic awareness (Lazerson 1980). We do not try roles where the chance of success is low. Some time ago, Rozelle Miller of the Maryland State Department of Education did extensive work in social studies with junior high emotionally handicapped. For social studies she used a "community" with various economic roles for the pupils to assume. Economic transactions between the banker, the oysterman, and so on were used to develop a sense of community and civic process. The tasks are problems designed to require certain interactions. She finds that the role enactment confines the overactive and induces expression in the reticent. She indicated both academic and behavioral progress from this methodology. A useful and comprehensive book in the area of simulations and games is by Horn and Cleaves (1980). Many of the theoretical sections and the over a thousand illustrations can be translated for use with children.

Minner (1981) describes the use of photography for therapeutic and creative ends. Constructing a slide-tape show has several steps starting with taking the pictures and then writing the script. Presenting the "show" gives the SEI group a chance to perform before their peers. He also proposes a visual arts gallery for the school. There are also examples of a class writing and taping a movie as a project with skill learning.

In truth, the first and continuing curriculum is the self, which can be the core of the curriculum. The first spelling lesson is one's own name. There are readers based upon the development of the self. We have already discussed the way language and literature can be used, teaching through fairy stories. A similar methodology is *Bibliotherapy*. Bibliotherapy is an oblique process and much akin to what has gone on in good English classes since time immemorial. When students read *Julius Caesar*, or any work of literary merit old or new, the discussion should have dealt with the essential problems and solutions that were depicted in the work. The problem might be of social organization or personal. SEI pupils recognize their own situation in appropriate stories and incorporate solutions that are depicted. There are now books especially written for various specific problems youngsters face (divorce, death, etc.) in addition to the many reflections found in literature (Creative Therapeutics, P.O. Box R, Cresskill, New Jersey 07626). Good source materials are found in Baskin and Harris (1977), Dreyer (1977), and Fassler (1978). Fassler lists literature related to fears and anxieties.

Physical education is a frequent source of difficulty to SEI pupils. There is a new synthesis of regular physical education and special education, with teachers who are dually trained. Once physical education becomes a success story there are dramatic changes—one person has written of therapeutic jogging! Usually competition is played down and individual as well as group games are included. A review of the therapeutic potentials of physical education has been prepared by Andrew Bennett (1977) with considerable detail on programs and research on effects of participation in sports. A government bulletin, *Recreation for autistic and emotionally disturbed children* (1973) provides practical suggestions for recreational activities geared to autistic children.

The importance of physical awareness and body management for its own sake is a significant area relative to self-concept. Body image, body control, and physical skills orient one to space outside the self. We have witnessed the growth of outward bound programs for adolescents, which are therapeutic programs based upon the contest with physical challenges. There are natural non-man-made dangers to conquer that provide healthy challenges. Jeff Flynn (Dexter, Michigan, Schools) bases a program for delinquent and disturbed youth on outdoor adventure because the environment is a neutralizer with natural consequences for all. Camaraderie, group problem solving, and accountability are utilized. Close to this is less strenuous therapeutic use of the camp setting where the high gratification of fun activities are coupled with group life and adult relationships, a milieu program but a positive placement (Gump, Schoeggen, and Redl 1957; Herr 1975; Hobbs and Radka 1975). Short-term camping during the school year is an alternative.

The Greeks valued physical skill in and of itself, as an awareness, pride, and concern for one's body's performance. The motor curricular range is very broad, from walking to dancing, from swimming to games and sports. Movement education replaces the old-style gym class. Geddes (1980) covers individualized physical education programs for all ages.

With many of her SEI pupils continually tense and over-stimulated, one teacher organized a program around relaxation training, a skill that everyone can use. The pupil practices tensing a muscle and then relaxing. All areas of the body are included. At the same time as the physical act, there is a cognitive component of imagination of a relaxed, peaceful condition, using channel D on the chart (figure 3).

A direct attack on the need for rules is not always the best approach. When her class refused to cooperate, one teacher decided to use rules for the games they devised. Since they wanted to play, she used the rules they set up (and often broke) as the teaching material. The fact that so many disturbed youngsters blow the games indicates our need to select activities at the particular level that our groups can utilize. They have often been denied participation because they are high risk and mess up the orderly expectation of a gym teacher. Some high-organization games must be delayed.

The teacher also uses game therapy described by Gump and Sutton-Smith (1955). It is possible for a pupil to be put in a low- or high-status role in a game. A bully can be regulated by the rules when he is "it" in a low-status "it" game. A low-status "it" game is one where the rules put the person who is "it" at the mercy of the others. An example is a scapegoat game, where the "it" can be teased and taunted. On the reverse side of the "it" role, an unassuming pupil may be given power in a game where he is in charge, as in king of the hill. In games, when the "it" role includes control of the game, imbued power is given to a low-status youngster who thus practices a new role in the social group. A high-visibility game such as baseball highlights and makes obvious any successes or failures. In addition, this game contains a lot of standing and waiting for every moment of personal action. In football it is often hard to know who is doing what but there are distinct roles. Tug of war is a no-loser game; even if your side loses, you pulled harder than anybody and have no personal sense of loss!

A teacher reported great difficulty every recess period when the class played baseball. In choosing sides the teacher had to "assist" the inclusion of all. Only one side had a pitcher who was not more frustrating in his wildness than no pitcher at all. To be "fair" the teacher ended up pitching for both teams. Thus he walked, struck out, or put them over for hits for each player. There was much overt expression of how fast or slow he pitched to "that guy but not me." He was also the umpire. At times, a very poor player needed extra dispensation to compensate for his inabilities. The teacher again had to decide how much to make it possible for him to hit. The teacher explained that unless he did all of these things the class would never have been able to play ball at all, but there was little time to work through decisions, interpreted by the youngsters as arbitrary. There was little playing going on. They went back to the classroom after recess with a high level of bickering. The teacher then would read them a story, an activity that they liked, to get them over their tension. Would a thorough prediscussion have been in order? Or should a less taxing game have been tried?

A teacher of junior high was taken aback to discover how few nonacademic extracurricular or community activities members of his class had experienced. They made funny noises in music class, quit the play at the last moment, wouldn't draw "right" in art, or boycotted the "naked" locker room in gym. To the able belong the opportunities in extramural and enrichment in school. When a youngster panics and won't play his part in the play opening night, once is enough. What teacher does not want a good show for the parents or other audience? Often these youngsters do hold together well, but when they don't we should be prepared. In the same way, the broader community acculturation through activities may be restricted.

A child may be kept in his own yard because the neighbors are afraid of the way he hits. The religious institutions may find it difficult to include him. The teacher organized an after-school program using scouts, a big-brother and big-sister program, got free tickets to community activities, and organized a camping expedition. He felt he knew his pupils better as people and had created bonds that helped in traditional classroom interactions as well. His first thought was that because he had found all of these good things for them, they would show their appreciation by acting properly. But it was not that simple.

This game-quality analysis should be applied to all methods we use to teach skills. A spelldown with one winner emphasizes competitive feelings not likely to be aroused when each pupil uses his own personal list for his own spelldown with everyone a possible winner. All the pictures produced by the class put on display generate a different role for the teacher and pupil than selecting the best one to put up each week. Reading aloud before a group is more visible than the same activity with one other child and the teacher. Being read to is a giving experience for teachers at all levels, and for most children it is not only pleasurable but it also engenders fantasy. Every choice of an activity and method carries psychological implications.

The major researcher on games who has studied every type from worldwide children's games to video games is Bower, mentioned earlier (in Shears and Bower 1974). He has evolved ways for analyzing how games work and what they mean to children. Incidentally, he first became interested in the topic while he was working with disturbed children, which is still his profession. One of his interesting ideas is to ask youngsters how a game may be changed to make it more fun.

The Affective Curriculum

SEI pupils, by definition, must have deficits in social and emotional accomplishment. For this reason, certain curricular activities focus directly on these problems. Brown (1971) calls this confluent education, integrating feeling and thinking.

There is a covert and overt affective curriculum. The covert aspect includes identification with the teacher and the many indirect group and individual support conditions we have discussed. In fact, this has been the theme of this book. We have already illustrated some overt curricula as in the case of teaching self-control. *Affective education for special children and youth* (Morse et al. 1980) covers the preschool, elementary, and high school ages, with goals related to the particular developmental period and an extensive list of programs, materials and methods. More recently an issue of *Teaching Exceptional Children* (Morse 1982) was devoted to recent theoretical issues and examples of practical programming. The application of affective education to SEI children was the subject of the Advanced Institute at the University of Minnesota in 1977 (Wood 1977). This publication illustrates the amorphous state of affective education in SEI teaching. Included are broad philosophical issues on the nature of normality, discussions of specific programs for affective development in normal youngsters, training methods for child self-control, and a classroom management and relationship program, all germane in one way or another to affective education. Some associate affective education with the psychodynamic approach. This is in error, since education of the affect is possible in many different ways, including highly behavioristic ones as already illustrated in figure 3. Affective education programs cannot just be pushed into the curriculum. When and what are relevant to a particular group has to be thoroughly considered because of the potential arousal quality of affective material for SEI youngsters.

One preference is for integrated affective educational work included in the normal course of events, such as found in *Fantasy and*

Feeling in Education (Jones, 1968). Here affective matters are incorporated into the normal educational experience by including how youngsters feel about what they are reading or doing. In fact the way we traditionally ignore the feeling side is as much an insult to complete learning as ignoring the cognitive. Most SEI classrooms are at least hip deep in affective experience of various kinds already, though much of the affective component is hardly creative.

Most writers do not feel that indirect teaching is adequate for these times. Cartledge and Milburn (1978) have made a strong case for teaching of prosocial behavior in a democratic society. The author says that at present there is a "hidden" curriculum having to do with social behavior and values in the media through drama and the news reports. They demonstrate that it is possible to teach skills of social interaction, altruistic behavior, and control of aggressive behavior. Modeling is the primary media. They also find that these behaviors are highly correlated with academic achievement. Some affective education programs are designed to "educate" pupils, while others are aimed at increasing the sensitivity of teacher. Various specific designs are reviewed by Morse and Ravlin (1979).

Affective educational programs have been criticized for their vagueness and generalities. Barclay and his associates (Stilivell and Barclay 1979) propose integrated affective education starting with a system of assessing the climate of classrooms and mental health status of individuals. It is argued that environmental press, individual pupil nature, and the intervention must be synthesized to make affective education more than hit and miss. By using their scales they believe it is possible to focus on individual needs.

There are many processes that will net affective changes, but it is particularly difficult to assign specific linkages. A review of thirteen specific programs found that over thirty concepts were used to describe the various affective goals. These psychological concepts included self-concept and self-esteem, creativity, locus of control, personality, empathy, causal thinking, self-awareness, and achievement, among others. The high-frequency goals were self-concept–self-esteem, acceptance of self and others, and awareness of feelings. It will be noted that some attributes were goals for teachers, most for pupils, and a few for both (Wagman 1977).

Four popular programs, "Human Development," "Developing Understanding of Self and Others," "Toward Affective Development," and "Dimensions of Personality," were subject to critical study by Medway and Smith (1978). While they point out that there are severe limitations in these programs, there is evidence of merit if they are used as the authors intended. The techniques used include the magic circle, where children sit on the floor in a circle with the teacher for discussions of their thoughts and feelings, which are clarified by the teacher. Another method is the use of units with stories, recordings, posters, and puppets. Problem situations depicted in stories and role playing are included. Another method uses a series of activities for each unit, which include a reading selection, workbook for responses, and group discussion of answers. The teacher maintains a nonjudgmental stance.

A stepwise sixteen-phase-program social-learning curriculum is available to develop self-identity and social adaptation that covers the self of the special child who is working toward independence in the family. There is a complete kit of pictures, charts, and guides in this material by Goldstein (1974). One hopes that the teacher will select and adopt from general programs and not kill the potential by a thirty-minutes-a-day course, here we go ready or not. This need for teacher selection and reworking is especially critical for SEI classes where there are so many unique conditions.

One of the few programs designed with a basic conceptual theory is TAD (Toward Affective Development), which will eventually have materials for all grades. The authors, Henry Dupont, a special educator, and his colleagues (1974) have a sophisticated seven-stage affective development model related to Piaget, and age-level competency. The curricular materials have been carefully researched and consist of audiovisual materials and stimulants for discussions. There is brainstorming, role-playing, and group activity. The teacher models correct behavior, reinforces correct pupil responses, and directs the student activities. Communication, group roles, needs influencing behavior, and the nature of values and value choices are emphasized. There are scales to evaluate development. This program actually came out of the author's work with SEI youngsters. Teacher training is part of his program, as it is in several others.

There are programs to improve self-concept, such as *One Hundred Ways to Improve Self-Concept* (Canfield and Wells 1976), but self-concept is so much a part of the person's totality that it is hard to imagine a specific curricular method that could accomplish this. Target programs are common, however, as one to increase self-responsibility for one's own learning in school (as opposed to the teacher's responsibility) by way of interviews and a self-scheduling system (Wang and Stiles 1976). There are certain target programs that SEI teachers may prefer because they are aimed at particularly common problems of SEI pupils: self-control, values clarification, and sex education.

There are several film series and curricula that are available for teaching social skills to adolescents: *Skill Streaming the Adolescent: A Structured Learning Approach to Teaching Prosocial Skills* (Goldstein 1980) includes social skills, skills to deal with personal feelings, and alternatives to stress and aggression.

The SEI teacher does not take for granted that given behavior will change following a teaching strategy. Many behaviors can be changed with relatively simple strategies, and others require multiple and extensive interventions. Self-control starts with the incorporation of the value to want to behave in a given way, and we must be certain the pupil really does wish to manage himself in the way we imply. This may take some deft LSI. Lip service to conformity is one trademark of the sociopath. When a youngster fails in self-control, this does not indicate that he does not want to behave, although there may be conflicting motivations of which he is not aware.

Sex Education as a Target Area

In a society such as ours, sexual aspects enter into life in manifold ways. SEI pupils will have an overquota of sexual problems. Attitudes toward sexual matters are an important target area in affective education.

One is reminded that there is no lack of sex education: certainly this culture provides messages. As Thurman and Yard say (1978), these random messages result in exceedingly poor sex education for the behaviorally disordered. Surveys show that parents and professionals know of the need but little is being done about it. Thurman and Yard's position is that this task should be met by parents and professionals together. This requires training of both, and the authors discuss the conduct of workshops for this purpose.

Until recently special children were supposed to be sexless, even though many of their behaviors stemmed from sexual problems! As with all other important areas of life, sex education starts with preschool and continues not only through formal schooling but throughout life. The significance of gender in a world with fast-changing and multiple attitudes toward differentiated roles is not easy for normal children. The use of sex for aggressive purposes, for relationships, and as a substitute for love is epidemic with adolescents. What to do about intimacy, contraception, and what used to be common-law marriage are issues for normal and special pupils. There are groups of society publicly espousing almost every sexual expression invented. Many parents model behavior that a teenager is not supposed to know about.

It is doubtful that the school with or without a program of sex education can counter negative social forces for all youngsters. But reasonable sex knowledge is a birthright. While youth now reach sexual maturity at an earlier age (12.5 for girls) and live in a sexually stimulating environment, Anastasiow (1983) states that maturation of the control centers in the brain follow two-and-a-half years later. Of the 1.1 million teenage pregnancies, one-half end in spontaneous or induced death of the fetus or of the mother. The live babies born are at high risk. He advocates starting at junior high with education concerning child development and experiences to ensure a recognition of the responsibilities involved in child care and recommends the FEED program for special-education teachers. This certainly should be combined with information regarding contraception and especially the psychological significance to both participants. The fact is that SEI teenagers with their tendency to use sex as a substitute for caring are especially susceptible.

SEI children are less able than normal children to recognize the emotional component in facial expression and do not pick up some of the messages on an informal basis. They need to be taught a considerable amount of what normal children acquire informally (Zabel 1979).

The preadolescent is very interested in the human body and how it functions, including reproductive information. Who teaches it is as important as what is taught. There are resources available to provide curriculum for special education such as the Iowa State Department publication, *Social and Sexual Development: A Guide for Teachers of the Handicapped* (1971). SEI pupils have all of the misinformation of the normal child about sex, and even more. Bizarre notions are common. For some children, their own pathology may lead to obtuse speculations, as with some schizophrenics. With others, their essential mixup is sexual as in the case of the fear of impregnation in some cases of anorexia. We do not expect that the traumatic sexual cases of incest, rape, and seduction are going to be "cured" by an affective education program. Nor are youth expected to stop just because they have information after they have become sexually active and have found the experience exciting. One youngster said, "I like it. That's why I do it."

Regardless of the societal openness about sex, every adolescent goes through the sexual maturation process for the first and only time. Sensitivity to sexual stimulation increases. Erotic dreams and masturbation often bring simultaneous excitement and guilt. The differences in various youngsters' knowledge base about sex is amazing; the range of feelings is even more diverse. Sex education, in addition to facts and exploration of feelings, is tied up with the capacity to care and form intimate relationships. Often special children anticipate rejection from the opposite sex. Films such as *Sex Roles: Redefining the Difference* and *Contraception* (from Media Fair, Vienna, Virginia) can be the basis of classroom discussion.

Kalma (1976) describes a program conducted for SEI adolescents. Because sex education includes both factual information and values, there are issues to which no right answer can be assigned. The topic should be presented only by a teacher who has rapport and trust from the students. She found many erroneous ideas, lack of information, misinformation, misinterpretation, distortion, and fantasies. There was considerable anxiety and anger. Topics were often personalized and there were some very frank discussions of their own sexual activity. The teacher identified the sources of anxiety and gave personal support. A great deal of choice was given to students concerning materials so that they were not forced to deal with material too difficult for them at the time. Films allowed passive absorption of information. Overall interest was high.

There are many resources for adolescent sex education; SEICUS, the Sex Education and Information Council of the United States (84 Fifth Avenue, New York City, New York), publishes bibliographies and information including an excellent series of packets covering almost any topic in this area. Macdonald (1979) has a curriculum and a report to aid SEI teachers. Body curiosity may be the interest rather than sexual behavior in the true sense. Masturbation may be a problem. Menstruation obviously can be a traumatic event. Whether they ask or not, clear explanations of birth and related matters should be presented.

Values Clarification

One of the most popular affective education programs is directed at values, a significant issue with SEI pupils. The implication of "teaching" even conservative values so concerns the educators that for the most part the attention has been directed to values clarification or learning about how one comes to value, although we inadvertently are busy in school all the time trying to inculcate various values. Thus discussion of what one believes, sharing, evaluating, and applying values are common school experiences. As we have seen, there are some SEI pupils whose problem is lack of values. In fact, the peer group often share their "nonvalues" quite vigorously. Adolescents tend to be pragmatic about values and behavior. Feeling that parents just don't understand, they have to cover up. For those children who have values but in a mixed-up context and are unclear about what they believe, value clarification discussions can play a significant role. While moral growth cannot be given in a course (Reimer, Paolitto, and Hersh, 1983), it can be fostered.

Kohlberg's moral dilemmas have been prepared for special children by Simon and O'Rourke (1977). These deal with feelings, emotions, love, and values; included are suggestions on how to use these ideas. Special children also have the problem of handling attitudes they encounter toward special people. It is interesting to see a group come to recognize that they are doing the same scapegoating within their own group as they receive outside.

Glasser's class meetings can be used for value clarification. It is difficult to think of a topic or problem that does not involve a moral or values issue. At least in SEI classrooms, values come up all the time. Values clarification exercises are presented in the classic book *Values and Teaching* by Raths, Harim, and Simon (1966). A more recent values teaching guide is McPhail, Ungood-Thomas, and Chapman's *Life Line/Learning to Care* (1975). Here the expectation is that awareness of self and others will actually induce new values.

Important psychological considerations related to values creation versus values clarification go back to our figure 3. Values result from observation of others and identification as well as modeling. Also, one extends the basic values one already owns to new settings by relating new conditions to old values already internalized, an example of cognitive learning. But this is not really creating fresh new values. When it comes to most SEI pupils, especially the sociopathic group, standards have to be set and enforced, hopefully eventually to be functional so that they will be internalized or at least abided by.

Drug Education as a Target Area

For adolescents and in some locations preadolescents, use of drugs, alcohol, and sexual acting out are three most alarming symptoms. Ergo, the school is expected to have programs designed to prevent or control such behavior. After all, schools teach driver education to make safe drivers, so it is said. Whenever the anxiety and guilt about a particular symptomatic behavior arouses the public (and rightly so), then the schools are expected to provide a cultural prophylaxis. Drug programs have moved to drug education efforts involving affective education. The special teacher recognizes that these practices that society wishes to curb in adolescents are not just adolescent behaviors; they are symptomatic behavior in our culture. Only adolescents are not supposed to be involved in these cultural practices yet. We live in a drug culture—which is legitimized, characterized by overuse for easy solutions to difficult problems and extensive abuse. Schools may find that as many parents as pupils abuse drugs. Schools may be in a setting where the heroes and adults with money are likely to be drug pushers or pimps. The work of Jessor and Jessor (1977) indicates that many "transgressors" are "normal" youth and implies these behaviors are not as atypical as some would imply. Community mores on these behaviors differ vastly in various locations.

It has been estimated that some 5 percent of the teenage population are problem drinkers and chronic users of drugs. SEI pupils are overrepresented, and it is good to remember that drugs play a medical role in special education.

Those who are to teach or educate in this area should be well informed about the drugs, their effects, local accessibility, and the names that are used in the peer culture, which differ from place to place. While the research on the effects of various drugs is not always definitive, the devastating social, educational, and physical consequences of extensive use are clear. Supporting the habit brings a high risk of engaging in delinquent behavior. The OD problem is one for which schools need to have a handling procedure. Detecting the pupil under influence in the classroom may be difficult at times.

When one looks at the consequences of using drugs, the differential diagnosis of possible causes for addiction can be begun. Drugs can enable a youth to avoid pain, feel excited, be part of a group, talkative, have high sensory stimulation, alter appetites, hallucinate, become apathetic, feel euphoric—to say nothing of making it possible for him to panic, become sick, or have seizures. The difficulty of policing is evident when glue or lighter fluid are available to children for sniffing. However, experimentation or trial out of ignorance have to be considered as well. A popular high school student responded to his anxious mother with the following considerations. He had tried the "mild stuff" on his own. Of course there was a lot of drug taking going on in school. Yes, they tried to get him involved. No, they couldn't. Why? Because he just didn't care to but he had a policy of live and let live. Yes, he was one of the gang but they let him alone about drugs now. Sociable, independent, forthright, and nonjudgmental, he kept his social role because he was an engaging individual. Not all teenagers are that fortunate or inner directed and independent. Recently it has been recognized that the most effective drug education is probably combined with interest in one's own physical body and in keeping it healthy.

The first question to ask is What is the relationship of the drug use to the self of the user? In this day of instant everything, it is not surprising that there are many youths who look for a fast-food approach to solving growth struggles. We ask if drugs are a substitute for normal gratifications in life, social contacts, and activities. Is there a particulr stress with which the person cannot cope? Is it rationalized as a spiritual experience? Peer pressure is usually a potent force. Drug education is the development of selective interventions based upon self-concept of the potential abuser. The amount of frustration and depression present in adolescent society is seldom recognized. Adults forget what it is like.

FIGURE 7. Aspirations for work may not be fulfilled.

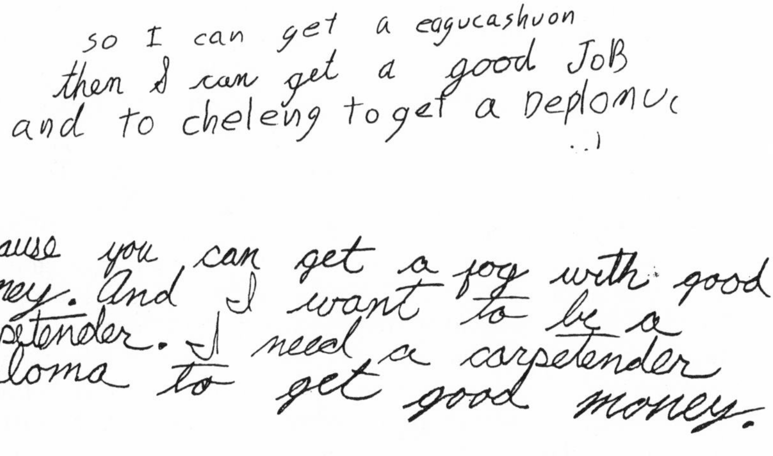

so I can get a eagucashuon
then I can get a good JoB
and to cheleng to get a Deplomuc
...)

Because you can get a joy with good
money. And I want to be a
carpetender. I need a carpetender
diploma to get good money.

Career Education

Many SEI adolescents are very aware of the need to find a place in the world of work. As illustrated by the two statements in figure 7, they face serious difficulties.

If we take the LEP seriously, career education has a role at childhood as well as adolescence, but a teacher will not expect pre-high school pupils to do more than explore the world of work. With adolescence, one's work goals assume dominance even if it is to be a long-delayed entry into a profession. There are a myriad of issues that bear upon this neglected area. It is just as important to prepare for a sheltered workshop final placement as for a more typical job. One's work becomes a significant part of the self.

As we will recall from *400 Losers* (Ahlstrom and Havighurst 1971), there is no magic in work that automatically solves SEI problems. Pupils foul up a vocational class as well as a history class, and the tolerance of their behavior soon wears thin. Rescuing youth who are on job placements requires a full-time effort. In one training sheltered workshop there was a crisis worker on hand both to make it possible for some to attend and to use the contentions and problems as a means of helping the disturbed adolescents come to terms for survival. On the other hand for many youngsters the job is it—you earn money, independence, and become an adult. Since having a job is so critical, many otherwise difficult youth do put forth great effort to do well and not blow it.

A comprehensive monograph is *Career education for behaviorally disordered students* (Fink and Kokaska 1983), published by the Council for Children with Behavioral Disorders of the Council for Exceptional Children (1983). Career education includes the many things pupils need to know about the work world as well as the specifically vocational aspects. Developing work values is included. The monograph covers all aspects of career education and includes model programs for various populations including the autistic.

One of the problems is getting acceptance in training programs for our pupils because they have both emotional-social problems and academic limitations. There are supposed to be guarantees for them built into the use of vocational rehabilitation resources. Yet many services for SEI have found it necessary to organize their own training stations (sheltered workshops or selected community placements) and have developed their own cooperative on-the-job training. Perhaps the single example of the full promise of such a curriculum is found in Shore and Massimo (1979). This and prior publications by these authors give the specifics of a community-based job placement training program for delinquents, who are a most taxing clientele. In addition to job placement, the program included remedial education and psychotherapy. The fifteen-year follow-up demonstrated the value of the program in the higher adjustment of the treated group over controls. The program was administered by one person, jobs were carefully selected for each boy, intensified individual learning was related to the job, and the therapist was available at any time of the day or night. The educational component included field trips, writing job applications, and accompanying the youth on the first job interview.

In vocational planning for SEI adolescents the concrete is emphasized. True, there are training stations, specific places to learn the skills. But the place does not a program make. The same problems that face an SEI pupil in academic studies are likely to be in play here. Motivation is usually higher and there is the concrete reward of an object made or a dollar earned. But pupil problems such as giving up easily, putting forth little energy, needing continual support, or not grasping the social interplay, can confound the situation here as well. The special teacher's skills for this area are the same as in other areas. Vocational training can provide the essential rescue channel for a pupil. One very disturbed adolescent girl found herself first truly "being needed" as a person in a sheltered workshop where she was part of a "production line." The Council of Exceptional Children has published a series of career and vocational education materials dealing with all elements of this expanded concept.

Some advocate special classes devoted to the study of careers throughout all school levels. Others would integrate topics in the regular curriculum. Reading can use vocational materials, and writing letters or reports on jobs can be part of the language curriculum. There are adequate resources available to make vocations a school subject. Career educators see this as a way to work on self-concept and self-esteem. Typical career education, just as all other education, will need to be adjusted for SEI pupils.

Although work world awareness is essential at all ages, by junior high and certainly in senior high, the prevocational and vocational side of schooling should be included. A basic curricular decision at this point is to what extent the pupil will be absorbed in the mainstream. Some SEI youngsters will end up in the professions and be able to use the resources of higher education as do normal young adults. Others will enter trade and business or sheltered workshops.

Adolescents require more vocational experience; other subjects and skill areas can be related to this goal. From prevocational exposure the pupil moves to practical direct experience in a sheltered workshop, a job placement, or the services of vocational rehabilitation for a career. Whatever the future, the adolescent must be given some way of earning money or independence will be low. Finally, with the LEP in mind, the proof of rehabilitation is for the pupil to graduate into the world of work, even if in a protected setting. With the changes in the economy and the increasing number of job seekers, it will take a great deal of effort to meet the goal of every special person employed. Transition to the world of work is the goal, and so far the record is poor.

CONCLUSION

The curriculum and method axis has been presented from both traditional and creative viewpoints. There are innovative ways to learn skills and there are innovative things to learn, but none of this in any way depreciates the specific methodologies that embody principles suited to SEI teaching. Much of what a youngster must learn will not be acquired by indirection or osmosis. The methods for teaching skills described earlier are just as essential as the creative phases. There is a lot of rote learning and drill as part of the school day to ensure that skills are learned.

As we have seen, there are designs for classrooms and specific methodologies that expedite the curriculum and method dimensions. While there are scattered research reports on efficacy of this or that program, for the most part the matching of pupil need and activity are still the responsibility of a teacher's judgment. The essence of teaching SEI youngsters is creative teaching, introducing innovative ideas that make the classroom an exciting learning place for all of the areas on face 3 of figure 3. The long-term solution to motivation and discipline problems lies in curriculum and method.

Teachers are constricted in experimenting by the possibility of negative contagion. When a pupil announces that he isn't going to work that day, would it spread? Meeting this head on with countermanding joins a battle. The real protection is insulation provided by activities of value to most of the class. Then the divergent announcement has less inductive power. When the instigator is of low status and the others are involved in work important to them, the announcement will probably be ignored. When the individual expresses feeling lurking just under the surface in the others, such a statement picks up followers. If the statement is designed to test the teacher's authority, the group may become an interested audience to see what the teacher will do. Regardless of the verbiage, the teacher behaves as if he or she expects everyone to work. Some pupils even do the first problem on the assignment while announcing that they are not going to do any work.

An integrated, multimodal experience involves children. Ecology from a book or even a movie is quite less moving than a direct experience in the actual world about them. Classrooms with plants, animals, and fish develop primary experiences. It is well to remember that no device will solve the problems of the classroom, or be easy to apply. But the oversupply of worksheets and mechanical exercises can be the bane of special teaching. Seeing the child bring in an animal or insect he has captured (even though he frowns when called upon to study the same thing in the classroom) or feeling the excitement over a play that is to be put on or an exhibit that is nearly finished reminds us that SEI children respond much of the time as do non-SEI children. In fact, the teacher may have to tone down the excitement or exaggerated expectations. Some respond to music and artistic experiences even more intensely than the normal child. Going to school is an indication of normalcy to the child.

Multiple-level units have solved a problem faced by many teachers who have a wide diversity of ability in the same class. If all learning was individualized there would be no group learning situations and pupils would miss an essential school experience. Dr. Milton Sakorafis (Hawthorn Center, Northville, Michigan) developed multilevel health units that incorporated tasks appropriate for the range from nonreaders to sophisticated students. The unit booklet for each pupil included simple tracing tasks, levels of vocabulary (from recognition to searching out dictionary meanings), and advanced topics for brief papers. Each student did what his level of ability allowed, but all worked together on the same booklet and discussed matters together. The more advanced students provided information from their individual work for the others. Those who read at a very low level were able to hear information at a more advanced level. An SEI classroom often represents the range of the old one-room school regardless of administrative efforts to ensure homogeneity. Group units complement the individualized work time.

Children and youth have a developmentally instigated curriculum as is described in *Teach Us What We Want to Know* (Byler, Lewis, and Totman 1969). This survey provides the topics that pupils of each grade list to be of personal interest. IEPs should also contain topics and skills that individual pupils have as concerns. The more relevant the tasks, the more interesting the presentation, the more the class will be on track.

For example, the goals of a program at Judge Baker Guidance Center, in Boston, were to improve self-control, self-esteem and social skills. Rather than approaching this abstractly, youth "practiced" making decisions around adolescence, getting and keeping a job, sexuality, drug use and abuse, and juvenile law.

The special class is replete with interesting materials. Individualization anticipates the widest variety of activities, which are sometimes self-administered. There are endless aids that teachers use, including computers, games, units, kits, and books to teach skills in language, reading, spelling, and arithmetic. Every teacher begins to accumulate a bank of individualized materials. One teacher had sequential worksheets for all academic skills.

The critical thing is to use all of the available ego for schoolwork at any time, but one is never sure how much ego is available to the pupil at any moment. Teachers become keen at telling the signs, even as a pupil comes in the classroom door. Today may be one of "those days" or one of those "other type of days." Teachers learn that this one can be kidded out of his mood and will then have energy to devote to school, while another will be in a depressed state for several days or a long period before he relaxes. Always encouraging but never overdemanding, always expecting but never being dominated by expectation, the teacher meets the situation moment by moment. This is the profession of SEI training. Making these continual decisions in a stream of events is psychologically draining. The pupil's position in the teacher's regard and in the classroom is secure regardless of his production rate. There is no hierarchy of the "first chair" where the director beams on the most proficient member, while the others are supposed to strive harder to catch up and overtake the leader. Thus, the teacher is after maximum production but does not resort to competitive devices with inevitable losers. Those who fear that the child will never have to face the reality of competition need have no anxiety; peer society and inevitable comparisons force competition, so there is no insulation from reality—only mitigation. As the pupil is able to cope with competitive conditions, he enters into such "contracts" on his own.

8

Teacher Roles

TRANSITION

THE SECOND FACE of the cube (figure 3) and the elements of figure 4 indicate that there are several settings where SEI teachers function. The range is from mainstream consulting to a special class in an institution. Different settings imply differences in role. Yet the diagnostic processes are the same, there is considerable overlap in clientele, and the basic teaching methodologies are similar. There is a naive assumption that a setting defines the program. We speak of mainstreaming, a special class, or an institutional setting as if this ensured what resources would be available. Theoretically different settings should generate different resources and thus have relevance for placement; in truth the variation in resources between two of any one type of setting may be greater than between different settings. There are good-quality programs and poor programs in each type of setting. The study by Leinhardt and Pallay reviewed on page 171 is germane here. In this chapter we first consider the problems in deciding the proper SEI placement and then the implications of various settings for SEI teaching.

PLACEMENT DECISIONS

Once a pupil is designated as SEI, the question then becomes Where is the proper placement, presuming there are options? This often ends up being whatever is available. Then the pupil is made to fit, even if the result is exacerbation and more costly interventions in the future. The range of possibilities should cover the cascade from mainstream to institution, with guidelines for decisions. In reality, few communities have an articulated hierarchy of settings. What should govern the placement service is a match between the needs the pupil has and the resources to meet those needs. How many interventions will be necessary to maximize the pupil's potential for growth? Where can these interventions be expeditiously brought to bear? These questions are guided by the IEP and, one hopes, the LEP. Some SEI pupils require total environmental control, others find solutions through intensified academic help. Where can behavior problems best be handled, in a regular class with crisis intervention or a special class? Is counseling or group work required? Intervention in the family? In a word, as we consider the multimodel intervention possibilities discussed previously, where can the necessary ones be applied? Where will there be the store of energy to make changes and who will be responsible? Of course it is not this neat. The cues for interventions may be incomplete and the actual settings may offer other than what is supposed on the administrative chart. Why are proper placements so hard to come by for a pupil? There appear to be a number of reasons stemming from our skills, philosophy, budgets, and diffusion of decision-making power.

1. Diagnostic studies are frequently inadequate, not providing the depth and scope of information needed to understand the pupil's needs (chapter 3).

2. The resources may not be available. What does "education" include in PL 94–142? Are there contracts with other community services? How many and what type of services are to be included? This is often a local decision with court action an option to expand what a district may offer. Particularly with SEI pupils, there is the matter of including therapy, which was discussed.

3. There is the question of who will pay for services. If the IEP does not stipulate the service, the school is not obligated, which means restricted IEPs are common.

4. There are philosophical considerations that often override psychological reality. PL 94–142 states that placement should be in the least restricted environment that will meet the child's needs and the least restricted part has caught the fancy of special educators, resulting in extensive mainstream placement. Not incidentally, the mainstream is also the least costly placement, with minimal service. Many special educators behave as if the less special education the better for the pupil, an interesting commentary on the profession. When a pupil or parent requests a class over mainstreaming they are incredulous! There

is also a tendency to classify all special classes and all institutions as "bad" for children regardless of quality of program or pupil need. There are regular teachers so negative about special education that they hesitate to make a referral.

5. The power of decision is split, which can produce strong conflict around placement. There may be disagreement over what services should be made available. Those few cases that cannot be worked out at the local level can become legal suits. The professionals define the services needed, the system decides availability and has to provide the money, but in the last analysis, if the parents disagree, it can become a court case after the informal processes of the district and state have been exhausted. This conglomerate of powers can cause conflict concerning where the child will be placed. Parents have the right to refuse the placement and/or the quality of service. While lawsuits are few in number, they are costly in time and money so that systems sometimes acquiesce even to plans their professionals oppose. When the courts mandate a service, the schools are legally bound by the decision though they may drag their feet. Someplace there has to be funding. At the national level and sometimes state level, the actual budget may be under the proposed appropriation.

Parents do and should advocate for services for their children: parent groups doing this are the allies of the profession, not the enemy. The rare parent who presses an unwarranted case or wants to send the child away for placement constitutes the price we pay in a democracy for shared power of decision. For the vast majority of the cases, there is no problem.

The power of the pupil is lowest in placement decision making. They may not even be consulted. Pupils do express their reactions however; in one way or another they react to what we do to them when we ignore their concerns. It never has hurt adults to listen and work through the pupil's ideas.

Youngsters may request a lawyer. The right not to have treatment (including special education) is still in limbo. All children in institutions must have their legal rights explained to them by a neutral person.

Three examples will illustrate the impact of being told their rights. One psychotic boy began to cry and ran to his school principal, whom he trusted most of all, asking why they were making him leave, saying "You know I got no place to go and I can't live out there." It took a great deal of reassurance to reduce his panic and misinterpretation. Another youngster, quite disturbed, carried his patient rights book with him and looked up any request made by an adult. If it did not say so in the book, he said he wouldn't do it (assigned homework is an example of this). This was a little difficult for a while, but it eventually worked out. A third homicidal adolescent, considered to be a virtually untreatable sociopath, went to court to get "sprung." He went back on the street.

A concept of the right to treatment is developing. A *place*—mainstream, special class, institution, or wherever—does not define needed treatment. A person must be given a legitimate remedial program. The essential argument is over what is adequate treatment, and punitive and abusive interventions are not an adequate program. The right to adequate educational treatment is also seen in legal suits for an extended school year and sometimes an extended school day. The argument is that pupils lose gains otherwise.

Special educators should not be dismayed over the problems brought by new rights and a redistribution of power. Especially, the youngsters should be given as much decision making as possible rather than have things happen to them on an external basis. Any teacher who spends a year dealing with pupil resistance generated by forced decisions knows that when a helper is not seen as a helper, treatment effort gets absorbed in contention. It will take time to learn how to deal with these placement issues on the problem-solving basis rather than roles, raw power, anger, or fear. We are evolving more humane and productive ways of making decisions in special education, which is well worth the price.

(6) Finally, money will doubtless be an increasing under-the-table issue in the next decade. School budgets are being reduced, regular teachers are reacting to the cost of special education, and there is an increasing tendency to farm out school psychological and social work services to outside contract personnel, which provide the minimum required by law for diagnosis and support at less cost than integrated in-house services. Also, if insurance will pay for treatment or institutionalization, this may enter into a decision, but when the insurance runs out so does the service, whether or not recovery has taken place.

Mainstream Placement

Often, all things considered, we are unable to predict just what placement would be best for a given pupil. This is why cyclic reevaluation is essential regardless of initial placement. But, as Gickling and Theobald say (1975), "Neither the results of articles which were critical of mainstreaming . . . nor the admission of methodological inadequacies within efficacy studies. . . . has slowed down the mainstream movement" (p. 317). We do know that SEI pupils are generally the least desired special-education mainstream candidates, since social skills are so critical in the regular classroom. Most advocates of mainstreaming think of the more mildly disturbed pupil. Philosophically, it has been held valuable for normal children to learn to live with SEI and other impaired children as a part of their democratic heritage (which, incidentally, adults usually avoid if possible). They will learn tolerance and humanitarian attitudes toward those who are different. But there is a wide range of reactions. Normal pupils have been known to express resentment over the undue time these youngsters get and the difficulties they present in "living together," even to disrupting learning. Some very empathic children reach out and try to help. Peer therapy can be the greatest asset or a time bomb (Guralnick 1976). The philosophical value has to be converted into a psychological reality. The youngsters learn what their actual experience teaches, not what a philosophy intends. We can include acceptance of differences in what we teach regular pupils. We can protect their rights as well as the rights of the SEI pupil, but it does not happen automatically. Thurman and Lewis (1979) suggest that response to difference by rejection and prejudice lies in early learned responses to differences and is not easily eradicated. Propinquity by and of itself will not solve the problem. We can take nothing for granted.

An interesting experimental study suggests that partial integration (in this case of the academically handicapped) may provide pupils with two reference groups (special and mainstreamed) and result in improved self-concepts. Those with only the mainstreamed reference group were found to have diminished self-concepts (Strang, Smith, and Rogers 1978). This again illustrates the subtle nature of psychological influences. School adequacy and general adequacy may not function the same way. Both mainstreamed and special-class pupils had significantly lower school adequacy self-concepts. However, only the mainstreamed group had a significantly lower general sense of self-competency (Ribner 1978).

The acting out emotionally disturbed child has been found not to contaminate other children in a normal elementary public school classroom, which is fear evidenced by the "germ" theory in mainstreaming (Saunders 1971). The exposure was limited. Certainly the character of the mainstream class would make a difference here. Special educators should take pride in their humanistic philosophical base, regardless of their psychological persuasion. We serve as a social conscience for the impaired. Still, mainstream placement is an individual decision, not a policy.

The Special Teacher and the Mainstream

One can start by asking So what is new? The concept of mainstreaming is older than special education, for it used to be "make it in the mainstream or out," no matter what the problem. In many instances pupils were physically present but psychologically absent and not part of what was going on, which is incidentally a condition that is true of many regular pupils as well. Some schools practiced "lifting" students from grade to grade regardless of achievement until the age of legally required attendance was reached. This was mainstreaming after the old style.

Professionals have advocated that at least a half of the SEI pupils should remain in regular classroom. The value of interacting with normal peers and using them as models is one of the strong arguments. A most comprehensive definition of mainstreaming is that by Kaufman et al. (1975): "Mainstreaming refers to the temporal, instructional, and social integration of eligible exceptional children with normal peers" (p. 40). These writers include the coordination of special and regular personnel in joint responsibility. "Eligible" touches off a quandary. The book *Mainstreaming: A practical guide* (Paul, Turnbull, and Cruickshank 1977) holds that the process, pro and con, must be understood by parents and the community as well as the professionals if it is to be effective. A special issue of *Exceptional Children* (1980, vol. 47) reviews the status of mainstreaming including possible misconceptions of the least restrictive environment, integration, and such matters as peer relationships and teacher training strategies.

Mainstreaming implies meeting the child's needs through the regular system, often the very system where he was unsuccessful to start with and even the system that critics have cited as the cause of the child's problem! If nothing changes in the system, will it benefit him to put him back in the polluted mainstream? Diamond (1979) says that understanding of special pupils and individualized instruction are myths about the mainstream. Some teachers and teacher's unions have objected to including special pupils in the mainstream even if the count was weighted three for each SEI member. They say that they were given too little practical help with these children both before and since the formalizing of mainstreaming. Sometimes their complaint is a lack of help for other "nonspecial" special children. When a system is rigid and will not introduce the flexibility to accommodate special pupils, it is a gross injustice to make hapless children the political pawns of confrontation. Hundert (1982) argues for the selection of the right candidates for mainstreaming and the preparation of the pupil for the experience. Thurman (1980) points out that mainstreaming is a serious issue because it affects *all* school children, not just special pupils.

Obviously, being separated from the mainstream can have harmful effects on particular pupils that outweigh the benefits of the special provisions received in a more specialized service. There are also the negative consequences of labeling previously discussed. In a recent study that replicates earlier findings, Gillung and Rucker (1977) found that adding the label to the description of behavior resulted in lower expectations by both regular and special teachers. The evidence is that the teacher responds differently to pupils labeled with any of the many SEI derivatives (Herson, 1974). There is an inevitable peer labeling process with such terms as *nuts, retards, queers, crazy,* and the like. These are often harder on the SEI pupils than their formal labels, which they may never directly know.

A "natural" regular teacher (she can help troubled kids—has a way with them) may be the crucial ingredient in mainstreaming. Schools should utilize such natural talent rather than mechanically force teachers to accept the SEI pupils. Regular teachers are more effective in increasing prosocial behavior of withdrawn children than in decreasing inappropriate acting out behavior (Weinrott & Jones, 1977).

Macy and Carter (1978) studied a variety of special pupils, including SEI, using small N-matched pairs as well as a larger general sample. The mainstream proved a viable alternative to special classes for most of the students. Teacher ratings on performance were equal, but the curriculum for the mainstreamed students was more advanced. West (1980) studied elementary mainstreamed emotionally impaired children and normal pupils matched in ability, sex, age, grade, race, and IQ. She found the SEI pupils were off task more often but usually quietly self-involved. They took more teacher time. Those who were having a positive experience themselves and in the classroom were perceived as well behaved, more on task, motivated, and relating well. The converse was true for the more off-task, conduct problem, and antisocial individual SEI pupils. The results suggest that limited ability is not the critical factor in the elementary classroom, but the more normal your behavior the better. There is a logical inverse relationship between sociometric status and aggressiveness (Hutton & Roberts, 1982). Younger children are more accepting than adolescents, and girls more so than boys. Also information about handicapped children facilitated positive interaction. Both aggressive behavior and highly bizarre behavior on the part of special pupils reduced the interactions. They conclude that mainstreaming required work with attitudes of normal students.

Some have claimed a violation of PL 94–142 in mainstreaming. Silverman (1979) holds that it is a simplistic argument to maintain that equal rights equals mainstreaming. Mainstreaming has limited potential; the SEI pupil has a right to his difference for as long as it persists. Special-education placements should not be overused (as in the case of minority groups) or underused (as in the case of the seriously disturbed).

Forness (1979) reviews the clinical criteria for mainstreaming the *mildly* handicapped. His list of "shoulds" includes being young and early in identification (against older and long term); the problem is mild and exists in the school context (against severe and pervades other ecological areas); the problem is in a single area (against multiple); remediation can be done without complicated materials; if the pupil has normal friends or ability to make them (against repeated social difficulties); if the regular classroom is no larger than thirty; if the regular teacher is willing and able and if the family is supportive. How many mainstreamed decisions could pass this test?

If we apply ecological theory to mainstreaming, a great deal of attention would be placed on the ecology of the person-environment fit (Levine, Hummel, and Salzer 1982) and less on the pupil's diagnosis per se. Curran and Algozzine (1980) found teacher tolerance levels to be an important consideration.

One does not separate a child from the mainstream on the basis of a diagnosis of severity of the problem alone; the case for separation is that his needs cannot be met in the regular setting as adequately as in a more intensified service.

Kendall (1971) examined the conditions for effective mainstreaming and the extent to which the mainstream educational programs encompass the needs of special children. Drastic "changes in curriculum and organization" will be necessary for effectiveness. Kendall holds that schools are notorious for rigidity although they are opening up. Mainstreaming is on a personal prescription basis. Regular classroom teachers will need training, available consultants, and aides. It is a social phenomenon, a matter of social integration beyond academics.

Among the obstacles to overcome are attitudinal hangovers. Traditionally, the SEI child was the responsibility of mental health agencies; teachers were not to interfere. Another pressure coming out of mainstreaming is that on classroom teachers with responsibility for larger and larger classroom groups, partly accepted as a way to increase salaries. There is inadequate money for on-the-spot aides and other assistants to individualize curriculum and interpersonal relationships. It is expecting a lot to add this to a regular teacher's work load. In some schools special pupils are double or triple counted in class enrollment figures, aides are added or increments are made to salaries. Note that any such procedure increases mainstream cost.

The hope is to obtain the best of both worlds for the emotionally disturbed child, somehow give him a normal educational experience and special treatment simultaneously. While we serve more children, we serve them less intensively and have a budget solution to the cost of mandatory legislation. Vacc (1979) says the best answer is to consider our pupils as unique learners, an extension of individualization. The sequence is (1) observing and prescribing a planned course of teaching, (2) establishing good rapport, (3) defining the reality of the life situation, (4) assuring the child that she/he can be helped, (5) praising, encouraging, and negotiating changes in the child's environment when necessary.

All of this is not to gainsay the fact that many disturbed children find a good regular school experience an oasis, a compensatory place from tribulations that they face elsewhere, often at home. Schoolmates can be a source of much good response and the school activities lend themselves to a sense of positive growth. Enright and Sutterfield (1979) see the behavior of normal pupils to special peers as a chance for both moral and interpersonal education. This certainly indicates the importance of a finely tuned general educational program.

We could reverse mainstreaming by having regular pupils go to the special class to help a friend (Poorman 1980). Stephens and Braun (1980) studied the willingness of teachers to integrate special pupils. Sixty-one percent were willing. Factors of confidence in teaching them, a belief exceptional children were capable of becoming useful societal members, and belief that the public school should educate exceptional children were significant determiners. Those who had taken special-education courses and were elementary teachers were more willing to integrate. It should be noted that there may be a self-selection factor in those who took the courses. Junior and senior high school teachers are also faced with subject matter pressure not always found in the elementary situation. There is some indication that rural schools are less accepting (Tonick, Platt, and Bowen 1980). Since the school attitudes reflect the community, we are asking the school to make changes and influence community attitudes, which is no mean task.

Alterations in the Mainstream to Accommodate SEI Pupils

There are many possibilities for change in the mainstream to make it more useful for special pupils. Certain administrative conditions can be altered to increase flexibility. This requires a reconsideration of the basic practices that have become sacred over the years such as time of the school day, special placement in highly selected classrooms, added curricular variability, and variable group size for given classrooms. When we make classes numerically equal we usually make them psychologically unequal. There is also double counting of the special pupil mentioned before. We are not suggesting that these variables in themselves can in any wise solve the problem of mainstream schooling for the disturbed child. What we are suggesting is that these variables should be considered. For example, some disturbed children cannot take a full day without disintegrating, but schools often have time rules that require a common hour of coming and going for each and every pupil. There are, in placement, teacher-pupil pairs that generate natural friction while other pairs are facilitating. Can we use the talents of teachers and take advantage of natural affinity? Sometimes teachers and administrators view reassignment requests as a sign of failure rather than evidence of insight about grouping. A pupil with a very poor reputation may even need an entirely new school opportunity to provide a fresh start. A junior or senior high student may be able to take the typical courses, but the rate at which he proceeds may be far short of his normal peers; two semesters are needed in place of one. The challenge to administrators is how many written and unwritten rules can be reconsidered? How different can the school become in order to serve the differential needs of SEI pupils? Rules and regulations made for normal children may ill suit the needs of the disturbed.

In work with a high school staff, it soon became apparent that almost every teacher had already gone out of his way to help particular "different" pupils. There are these self-chosen pupils who appeal to some facet in a teacher. The problem is to extend this feeling to all special pupils. The teachers indicated what they needed to help special pupils: specific handling plans, a benign place to send the pupil if he got into trouble, alternative curricula provided by special educators, decisions on differential grading agreed to by the whole staff, and ongoing consultation on the nature of the pupil's problems and handling.

1. *Control Backup for the Mainstream.* Especially critical for the regular classroom teacher dealing with SEI pupils is willing and omnipresent help when needed. This includes a chance for nonpunitive exclusion when that becomes necessary, for a few minutes, hours, or even days. This is not a primitive teach-him-a-lesson technique but is done with a view to both his temporary needs and long-term progress. Usually the school principal functions as the gatekeeper, although in some schools with a built-in clinical team the crisis teacher, the psychologist, or other worker may provide the help. Sometimes the pupil can work when out of the classroom; sometimes he may be very upset and need to talk out his feelings before anything else. It is most important that the second-level control person does not "split the team" by overidentifying with pupil feelings versus the teacher, thus becoming the "good mother" against the "bad father-teacher." Nor should the child be punished or chewed out. When exclusion is used in a power play the child returns with even greater anger and confusion than was present when he left.

There are other types of support that the classroom teacher needs. For example, the authority of the principal may be useful in moderating a parent inclined to severe punishment. Perhaps the need is to make certain school requirements more flexible and allow this particular child to be a patrol boy to help his sagging self-esteem.

There are regular classroom teachers who already have one or perhaps two children who are disturbed but not identified as special pupils. There are classes that already have a critical mass of marginal children, or the whole class may exhibit divergent behavior. At any rate, when there are multiple problems, the classroom operation needs to be altered before mainstreaming additional pupils into it. Group codes must be taken into consideration in such instances. Adjustment to the special pupil is a particular case of extended accommodation to individual differences to give the disturbed pupil a new lease on life. Many a school milieu could be overhauled and individualized to the benefit of normal pupils as well. There are resources in junior or senior high school that we need to obtain for SEI pupils. Some need double periods in shop or art where they can function reasonably well, but this "cannot be done" because of system rituals.

2. *Utilizing the Mainstream Teacher-Pupil Relationship.* The interpersonal reactions between the mainstream teacher and the special pupil are a particular concern. SEI children are more highly sensitive than most to the nuances of interpersonal interactions, some being

constantly involved in transference responses. Things that can be passed over and forgotten with most pupils must be worked through with the disturbed pupil.

The behavior of the typical disturbed child is not easy for a mainstream teacher to take without understanding the dynamics. This means the application of relationship phenomena from axis 1 (figure 6). Countertransference seduction will be tried on the regular as well as the special teacher. The regular teacher of the SEI pupil becomes a special-education teacher because of the presence of this pupil. All of this can be very perplexing to the regular teacher. You extend yourself only to be further tested. This the special teacher of the disturbed understands and this the mainstream teacher must also understand through consultation or inservice education.

While the teacher is as tolerant and accepting as the situation can permit, the expectation is still for the pupil to produce school-appropriate behavior for the most part. It is, after all, the mainstream and not a special classroom. If this cannot be, the pupil should not be mainstreamed. Most adults have particular situations to which they overrespond because of personal sensitivity. For example, one teacher may find it difficult to be rejected by a disturbed pupil. Another may find defiance particularly upsetting, or it may be clinging, aloofness, a temper display, or aggressive behavior toward peers. The behavior of SEI children can produce feelings of disgust, anxiety, helplessness, frustration, anger, or overinvolvement in a teacher. The pupil senses what it is that bothers the adult and engages in a contest. Thus the regular teacher must appreciate countertransference. Normal adults learn to control their interpersonal relationships to keep them overall warm and accepting. Tension may result from trying to help the whole class and at the same time help the disturbed child adequately. The axiom that underlies the right to give the disturbed child differential treatment is that every pupil gets as much as possible of what that pupil needs. Only when all are adequately served can any one be served differentially. While this sounds simple—to teach as he needs—it is often not the mode. The primitive sense of equality is to each exactly the same regardless of the individual differences. Equality means giving each as much as possible of what each needs. Unless this is done, the attention to and allowance for the mainstreamed disturbed child will upset the others.

3. *Developing Group Tolerance for the SEI Pupil.* The regular classroom is a group setting. What does it do to the classroom to have a SEI pupil? Gresham (1982) asserts that mainstreaming is postulated on three erroneous assumptions: increased interaction of normal and

handicapped, modeling of normal behavior, and increased social acceptance of the handicapped. The research refutes these assumptions. Gresham then describes social skills training, which is a necessary component.

Obviously there is no one answer in mainstreaming but certain fears seem unfounded. There are so many variables. Kounin, Frusen, and Norton (1966) put a great deal of emphasis on the regular teacher's capacity to manage behavior; if he is successful overall, he will also be successful with the disturbed member, and there will be less contagion.

Newberger (1978) emphasizes the self-concept in his paradigm for improving socialization, utilizing "a shared collective of teachers, parents, children, school officials and community resource personnel" (p. 120). He combines how the person thinks of himself, affective education, and interpersonal modes of the teacher and peers. A positive functional relationship is needed between peers to facilitate mainstreaming. Propinquity alone will not suffice. Nor will admonitions or hope for good will. Johnson and Johnson (1981), in a carefully controlled study, compared cooperative versus individualistic instruction in math. The cooperative procedure resulted in more interactions, more giving of assistance and encouragement (to the handicapped), and more cross-friendships and free-time interaction. There is a caveat: it depends upon the quality of the experiences that actually take place in the cooperative setting. If these turned out to be hostile or nonproductive, one could not expect method to produce magic.

The characteristics that are associated with peer status are of course a reflection of the peer mores. Aggressive, anti-adult hostility and threatening behavior can be highly admired and the source of high status. Educators are prone to think of peer values as being those desired by adults. Antisocial behavior can produce low status in "normal" groups. Gold (1958) found positive status is a function of expertise in relevant dimensions, physical attractiveness, and interests—all again peer related in substance. Novack (1975) shows that children can distinguish normal behavior from various SEI patterns. Aggressive and withdrawal behavior were viewed most negatively.

A series of very interesting studies on peer reactions to emotionally deviant children has been developed around the initial work of Marsden and Kalter (1976). Elementary-age children were able to distinguish levels of pathology. Hoffman (1976) found that liking and disliking are independent of the level of pathology. Normal pupils are apparently threatened both by aggression and regression. A study of the emotionally disturbed in a treatment setting revealed a similar picture with rejection being related to physical and verbal aggression and intrusive acts (Kaplan and Kaufman 1978). Trinka (1978) studied the language used in discriminations by children. She found children used terms that referred to general mental health status *(weird, crazy, queer, dumb)*, norm deviation *(crybaby, sissy)*, behavior *(bully, big shot, mean)*, personality characteristics *(selfish, self-centered)*, and inner feeling states *(worried, insecure, feels bad)*. Peer responses are a major concern in mainstreaming.

The acting-out disturbed child is most likely to produce a high incidence of peer relationship irritations. They are often embroiled with their peers who find them hard to live with. First off, the teacher's own perception of difference is likely to be communicated to the pupils. If the teacher feels the disturbed pupil has no right to be in the classroom, cues are sent out that pupils pick up. The covert feelings of the teacher will become overt and acted out by the peers, further alienating the special one. Sometimes a teacher feels the special pupil usurps the rights of the others. It is safe to say that if the disturbed pupil is unwanted by a teacher and that teacher is respected by the class, the pupil will be unwanted by peers as a consequence, even if he is not already rejected by them on their own.

The answer is not to say "he is not like us, therefore tolerate him," implying that he is a member of an undesirable subgroup. The more valid explanation is that we are all different in many ways—the special pupil is only a particular case of individual differences. The classroom is presumed to have gratifications for the regular pupil; there is achievement, satisfaction, and acceptance enough for everyone if the classroom is as it should be. Then the extra dispensation for the disturbed pupil does not deprive the others.

But an establishment of peer code of acceptance is not enough. It must be backed by the teacher's handling of the critical point of conflict. This requires understanding the individualized role the disturbed pupil plays in the particular group. It is not uncommon for a teacher to say, "Well, he finally got his. I've been waiting until they all jumped in." If such "therapy" is actually part of a design for treatment, that is one thing. If it is letting the peer impulses do what we would like to do ourselves but consider it too primitive, that is something else again. Just where does the disturbed pupil cause trouble? "He busts up our games." "We all laugh he acts so nutty." "He won't play with us." "He does bad things" (said of an early adolescent who masturbated openly). "He won't work so why should we?" "He says mean things even when you try to help him." "How can you study with him talking?" "He makes the teacher mad and we all get it." Unless the teacher does something about the specific behavior at the point of tension, pupils cannot be expected to continue to accept the different one. He will become a scapegoat. The teacher first uncovers the issue by helping the others express their resentment. Then at this point the teacher must step in with a tactic to reduce the intolerable behavior, even though the special pupil may not appreciate the action and even though such drastic steps as temporary exclusion may be required. But whatever is done and why becomes a plan to meet the condition, not punishment for bad behavior per se.

It is unfortunately true that disturbed pupils will also upset other teachers by their behavior, and the regular classroom teacher must intervene here too, again at the point of concern. Perhaps he cannot have the freedom of the playground, lunchroom, or halls at passing time if these situations cannot be monitored satisfactorily.

4. *Adjusting the Academic Tasks.* Mainstreaming requires the regular teacher to deal with the curriculum-method axis. By and large, disturbed children are academically retarded. Reading is especially vulnerable. Usually they require far more supervision than the normal pupil because they make more errors and become discouraged so easily. To the teacher who expects pupils to be on an academic assembly line with each station adding the next part in systematic fashion, the disturbed child's irregularity will be a particular problem. There is unevenness in what he knows and can do. Progress is by spurts and starts, days of absence may be frequent. Motivation is difficult. The axiom is to adjust and individualize the requirements to the level where the pupil can function at the present time. He may fluctuate, doing well one day but not for the rest of the week. When he is upset, the teacher does the things described for the special teacher, which take time.

To tailor the curriculum to the level of possible functioning may mean significant alterations, to the point of unrecognizability. Rather than the pupil bending to meet the set curriculum, the disturbed pupil requires the curriculum bend to him. Themes can be hard for a teacher to get excited about if each is on one topic—the Civil War, or hot rods. Since wherever the disturbed pupil is becomes a special class by virtue of his nature, techniques described in the previous two chapters are germane to the regular teacher too.

Further, usual evaluation procedures will have to be altered or ignored entirely for many of these children. This runs into school standards and the move toward competency level performance for graduation sometimes set by a district or even a state. Grading is a primary concern for high school teachers. Individual competency-based progress charts are most valuable. The teacher has control over the task, methods, evaluations, and relationship dimensions. If the ultimate flexibility is applied in these areas, regular classroom accommodation will be increased: this is the essence of mainstreaming.

5. *The Place of Clear Limits.* All of the discipline factors discussed previously are relevant to the mainstream. The regular teacher, even as the special teacher, needs control of classroom immigration and emigration to set limits. A clearly stated set of requirements can sometimes be established by the teacher alone, but participation of outside forces may be required as it would in special classes. Neither a punitive nor permissive design is the goal. While temporary outbursts will be anticipated and passed over, constant war on authority cannot be ignored. A shorter day or period may become part of the regulatory design. Often a place of retreat, a special space where the disturbed child can go, reduces distractibility and potential for upsetting the class.

One secondary school special educator developed a process, accepted by pupils and teachers, called "three times and help" to prevent hostile exclusions. When a pupil's behavior was deemed inadequate by the teacher, he was pleasantly asked to respond within the limits once, twice, and yet again. If he did not or could not on the third request, he was then to go for help to the crisis teacher. This was not exclusion, punishment, or a lowering of the boom. It was explained that he needed a different setting at this point in time and there was a place. After a possible solution was worked out, a three-way conference with the pupil, teacher, and crisis teacher was the road back. Both mainstreaming and separate special education for adolescents is a more complex situation, based upon the psychology of the adolescent period. Failure is devastating. Who wants to be different? Peers are going through a sensitive period themselves and are more protective. The volatility of this age group requires intensive planning with each pupil to provide the least provocative form of assistance.

6. *Mainstreaming Evaluation.* Evaluation is very difficult, with loose variables dominating the efforts. The ecological conditions are not the same, even in the same setting, for two pupils. Theoretically, if the match of needs and services is correct, the results should be positive. One does not evaluate a teacher of mainstreaming or a pupil; one assesses the system, and beyond that there is the ecology of the pupil's total life span and extraneous events. All of this is why the N of 1 technology previously described is required, emphasizing the match of the need profile and resource profile. The issue is really not what percent of SEI students survive mainstreaming or even what percent improve. There will be natural remissions and various external changes. The issue for evaluation is for whom and in what explicit

ways is mainstreaming the treatment of choice? Can we predict the conditions that will guide placement decisions?

A few studies have been mentioned in prior pages. Hauser (1979) emphasizes that there is no adequate conceptualization of the evaluation process to start with: both formative and component processes have been advocated. MacMillan and Semmel (1977) outlined an evaluation design including support processes used in the classroom, impact on regular pupils, appropriateness of the goals, and effects on the school professional personnel. Hauser supports these proposals but says that the conceptualization is complex and intricate, involving the social organization of the school. He considers several factors in an instrument called Victory: ability to carry out a program, values of persons in the program, information factors working for acceptance or rejection of the program, fears and resistance, rewards and benefits, and finally an assessment of benefits to all who are involved.

One aspect of evaluation is the impact on the regular teacher. Not surprisingly mainstreaming mildly handicapped students requires higher teacher involvement than with normal pupils. Much of this involvement, as one may anticipate, is dealing with behavior incidents rather than giving academic assistance (Thompson, White and Morgan, 1982). It might be helpful to note that certain student behavior has a lot to do with pupil mainstream survival (Bloomer and King, 1981). When the teacher is instructing, attend and do not scan the social scene. Not listening or interfering at these times is a blatant irritant.

Many evaluations of mainstreaming have to do with reintegrating pupils who have been in special services of one type or another. The Iowa group (Smith, White, and Peterson 1979) with a large sample of SEI pupils, report that during one school year a relatively high number from special classes were partially integrated. Most teachers (over 64 percent) reported no full-time integration. The mean number of students served by each teacher was slightly over 10; the mean for partial integration was a bit over 5; for total integration a bit over 1; and for more restrictive program referral, the mean was 1. Thus about as many went to more restrictive environments as were mainstreamed. Another important aspect is how the pupil feels about reintegration. If the positive self-gains outweigh the anxiety and fears, as the child sees it, there is better promise.

To conclude on a positive note, the National Institute of Mental Health commissioned a study of mainstreaming from the mental health perspective (Hughes and Hurth, in press). The major mental health concerns of the least restrictive environment provision of the federal legislation are listed as:

1. How teachers will deal with these mainstreamed pupils;
2. How the handicapped will respond out of their restricted environment;
3. How the normal and handicapped children will relate;
4. How parents of both will understand the reasons and provide support.

They found the mainstreaming fraught with both positive and negative potentials for parents, pupils, and teachers. Six model programs are presented in intensive case histories. The following factors were critical: all levels of the administration must give support; development takes time; change is most likely when planned from within; and a school climate of trust and mutual respect is prerequisite. Further, the model programs had community, administrative, and parent support. Prior to mainstreaming they had experimented with the idea. There was a full complement of options for special pupils. Communication was stressed. Mental health goals were emphasized and there was ongoing coordination with mental health agencies. Finally, the programs had adequate support. This publication also contains brief reports of many additional programs, an extensive bibliography on mainstream problems, and lists of resources on all facets of the work.

One way special education can make mainstreaming effective is to reverse the process of "giving" the regular teacher "our" clientele and "accept their clientele." Until we advocate the mental health services for all children both in the school and in the community we will perpetuate the special education cul de sac. Teachers need help for all of their difficult pupils, specially certified or not.

There must be some psychological intervention employed to help the special mainstreamed pupil beyond a seat in a regular classroom. A lesson can be learned from the recent life-streaming of persons from institutions for the mentally disturbed. When they were put back home, many of them needed extensive maintenance support lest they should end up on the streets. It is the unusual seriously SEI pupil who can find a solution in the mainstream without altering its nature and/or adding to the services.

TEACHER CONSULTANT AND RESOURCE ROLES

The mainstream teacher is too often left on his or her own with minimum support, which is not according to the theory of how things should be. The teacher consultant role is designed to fill part of the gap. There are a great variety of teacher consultant-resource patterns; sometimes it is consultant to teachers only and at other times it is combined with operating a resource room.

A symposium on the Teacher-Consultant model was presented in the *Journal of Special Education* (1977, Vol. 11). Little (1978) claims efficiency for the consultant and change-agent concept in meeting the regular teachers' needs. Hobbs (1982) has a vastly expanded concept of the teacher consultant as a community liaison agent.

Miller and Sabatino (1978) contrasted the teacher-consultant and resource-room approaches. Pupil academic gains were equivalent. Both were found superior to no service. With consultant help, regular teacher methodology was superior. The regular teachers became more accepting and increased positive communication with pupils. The consultant model was very time-consuming. While many consultants are itinerant, going from school to school "advising and leaving," the best possible design is to consult in situ as an integral part of what is going on in a school. Thus one participates in the responsibilities of the school and has a chance to know intimately the resources and limitations of the system and perhaps have an impact on the total ecology.

Sargent (1981) found that resource teachers spent half of their time in direct pupil instruction plus 16 percent of their time in preparation for instruction. General school duties, assessment, and consulting with staff were about 8 percent each. Regular teachers wanted in-service workshops, special curriculum materials, and specific help from resource teachers.

Evaluation

When it comes to effectiveness likely variables are the individual experience and competency of the resource-consultant teacher, the acceptance of the program in the system, and the time available to work with specific pupil problems as well as consult with the teachers. Sindelar and Deno (1978) reviewed seventeen studies on the efficacy of resource rooms relative to both academic and social development. While the results are not definitive in either area, this format did seem to be of advantage to the mildly disturbed for academic gains. The more astute the studies, the more effective were the values of resource programs. Using a control group in the regular class of LD students, Rust and Miller (1978) found gains in achievement in both.

Harasymiw and Horne (1976) point out that the attitudes of

teachers—negative and stereotyped—reflect the general public attitudes. In general the SEI group is lowest on acceptance, and within this, the psychotic are lower than the neurotic. They find that attitudes can be modified by in-service programs based upon knowledge, mainly by reducing anxiety of teachers working with designated special children. Modifying the underlying attitudes is a far more complex matter requiring:

1. Awareness of the teacher's dilemmas that are not part of special education, such as a load of behavior problems.

2. Direct *service* from the special-education resource or master teacher working with the pupil is what the regular teacher wants, not being given advice (Bussis 1976). But direct help to a pupil outside of class is only one facet of the condition. Observe the pupil in the mainstream and offer help for what goes on there through mutual interaction.

3. The huge current investment in training mainstream teachers to be instant special educators must be carefully examined. Short courses, lectures, information giving, and so on are not looked upon with favor by most regular teachers even on released time. The special educator does well to avoid moralistic efforts to correct negative attitudes. Offer what the teachers themselves request based on a survey. Information has a role but must be done in new and exciting in-service ways with outstanding materials, leadership, and considerable time for discussion. Giving the teacher a direct opportunity to work with special pupils co-teaching with an expert is perceived to be of more value than courses.

Resource-room teachers should know that their views and mainstream teachers may differ on effectiveness. Graham et al. (1980) found that regular teachers judged communication less adequate than the resource teachers thought; the regular teachers were more favorable to the potentials of mainstreaming; neither group felt that the regular teachers had the needed skills; and regular teachers were more positive regarding the availability of assistance.

The same difficulties face evaluation of effectiveness of these programs as indicated elsewhere. In group comparisons there are added variants in the teacher skills and the adequacy of the match of groups. There have been a number of studies dealing with resource room from LD and MR pupils with equivocal results. In one of two instances using control groups (Rust and Miller, 1978), the mainstream pupils made equal gains; in the other (Jenkins and Mayhall 1976), the resource groups were superior.

A careful effort to analyze how the resource-room format works was conducted by Glavin et al. (1971). This was a rigorous, behaviorally designed, specific skill-teaching program. The immediate results were favorable in both academic and social gains, but on follow-up in the regular setting the gains did not maintain. Sindelar and Deno (1978) reviewed seventeen studies of resource-room effects on academic achievement and person-social development. Few studies met rigorous standards. They indicate that above and beyond the technical problems of evaluations are diverse populations and conditions. For academic growth, while the results were mixed, there was support, though not necessarily for all populations. Attention should be turned from the question about whether a program works to for whom does it work and how. Kerlin and Latham (1977) concluded that a crisis-resource program had a significant effect on reducing inappropriate behaviors. Beare (1981) presents an interesting thesis. It seems that the schools scapegoat these youngsters who in turn blame the schools for their plight. The crisis teachers and advocates facilitate a return to calm after episodes, and are a resource to pupils, teachers, and parents. The survival rate and attendance of the pupils improved even through some parent values are alien and denied the pupil's problem. Changes in school attitude are more likely than changes in parent or pupil attitudes. The chances are much better if the focus is resolving concrete incidents that arise.

4. Acknowledge the bank of human resource for special education already in the regular staff—many do not need to be made over but need to be located. There is already a natural inclination of individual teachers to reach out to particular types of children. This constitutes a significant resource. Respect the regular teacher's professionalism by sharing IEPs and other information germane to their contacts.

5. Provide ongoing services, including consultation, backup assistance for crises, and specific curricular help. Teachers, especially secondary, have asked to have adjusted material prepared and brought in if significant changes are required in course materials.

6. Grading and passing are a problem, especially to secondary teachers. It is not enough to have a "flexible" grading system. The teachers need an agreement among the staff as to how grading will be done. One method is a set of minimum requirements for passing a given course. When these are met (which sometimes takes much longer than for the normal youngster) the course is passed. This minimizes the judgmental and personal tension around evaluation.

When any of the conditions of mainstreaming discussed previously are lacking, the consultant or resource teacher must find solutions. We will need to explore with the youngster how he will feel going out for extra help or working on material different from the others in the group.

Internal versus External Consultation

The teacher consultant role when one is a peer is very different from the external consultant coming from a related discipline such as psychology, where the different knowledge base and expertise covers over many a difficult situation (Meyers, Parsons, and Martin 1979). Admitted or not, most consultants work from a base of presumed superiority in the professional hierarchy. Thus in training to be a consultant, they are told how not to be overpowering, unconsciously arrogant, and the like. This embodies a covert presumption that the consultant does have knowledge and solutions that have escaped everyone else. A consultant who is really useful is coveted by teachers or parents. A special work dealing with educational consultation specifically is *The Educational Consultant,* which deals with all facets of the process (Heron and Harris 1982).

The SEI teacher as consultant operates from a relatively common knowledge base with the regular teacher. A mutual problem-solving approach replaces expert role power. In fact mutual problem solving should be the basis of all consultation. The first step is to work with the situation as the teacher sees it and attempt to provide solutions to the problems that are apparent. From there on in it is similar to any helping situation that follows the nature of the problem, wherever it migrates, in searching for a solution. The power resides in the ability of the consultation to help, not in the consultant role.

ACTION CONSULTATION: THE HELPING TEACHER ROLE

Consultation through direct service is a highly desirable option. A series of techniques have been developed to facilitate maximum support needed by special children regardless of placement, mainstream, or institutional class (Morse 1976). The original concept of crisis assistance evolved from Redl's concept of life space interviewing to assist the child when he was unable to function in a situation either because he could not cope with the learning tasks, the social situation, or both.

At times of crisis there is need for an immediate rescue provision, not later when the event has been dissolved by the passage of time. Time, for children, serves as an eraser.

Principals seldom have the time for involvement with pupils that they once did. Some are exhausted by hole-in-the-dike disciplinary actions. As the top authority in a school, they are still critical in setting the tone and climate of the school, being a backstop for the teacher, working with specialists and parents, and being an overall advocate and help for disturbed pupils. These matters have been detailed in *Classroom Disturbance: The Principal's Dilemma* (Morse 1971).

In the old days, before the paper avalanche, school administrators often dealt with the crisis situations. So great was the suspicion of the mental health approach that some administrators demanded a first look at all problems lest the soft headed mental health types ruin discipline by permissiveness, an echo of adherence to punishment as intervention. In actuality, the person who often takes over in the crisis in the principal's absence is the office secretary; some do an excellent job as a layperson and enjoy the activity. They can say things to youngsters that professionals often cannot. In secondary schools there is the vice-principal in charge of discipline who is the first line of defense in crisis time.

The new concept of crisis intervention is quite other then "discipline" or haphazard response. The crisis intervener converts problems into prime social learning events; is an advocate for all parties, including both the teacher and the child; serves as an ombudsman and sometimes as a consultant to the milieu or particular persons. The basic reason why a school needs a crisis clinic is that it is a group-work agency, with an adult-pupil ratio that does not permit extensive time of the person in the group leadership role (either regular or special teacher) to work through the incidents that come up with either regular or special pupils.

There are two types of crisis; the first is developmental. In the original work by Caplan (1961) the concept of crisis was that life periods of significant stress produce new conditions for which new solutions must be found. The basic life crises for adults are career selection, marriage, divorce, the birth of a child, the death of a loved one, a move to a new location, a change of jobs, and so on. Of course not all such events constitute an overload for all persons. Each crisis condition is also the open door for possible growth. This is somewhat like Erikson's stages of growth. With children, life crises can accompany growth cycles such as learning to walk, the birth of a sibling, use of language, and adolescence, as well as those induced by family crises. In a study by Yamamoto (1979), children rated twenty life events for stress. The most upsetting were loss of a parent, loss of sight, failing a grade, wetting in class, parent fights, and being caught in a theft or lying. The least were a new sibling, giving a report in class, going to the dentist, being picked last on a team, or losing in a game. In the middle were scary dreams, a new school, ridicule, and being sent to the office. Experts and children do not always work from the same list. These were normal children. Major decisions about vocational choices are fraught with tension. Relative to school, the first crisis is the initiation of schooling with an instant host of siblings (at all levels of socialization) and a new "mother" (teacher) who sets up strange expectations, and you can't go home if you wish to. Then there is the trauma of the first grade where usually fun and games are replaced by expectations of achievement, and comparative progress evaluation is implicit. At the third-grade level there is shifting from rote to more conceptual learning, which incidentally is also related to a physical growth cycle and now memorization (even if you could do it well) is not enough. Then comes leaving the elementary format (ready or not) for the more diverse environment of a school with many teachers, many more peers, and expectations for both independence and skill performance. Finally, there is high school, in which, theoretically if not in reality, a no-nonsense, get-the-work format is the priority. Of course crises come in children's lives from many other factors than school, and sometimes school is only where the problem is acted out more conveniently than at home or inside one's self. Developmental stages produce special problems for SEI pupils.

In addition to developmental crises is a crisis coming from a conflictual incident (which may at least in part overlap a developmental cycle). The crisis may be the result of the pupil's lack of experience in dealing with a situation or use of a self-defeating method. Redl (1959) spoke of giving children "hurdle help" to overcome an obstacle. He wanted a way to deal with life situations hygienically and utilize them for teaching more adequate behavior. Because of the problem-solving approach to learning through crises, it is not a matter of adults saving face but of analyzing a situation.

Crises are not new to schools. In fact some schools and some classes are crisis saturated and little else happens but one crisis following the other. Special classes and institutions have such periods. However, responses tend to be reflexive and punishment oriented. One asks after such an episode What did we assume we were teaching? Often it is obvious that we are expecting instant change at the cut-rate counter. Authority figures are often under severe role pressure to "solve" the situation, usually implying unholding the rules of the school, come what may, or defending a teacher, come what may. A crisis is evidence of some maladaptation, some lack of insight on the part of the adult or system, some demand put on the pupil beyond his capacity at that point in time.

Schools also tend to favor cooling-off periods ("Let him sit for awhile"). There are of course times when this is advisable. But in general, the time to interact is when the real feelings run high, when the raw emotions are visible. Cooling off also allows time for repression, and the real precipitating condition disappears into limbo until the next time. Often a youngster returns to the identical scene that produced his confusion after being dressed down. The adult who participated in the altercation may have to reaccept the pupil without having had any direct interaction with the pupil.

At a time of crisis the pupil has run out of useful resolutions to the dilemma and experiences an overload. When we are in a crisis most of us "tell more" and "respond more" than in ordinary states. We are, as Caplan and Lindsay (1975) say, more labile. The self-system is permeable at the point of crisis.

Crisis intervention is teaching satisfactory coping mechanisms using the generative forces of the elevated emotional state at that time to move past usual defenses to the heart of the matter. Diagnostically, times of crisis are very revealing of our inner natures, before the shade of cooling off is pulled down. Some crises are of the direct, explosive type. Others are of a slow burn, sustained nature, festering over a period of time.

There are unique aspects of crisis work with children. First, the crisis may be only in the teacher's perception and not in the pupil's. In fact, there are times when a pupil finds considerable satisfaction in an event that the adult sees as a crisis. The adult may be the target. Or the results of the act may be worth it to behave in a given way. In common with adults, children are prone to project the crisis, ("It's their fault"). Also, pupils are not always more ready to accept help in times of crisis (nor are adults for that matter). Regression is common. What this all amounts to is clear: there is no easy out with children and crises. It is as difficult as any other teaching process. The astuteness of the intervener is still crucial, and LSI is the technique. A helpful book for teachers is *Children in Crisis* by Cochrane and Myers (1980), which deals with step-by-step handling of anger and various emotional upsets in children that are resolved to the satisfaction of child and adult. Long's conflict cycle, previously discussed, is also most appropriate here.

Special school "crisis teachers" or team programs have been developed. They must know the milieu, be free to deal with whatever comes up, and free to trace down possibilities to wherever they lead. A person cannot defend the status quo or take sides or be afraid to confront malpractice. The basic process is to examine the situation from a just point of view.

Classroom teachers with disturbed pupils in their classes have been quick to point out that many disturbed pupils can manage the regular classroom *part* of the time but *not all* of the time, perhaps days or even weeks. But when the child cannot function adequately, the impact on the classroom is disastrous, requiring exclusive teacher time to work through the problems. If the issue is settled by supervision only, classwork can go on, but the child's problem is not resolved. If a pupil is excluded, and no one helps him with both the emotion and the academic frustration, all he does is cool off and return until the next bout. Teachers need a service that is always available for the pupil at the time he is in consternation. The resource, crisis, or helping teacher adds new depth to accommodation of individual differences in the school milieu, though it is not a substitute for close teamwork with clinical personnel within and without the school.

The helping teacher provides an immediate school rescue operation at the point of problem origin to keep the regular classrooms as free as possible from teacher-exhausting, group-disrupting conditions. Itinerant service is not a substitute: it must be available at any time without stigma or recrimination. The service is also useful for the withdrawn, unhappy, quiet underachiever who is failing to make progress, too.

The crisis teacher must know the curriculum at the school level served, must be steeped in remedial teaching techniques, and must be skilled in life space interviewing (Martin 1979). The program is usually conducted in a small classroom with a pleasant anteroom divider for privacy when more than one child needs immediate attention. Books, materials, and educational games of all sorts are at hand. The exact modus operandi must be derived from the specific needs of a given school.

1. Another specialist alone will not make the necessary impact on the school environment. The crisis teacher can be effective only to the degree that this effort is part of a total school milieu dedicated to the maximum understanding and help of the deviant child. All adults who deal with the pupil share in constructing the plan and evolving the strategy with the pupil. Frequently, after an encouraging start an im-

provement plateau is reached and then new plans must be evolved based upon a more complete understanding.

2. Referral procedures are the responsibility of the total staff. When a teacher feels that a pupil cannot be helped in the classroom alone, this pupil becomes a potential candidate for the helping teacher. This should not await a complicated diagnosis. The behavior in situ constitutes the referral. When possible, plans are worked out in advance. When this is not possible, the regular teacher may take the pupil directly to the crisis teacher and present the reality situation in a nonrejecting, nonmoralistic, but frank manner. The two teachers discuss sympathetically with the pupil the educational complexity at hand. The pupil's attitude about the referral are faced directly and the crisis teacher goes over possible goals. The pupil returns to the classroom only when he is deemed intact and ready. Teacher teamwork is clear to the pupil in the referral back process.

The crisis teacher does not have a regular class or constant clientele; pupils may come and go, sometimes on a more or less regular basis as seems advisable but often on a episodic basis when pressure accumulates. At particular times there may be more than one pupil in a joint session. There are always SEI pupils to be given individual help when there are no demanding crises.

3. What goes on in the special setting is determined by the pupil's problem. Children seldom compartmentalize their relationships or their quandaries. The interacting adult may take on a role of a man-to-man confidante, a parental surrogate, or a counselor as well as the general teacher role. Perhaps it will be individualized tutoring, an informal talk, a diversionary activity, or an intensive life space interviewing session around the feelings and tension evidenced.

In short, what is done is what any teacher would want to do were they not responsible for a classroom. The difficulty may turn out to be a learning frustration, an interpersonal conflict, or an internal feeling. As the helping teacher sizes up the situation, plans are made for immediate and long-term steps. Outpourings of the child's inner conflict are not unusual. It is particularly important that the child learn he will be listened to and that his problem will be considered, even to the point of initiating joint sessions with his regular teacher to discuss conditions. There are few of the secrets and confidentialities which some professional workers make much of at the expense of the exchange of information necessary to solve the pupil's school problem.

Referral is not seen as classroom teacher inadequacy. The type of problems vary with the school. For suburbia the pressure on the child may be for more academic achievement than he can produce. He may demonstrate his difficulties by learning inhibitions that have to be worked through. Moodiness, depression, and sadness around learning may be the cue. The unmotivated child and the far-out dreamer as well as the acting pupil are also candidates. The concept of a crisis-helping teacher cannot operate on the exclusive basis of certified pupils only. It must be responsive to all of the flack in the system.

Sometimes this service is considered appropriate only for the elementary school; such is not the case. The job is much more complex in a junior or senior high and communication absorbs a great deal of teacher time. Troubleshooting, finger-in-the-dike operations, and crisis sequences are a bane unless reasonable long-term plans are integrated in the efforts.

Blom (1966) used a modification of crisis intervention in a day school for disturbed children. The crisis person assisted right in the room where the problem occurred. If this was not feasible, a quiet room was utilized for a life space interview with the child, so that he could return to the classroom. The Rose School uses this plan.

Some pupils have learned to make self-referrals before blowing up. Having a central person one can trust is a great help in working out school problems and in extending the opportunity to discuss other difficulties. Even with adolescents, SEI vocational placements usually require intervention from a person like the resource teacher to keep it from faltering.

ACTIVATING THE SCHOOL-BASED PSYCHOEDUCATIONAL TEAM FOR DIAGNOSIS, CONSULTATION, AND TRAINING

Schools are experimenting with realignment of their special personnel. One method is Ruckhaber's (1975) early morning and noon miniclinic sessions, specifically designed to bring very prompt attention to any pupil of concern to a regular or special teacher.

Another proposal is for a local psychoeducational team operation, outlined in figure 8. Such a program includes a special-education teacher or two, trained to manage both learning and behavior problems; a psychologist for diagnosis and management help; a social worker who understands the difficulties of the home situation as well as how to help a child in a crisis. Other possible school specialists include guidance workers and reading and curriculum workers, as well as

FIGURE 8. Model of psychoeducation team function.

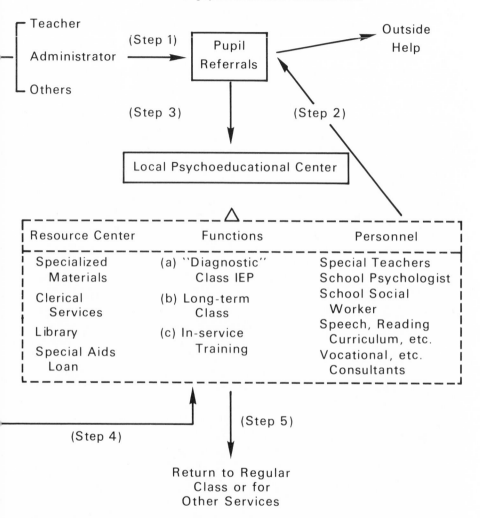

health and speech personnel. Finally, external neurological and mental health consultation is on call. This team is concerned with a pupil's behavior, the group process, and the total educational experience, not the pupil in a vacuum.

In step 1 the teacher, administrator, parent or others make the referral. A brief statement of the problem situation suffices. Referrals may have been seen previously by specialized personnel, since diagnoses are more common than actual interventions. In step 2 the team decides the most logical member to go to the classroom and observe the child as he functions in the situation where the problem exists. It may be that more detail is needed about the child's capabilities, and the psychologist would observe before testing. Or perhaps the pupil presented a severe learning problem and the special teacher competent for this category would be the first to visit. Personnel would actually go to the classroom and talk to the teacher and principal, but primarily study the ecology of the behavior. Many problems may be solved by steps taken at this point. If no strategy could be worked out over a period of time (such as placing the pupil in another classroom if special teacher-pupil conflict seemed evident) the pupil would come into the center *temporary* diagnostic "class." Here a special teacher would work directly with the child until the problems were in hand. Team functioning of all specialists brings to bear the knowledge of all the disciplines in this minimilieu where there is actual behavior as well as test data to analyze. The time might be brief or extensive, but the child would stay with the diagnostic class until he could be both managed and taught. It may prove a complex case soon referred to a long-term class or an outside sevice. Parents would be involved extensively from the start, but there would need be no labeling or categorization in this diagnostic service.

When the child is adequately understood and a design for educating and helping with his problems is evolved, step 3 is activated. The resource center would provide the special curriculum materials necessary (special readers, vocabulary devices, and so on). In many cases of learning disability it would be necessary to plan an extensive individual learning sequence. There are self-tutoring machines and computer programs that can be utilized. The plan might be a self-control course or a behavior modification program for home or/and school. Tape-recorded lessons, teaching machines, and other devices to individualize the work would be important to provide for the regular teacher.

After the team found a way to help a pupil, step 4 is brought into play. Here the regular teacher joins to work directly for in-service training with the special teacher and pupil until the new procedures are mastered. In the view of most school people, after diagnosis, present procedures are woefully weak in follow-through. Here the teacher does the actual follow-through after being trained. Certain children may be referred to other services rather than going back to the regular class, even as a first step if the problem looked that serious. More complete diagnostic studies, clinical analysis, and medical examination may be required. Parent involvement may be the crucial aspect.

A child returned to his regular class with his regular teacher does not mean the end of the team responsibility. Failure to function back in the regular classroom, regardless of the plan, means that the regular teacher needs additional help.

The next strategies would encompass academic, psychological, and ecological interventions. For example, suppose a child is given to outbursts of temper, exhibits a low frustration tolerance and a brief attention span. He disrupts the regular classroom. In the diagnostic class it has been found that this can be reduced if he is provided with special drill material since he has difficulty in assimilating the printed page. Temper tantrums have been reduced through life space interviewing at the center. These procedures are transferred to the regular class and things work out. On the other hand, a child who seemed dreamy and out of it might be found to be escaping a frightening life situation. The teacher can encourage involvement in classroom activities but the inner stress and outer press both must receive attention as well. Or a child with a severely pathological home situation and a long history of ingrained reaction may need a major therapeutic investment such as day school.

THE SPECIAL-CLASS TEACHER ROLE

Since teaching SEI pupils was the theme for chapters 6 and 7, the concern here is with the unique aspects of the public school special-teaching role.

The history of special SEI classes covers three phases. The first, born of necessity, operated on a pragmatic basis. Difficult kids were put with a tough teacher. Then came the first classes for emotionally disturbed, sporadic and struggling, highly diverse in style. Finally, phase three is the current status of classes as part of the legal mandate.

There were always pupils who, because of their behavior and alienation, could not be managed in the public-school mainstream. When mandatory attendance laws were enforced, something else had to be done besides neglect or exclusion. Homebound teachers might include some of these children if the pupils were receptive—but many were not. Delinquent and acting-out youngsters were often put in with the mentally retarded or sent to institutions for delinquents. Psychotic children were referred to state institutions, often put in wards with adults, or sent to institutions for the severely retarded child.

However, many schools did attempt to create classes for recalcitrant youngsters. It was not a result of diagnosis but on the basis of their symptomatic responses. The result was often a mixture of various disturbances ranging from psychotic to ego intact. Sometimes in the big cities, whole schools would be devoted to such classes. Minorities were overrepresented. Teachers were selected for their ability to "handle" difficult cases, often by physical force. One teacher put it, "Banging their heads against the blackboard a few times cures them." He also had actually pushed one "tough customer" through a closet door as an object lesson for the group. Of course there were also nonbrutal, well-meaning teachers, but provisions were often primitive. From one "ungraded" class they moved to the next until they dropped out.

Legitimate classes for the SEI pupils were late to be organized. In fact, until PL 94–142 there were states with no programs. Some schools depended upon school psychologists and social workers to treat these children, but most schools had nothing. Early classes were often permissive and sometimes based exclusively on an analytical orientation. However, a wide variety of practice emerged. In a study of the designs (Morse, Cutler, and Fink 1964) classes were classified as psychodynamic, teacher-based idiosyncratic, learning based, strictly educational, and primitive. There were some who believed that their pupils could not learn academics until emotionally cured. Others held that no therapy was needed—just remedial basics or punishment.

As states began to set up classes under the new legislation, standards were set for diagnosis. Many were planned for the "in-between," the psychotic being sent to institutions and the mildly neurotic being left in the mainstream. Expectations were for cures, often with time limits such as two years and out. There was an illusion of correlated independent therapy, which was not the case for over half. The essential working team was the teacher and principal, but for the most part, the teacher was on his/her own. Some schools used basement rooms to tuck the classes away. On the other side in the desert of confusion there were outstanding programs. Devoted teachers and other professionals performed the impossible. During this time, professional SEI teacher-training programs evolved and some state departments were giving support. But coverage was sporadic. Because of the particular split responsibility (education and mental health) and uneasiness about emotional problems, schools held back. Sometimes administrators left everything to a teacher fresh out of college to create a miracle. One administrator asked the author if it was OK to whip these kids as he did others. During this period many classes were developed and then died after failing to meet expectations. There was no eagerness on the part of sending schools to have pupils returned to their classes. Once gone never back. It was hard enough to get rid of them in the first place.

Pressure for special classes came from the mainstream—the same mainstream that is now expected to be the major educational effort. Teachers were being worn out by larger classrooms with increasing numbers of pupils who did not fit the typical routines. Special education encouraged the concept that special was different, requiring sequences of training that regular teachers did not have. Special teachers for special classes were to be the answer. With this history it is no surprise to find some regular teachers perplexed about the mainstreaming solution, now coming from the same experts! Most programs were developed for the later elementary age, when toleration for deviance lessened. Programs for adolescents lagged far behind, although there were some attempts (Long and Morse 1966). The final phase of special classes stems from PL 94–142. There are several logistical conditions that deserve attention in appraising special classes.

1. *Physical Setting.* Classes should be placed in schools with a high hospitality index for the program. In the elementary school, easy access to out-of-doors, washroom, and the principal's office are indicated. The room should be large enough to have the variety of corners needed, a crafts activity space, animal cages and aquarium, along with plants and places for individual work. A separate, teacher's glassed-in space for private conversations while still monitoring the group is important. A "quiet-room" space is needed though seldom used; if there is none the pupils sense the inability to control and exclusions are more frequent. These pupils consume large amounts of materials, so an adequate budget is needed. Access to television, computers, typewriters, taperecorders, and self-teaching machines is essential. It is interesting that regular children, seeing a well-designed program for only ten SEI pupils, sometimes ask if they can join. To them it looks like a very good place, which it is. Teachers differ on the value of independent desks versus group tables (or combinations), depending on the nature of the pupils. Team teaching and aides are an important consideration.

2. *Who Attends.* The largest groups for such classes include both neurotics and sociopaths with psychotics in the minority. There are diligent efforts to keep out the value-defective youngsters in some districts, but usually they are included in one way or another. The reactive syndrome should generally not be placed in such classes but often are.

The idea of ten as a magic number is unfortunate, since this depends upon how well a group functions. Aides are highly desirable but not always present. There is a real question of mix of pathologies.

However, grouping has more to do with manifest behavior and management than with the ideal. A significant recent development is the specialized public classroom for the autistic, preschoolers through adolescence with higher adult ratios.

Public-school special pupils are often as disturbed or more so than institutionalized children. Theoretically school clientele have supporting and workable families, but this is frequently not the case. Sometimes failures in institutional treatment are referred back to the public school, which legally has to take responsibility for all pupils. Theoretically the institution should be taking students when the home needs relief to survive or cannot be counted on to give adequate support to the child in working out his problems. The institutional pupil should need a total controlled milieu, which should not be true of the public school pupil.

3. *Supportive Resources.* SEI public-school teachers often say of the support provided that it is too remote and inconsistent. Too much is consultation and too little direct service ("Where were you when we needed you?").

Public-school classes are essentially educational enterprises, depending primarily on school resources and only secondarily on help from community agencies. A public school should not open special classes unless the basic school-related specialists are available.

Even with the rare consulting psychiatrist, few schools have the intensity of support needed unless school services are extended through use of all community services. For this reason working arrangements are necessary with a child guidance multidiscipline clinic and/or private practitioners. Take the simple matter of medication, which has been found useful in many cases. Without constant medical involvement, this would not be accessible to schools. Public-school special teachers are clear in stating their desire for regular, intensive consultation on educational programs and dynamics. They ask for help especially on group behavior and sometimes on their personal reactions.

The teacher and the "next in line," principal, constitute the typical working team. Others will be involved but seldom with immediate behavior and crisis management, unless there is a crisis teacher. The total backup process includes depth: it may be a quiet time-out place, referral for intensive therapeutic help, calling in parents, or even exclusion. It is not too much to say that the quality of a public-school classroom can be judged by the depth of support for the teacher.

The major initial problems in public classes are control and handling of aggressive behavior. Academic motivation and achievement matters come next. As time goes on the intensity of raw control problems should become reduced, but academic and motivational ones are still impressive. After a time, rather than fight, pupils bicker and resist more. In practice, classes are to have a restricted three-year achievement range, but this is very difficult to maintain.

At present, the majority of the time is spent in academics. Activities such as art, music, and gym come next. Considerable time, sometimes approaching half, is spent on group or individual "discussions" on discipline. Individualization is largely through workbooks and remedial programs. The school-day sequence for many of these classes closely approximates that of the ordinary classes for the given age except that for the high degree of individualization. Pressure for academic gain is felt by teachers, parents, administrators, and pupils. A major task of the teacher is to temper expectations with reality.

The typical teacher role in the public-school class often constitutes virtually the total service. Areas that in an institution would be handled by various disciplines are left to the teachers in public schools such as those overseen by the assessor, director of the academic effort, the tutor, the group leader, the counselor, the contact with parents, the discipline manager, and change agent for behavior alterations. Most teachers want so much more for both parents and pupils. Only about a quarter of the children and mothers (fathers much less) receive treatment while the pupil is in the special class. Of course there are those who do not need such therapy. The relief to parents brought about by the pupil's school success may be the first stage of therapy for the family. Even parents who may care little are faced with a social problem when their child cannot manage school.

4. *The Way Back.* The most effective solution to the way back to the mainstream is never to take the child completely out. However, some separation has occurred even if the pupil is "special" less than half of the time. Hewett (1968) advocated that the pupil always have his seat in his regular class, so that he is on "loan," as it were, to the special class. When the time comes, the pupil may be ready to return and want to return but fear failure. The teacher may wonder if he is ready and be ambivalent; after all his future success reflects on his teacher.

The return to the regular classroom is based upon the judgment of someone that the youngster is ready. This may be a clinical decision made by a team or one professional. The decision may be based upon better behavior rather than all-around ability (academic, etc.) to survive in the regular setting. The child's perception may be included or ignored. There may be parent pressure or political pressure by some part of the system. Smith, White, and Peterson (1979) propose particular elements: a summary of the original special-education placement data, criteria used to determine readiness for reintegration, responsibilities for decisions once returned, how the classroom (and teacher) were selected, strategies for continuation of the progress, and follow-up procedures. The road back is a process and not the decision. An excellent film done by Mason (n.d.) on the return of two elementary students is *He Comes from Another Room*. The politics of placement are often regenerated when reintegration is proposed. Sometimes there is a reluctance by the special teacher to let go. Termination of any therapeutic experience generates many personal reactions, as Redl (1966) discusses around the "threat" of improvement. Of course there are stages to return, or integration. Through continual but limited integration, the special student compares himself with the normal students, makes an outside friend, and knows other teachers. Minimum integration is on the playground, in special events and in the lunchroom, with special areas of art and music perhaps next. Regular teachers and classrooms should have the special-class program explained and be encouraged to visit.

It is easy to be glib about integration and the road back, but that would not be honest. There are times when the pupil has worn out a school before going to a special class. Reputations do not evaporate. The child may return to a very seductive atmosphere where he is virtually baited by old conditions. The care and nurture of the returnee deserves far more attention than it is given. It has been observed that the returnee often has to respond in a better-than-average way to be accepted again, such is the nature of psychological hangovers.

In conclusion, the most difficult special-education teaching role is that of the public-school special classroom. It includes:

1. Participation in screening and acceptance of pupils;
2. Set teaching skills along with the ability to negotiate for adequate resources;
3. Serving as an advocate for the child, pressing for help for the child and family from appropriate sources;
4. High-level teamwork ability. This includes not only the principal, but the school clinical personnel and community agency personnel. This means a knowledge of other roles in child intervention and vigorous equal participation as a teacher;
5. Ability to interpret the child's behavior to other teachers and to coun-

sel with them regarding "spillover" situations to mediate the school environment;

6. Ability to work with parents in many ways;

7. Consultation with colleagues to open up increased integration as warranted by the pupil's readiness;

8. Cultivating the return to the mainstream as soon as the pupil is ready;

9. Engaging in follow-through contacts.

Evaluation of Classes

The credit for the end of the primacy of classes for special-education pupils is usually given to Dunn's study (1968). Never has so much generalization resulted from one study of restricted variables on a particular population. Were there some who benefited a great deal and others not? Of course the changes were not singularly a result of this study; the study became the rationalization for the anti-establishment revolution in special education. The *quality* of the classes is the issue. If the classes were poor, who would expect many benefits? We must ask, also, are the classes meeting the individual needs specified in the diagnostic study and the IEP?

Vacc (1968; 1972) has assessed the efficacy of the special class versus the mainstream. He found the special-class SEI students made more academic and social gains. The disturbed children in the regular class were also less well accepted. In a follow-up study the advantages were not significant after a return to the mainstream. Kent and O'Leary (1976) did an interesting study with first graders with conduct problems who were randomly assigned to a special class or the mainstream. Both groups improved significantly on observed and rated behavior. The special group did do better academically, but many of the gains were lost on their return to the mainstream. They question the value of the special classes for other than severely handicapped.

In a survey of special classes based on teacher perceptions (Morse, Cutler, and Fink 1964) teachers and coworkers predicted that about one-third of the pupils would make a complete adjustment, one-half limited adjustment, and one-sixth would be complete failures. As to school adjustment, over half were expected to return to the mainstream, a fifth continue in special classes, and some 12 percent go to institutions or vocational training. Dire predictions were made for a few.

Brozovitch (1969) argues for the value of early involvement before adolescence; those who entered the adjusted study program after twelve did less well than those entering earlier. The more stable the home and the higher the IQ, the better the results. The withdrawn syndrome pupils did better than those who acted out. The average time in the special class was about eighteen months, which the authors see as inadequate. The prediction is that pupils who go back to the mainstream will continue to need an adjusted program.

McKinnon (1978) followed a mixed group of SEI young elementary pupils who had been in a special class for a year and a half. During this time their learning rate improved, though it never reached the normal rate. Fifteen percent were classified as highly improved, 67 percent improved, and the others not improved. Parents were positive about the class overall, and the pupils saw the experience as useful to them. After a period that averaged three years, 46 percent of this group were in the mainstream, 21 percent in some continuing special SEI program, 11 percent had been suspended or had dropped out, and the others could not be located. The students' self-concepts were slightly below norms. They were anxious about academics (they had serious academic problems) and felt that they had improved in peer relationships and were getting into less trouble. School and teacher relationships now were not viewed as less positive than in the special classes.

An exhaustive study was done on a program for elementary SEI pupils (Rubin, Simson, and Marcus 1966) using a control group. Many of the children made improvements according to teachers and parents; the majority of the improved were from the program but some from the control group as well. Academically they were still retarded. The experimental group held their gains for the one or two semesters at follow-up. When the psychiatric and psychological data were examined, there was no significant improvement in emotional adjustment. One of their conclusions is that the need is for different school programs for various syndromes, not a single class design for disturbed pupils.

It appears that with SEI pupils in special classes, the higher the IQ, SES, external support, and the younger the age, the better the prognosis. A 1981 report by Safer, Heaton, and Parker described positive results for a program of multisuspended junior high pupils. The program included a token economy, making contracts with parents for certain responses to behavior in the home, small classes and individualized instruction. Behavior and academics improved. In a high school follow-up four years later attendance and conduct favored the program group over controls, but there was a high dropout rate for both and similar graduation rates (Heaton and Safer 1982).

In a follow-up of over several years of one class where the author was consultant, 61 percent went back to regular classes (of these 88 percent made it, 6 percent were excluded, and 6 percent went to institutions); 15 percent went directly to institutions; 15 percent moved and; 3 percent went to classes for the retarded. Of course, what you take in is reflected in the outcomes of any special class. When pupils were interviewed, some said they had no problems to start with and others see themselves as cured in a few weeks. There are also those who feel their survival is the result of special-class placement. For LD youngsters Battle and Blowers (1982) found that gains in both self-esteem and perception of ability favored those in a special class over the mainstream.

Carlberg and Kavale (1980) did a meta-analysis of fifty studies on the efficacy of regular class and special-class placements. They found that special classes were significantly inferior for students with below-average IQs and significantly superior for the behaviorally disordered, emotionally disturbed, and learning disabled.

While there are some authors who report fabulous sprints, the general observation is that the rate of growth of SEI pupils is less than normal even when in the special class, and that a good many of them, while they make significant academic gains in the classes, are still behind and will continue to be so, though they will be within the range found in most mainstream classes. Some SEI pupils come to achieve normally, greatly assisted by the boost of the special class; and there may be as many as a quarter who are not academic problems in the first place.

Secondary Classes

Both Hauser (1978) and Nelson and Kauffman (1977) indicate that there is little published and currently an absence of guidelines for appropriate programming for adolescents. There is a rapid growth of programs according to Hirshoren and Heller (1979), who surveyed all the states. The formats are typical: special class, resource rooms, and vocationally oriented programs.

The junior high level presents an interesting set of contrasts. Too often after a protected elementary experience the child is dumped, ready or not, into a foreboding mainstream. Some for whom failure is predicted do make out well, and others disintegrate when faced with the choices, mass of peers, and continual movement from place to place. Even flexibility of selecting from many and varied courses and instructors may not offer a solution to the pupil's problem. A disturbed child can mess up in shop or art as well as English or math. One youngster spending his nonacademic time in shop was really serving well as a teacher's "aide" and learning a great deal until the administration became aware. This violated too many rules and the positive experience was forbidden. If there is a good crisis teacher program as described, more pupils may survive in the mainstream or special class. No one secondary teacher is likely to know the pupil as intensively as he is known by his elementary teacher.

Adolescents have a much stronger resistance to special class placement and will use cold war tactics in opposition unless they agree to the placement. It is an insult to their self-concept struggles to be different in such a way. The hope is to at least partially integrate adolescents, or as one teacher put it, not segregate them completely unless all other of the school resources have been exhausted.

Halpern (1979) discusses the sad plight of special education for adolescents and young adults. In his view, a balanced program should include academic skills (remedial or functional), personal social skills, daily living skills, and prevocational-vocational skills. There is a combination of teaching-counseling in most programs. Assessment should be tied to actual applied performance ability, not norms of tests. The mixture of "soft" (neurotic) and "hard" (value-deficient) pupils creates difficult group interactions.

To the adolescent being special means being negatively different, which is hard on the self-image. Even when a pupil cognitively acknowledges the need, the emotional problem remains. Being "special" is personal failure, an intolerable feeling. Efforts to return these pupils to the mainstream are often not successful because of lack of depth of support, the vulnerability of the age, and the impending life decisions (Deen and Porter 1965). Another reason for the difficulty is the very broad spectrum of psychoeducational needs of various pathologies. What is needed are programs, not a class. If a pupil can be mainstreamed with a resource teacher, all well and good. But frequently this is not enough, and there are too few alternative schools.

Recent basic resources for secondary programs include Towns (1981), Jones (1980) Cullinan and Epstein (1979) and the two-volume work by Sabatino and Mauser, *Specialized Education in Today's Secondary Schools* (1978). The first Sabatino volume covers the characteristics of delinquent and disruptive adolescents and methods of educating them. The second is devoted to diagnosis and remediation. Their approach includes primary prevention and general school procedures as well as special education. Conventional educational procedures have failed and a wide range of alternative strategies are necessary. They make the point that traditional instruments of assessment cannot provide the necessary data for planning and advocate teacher conducted, criterion referenced testing and observational studies. Programs include adjusted academic classes and special education with an emphasis on remedial and vocational work. But again, programs must be individually planned for each adolescent. While career education is seen as a most encouraging avenue, it is not an automatic solution, as we have seen. Since reading is a critical failure area for many of these youths, the authors deal with remedial programs in this area in considerable detail.

Specially trained teachers are important. Wood (1980) points out that since certification is across the grades in many states, it is assumed that generally trained teachers fit all levels. But there are some distinctive competencies for adolescent work. There is more emphasis on group skills, being a teacher-advisor, sophisticated management, promoting team support (including parents), and self-maturity.

Northcutt and Tipton (1978) point out that some adolescents will return to public school, some get an equivalency diploma, and some find job placement. Techniques for dealing with acting-out SEI pupils must be supplemented for those teaching psychotic adolescents. The adolescent participates in the goal setting. Classes are individualized and self-paced. Curricula follow the guidelines of the local school district. One-third of the adolescents in their program return to public school regular or special classrooms. Most of the others end up with equivalency graduation or vocational placement. As schools increase their proficiency tests for graduation, graduation will be more difficult. A recent issue of *Behavioral Disorders,* edited by Frank Wood, (1979, Vol. 4) was devoted to adolescent programs. The Madison (Minnesota) program (Bratton 1979) is multidiscipline, including special teachers for classrooms and a resource room with psychologists and social workers for counseling and classroom assistance. There are also assistants for the classroom teachers. There are three levels of classrooms with differential emphasis on communication, self-control, concern for others, and self-awareness with a progression to regular classroom operation. There are 230 sequenced behavioral objectives divided into five areas: behavior, communication, socialization, academics, and counseling. Special courses are given on drug and sex education. The nonacademic curriculum is broad and thirty electives are offered. Behavioral contracts and a point system are used. Efforts of parents and community agencies are coordinated. Safer (1982) advocates a multidisciplinary perspective in planning school programs for disruptive adolescents, including knowledge from sociology, education, human development, and medicine.

A special resource room and center program is described by Pearl (1979). Resource rooms use Glasser's reality therapy and a behavioral point system. High emphasis is put on self-responsibility. Time out and loss of points and privileges are used for infractions. Concrete and social reinforcers are given for goals achieved. The resource center is the last public school stop before residential treatment. Goals include learning to be one's own person and not being misled by harrassers and how to take direction from adults. Behavior modification and group counseling are included.

Mark Twain School, Montgomery County, Maryland (Laneve 1979) was previously described on page 243.

One of the most promising designs, albeit not a cheap one, is a team-and-integrated approach where two teachers work together, one handling the English and social study periods while the companion teacher tutors, counsels, does remedial reading or study assistance for those who need this help but who can take the English and social studies with regular classes. Then the second teacher takes over for periods covering math and science while the companion teacher becomes the tutor. Any possible nonacademic opportunity is utilized as well. These content classes are for pupils who cannot survive in even the most carefully selected regular classrooms for the given subjects. Otherwise they go to regular classes aided by tutoring and homework help along with supportive counseling.

A favorable impression of special classes seldom exists in the adolescent culture, though it is common to find, on interviewing them later, how much they realize the special class was the only survival possibility.

It is difficult at the junior and senior high level to get sufficient reality into the school design. While it is true that there are many pupils who will return to normal school channels and perhaps eventually even go on to college or a specialized training, it would be a mistake to see this as the universal expectation. Many of these pupils will need continuous protective planning in education and later life in keeping with their restricted prognosis. Too many special educators seem determined to make academic scholars out of virtual nonreaders.

Generally junior high is less complicated and more receptive to special education. In senior high there is the coming of age, which means that a pupil can drop out on his own if he cannot function in what is available. There has been some attention to a home-base class for the older high school pupil, so that there would be a place he could go and get help, or retreat to when under too great stress, while attending usable parts of the school. One thing is certain: support has to be always and immediately available both for the pupil and teacher if friction is to be kept to a minimum. Consultation with other teachers becomes a major effort of the special teacher at this level. One such teacher says he spends the greatest part of this time in "bailouts" and maneuvering for his youth. Group work may be more feasible than individual counseling at this age.

Preschool Programs

One of the most encouraging specializations developing in special education is in the preschool area. Merle Karnes (1979) has written *Small Wonder* with a kit that covers the period from birth to a year and a half. There are activities for "school" and home, covering enhancement of physical, intellectual, and emotional growth for special children. It must be said that working with emotionally disturbed infants is a professional subspecialty and cannot be left to materials or reading: supervised practicums are required.

Preschool work builds upon sound practice for normal children. Raver (1979) warns against "adding a dab or two" (p. 22) of special children and expecting good things to happen automatically. One must employ specific methodology and materials to encourage cross-peer interaction, using shaping and praise. She found that imitation of the normal child's behavior must be made a definite training procedure if it is to take place. Ten percent of the funds for federal preschool programs are legally dedicated to special pupils. SEI children are supposed to be included and given extra assistance.

Parent relationships are critical at this level. Because young normal children have as yet few skills to deal with atypical children, the teacher has to provide solutions. Curiosity about disabling conditions is one important aspect of the normal preschool child's world (Cohen 1977). The issue of early intervention and integration at the preschool level is discussed by Guralnick and his colleagues (1977) with various theoretical intervention models. The TEACCH Program, previously discussed, is an excellent model for long-term early intervention for the most seriously disturbed.

The preschool special teacher is more than an academic tutor, for there is in addition to the school readiness, cultivating relationship, personal growth, and socialization. Depending upon the nature of the family involvement, psychotherapy might be necessary. In early intervention, teachers give handling advice or have parents learn specific skills by coteaching. With seriously disturbed small children, two teachers are required for groups of six to eight. Curricular assistance for preschool programs has been provided by several authors, a main leader being Mary Wood and her team (1975, 1977). The series of publications cover academics and all pertinent areas of special education. Neisworth et al. (1980) cover all preschool domains for all areas of special education.

Another development is the diagnostic nursery, which some psychiatric centers have evolved. The children become members of a temporary nursery and a complete diagnosis of the child and intertwined family releationships is conducted. Developmental disorders are evaluated. Parents are intensively involved, often being trained in techniques to use at home. Some children are referred for long-term help. Others improve rapidly with changes in parental management.

Summer Programs

One of the things noticed in some public educational programs for the disturbed is regression over the summer. Parents are taking legal action to get full-year public schooling for certain SEI pupils. A few districts have experimented with less formal but organized day programs when the pupils cannot attend a special camp or some other facility. Summer-school programs include some academics and tutoring to keep the skills active and moving, but usually a larger amount of time is devoted to camping, outings, and group work. Thus, they provide the pupil with a broad socializing endeavor without at the same time losing contact with schooling. Such summer programs, being natural child experiences, represent less of an "extrusion" from normality and may be tried before a special-class placement.

Therapeutic camping is a growing enterprise. There are unique characteristics that make camping an excellent avenue for helping most SEI children. First of all it is a natural, prized thing for most pupils through adolescence and it has no stigma. Second there are many generic rewards such as activities and fun things to do. In fact it is a contingency-loaded situation. Certainly the camp environment is so different from a regular school setting in both the interpersonal arrangements, total living, and activities that it offers a new opportunity. The success of outward bound camps gives us insight about delinquency and alienation. In these camps youngsters suffer hardships, conquer danger, and develop a pride in themselves, which means a great deal to self-esteem (Brown and Simpson 1976).

One aspect of this work was revealed in very early efforts. "Last chance" children were taken to the north woods where the contest was survival against nature rather than against arbitrary imposed rules. You carry your load in order to eat, not because the adult says you should. You put up a tent unless you like to sleep in the rain. You do things for your creature comfort. There are few rules. A similar type of "live out" was used at the University of Michigan Fresh Air Camp for socially impossible, adult hostile, destructive children. A pair of "kings" became peasants when they cooked their own food and selected activities out of an available possible list without immediate adult supervision. Usually one of the pair had more than enough in a couple of days and came back requesting to rejoin society with a great list of complaints against his former colleague in disruption. One could not explain to them in weeks of LSI what the reality taught them in hours.

Camping is not only for the acting out; properly designed it can be useful to many types of children. Hung and Thelander (1978) conclude that "an intensive and systematic treatment program can be created for a group of autistic children in a short term summer camp" (p. 535).

A very useful paper reviewing the research on camping as a therapeutic tool for SEI children is available from Kralj et al. (n.d.) at the University of Virginia. This critical review of the literature makes it clear there is no magic in camping or even special therapeutic camping. The research points up the fact that the fit of child to the specific program, type of problem, and flexibility of the camp program constitute the key.

Consultation with Parents

SEI teachers find themselves consulting with others than their colleagues. These include persons from related disciplines, community groups, and especially parents of SEI children. Gesten et al. (1978) found among other things "that parent interactions are the most troublesome situations for teachers to handle" (p. 180). Graybill and Gabel (1978) noted that teachers nominated the parents of conduct problem pupils for counseling; however the teachers' perception of problems was frequently unrelated to parents' perceptions of problems.

Since the school is, for many parents, a less anxious contact than a mental health agency, teachers can often work with parents who would otherwise be resistant to intervention. In the school parents are not converted into patients. Problem-solving procedures are used that promote collaboraton. Parents are sometimes a problem to themselves and their youngsters but more frequently they are doing the best they can in what is for them a most difficult situation. For every "impossible" parent there are many who respect the teacher, ask for help, and come to room meetings (Menolascino 1980).

While there is no place for the common tendency to scapegoat families and blame them for every problem that disturbed children have, there are those conditions where the family dynamics are precipitating and sustaining causes. This is not to blame those parents; the presumption is all of us do the best we can given our assets and limitations. For every parent who has severe limitations, there are more who give beyond what seems possible. But the parents who are overwhelmed or are living out pathological life experiences on the child do exist. There are sociopathic, neurotic, and psychotic parents. This is not the usual condition, but they do occur. Many are very anxious parents, driven by fears for their youngsters, feelings of inadequacy, sometimes guilt, and often angry at what fate has meted out to them ("Why should I have to have a child with these problems?"). There are also parents who can deal with infancy reasonably well and not pre-adolescents or adolescents, and vice versa.

In addition to various forms of therapy for parents and supportive help through special education, the school may find itself cast as a major parent contact. Parents often ask the special teacher questions and seek help. If there is an outside therapeutic attachment, this request, whenever possible, is channeled back to the primary agent. It does no good to have a series of uncommunicating helpers trying to resolve an issue. If there is no outside contact, school social workers or school psychologists may be suggested as a point of reference. The teacher will want the consultation if indeed the teacher-parent contact becomes a major channel.

The school's basic approach to helping parents is not to convert the parent into a "case," even when it is obvious that he or she does need a great deal of help. Parents are still parents and can be dealt with on a problem-solving basis, though this will not necessarily be adequate to solve the difficulty. Using basically a sympathetic LSI approach, the specific issues that are causing abrasion can be approached, with feelings as well as process and possibilities to try. Often the issue is management of home discipline. Without probing for causes or interpreting, through LSI, the cues a parent gives of anxiety, anger, or fear of failure can be responded to, ventilated, and strategies can be suggested. The success of behavior modification is a case in point. Goals are target specific, methods explicit, and the parent training precise.

Every parent contact is an intervention for suggesting new concepts (Steinhauer and Quentin 1977; Loven 1978). The goal is to promote collaborative problem solving, and the special teacher may be an information communicator, facilitator, educational consultant, or educational counselor.

In the use of the Moos family games (1979), the helping person can stay at the ego level reporting the results of how the family played the game for them to talk over and resolve. The idea is to find what can be changed rather than to "cure" families. The concept of theraplay (Jernberg 1979) proposes a structured play situation for problem children and their families. It is especially useful when verbal techniques are not appropriate, and it is particularly adaptable to mothers with young children, although Jernberg has applied the procedure to adolescents and adults.

Those not experienced in dealing with families of disturbed children should be aware of the complications and depth of feeling embodied in even seemingly ephemeral family conditions. In fact, those of us who consider ourselves normal are usually still carrying within ourselves elements of family that persist as eternal emotional hangovers. The deeper the relationship the more complicated the interaction patterns for good and ill. The scapegoated children show how a child role can be created to balance unresolved parent antagonisms. Divorce rates are higher in special-education families. Emotional binding is not only love; it is hate, fear, and anger, as is demonstrated by homicides where anger flares among "loved ones." To know these things is absolutely necessary for teachers, even when they may function only as a holding service for a child who is the victim of a sorry family. There is no place for blame. We do not try to make them over, but we do not shrink from ego level, conscious problem solving. SEI teachers know this because often though there has been a pretense of there being no problem at home, it will all be dumped out. The teacher then tries to get the help needed but maintains a role in the particular strategies of dealing with the child's behavior.

The impact of a seriously disturbed child on an intact family should not be ignored. We do not have to postulate family "disturbance" to recognize family "consternation." For example, there is an overrepresentation of children with mental and physical handicaps in the abused child population. Marcus (1977) has reviewed the matter of impact of the special child on the family and listed the accusations made of parents, even when, as in the case of autism, the biological conditions are apparent. He points out that family characteristics seem representative of the general population. But these families undergo constant stress, worry and anxiety, hope and despair. Some cope in ways that add to personal growth of the parents and the siblings. Other parents become guilt ridden, try everything, and hide their problems. It is interesting that not only the family, but the attitudes of the extended family (i.e., relatives) have a great deal to do with family equilibrium.

It has been found helpful to get the modes of dealing with the SEI child out into the open and recognize what is actually going on. Then one looks at the parent support system to find out what is being done through parents, siblings, or family for support and whether there a role for a specialist. Any worry about siblings is explored. In helping parents, particularly mothers, to be effective in interventions, it has been found that their ecosystem or family network must be considered (Salzinger et al. 1980). The greatest changes are likely to be in parents' self-confidence in their ability to evaluate and handle their children's problems. It is useful to discuss how hard it is to make changes, not only for the child but for adults as well. There is often great relief in getting matters into the open problem-solving arena even though the difficulties persist. We learn to live better with what we must tolerate.

There is an organization, Closer Look, a project of HEW, Bureau of the Handicapped (Box 1492, Washington, D.C. 20013) primarily for parents and to help others work with parents of special children. Their publications cover legal aspects but go into all issues related to parents and special children. There are three other books of particular value to teachers in their work with parents, Cooper and Edge's *Parenting* (1978); Stewart's *Counseling Parents of Exceptional Children* (1978); and a parent's side, Turnbull and Turnbull's *Parents Speak Out: Views from the Other Side of the Two-Way Mirror* (1978). A guide to literature for parents has been produced by Moore et al. (1983). *Closer Look* is a parent advocate publication with many ideas to strengthen parent involvement.

The consultation may take the form of support for parent groups related to a room or group of SEI children, or a national organization such as those for the autistic or learning disabled. Michigan has a statewide organization, the Michigan Association for Emotionally Disturbed Children (MAEDC). Parents and professionals join in local units and those on the state level to advance the care for these children through lobbying, special projects, and parent support activities. Such a group is a great help to teachers. Obviously every reasonable effort is made to refer parents to community sources of help, but regardless of parent agreement, special education maintains a responsibility for the pupil.

CONCLUSION

Actual programs never appear on paper. Programs are people and events. Obviously no changes will take place in the child unless something of his present internal or external situation is altered. When parents are said to be noncooperative, do we still make repeated calls to them? We say the pupil should be temporarily sent home, but he comes by bus and knows we cannot exclude him until the bus comes. And is someone home and what will they do? The clinical personnel may not communicate what is happening in therapy. Is teacher time provided to go to the clinic and wait out the needed appointment? He does not learn to read after a year's help. Can we alter the procedures to get more intensive help and keep at it? A special teacher must be able to generate forces to overcome the workaday resistences or the effort will soon become mundane. Like other resistances, program resistances have a way of showing up again in a slightly different form after the initial bout. The psychological mortality and limitations of public-school programs should be recognized as stemming from a complicated set of variables, only one of which is the teacher.

9

Out-of-School Placements

TRANSITION

IN SCHOOL AND OUT-OF-SCHOOL placements merge in the day-school format. Day schools may be operated by a school system or a mental health center, public or private. Designs are highly idiosyncratic. The next intensified placement is a total "living-in" institution. To complete the circle, we consider the Halfway House concept, as one way back toward the life stream. The SEI teacher has different roles in these settings.

DAY-SCHOOL PROGRAMS AND THE TEACHER'S ROLE

SEI teaching in a proper day-school program constitutes a role differing somewhat from roles within the school setting. While there are day schools that are nothing but a collection of classes with no more complete service than the single class, this is not the true day-school concept. Custodial day-school programs do exist in both the public and private sectors. A day school is a multidiscipline unit with educational and mental health personnel on the grounds working together to create a therapeutic milieu. The nature and severity of certain pupil problems prescribes such dual involvement. With youngsters, the live action setting offers potentials for getting at behavior not possible in outpatient contacts. There is also the fact that with the larger number of students in such a day school, it is possible to provide a wider range of services and experiences. Day schools are usually sponsored by some combination of community mental health agencies and public schools.

There are true joint enterprises and others where teachers are supplied to a program run by mental health. The day-school approach offers the opportunity for maximizing intensive educational mental health intervention short of removing a child from his home. Theoretically there should be both day programs and night programs available for children as there are for adults. Some children can cope with school and other activities during the day but experience their primary exacerbation in the home setting. Such programs for night care would of course be mental health sponsored rather than school sponsored. Providing the home is a positive place, day schools minimize the extrusion of the youngster and of course cost much less to operate than total-care institutions.

Day schools may operate half a school day, a full school day or on an extended-day basis, providing after-school activities for youngsters who would otherwise be likely to have a destructive experience during recreation or free time. They may be designed for short-term or long-term treatment and education (Littlesand 1977).

One essential difference between the day school and a residential setting is in family-community contact. In the day-school setting the youngster is still in the family setting (and community life) after school, even if school means an extended day for him. One hopes that the family is not entwined in the problem or that the family is involved in corrective efforts at the same time as the child. If the pupil can manage school adequately and the family is supportive, day school should not be necessary. When more milieu control is necessary and where more intensive resources are involved, the day-school format becomes useful. It also serves to reduce the impact of a devastating home situation and provides a channel for increasing family involvement in corrective processes. If the family is the major source of provocation and nothing can be worked out to reduce this negative input, day school will not be the indicated mode of treatment. If the child goes home to a situation that generates or exacerbates the problem, the potential of the day-school effort will be eroded. Some day-school programs are built for a particular clientele, such as delinquents, where controls become the central feature (Jacobs and Schwertzer 1979). Others may serve autistic or schizophrenic youngsters. However the usual clientele is broad ranged. The length of day can be extended to take the great share of the waking time including after-school group work, clubs, recreation, and evening help with schoolwork.

The age range for such programs is from preschool through young adulthood, though there is considerable reluctance to having very young children on a full-day or extended-day basis even when it is necessary for the mother to work. At the other end, there are late adolescents and young adults who can go out in the work world but need a protected night home.

Usually every effort will be made to involve the family to resolve any unfortunate relationships as the pupil attends the day-school program. Parents may learn how to give more help to the child, even when they have *not* been the cause of the youngster's problem. The family may never reach the level of perfection some would like, but there should be adequate sustaining elements to make it helpful for the child when at home.

The day school offers the chance for an integrated milieu for the total school day: resources are similar to those needed for total care in most respects. Of course no child-care workers or dormitory facilities are required. Hence, communities can more easily afford such programs (Savicki and Brown 1981). The components must be broad and rich to take care of growing needs of the youngsters as well as provide remedial conditions. Recreation, activities of a crafts nature, facilitation of group life, and food provision are added to special education and therapeutic intervention.

Many day schools have a multidiscipline base under the leadership of educational personnel. The League School format, created by the late Carl Fenichel, is a prime example (Fenichel 1966; 1976). This well-known and successful day-treatment program was the inspiration for the spread of a series of such programs. Before his untimely death, Fenichel was an outstanding leader in the field and particularly adept in the work with autistic and seriously disturbed children. Such autistic and schizophrenic children were considered unreachable when he began his work. In the League School program, the teacher is the key person who provides the structure, security, and organization for the pupil. The children are usually totally indifferent when they first come to the League School. There are close relationships with parents in all of the work, and a home-training program has evolved for preschool children. The children are first taught to listen, and communication is simplified. The curriculum ranges from self-care to academics depending upon the pupil's capacity. Group activities and the eating times are utilized for teaching as well as the usual pre-school and academic work. Therapy of a traditional nature is also included. Excursions into the community continue in a conversation clinic to teach social skills and proper use of language. Vocational skills are part of the adolescent's program. Results range from "success" to graduated but limited accomplishments, but Fenichel always stressed that *every gain* means a better life and no child is hopeless. While the teacher is key, this is an exemplary multidiscipline program.

The league's *Home Training Program for Young Mentally Ill Children* (Doernberg, Rosen, and Walker 1968) is based on cooperation of parent and professional on an equal basis. No child was dropped because of behavior; honest, frank opinions and evaluations were given; and a maximum effort was put into working with the child and family. The family came to work at the center every week. The parent may observe or work directly with the child in thirty to forty sessions. There were biweekly meetings of parent groups. The program included teaching self-help, communication, socialization, and preacademic skills. They found this approach to be practical and effective for even the very disturbed. The goal was to keep severely disturbed children in the community by providing a school and home program. Many of these schizophrenic, autistic, and multiply handicapped children had not been receiving either the education or therapy that they needed. The design is a highly individualized educational program with interdisciplinary clinical participation.

With mandatory special-education legislation and the negative feeling regarding institutions, there is no question that the day-school pattern will see increasing development. There is no way to have a cheap day school program with adequate personnel, though the cost is but a percentage of institutional care.

There have been some day-treatment programs that are designed for total impact to serve very disturbed adolescents. Linniban (1977) describes such a program, which includes family therapy *in the family's own home.* Because this group believes in community involvement, the program itself takes only part of the day with an effort to get each youngster in a public, private, or vocational school taking up the other part. Outreach by the staff supports teachers and other agency personnel. Since they accept so seriously disturbed and psychotic youth, eventually some must be referred for long-term hospitalization, but most are able to be maintained in the community. A casual atmosphere, "educational" activities, and a relaxed informal staff attuned to working with adolescents are seen as essential. Flexibility is the basic process in planning for individual needs.

Hoover (1978) describes a program for those who are very hard to reach, persons over eighteen, a special concern for states where the age of special education responsibility continues after high school. An open approach following the Summerhill philosophy is utilized. What this means in practice is that students must have freedom to assume responsibility and face the consequences of their decisions. The teacher helps the student identify his problems and locates adults who can provide help, while the student determines which of the possible solutions seems appropriate. Counseling psychology is combined with special-education training for teachers in such a setting. A great deal of effort is devoted to student self-governance, group discussion, and group decisions.

Certain mental health settings develop day-school programs as a viable addition to treatment alternatives. The pupils are from the geographical area and arrive by bus. They comprise a group the special education programs in the public schools have not been able to help, sometimes because of their acting out and because of the complicated nature of their behavior. The mental health setting can sometimes pressure parent cooperation that would be impossible to attain in the public schools. Such a day-school program is operated at Hawthorn Center (Northville, Michigan) in conjunction with an extensive inpatient and outpatient service. Schooling is the core of the experience with added therapeutic attention of two kinds, crisis exploitation and tradition therapy for pupils and parents as indicated. The events in the setting are used to foster insight as they occur in the group life, authority relationships, or schooling. Because so many of the pupils have not only behavior but learning problems as well, special language-reading help is provided on a tutorial or small-group basis. Recreational activities are included. Integrated with the inpatient population, the size of the school is large enough to offer a wide range of educational experiences. All of the educational opportunities of the best schooling are utilized, appropriate to the age. Though some youngsters have limited ability to function academically, others can, in spite of their problems, accomplish normal skill and knowledge development. A great deal of emphasis is put on the nonacademic areas as well, in both the curricular and extracurricular areas. Music, dance, drama, and arts and crafts are incorporated. There are shop activities, even for the young children, which moves along with older children to prevocational and vocational aspects. The auto shop is very important for adolescents as are the courses in food preparation and beautician skills that they can use in personal and professional ways. Food preparation training includes both home economics and vocational skills. A greenhouse is used for both formal and informal teaching of plant life as well as certain vocational skills. A complete indoor and outdoor physical education (including swimming) program is included. Special days are celebrated and seasonal activities emphasized to prevent the institutional syndrome. For the more limited youth an "in-house" sheltered workshop program provides carefully organized graduated work skills for both boys and girls. The earning of wages is not taken lightly; this may be the first time many of these youth have felt important to society. Needless to say pathology does not dissolve in a work arena, but even for some very disturbed children the money incentive is real, and with skillful planning of "jigs" and "work stations" the motivation of the work can be used for skill education including math and writing. The con artist is still an operator, the delinquent still tries to use his talents to confound the system, and the schizophrenic youth has little awareness of the whole situation, but they do their routine tasks and have real jobs. For many disturbed children the sheltered workshop is the bridge to the final step where in cooperation with the vocational rehabilitation, the young adult who can goes to on-the-job training. A thorough exploration of the youngster's potentials comes first. Again, the problems of the youth go with him but the work setting is an excellent place to teach social behavior as well as vocational skills.

In the Hawthorn program, clinical personnel are available to the action areas and move in when a crisis occurs that cannot be resolved on site. Group work programs are included as well as traditional therapy. This enables a combination of classical and situational support. The diagnostic needs for the day-school pupil are no less than those we have described previously. Since many day-school pupils are already in non-family-caring institutions, there is a great deal of effort to coordinate life plans for particular children. Every effort is made to keep contact and provide help for the parents.

The Special Teacher's Role in the Day School

In addition to the overall skills of the SEI teacher, day-school teaching requires particular functions. There is an extended distance between day school and regular schooling where the hope is that many of the pupils will eventually be able to return. Consequently the teacher emphasizes liaison with the sending school and for those who return, with the receiving school. As much as possible the day-school curriculum is articulated with that of the home school. With the diversity of educational curricula, this constitutes a significant effort. Pupils worry about what they may miss and need assurance. The teacher discusses the contacts with regular school and whenever possible uses the same or similar materials to reduce the pupil's anxiety. When the time comes, the receiving teachers in the public school must be counseled and supported. It has been found that teacher-to-teacher communication is more effective than leaving such a crucial relationship to other disciplines. Regular school survival becomes a critical part of any recovery program for the child, and the ability of the child to cope with school may determine whether he returns to a regular or special setting after treatment. Unfortunately, many times a compromise is necessary. Both continued supportive tutoring by day-school teachers and therapy will often be necessary after the pupil leaves the day school.

Certain functions of day-school teachers depend of course on the particular setting, but all day means eating with youngsters—a therapeutically valuable but emotionally taxing time—and playing with children in informal times. Especially for adolescents the teaching team has to assess any special talents or particular abilities in order to provide the greatest possible assortment of opportunities. Frequently teachers have to be responsible for more than the usual number of subject matter areas to provide a range of high school subjects.

Control factors often become critical in day schools unless there is a place to send a child. Temporary exclusion is complicated. The transportation problems may mean he cannot be sent home even if he cannot manage the school day. There may be no one at home if he could be sent. Crisis help on the spot replaces exclusions.

If a day-school setting has inadequate resources, the teacher turns out to provide everything the pupil gets by way of help, serving as teacher, remedial tutor, crisis helper, and quasi therapist as well as parent contact. In a properly organized day school this is not the case. Classes are small and the staff members work as a team. Aides may be available. The essence of the adequate day school is the multidisciplinary approach for disturbed children. The teacher both contributes knowledge and observation to the team and has the major responsibility of working out the dynamic information in terms of an educational design. In some instances the teacher will also be a major parent contact around the school performance. With those pupils who are academically intact, behavior may be the major concern. The teacher will see the transference of authority relationship, peer problems, and fear of failure that are brought to planning meetings. With some of the very disturbed youngsters, the concern may be over self-destructive behavior. Out of the team staffing meetings comes not only specific goals and methodology but concepts about pacing and pressure to be exerted as well as what to do if plans prove inadequate.

As a full member of the therapeutic team, knowledge about other professionals and their skills is essential to the day-school teacher. More than this however is the ability to present one's ideas, observations, and problems in an open and professional manner to other disciplines. Significant time must be provided for interdisciplinary team exchanges. As with all multidiscipline programs, mutual trust and respect becomes particularly important. The teacher has unique individual and group skills and knows curricula. The point of the team is to blend this area with other professional contributions to provide the best help for each particular child. In many public school programs the teacher tends to be the king or queen of the hill: in day school the teacher is a team member.

Interprofessional relationships are not always smooth. The clinical member is usually in charge of the overall therapeutic plan. Frequently he or she has poor appreciation of the teacher's classroom as a group operation. Somehow the pupil is to get up to grade level or beyond. The teacher may expect miracles from a therapeutic session. There are also questions of where one role leaves off and another begins. Mutual respect develops only over time. When there is not a conscious trust level there are possible divergencies that children are quick to exploit with comments like "My teacher says . . ." or "my therapist says. . . ." Three-way conversations should be held frequently to integrate effort. There can be interdisciplinary exchanges that are depreciative rather than supportive in the difficult task of working with SEI children.

In summary the role of the SEI teacher in a proper day-school setting emphasizes the following:

1. Utilization of the skills described in the teaching chapters;

2. Participation in educational placement and planning conferences;

3. Joining as coequal with a multidisciplinary team in working with children. Since all disciplines are on the grounds, the depth of team functioning is more intense than in prior school settings. This demands considerable personal and professional self-understanding. A defensive stance will not be effective;

4. Contributes information on the school behavior to other disciplines;

5. May have a significant role with parents but not the major role, which is usually that of the social worker. At least communicates educational information;

6. Must be able to share responsibility with other disciplines, find satisfaction in the child's growth through a team rather than be tied to gratification coming solely from one's own individual effort;

7. Cultivates contacts with mainstream for articulating present school-

work and for future return of the pupil. Teachers talk to their counterparts rather than leave this to others;

8. Engages in follow-up to continue support for the student.

THE INSTITUTIONAL SETTING AND THE SEI TEACHER

No aspect of special services has aroused emotional reaction equal to that focused on mental health institutions for children, save perhaps the feelings regarding institutions for the retarded and seriously multiply handicapped. Historically, many mental hospitals have been terrible places for children and adults, as we all know. Even now the more destitute and needy the children, the harder it is to get sustained adequate care, and there are scandals even in so-called good programs, which are supposedly carefully monitored by the highest paid mental health personnel. Even when children and adolescents were finally taken off adult wards and given their own place, it was often substandard, in old buildings ill adapted to growing children's needs. There are still states with virtually no programs of merit.

Any good residential program for children will be far more expensive than an adult service; costs equal attending an Ivy League college. The ratio of total institutional staff to children is three adults to one child. On the other side of the coin there are beautiful settings for children and milieu programs that offer a richer life than elsewhere, far more than the home setting offered many children. There are excellent public and private caring places.

The old idea of hundreds of children in large holding institutions is no longer legitimate. There are a great variety of institutional formats including hospitals, schools, small residences, cottage programs, and "homes." No matter what the architecture or the quality of the furnishings, the real problem is the quality of the daily care, the educational program, and the therapy for the youngsters. Quality programs are expensive in money and in psychic energy. Staff burnout is all too common. In fact one famous director considered it necessary to match child turnover with staff turnover, such was the strain.

Very few children and youth need to be under lock and key if the program is adequate. For those few who do, closed units are required until they can manage freedom. Powers (1980) has described in telling terms, with cases, the nature and difficulties of providing good institutional treatment. He follows the humanistic approach we have depicted. In his view the goal of therapy is to help the child understand the causes and consequences of his dilemma and then to allow him to experiment with new solutions. Each professional person in the milieu "must become bigger than his or her craft, bigger than himself or herself" (p. 5). To create and maintain a therapeutic milieu is a formidable task and a maximum effort must be directed to the persons with the long, sustained contact hours such as child-care personnel and teachers. State institutions have a double problem with staff, since civil service now has a goal of using the least expensive and least trained with mechanical advancement in pay scale, which is all designed to save money. The first element one looks to in appraising a setting is the leadership. The overall criterion is Would you have a child of your own placed there, given the need?

How do we know who needs complete institutional care? Foster placement with special education is gaining ground and will be a significant part of the complement of needed services. But foster care for many very seriously disturbed youngsters is impossible to find, and when it is available for the appropriate group, it will require ancillary support for the parent as well as therapeutic intervention for the child. It is easy to propose alternative solutions if you are not responsible for finding those resources and making them work. A local home or family group home may be the choice for many children. These can also be solutions or disasters just as well as in a larger institution. The professionals who have undertaken group home treatment can attest to the trials of keeping the home hygienic, the staff adequate, and ancillary services in order. Some small centers have schooling on grounds but most utilize community special education. Not infrequently pupils who need particular special education are mainstreamed, resulting in general consternation. Recently, to reap insurance money, there have been a rash of institutional programs that take in the disturbed child for "short-term treatment" which means until the insurance runs out. Few of these have school programs or any program for that matter. In contrast there are local group homes with unbelievably dedicated leadership and personnel. There are reputable nationally affiliated programs that advertise in respected professional journals. An SEI teacher had best do some research before accepting a position in any institution, however.

It is reasonable to ask why should a youngster be placed in a psychiatric or other residential setting. The answer is simple to state but the conditions hard to discern: such placement should be done only when other processes already discussed are not adequate to help the child. While it is possible to have an equivalent school program in a day school, it is not possible to have a totally planned milieu, which the remediation of some problems requires. Conjoint educational and therapeutic and designed living experiences are necessary for conditions where children are a risk to themselves; children are a danger to others, and finally where it is not possible to do the intensive work necessary to change patterns unless the whole life-space is utilized. Being totally cared for, eating times, informal times, and nighttime expand the situations for help if one understands that these functions offer needed conditions for relearning life patterns. The fact is that there are families who cannot respond to their children without adding to damage already done and families where it is impossible to intervene, even by sending workers into the home. Children who are overtly and covertly rejected cannot build self-regard without intensive adult acceptance. Other disturbed children put such demands on the home that they wear out the best-intentioned parents. For the child and the family, placement becomes the only solution. The interventions needed imply not only specific therapies and special schooling but adult figures for identification, group living experiences, and the kind of psychological and physical diet that one would wish for all children.

Now, why not provide all of this in the natural home setting or the surrogate "homes" design? Because it is not possible to provide the twenty-four-hour-a-day integrative surveillance needed. It also may not be possible to watch over and utilize certain events with peers or in the neighborhood. While peer influence may be helpful in some instances, in others running with the herd may be a catastrophe. There may be too many seductive things beckoning difficulty in the external, uncontrolled world.

Many deviant youngsters are master escape artists. They slip through the controls. They will learn only where there is continual clinical exploitation of live events. Inpatient care can be needed, even with intact, integrated families who are willing to work with the therapists, because the child may cause such catastrophic interaction that parents and siblings cannot respond properly. There are also children for whom placement is necessary because pathology of the family interaction cannot be changed. Children can be part of a negative interaction pattern in the family. There are also examples of cases where the family is not causal in the chain of events leading to the child's problem behavior but yet the family cannot mobilize the extra resources needed to cope with the problem. Well-meaning families are not always adequate even with outside support. While there are parents who act out their own problems on the children, it is more common to find parents who mean to do the right thing but cannot sustain corrective influences even with the right intent. After all, if they were adequate in the first place, certain difficulties might not have appeared. Rabinovitch (1971) discusses indications for admission as a matter of quality and degree of functional disturbance and environment, not diagnosis per se. There are four categories of admissions: (1) emergency, where there is no clinical alternative; (2) chronic and severe acting out in home, school, and/or community; (3) chronic and severe withdrawal, depression, and anxiety; (4) pediatric management problems. He cautions against separation from families without due cause. The admitted children suffer from severe biological or social disturbances. They have failed to respond to treatment efforts.

Rabinovitch (1971) discussed the role of inpatient treatment by reviewing fifty consecutive admissions to Hawthorn Center, ranging in age from six to sixteen. Sixteen were emergencies for which no alternative could be found, twenty-two were severe chronic acting-out children, seven severe withdrawal and depression, and five psychophysiologic cases. In every instance a long series of efforts had already been exhausted. There are many examples that indicate the need for greater prevention efforts, but *until that is accomplished* someone has to take on the most difficult cases. It is not a matter of a community service *or* a mental hospital; it is the need for more complete services of both kinds. Hoffman (1982) advocates joint evaluation and treatment of both the child to be institutionalized and the family.

Whatever the locale there must be special education. While some institutions use public school special education, most integrated milieus have their own schooling because education is such a central element of a child's life and provides so many helpful activities (Forness and Langdon 1974).

A 1977 report titled *The Education and Socialization of Institutionalized Emotionally Disturbed Children and Youth* is available on the status of programs for institutionalized SEI children and youth. The major problem areas are conflict between clinical and educational staff regarding the control and philosophy of the educational program; lack of resources (staff, space); and restricted coverage of educational opportunities. Model components suggested include no-fail grading systems, outdoor education, community involvement, and vocational education. This document also includes state laws governing such programs.

Descriptions of particular programs can be found in *Growing Up in a Garden City* by Murphy (1974) on the Menninger School. Mayer

(1977) has discussed group care. Hoffman, Becker and Gabriel (1976) have written on the hospitalized adolescent. Hawthorn Center has a film portraying an extensive program.

Special Aspects of Institutional Teaching

It has been observed that the adolescent residential treatment population has become significantly more disturbed in recent years (Weintrob 1974; 1975). Probably the same could be said for preadolescents. This may be due to the general desire to prevent institutionalization and waiting too long. It does mean that institutional teachers (as well as other workers) will find it necessary to adjust their methods and expectations to working with students of more limited prognosis.

Doxiads (1976), in discussing institutions for young children, points out it is the staff quality and relationships that make for the character of the institution, and the same can be said for the school segment.

The cooperation between disciplines varies greatly from institution to institution. The prior discussion of day-school politics is intensified, adding now all of the persons who provide food and supervise living times. Thus child care and nursing are significant new disciplines. There are places where the authority is vested in treatment teams and even rotated among disciplines. On the other extreme, there are those where the authority rests in one discipline, usually psychiatry, with all others subservient. When the psychiatrist understands and appreciates the potentials of education (as well as other nonpsychiatric areas), this presents no problem. The breadth and personality of the individual is more important than the specific discipline of the person in charge, be he psychiatrist, psychologist, educator, social worker, or nurse.

In some settings the teacher does not even make the educational plan for the child. The power priorities are evident when one sees who participates in assignment of pupils to classes, changes in rooms, and what is to take place in classrooms. On the other hand, teachers can ask too much from therapists to manage discipline and exclude pupils, etc. Collaboration is the only answer. As in the day school, if there is interdisciplinary trust and respect, all will have a contribution to make through case analysis and problem solving. The teacher is not an independent agent to go his or her own way; however, collaboration should be a two-way matter. Incidentally, the clientele are not expected to be the same in every institution and one expects differences in what goes on in therapy and the classroom. Overidentification of workers with "their" child can be a source of conflict.

In interdisciplinary work a distinction should be made between discipline role conflict and interpersonal conflict. A dictatorial or subservient individual becomes a problem to others of the team whatever the profession. Unfortunately the educational and mental health fields are not renowned for the superior personal adjustment.

Forness and Langdon (1974) see limitations coming from the medical hospital settings, which makes teaching in them more difficult. Teachers' roles are more diverse and teachers work in relative isolation, seldom having primary responsibility. The other professions do not know how to work intimately with educators. Since school is a pivot for eventual survival for many children when they leave, the teacher must play a vital role in placement proceedings. They report teachers' problems include jurisdictional questions on overlap of function and being "belabored" with advice on how to conduct the classroom. Forness and Langdon would give the teacher control over the academic but not the social behavior decisions. Behavioristic methodology can be a source of conflict in psychoanalytically oriented institutions.

The fact is that there are all levels and types of institutions. Some are departmentalized and dominated by one discipline. Others are run by educators. In some, one particular treatment theory dominates, either psychoanalytic or behavioristic. Token economies may be used in the living areas and school combined with behavior therapy. Then again, child management may follow one course and the therapy another. Most institutions find value in flexibility. If the diagnosis has been thorough, it should determine a multimodal process rather than applying an arbitrary concept to all. In matter of fact, most institutions will find it difficult to accomplish the goals for all children even with a wide spectrum of treatments they may devise. Just having the children under one roof is in itself no guarantee of integrated programming.

Adolescents present certain unique problems to institutional treatment and teaching because of age, size, and the adolescent phenomena (Hoffman, Becker, and Gabriel 1976). This age is most easily upset by being different, freedoms being curtailed, and a hazardous future. In a not so perfect but better than most institutional program, an adolescent girl expressed her perceptions in the following way to her college "friend" who visited and took her outside the walls. She is seventeen and describes a picture she drew. The drawing was of squares: "The square are crazy people. They have four rough edges.

The squares with circles in them are crazy people who are getting well. They have rough edges but a smooth circle is deep inside. The triangles are "staff." They have some rough edges but they are sharp on top." When asked how she would draw well people she said, "Circles with a square inside. All people have some rough edges deep down." Then she pointed out the difficulty when the squares go outside to the world of circles. "You think you are no good like other people. It is no use trying when you are crazy." The person thinks everyone outside can tell and they judge you on that basis. Later when a group of these girls were at a halfway house, they found it most difficult to act "normal" on their jobs. They said that they were being looked at and labeled, some of which was projection and some reality. They expected to fail in the regular class or the regular society on their road back. This is the broadened concept and challenge of education for the emotionally disturbed: the goals are as broad as life itself.

Hoffman (1976) lists adolescent heightened narcissism, ambivalence in dependency-independency, desire for privacy, and power struggles among the particular issues and each is found in classroom situations. Certainly sexuality of the age creates anxiety for both pupils and the staff. The teacher who works with adolescents would do well to consult *Adolescent Psychiatry,* an annual for the most current studies of this ever-changing field (Feinstein, and Giovacchini, 1971–82 and Looney et al. 1981). Every adolescent (as well as younger patient) must be given an explanation and printed copy of their rights. Rights include a discussion of the right to safety, treatment, a physically good place to be, to go to school, practice one's religion, to be treated with respect, and to communicate with a lawyer if desired. Processes for handling complaints are required. All staff are responsible for following the code.

Institutional Schooling

There are many variant educational designs in inpatient schools. In general the schools tend to be traditional and reality oriented, even more so than the progressive educational formats in regular public schools. Others are designing exciting and different modes of teaching. The quality and creativeness of the teacher is critical in building a significant school. The institution should be the last place for dull teaching. But even in the institution, average educational growth is usually less than the normal pace though far better than it had been previously. School success pays off not only in the skill development itself but in enhanced self-esteem. The school components also contribute to a broader view of the child since here is an ongoing real-life projective test of his personal state, relationship capacity, and task-meeting competency.

While the disturbed child lives for a time in this special place, the special place is always a part of the community. Supervised by staff, youngsters go out into the community to participate in the many appropriate activities. Trips, camping, and excursions into the community for various activities reduce the separation from normal life. Concerts, trips, restaurants, visitations to stores, and everything a child can manage is incorporated into the acculturalization. We see the importance of the teacher as an educational representative of the broader culture, an adult who can interpret the events on television, who can help pupils understand more than 2 + 2. Bringing people into the classroom both on given topics and as general volunteers adds to the quota of human relationship available. Thus the institutional teacher's role becomes broad; in essence he becomes part of the doorway to the community. While some inpatient programs use schooling in the community as a general thing, if the youngster can already utilize regular or special education, he is unlikely to have the severity of problem signifying the need for inpatient service. Sometimes, with adolescents, the experiences needed may be available only in a regular school system. There are institutions that, late in the treatment, use external school as part of the transition back.

The most complete analyses of schools in residential centers is a task force report *Chaos to Order* (Task Force Four 1972). It is clear that there is no "type" of residential center; originally many of such institutions were called "schools" since education was considered the essential element. At present the school is seen as a central element in the treatment milieu program. The range of schooling includes sending children and youth to external schools, to a "typical" school within the residence, or to teachers functioning in the living areas teaching life survival skills. Chronic school failure is characteristic in residential care populations; this explains why school success, if it can be brought about, provides so much of the therapeutic gain. *Chaos to Order* suggests a far more constricted concept of the school than is presented in this volume. Primary emphasis is on intellectual tasks, though social behavior and acceptance of authority are also recognized goals. In fact, the integration of cognitive, emotional, and motor behavior is advocated with a diagnostic-prescriptive base of operations.

The Hawthorn program described in the day school section

(p. 320) is also an impatient program and represents the basic elements depicted in *Chaos to Order*. School in the institution is seen as different from regular school because the pupils will be more anxious about learning, be defensive, and dump other anxieties on school. Many school behavior problems come from the anxiety provoked by just being in a classroom, which previously has been a place of failure. The pupil responds to the teacher with overdependency or high resistance. As a result the in-house school should keep its educational character while educators participate as an equal discipline within the milieu. The physical nature of the school part of the establishment does much to establish its identity. The goal is to have, in a microcosm, a complete total school program: this is the problem with only a small group of teachers and pupils—especially at the high school level. In addition, the task force sees a need for small tutoring rooms, quiet rooms, and a materials center. The teacher will find institutionalized pupils with serious and long-standing pathologies and academic deficiencies. A great deal of emphasis is put on the collaborative role of the teacher with other professionals. The emotional strain of teaching disturbed pupils needs to be recognized in work loads and relationships. Because the pupil and teacher share goals, the teachers and pupils are aligned in purpose, which is one of the few times that this happens in the pupil's life. School is reality oriented. Classes average seven pupils. School is to run the year around to help recover lost time.

The psychoeducateur program described before, developed at the University of Montreal by Jeannine Guindon (1969), also has an institutional counterpart that is in high contrast to the commission report just discussed. The teacher plays multiple roles (teacher, child care worker, group leader, counselor, and parent surrogate). The adults develop skills in various areas of youth life. The objective is help the youngster develop a new and positive identity. The start is a highly organized program that gradually opens up to match the pupils' developing internal resources, ending with integration into the community.

Project Re Ed is an institution following the educateur concept, designed to prevent isolation from the community and operating as a residential placement except for weekends when the pupil goes home. It is ecological in concept and includes the Re Ed center, the family, school, and neighborhood. The unity is maintained by liaison workers. It is based upon a school educational model rather than a medical paradigm. Nicholas Hobbs, who was the generator of the concept, has written the definitive statement on Re Ed (1982). Re Ed is designed to deal with the total life system of the child. In addition to the school per se, teacher-counselors reach out into the community to work with families and community agencies, which means a new professional role for SEI teachers. The goal is to develop support systems for children and families so that changes can be maintained. Consultants function to formulate plans around specific problems.

RETURNING FROM THE INSTITUTION

While we know not all institutionalized pupils will return to the mainstream, there will be those who do. If the road back is difficult for the special-class pupil, the return for the institutionalized child is far more complex. New peers ask where you were before, and being in a detention home or place for nutty kids will be difficult to explain. Ferdinande and Colligan (1980) say that the adolescent should be kept oriented to the mainstream [sic], apprehensions should be dealt with, and actual reentry starts with a case manager who will be the advocate for the pupil in the new system and provide direct support. As they see it, continued support is part of treatment and an obligation of the institution.

Administrators and teachers in receiving schools ask about achievement, management, and what strengths and weaknesses the youngster has in addition to psychological data. Successful reentry into the mainstream is fraught with many conditions: the intensity of the original disturbance, treatment and educational effectiveness, the climate of the receiving setting, and of course the overall support system external to school. Bloom and Hopewell (1982) report on eighty-eight adolescents discharged from a state hospital, *exclusive* of those transferred to another institution. The pathologies included transient situational disorders, and personality, neurotic, organic, and psychotic disorders. Within six months, 43 percent were reinstitutionalized. Over half of the successful reenterings were enrolled in public school, helped by more supportive external conditions. While they did not find the diagnosis differentiated by groups, the longer the hospital stay the more likely the recidivism.

The point at issue is where they go to school after they leave the institution. Many are still high risk, needing careful support from the institutional school when they do return to a day or public school. Liaison teachers visit the placement and counsel with the teachers. More than that there is serial contact between the institution and the regular or special school. Since school is critical for survival, every youngster must have the educational help needed to make it. School is second only to the home in power to help or hinder.

Teacher Role

In the inpatient school the SEI teacher's role emphasizes certain functions:

1. Uses basic SEI teaching techniques outlined in previous chapters. Every child is to be given appropriate education.

2. Intensive interdisciplinary cooperation is required, this with the child-care personnel as well as the clinical persons for a school problem may have its genesis in the living unit. Depending upon the primary discipline in charge of the unit, the educational staff may be responsible to the clinical person in charge of the pupil's treatment. Teaching in inpatient units is not easier because of the support from the total milieu; it is just different. The children will be of the most severe disturbance. The divided responsibilities make liaison meetings of all who are working with a child a time-consuming enterprise.

3. The educational program for the child must be the teacher's responsibility and an IEP meeting should take place with entrance. School personnel handle the first line of behavior problems and collaborate about or refer persistent difficulties.

4. There should be teacher participation in school placement decisions although intake and screening are usually done elsewhere. The inpatient school program begins with as much information as possible concerning the school experiences of the youngster before he came to the institution; achievement, learning style, relationship to authority figures, and appropriate materials are included.

5. Ability to contribute the educational behavior in team meetings is necessary. There is a coequal liaison in working out the therapeutic plan for each youngster as the evidence is compiled. The goals and strategies are discussed and appropriate efforts for the school become assigned, but only the teacher knows what is feasible in the given classroom. It may be that the youngster needs to be tolerated at a given level, or it may be that conformity in the group is the planned mode of helping. Handling procedures must be agreed upon and feasible.

6. Participation in follow-up and contacts with school is a teacher function.

7. Expanding the perimeters of school to a broad education, not just "schooling," and to design commensurate broadening curricula depends on the teacher. The teacher responds to the child's life questions as well as to his school questions. This helps to provide information that the normal child gets as he moves around the community, watching events and observing how things are done.

8. Since the children are growing up for a time without their natural parents, teachers anticipate more intensive needs for adult interest and encouragement in their lives. Teachers stand ready to supply more of the sustaining influences otherwise missing in the child's life, realizing at the same time that the child seeks out of all available adults certain ones for deeper relationships, and it may be a teacher.

Evaluation

The most sophisticated analysis of the many problems of evaluation of institutional programs is found in a classic volume on evaluation by Durkin and Durkin (1975). There are good residential programs and poor ones; there are children and youth who are properly placed and those who are inappropriately placed; there are behaviors that can be remediated and other syndromes that are biological and can only be mitigated. The organic and psychotic have the poorer prognosis: the sociopathic are also less likely to change. High IQ and parent cooperation are assets for positive results in institutional placement, as well as the quality of relationships with the therapeutic staff, success with peers, and support after treatment. The institutional teacher should be dealing with the most seriously maligned children where prognosis is more limited than in other services. One recognizes that children placed in total care settings should be those who are the most difficult to treat and those with the least environmental support. Often placement is the last effort after everything else has failed, which again is far from a good prognosis. If the institution, as is the case for many state institutions, gets mostly sociopaths or regressed schizophrenics or low-functioning autistics, can the program be evaluated simply on the basis of "cures"? We have already reviewed the prognosis of syndromes in earlier pages. One evaluates the process and the quality of the service provided rather than counting those who are eventually returned to the mainstream.

In one of the few evaluations in the new field of day treatment, Grimes, Weiss, and Mazuryk (n.d.) report on a six-month follow-up study of 153 children. The Bristol Social Adjustment Guide for School and a parent questionnaire for the home were used for evaluation. The clinical team had judged the children ready for discharge. The results indicate the program "does well with depressed, withdrawn and even psychotic children." The acting-out children were seen as improved in the school and home and yet not by the clinicians. Some outcome studies show awareness of the complications of efficacy research. Prentice-Dunn, Wilson, and Lyman (1981) have related preadmission variables of day school and inpatient treatment to behavior and academic improvement. Parent involvement and IQ are related to improvement in both areas. In addition, age and living conditions were predictive of behavior gains and race of academic gains.

Project Re-Ed, as we learned, is designed as a short-term, educationally based, high community interaction residential program. Weinstein (1969; 1970) has done several follow-up studies. The Re-Ed children were found to have improved control, behavior, and self-concepts. The program was particularly useful for children with combined academic and behavior problems. Agencies saw 80 percent improved social gains, parents 85 percent, and the school 75 percent. Their continued below-the-norm academic performances appear, in teachers' perceptions, to reflect lower pupil ability.

In a recent study Davids and Salvatore (1976) used a questionnaire to parents for a follow-up study of residential child patients with varied and complex pathology. Initial acting out and aggressive behavior were not predictive of subsequent adjustment. Argumentativeness was related to poor prognosis; fearful and withdrawn children tended to end up with better adjustment while thinking disorders and peculiar behavior were indicative of poor subsequent adjustment. Age, duration of stay, or place of subsequent residence were not indicative. Of the seventy-one cases, twenty-nine were judged making good subsequent adjustment, twenty-two fair, and twenty poor. The good group had become better subsequent to discharge while the poor one had become worse. Also predictive ratings at time of discharge were not related to subsequent status, although accuracy of prediction of poor adjustment is better than the accuracy of predicting good adjustment. Garber (1972) reviews literature and then reports in detail on 120 adolescents from admission to one to ten years after discharge. Interestingly, 70 percent were at grade level on admission. One-fifth did excellent schoolwork in the hospital, one-sixth average, and one-third poor. Psychotic patients were least improved; they had shown the least involvement with peers and program and were treated with medications. The reverse was true of patients who were remarkably improved. A surprising number were rehospitalized.

Lewis et al. (1980) raise questions regarding the discharge of children going into the vulnerable adolescent period. Of the fifty-one preadolescent admissions, with an average of about two years of treatment, most had poor subsequent social adaptation. Children with good outcomes tended to be younger and not psychotic. Gosset and his team (1973) reviewed thirteen studies and concluded that the factors that were important in outcome were severity of psychopathology, situational forces, intelligence, adequacy of treatment, and continuation of psychotherapy after hospitalization.

In a provocative report Bloom and Hopewell (1982) trace the reentry into the mainstream of eighty-eight adolescent patients from a state mental hospital. Only those discharged to their homes, foster homes, or group homes were included. By six months, 43 percent had been rehospitalized. Sex, diagnosis, and prognosis were among the nondiscriminant variables; proper educational/vocational placement, and at least one parent in the home were positive indicators, and other family members hospitalized and the longer the stay were negative indicators of survival.

Fineberg and colleagues (1982) report a study of their own and review recent evaluations of adolescent inpatient treatment. The majority report improvement from admission to follow-up. They report overall improvement rates of 62 to 87 percent, with the most astute studies ranging from 66 to 75 percent. The median rate quoted from previous work on adolescent improvement without psychotherapy is 39 percent.

Overall, the multitude of entry variables, treatment variables, and post-hospitalization support variables make discriminant predictions dubious. What comes out in general is that the younger the application of treatment, the less the disturbance, the more family involvement and subsequent support, the more targeted the treatment, and the brighter the child, the better the prognosis. Positive adjustment to school and the ability to find a suitable educational experience (i.e., vocational) are indicators of successful intervention. Unfortunately there is relatively little attention to the crucial role of education in the follow-up studies.

THE HALFWAY HOUSE

We would like to believe that most SEI pupils will be able to return to a normal setting. They may need to go through the hierarchy of educational services in reverse rather than make a jump from where they are into the mainstream. Some need a time after intensive treatment to consolidate their gains. Others can never make it all the way back. One after-care program is described by Harding, Bellow, and Penwell (1978). The team consists of a social worker, special educator, and a community service worker. This program came about because of a study of the post-hospitalization records of discharged patients, including those who had made significant gains. Problems in school, home, and community continued. Thus specific professional help is needed for each of the three major domains of life. The teacher works to a considerable extent with vocational planning, starting several weeks before discharge, and this is a very specialized SEI teaching role.

Children and youth with a limited prognosis for a normal independent life need a protected placement. In place of continuing institutionalization, they need a small benign "living-in" center, perhaps for life. There will need to be competent, trained staff. It was stated that half of the children in one state could be deinstitutionalized were there such places for them to go, since so many had no home to return to. A sheltered workshop or protected job placement is added to increase their capacity to live normal lives even if they still need at least some quasi-mental health support for their general living. Counseling, group life and above all useful work must be provided. More than the normal young adult, these young adults are in need of vocational rehabilitation and continuing education. SEI teachers have a role to play with young adults. When the emotionally disturbed youngster is brought into maximum participation, whatever his life pattern turns out to be, there will be continuing educational needs.

EPILOGUE: WHAT OF THE FUTURE?

Eli Bower, in one of his many creative papers regarding special education, *Sacred Cows, Fuzzy-Wuzzies and Handicapped Children* (1979), describes certain beliefs that encapsulate special education: laws educate handicapped children, more laws equals more education; diagnosis must always precede placement; and nothing can be done until we know the complex developmental and ecological factors causing the problem. Hobbs (1974) proposes a total overhaul of classification and services for special children, based upon the Re Ed model and more concentration on the child's environment. Forness, et al. (1984)

propose several needed changes to improve SEI education. First, we need to overhaul eligibility, which is now focused on definitions and categorization. Rather, that effort should be put on data that will individualize the pupil's program. Second, the primacy of the teacher should be restored. There will be master clinical teachers who supervise aides and oversee programs, making the critical decisions about the youngster. Third, we need cooperative interagency agreements to fill in the gaps of services to children and families. Finally, controversial treatments should be monitored because there are many dubious procedures advocated for teacher use.

What is perhaps more important for SEI teachers, Where is special education for the SEI headed? Some have even said we should have a recess until we have digested our present efforts.

With ideological and financial retrenchment abroad in the land, the old solution of more laws and all of the needed money is no longer a probable course. Program surveillance by authorities is predicted to decrease. Of course there will be new fads, new curriculum aids, and new arrangements of service, all purporting to be the final solution. With the need to serve more pupils with less resource, there will be pressure toward the superficial and consultation rather than hands-on service to pupils. A survey of trends expected by the experts indicates the following, presented here without evaluation. Mainstreaming will expand and include more serious pupils and regular teachers will have to take special-education courses. Parental involvement will increase. There will be more attention to life skills and especially the vocational futures of our charges. With the move toward competency in graduation requirements, we will have to defend the rights of our pupils to their handicaps. There will be a vast surge of technological/computer-assisted instruction. Educational programs will be extended to preschool and young adult levels. Noncategorical grouping for teaching will increase in contrast to present categorical emphasis. Related to this, special teachers will be trained to teach across categories, perhaps being certified for all types of mild disabilities or all severe. If some of these changes come to pass, there will be obvious alterations in the role of the SEI teacher.

What Can the Individual SEI Teacher Do?

The challenge is what can one do to improve special education for the SEI pupil which will not cost more money? We can examine our beliefs, search for creativity, reduce the isolation of special education, expand our insight, and above all keep our morale, avoiding the zombie burnout syndrome. If burnout of SEI teachers is to be prevented, it will be up to each individual teacher, for little is being done to provide external support. In Zabel and Zabel (1981) the highest risk is for junior high school teachers, but all SEI teachers suffer the highest level of occupational distress. Less distress was reported by older teachers and those with master's degrees. Consulting teachers were at highest risk, followed by institutional teachers. The consulting teachers reported heavy caseloads, multiple bases and middle-man status. Discrepancy between expectations and school realities produce stress and burnout (Zabel, Boomer, and King 1984).

Obviously, the first thing a teacher should do is to look at his support system as it exists and explore ways of obtaining more thorough support if it is inadequate. One also looks at the specifics where one feels pressure and then gets consultation. While some conditions are personal ones, the evidence is that most fatigue is in response to external conditions. Taking a burnout scale once a year is one method of self-monitoring.

Examining Myths, Values, and Beliefs

Much practice is stultified by holding on to beliefs that are limited or erroneous. Do we think too superficially about the complex problem of helping children with socialization and self adequacy? We remember the effort that went into our socialization, and ask how we can provide this for SEI pupils. Schools have to change and become, for some youngsters, a family surrogate in the limited ways possible. We are generic child raisers as well as special educational personnel. There are also myths that mainstreaming will meet more problems than it can, that a placement is a program, or that an assigned role means the person is equal to the conduct of the role, certified or not. There is also the myth that the past can explain everything about behavior when we know most pupils are operating on their prognosis of their future. This leads us to more attention to sources of vulnerability and risk, not of the past but of the future. There is the prevalent mental health myth that we *cure* children. At best we help them improve their lives. Many will have to become responsible for their own survival with little help from the normal support systems for children.

The Search for Creativity in our Practice

Professionals alone cannot supply the necessary help. Can we selectively enlist the participation of latent human resources from peers to grandparents and find ways to train, to support, and to gratify those who give such assistance? There are service clubs dedicated to helping youngsters and there are religious and humanistically oriented persons in the society we must tap.

If we will substitute the life-stream thinking, advocated here, for mainstream thinking there will be a significant realignment of forces. This does not require a new law but it does require venturesome thinking and incorporating such thinking into our actions.

The Foundation for Exceptional Children (CEC, Reston, Virginia) has reported that of all handicapped who graduate or terminate public schooling, 21 percent will become fully employed (earning less than average adults) or go on to college, 40 percent will be unemployed and at the poverty level, 8 percent will be idle much of the time ("wasting," as we say), 26 percent will be on welfare, and 3 percent will be totally dependent and institutionalized. They also report that the government spends 10 percent as much for rehabilitation to independent living as in other support to the handicapped. It is a telling evaluation of IEPs when one thinks in terms of LEP outcomes. The studies reported here on the prognosis for SEI youngsters give little reason to think our situation is better.

Another avenue for creative effort is to maximize the use of crises. Again, it means a shift of emphasis. The woeful lack of positive use of group process is another opportunity for creativity. The cutting edge is the search for wholesome, positive group experiences and the need for youngsters to understand group life.

We have made a significant issue of rethinking assessment but again it will take a concerted effort to realign the procedures around PL 94–142. Meetings often resemble a role-dance gavotte. The teacher can keep the focus on the self-concept of the pupil as the key issue, so that the purpose of the whole discussion will not get lost. Parallel to this is the need for creativity concerning interventions. Clashes of ideology are out of place; we can guard against dissociated fixation on given methodology.

The difficulty and promise in following even these simplistic notions in our practice is not to be underestimated. One can go further and suggest iconoclastic teaching. To do this requires a degree of freedom that many teachers neither have nor seek. Following an existential feeling on an inviting spring day and going on a little trip because the time is right is an example of this. As a teacher said, if one followed all the rules all the time, programs could never emerge from dull mediocrity.

A third area to work on for the future is *counteracting piecemealism*. There is possible improvement through integration of services and filling in the missing spaces. On one hand, this is an advocacy role both personal and organizational for a local complement of necessary resources. If we don't advocate for what we need, whatever we have will be used for whatever the problem, regardless of fit. It is not enough to do one's own job well if there is a paucity of programs at the various levels from prevention to aftercare.

An excellent self-educational process is to do follow-up. A small study done for one's self and for reporting to colleagues is a step in professional maturity. Interviewing past students can reveal as much to a professional as formal courses. What did we do right and what did we do wrong? We also recognize that whatever our effort, it is but a part of a milieu treatment, since the ecological position recognizes the total life-space of the pupil. This reduces the piecework approach.

Professionals can also always work on *knowledge base*. In a manner of speaking, this includes all of the above. We practice only the psychology we really know and believe. Each child is an experiment, an N-of-1 experiment. The children spike many new searches. What is the psychology of attachment? What fosters growth relationships and prevents morbidity? Our fixation on pathology ignores prosocial behavior. There is so much more to communication and talking with youngsters than most of us know. Attribution theory has a primary role in a phenomenological approach. Family dynamics constitute an essential knowledge area. This is more than family pathology. What underlying strata produce child deviance? The change in the male good provider role, the impact of the working mother, and the family in transition are all germane and point the way to helping families without converting them to clients.

Finally, there is *morale,* the emotional tenor of programs. There is the morale of an often angry mainstream where many teachers are doing great things but others are not. How can all mainstream children who need some intervention be served, not just our categorical few? Those who are responsible must energize the system—replace hopelessness with hope. There are many changes that schools will need to make, each generating resistance. There is a lifelong agenda of unfinished business for the SEI educator.

Preventing Burnout

So much depends upon not being burned-out professionally. Our own analysis of burnout in SEI education suggests several aspects. One is that there is too much emphasis on teacher evaluation and too little on program evaluation. Many teachers today have no other employment options so the rapid turnover of the past is no longer feasible. Good teaching positions are scarce and pink slips are prevalent, so people stay on. It would be nice to have a sabbatical to work in a different way and with normal children every few years.

Professionals burn out for many reasons (Edelwich and Brodsky 1980). Some start burned-out (Rothman 1977). Often their training was idealistic, fitting with the rescue mission complex, which doesn't really take place in mental health work. Lawrenson and McKinnon (1982) found almost a 50 percent attrition rate of teachers of the emotionally disturbed in three years, the main reason being "hassles with the administration." The major satisfaction was in student relationships. Because of the nature of these pupils, a teacher should not depend upon that return for their mental health, however.

Some professionals are depressed by the trends in society or their own personal lives and dump it on their work. For others, there is a series of real frustrations in the job, brought on by the regulators or martinet superiors. This could change if only "they" would. It appears to be a confrontation society where a union organization is necessary to press effectively for removal of some of the useless requirements. We can engage vigorously in shaping of the goals of our several professional organizations, particularly the Council of Behavioral Disorders of the Council for Exceptional Children, and the interdisciplinary American Orthopsychiatric Association. The fact is, regardless of the voluminous literature, burnout is another of our series of symptoms and has no common syndrome. But the condition will undermine any program and tends to be contagious. Some meetings are more like bitch sessions, which make those with a positive outlook feel alone.

The dedication to helping others, particularly children and youth, is too easily assumed. It is a consuming profession, taking a great deal out of the person who would help. This tax on our personalities is there whether or not we recognize it, and only the very uninvolved, defensive individuals escape the price in human energy. Do not try to help anyone unless you can empathize with his state. Do not try to help those to whom you feel alien. While the rewards are great, SEI teaching is trying and exhausting, in keeping with any mental health profession.

Finally, the quality of the SEI pupil's experience in the future will depend more and more on the teaching profession. The advances brought about by legislation have about run their course. The recent United States Supreme Court decision, in a 6 to 3 vote, reversed the obligation of schools to provide an opportunity to achieve full potential. The court's view is that congressional intent was to open up public education to handicapped children, not to guarantee any particular level of education.

Who stands guard over the achievements from PL 94–142? It is the parents and the professional special educators. It was ever thus that what is gained must be continually protected. Engaging in struggle for the welfare of children presents the ongoing challenge for SEI teachers. This profession is not for an average professional. We cannot solve all of the problems these children and youth bring with them, but when we help even a few—which the record shows we do repeatedly— we have made a significant reduction in amount of human pain and saved our social order strain. In plain dollars, when we turn one youngster around we have paid back our salary to the society. Frank Wood, from the University of Minnesota, has put it succinctly. About people who work with severe behavior disorders and their overfilled days, he says, "Laughter rides on tears."

Bibliography

Abeson, A., and J. Zettel, 1977. Quiet revolutions: Handicapped children act of 1975. *Exceptional Children* 44:115–28.

The Advocate. 11 (May 1979).

Agee, V. 1979. *Treatment of the violent incorrigible adolescent.* New York: Human Sciences Press.

Ahlstrom, W. M., and R. J. Havighurst. 1971. *400 losers.* San Francisco: Jossey-Bass.

Albion, F. M. 1983. A methodological analysis of self-control in applied settings. *Behavioral Disorders* 8:87–102.

Algozzine, R., C. N. Mercer, and T. Countermine. 1977. The effects of labels and behavior on teacher expectation. *Exceptional Children* 44:131–32.

Algozzine, R., R. Schmid, and R. Conners. 1978. Toward an acceptable definition of emotional disturbance. *Behavioral Disorders* 2:48–53.

Allport, G. W. 1968. *The person in psychology: Selected essays.* Boston: Beacon.

American Psychiatric Association. 1980. *DSM III: Diagnostic and statistical manual of mental disorders.* Washington, D. C.: American Psychiatric Association.

Anastasiow, N. J. 1983. Adolescent pregnancy and special education. *Exceptional Children* 49:396–401.

Anderson, E. 1973. *The disabled school child.* London: Methuen.

Anderson, L. H., S. L. Barner, and H. J. Larson. 1978. Evaluation of written individualized educational programs. *Exceptional Children* 45:207–208.

Anderson, L. W. 1981. *Assessing affective characteristics in the schools.* Boston: Allyn and Bacon.

Anderson, N., and R. T. Marrone. 1979. Therapeutic discussion groups in public-school classes for emotionally disturbed children. *Focus on Exceptional Children* 12:1–15.

Anthony, E. J. 1974. *Children at psychiatric risk.* New York: John Wiley and Sons.

——. 1978. *Vulnerable children.* New York: John Wiley and Sons.

Anthony, E. J., and C. Koupernik. 1974. *Children at psychiatric risk.* Vol. 3, *The child in his family.* New York: John Wiley and Sons.

Antonovsky, A. 1979. *Health, stress, and coping.* San Francisco: Jossey-Bass.

Applied Management Science. 1977. *The education and socialization of institutionalized emotionally disturbed children and youth.* Silver Spring, Md.: Applied Management Science.

Apter, S. J. 1982. *Troubled children/troubled systems.* Elmsford, N.Y.: Pergamon Press.

Arieti, S., and J. Bemporad. 1978. *Severe and mild depression.* New York: Basic Books.

Arkes, H. R. 1981. Impediments to accurate clinical judgment and possible ways to minimize their impact. *Journal of Consulting and Clinical Psychology* 49:323–30.

Arnold, L. E., ed. 1978. *Helping parents help their children.* New York: Brunner/Mazel.

Arter, J. A., and J. R. Jenkins. 1979. Differential diagnosis-prescriptive teaching: A critical appraisal. *Development of Educational Research* 49:517–55.

Ashcraft, C. W. 1970. *School achievement in emotionally handicapped children following clinic treatment.* Research Report OEG-32-52-0120-5026. Nashville, Tenn.: George Peabody College for Teachers.

Aspy, D. 1972. *Toward a technology for humanizing education.* Chicago: Research Press.

Axelrod, S., and S. L. Bailey. 1979. Drug treatment for hyperactivity: Controversies, alternatives, and guidelines. *Exceptional Children* 45:544–50.

Babad, E. Y., M. Birnbaum, and K. D. Benne. 1983. *The social self.* Beverly Hills, Calif.: Sage Publications.

Bachrach, A., F. L. Mosley, F. L. Swindle, and M. Wood. 1978. *Developmental therapy for young children with autistic characteristics.* Baltimore: University Park Press.

Bagnato, S. J. 1980. The efficacy of diagnostic reports as individualized guides to prescriptive goal planning. *Journal of Exceptional Children* 46:554–57.

Bagnato, S. J. and J. T. Neisworth. 1980. The intervention efficacy index: An approach to preschool program accountability. *Exceptional Children* 46:264–69.

Baker, A. M. 1979. Cognitive functioning of psychotic children: A reappraisal. *Exceptional Children* 45:344–48.

Baker, E. H., and T. F. Thomas. 1980. The use of observational procedures in school psychological services. *School Psychology Monographs* 4:25–45.

Ballard, J., B. Ramirez, and F. Weintraub. 1982. *Special Education in America:*

Its legal and governmental foundations. Reston, Va.: Council for Exceptional Children.

Ballard, J. B., and J. Zettel. 1977. Public law 94–142 and section 504: What they say about rights and protections. *Exceptional Children* 44:177–97.

Balow, B., and G. Reid. 1978. *Autism sourcebook.* Minneapolis: University of Minnesota Press.

Bandura, A. 1974. Behavior theory and the models of man. *American Psychologist* 29:859–69.

———. 1977. *Social learning theory.* Englewood Cliffs, N.J.: Prentice-Hall.

———. 1982a. Self-efficacy mechanism in human agency. *American Psychologist* 37:122–48.

———. 1982b. The psychology of chance encounters and life paths. *American Psychologist.* 37:747–56.

Baron, R. A. 1977. *Human aggression.* New York: Plenum Press.

Barr, A. S. 1948. The measurement and prediction of teaching efficiency: A summary of investigations. *Journal of Experimental Education* 16:203–283.

———. 1955. The measurement and prediction of teaching efficiency. *Review of Educational Research* 25:261–70.

Barth, R. 1979. Home-based reinforcement of school behavior: A review and analysis. *Review of Educational Research* 49: 436–58.

Baruch, D. 1964. *One little boy.* New York: Delta.

Baskin, B. H., and K. S. Harris, 1977. *Notes from a different drummer: A guide to juvenile fiction portraying the handicapped.* New York: Bowker.

Battle, J., and T. Blowers. 1982. A longitudinal comparative study of the self-esteem of students in regular and special classes. *Journal of Learning Disabilities* 15: 100–102.

Bauer, H. 1974. *Learning to be: The psychoeducational management of severely dysfunctional children.* Seattle: Special Child.

Bauer, W., and J. L. Bauer. 1982. The development of self-concept boundaries. *Adolescence.* 17:685–93.

Beare, P. 1981. Mainstreaming approach for behaviorally disordered secondary students in a rural school district. *Behavioral Disorders* 6:209–218.

Beare, P. L., and E. C. Lynch. 1983. Rural area emotional disturbance service delivery: Problems and future directions. *Behavioral Disorders* 8:113–19.

Beck, A. T. 1976. *Cognitive therapy and emotional disorders.* New York: International University Press.

Beebe, M. C. 1978. The development and evaluation of one process of diagnostic-prescriptive programming. Ph.D. diss., University of Michigan.

Behar, L., and S. Stringfield. 1974. A behavior-rating scale for the preschool child. *Developmental Psychology* 10:601–610.

Behavioral Disorders 4 (February and May 1979).

Belsky, J. 1980. Child maltreatment: An ecological integration. *American Psychologist* 35:320–35.

Benezon, R. O. 1982. *Music therapy in child psychosis.* Springfield, Ill.: Charles C. Thomas.

Bennett, A. 1977. Therapeutic implications of physical education and competitive sport for child-care practice. Study, Cortland County Mental Health Center, Cortland, N. Y.

Bermann, E. 1973. *Scapegoat.* Ann Arbor: University of Michigan Press.

Bettelheim, B. 1976 *The uses of enchantment: The meaning and importance of fairy tales.* New York: Alfred A. Knopf.

Blom, G. E. 1966. Psychoeducational aspects of classroom management. *Exceptional Children* 32:377–83.

Bloom, R. B., and L. R. Hopewell. 1982. Psychiatric hospitalization of adolescents and successful mainstream entry. *Exceptional Children* 48:352–57.

Bloom, R. M. 1976. Teacher-pupil compatibility and teachers' ratings of children's behavior. *Psychology in the Schools* 13:142–45.

Bloomer, L. W., and T. R. King. 1981. Teacher identification of behavior problems among junior high school students: A preliminary study. *Behavioral Disorders* 6:219–22.

Boucher, C. R., and S. L. Deno. 1979. Learning disabled and emotionally disturbed: Will the labels affect teacher planning? *Psychology in the Schools* 16:395–402.

Bower, E. M. 1960. *Early identification of emotionally handicapped children in school.* Springfield, Ill.: Charles C. Thomas.

———. 1979. Sacred cows, fuzzy-wuzzies, and handicapped children. Paper presented at Conference of the International Association for Children with Learning Disabilities, 3 May, at San Francisco, Calif.

———. 1982. *Early identification of emotionally handicapped children in school.* Springfield, Ill.: Charles C. Thomas.

Brand, A. G. 1980. *Therapy in writing.* Lexington, Mass.: Lexington Books.

Bratton, S. 1979. The Madison School program: Programming for secondary level severely emotionally disturbed youth. *Behavioral Disorders* 4:153–62.

Brennan, T., D. Huizinga, and D. S. Elliott. 1978. *The social psychology of runaways.* Lexington, Mass.: Lexington Books.

Brickman, P., V. C. Rabinowitz, J. Kayuza, D. Coates, E. Cohn, and L. Kidder, 1982. Models of helping and coping. *American Psychologist* 37:368–84.

Brim, O. G., and J. Kagan, eds. 1980. *Constancy and change in human development.* Cambridge, Mass.: Harvard University Press.

Brolin, D. E., and B. J. D'Alonzo. 1979. Critical issues in career education for handicapped students. *Exceptional Children* 45:246–55.

Brown, G. I. 1971. *Human teaching for human learning: An introduction to confluent education.* New York: Viking Press.

Brown, W. K., and B. F. Simpson, Jr. 1976. Confrontation of self through outdoor challenge: Pennsylvania's outdoor experience for juvenile offenders. *Behavioral Disorders* 2:41–48.

Brozovitch, R. 1969. *A descriptive follow-up study of a public school program for the emotionally disturbed.* Research report OEG-0-8-085068-3628. Pontiac, Mich.: Public Schools.

Bussis, A. M. 1976. *Beyond surface curriculum.* Boulder, Colo.: Westview Press.

Byler, R. V., G. M. Lewis, and R. J. Totman. 1969. *Teach us what we want to know.* New York: Mental Health Materials Center.

Cameron, J. A. 1977. Parental treatment, children's temperament, and the risk of children's behavior problems. *American Journal of Orthopsychiatry* 47:568–76.

Canfield, J., and H. C. Wells. 1976. *One hundred ways to enhance self-concept in the classroom: A handbook for teachers and parents.* Englewood Cliffs, N. J.: Prentice-Hall.

Caplan, G. 1961. *Prevention of mental disorders in children.* New York: Basic Books.

Caplan, G. and R. S. Lindsay. 1975. *Crisis theory: A critical overview.* Nedlands, W. A.: University of Western Australia Press.

Carlberg, C. and K. Kavale. 1980. The efficacy of special vs. regular class placement for exceptional children: A meta-analysis. *Journal of Special Education* 14:295–309.

Cartledge, G. and J. A. F. Milburn. 1978. The case for teaching social skills in the classroom: A review. *Developmental Educational Research* 1:133–56.

Cass, L. K. and C. B. Thomas. 1979. *Childhood pathology and later adjustment.* New York: Wiley-Interscience.

Cautela, J. R. and J. Groden. 1978. *Relaxation: A comprehensive manual for adults, children, and children with special needs.* Champaign, Ill.: Research Press.

Chandler, L. A. 1981. The source of stress inventory. *Psychology in the Schools* 18:164–68.

Chappell, G. E. 1977. Cognitive-linguistic therapy: Comprehension and problem solving. *Journal of Learning Disabilities* 10:21–25.

Charles, C. M. 1980. *Building classroom discipline.* New York: Longman.

Chassan, J. B. 1961. Stochastic models of the single case as the basis of clinical research design. *Behavioral Science* 6:42–50.

Cochrane, C. T. and D. V. Myers. 1980. *Children in crisis.* Beverly Hills, Calif.: Sage Publications.

Cohen, S. 1977. Improving attitudes toward the handicapped. *Educational Forum* 42:9–20.

Compas, B. E., R. Friedland-Bandas, R. Bastien, and H. Adelman. 1981. Parent and child causal attributions related to the child's clinical problem. *Journal of Abnormal Child Psychology* 9:389–97.

Cone, J. D., and R. Hawkins, eds. 1977. *Behavioral assessment.* New York: Brunner/Mazel.

Cooper, J. O., and D. L. Edge. 1978. *Parenting.* Columbus, O.: Charles E. Merrill Publishing Co.

Corsini, R. J., ed. 1979. *Current psychotherapies.* Itasca, Ill.: F. E. Peacock Publishers.

Council of Exceptional Children. 1974. *Careers.* Reston, Va.: Council of Exceptional Children.

Craig, E. 1972. *You're not listening.* New York: Baron.

Creative Therapeutics. 1973. *The talking, feeling, and doing game.* Cresshill, N.J.: Creative Therapeutics.

Crisp, A. H. 1980. *Anorexia nervosa: Let me be.* New York: Academic Press.

Critchley, D. L. 1979. The adverse influence of psychiatric diagnostic labels on the observation of child behavior. *American Journal of Orthopsychiatry* 49:157–59.

Cruickshank, W. M., W. C. Morse, and J. O. Grant. 1983. The IEPC meeting: A step in the history of special education. Typescript.

Cruickshank, W. M., W. C. Morse, and J. S. Johns. 1980. *Learning disabilities: The struggle from adolescence toward adulthood.* Syracuse, N.Y.: Syracuse University Press.

Cullinan, D., and M. H. Epstein, eds. 1979. *Special education for adolescents.* Columbus, O.: Charles E. Merrill Publishing Co.

Curran, T. J., and R. Algozzine, 1980. Ecological disturbance: A test of the matching hypothesis. *Behavioral Disorders* 5:169–74.

Davids, A., and P. D. Salvatore. 1976. Residential treatment of disturbed children and adequacy of their subsequent adjustment: A follow-up study. *American Journal of Orthopsychiatry* 46:62–73.

Deen, M. A., and W. R. Porter. 1965. Development of a program for the reeducation and rehabilitation of emotionally handicapped male adolescents within a public-school setting. Research Report OEG 32-30-0000-1025. Rockville, Md.: Montgomery County Public Schools.

Dehouske, E. J. 1979. Original writing: A therapeutic tool in working with disturbed adolescents. *Exceptional Children* 11:66–70.

DeMagistris, R. J., and S. C. Imber. 1980. The effects of life-space interviewing on academic and social performance of behaviorally disordered children. *Behavioral Disorders* 6:12–25.

Dembo, M. H., R. K. Yoshida, T. Reilly, and V. Reilly. 1978. Teacher-student interactions in special-education classrooms. *Exceptional Children* 45:212–13.

Dennison, G. 1969. *The lives of children.* New York: Random House.

Deno, E. 1970. Special education as developmental capital. *Exceptional Children* 37: 229–37.

Deno, S. L. and P. K. Mirkin. 1980. Data-based IEP development: An approach to substantive compliance. *Teaching Exceptional Children* 12:92–97.

Diamond, B. 1979. Myths of mainstreaming. *Journal of Learning Disabilities* 12:41–45.

Dickenson, D. J. 1978. Direct assessment of behavioral and emotional problems. *Psychology in the Schools* 15:472–77.

Dickson, R. L. 1976. The relationship between attitudes and reinforcers: An investigation with emotionally disturbed children. *Journal of Special Education* 10:365–71.

Doernberg, N., B. Rosen, and T. T. Walker. 1968. *A home-training program for young mentally ill children.* Public Health Service Research Grant RO1 MH-14794. Brooklyn, N.Y.: League School for Seriously Disturbed Children.

Dorward, B. 1963. A comparison of competencies for regular classroom teachers and teachers of emotionally disturbed children. *Exceptional Children* 30:67–73.

Doxiads, S. 1976. Residential care for normal and deviant children. In *Psychopathology and Child Development,* ed. E. Schopler and R. J. Reichler. New York: Plenum Press.

Dreikurs, R., and L. Grey. 1968. *A new approach to discipline: Logical consequences.* New York: Hawthorn Books.

Dreyer, S. S. 1977. *The bookfinder: A guide to children's literature about the needs and problems of youth aged two through fifteen.* Circle Pines, Minn.: American Guidance Services.

Duffey, J. B., and M. L. Fedner. 1978. Educational diagnosis with instructional use. *Exceptional Child* 44:246–51.

Duggan, H. A. 1978. *A second chance: Empathy in adolescent development.* Lexington, Mass.: Lexington Books.

Dunn, L. M. 1968. Special education for the mildly retarded: Is much of it justifiable? *Exceptional Children* 35:5–22.

Dupont, H., D. Gardner, and D. Brody. 1974. *Toward affective development.* Circle Pines, Minn.: American Guidance Service.

Durkin, R. P., and A. B. Durkin. 1975. Evaluating residential treatment programs for disturbed children. In *Handbook of evaluation research,* ed. M. Guttentag and E. L. Struening. Vol. 2. Beverly Hills, Calif.: Sage Publications.

Dyer, C. D. 1974. Socially and emotionally handicapped. In *Psychoeducational diagnosis of exceptional children,* ed. M. V. Wisland. Springfield, Ill.: Charles C. Thomas.

Edelwich, J. and A. Brodsky. 1980. *Burn out.* New York: Human Sciences Press.

Eggers, C. 1978. Course and prognosis of childhood schizophrenia. *Journal of Autism and Childhood Schozophrenia* 8:21–36.

Ekstein, R. and R. L. Motto. 1969. *From learning for love to love of learning.* New York: Brunner/Mazel.

Elitov, P. J. 1984. Persistent and transient behavior problems in elementary school children. Ph.D. diss., University of Michigan.

Emery, G., S. D. Hollon, and R. C. Bedrosian. 1981. *New directions in cognitive therapy.* New York: Guilford Press.

Emery, R. E., J. A. Binkoff, A. C. Houts, and E. G. Carr. 1983. Children as independent variables: Some clinical implications of child-effects. *Behavior Therapy* 14:398–412.

Englemann, S., A. Granzon, and H. Severson. 1979. Diagnosing instruction. *Journal of Special Education.* 13:355–63.

Enright, R. D. and S. J. Sutterfield. 1979. Treating the regular class child in the mainstreaming process: Increasing social cognitive development. *Psychology in the Schools* 16:110–18.

Epstein, M. H., D. Cullinan, and D. A. Sabatino. 1977. State definitions of behavior disorders. *Journal of Special Education* 11:417–23.

Epstein, M. H., A. C. Repp, and D. Cullinan. 1978. Decreasing "obscene" language of behaviorally disordered children through the use of a DRL schedule. *Psychology in the Schools* 15:419–23.

Epstein, N. B., and L. A. Vlok. 1981. Research on the results of psychotherapy: A summary of the evidence. *American Journal of Orthopsychiatry* 51:1027–38.

Erickson, K. 1977. Disruptive youth and the rights of others. *Today's Education* 66:121–22.

Erikson, E. 1963. *Childhood and society.* New York: W. W. Norton.

Exceptional Children 47 (1980).

Eyde, D. R., and A. H. Fink, eds. 1979. *Behavioral Disorders 5.*

Fagen, S. A., and N. J. Long. 1979. A psychoeducational curriculum approach to teaching self-control. *Behavioral Disorders* 4:68.

Fagen, S. A., N. Long, and D. J. Stevens. 1975. *Teaching children self-control in the classroom: A psychoeducational curriculum.* Columbus, O.: Charles E. Merrill Publishing Co.

Fareta, G. 1981. A profile of aggression from adolescence to adulthood. *American Journal of Orthopsychiatry* 5:439–53.

Farkas, G. M. 1980. An ontological analysis of behavior therapy. *American Psychologist* 35:364–74.

Fassler, Joan. 1978. *Helping children cope.* New York: Free Press.

Federal Register. 1977. Washington, D.C.: U.S. Government Printing Office.

Feinstein, S. C., and P. L. Giovacchini, eds. 1971–75; 1979; 1982. *Adolescent psychiatry: Developmental and clinical studies.* Vols. 1–4, 6, 7, and 9. Chicago: University of Chicago Press.

Feinstein, S. C., and J. G. Looney, eds. 1982. *Adolescent psychiatry,* vol. 10. University of Chicago Press.

Feinstein, S., and P. Giovacchini, eds. 1971–83. *Adolescent psychiatry, developmental and clinical studies.* Annals of the American Society for

Adolescent Psychiatry, Vol. 1, 1971; Vol. 2, 1973; Vol. 3, 1974; Vol. 4, 1975; Vol. 5, 1977; Vol. 6, 1978; Vol. 7, 1979; Vol. 8, 1980; Vol. 8, 1981; Vol. 10, 1983. New York: Aronson.

Fenichel, C. 1966. Psychoeducational approaches for seriously disturbed children in the classroom. In *Intervention approaches in educating emotionally disturbed children,* ed. Peter Knoblock. Syracuse, N.Y.: Syracuse University Press.

————. 1976. Socializing the severely disturbed child. In *Psychopathology and child development,* ed. E. Schopler and R. Reichler. New York: Plenum Press.

Ferdinande, R. J., and R. C. Colligan. 1980. Psychiatric hospitalization: Mainstream reentry planning for adolescent patients. *Exceptional Children* 45:544–48.

Fernald, G. 1943. *Remedial techniques in basic school subjects.* New York: McGraw-Hill.

Feuerstein, R. 1979. *The dynamic assessment of retarded performers: The learning potential assessment device.* Baltimore, Md.: University Park Press.

Fick, L. 1979. Self-control strategies for emotionally disabled students. *Iowa Perspective* (May).

Field, T. M., ed. 1979. *Infants born at risk.* Jamaica, N.Y.: SP Medical and Scientific Books.

Fineberg, B. L., P. W. Kettlewell, and S. K. Sawards. 1982. An evaluation of adolescent inpatient services. *American Journal of Orthopsychiatry* 52:337–45.

Fink, A. H. 1970. An analysis of teacher-pupil interaction in classes for the emotionally handicapped. Ph.D. diss., University of Michigan.

————. 1972. Teacher-pupil interaction in classes for the emotionally handicapped. *Exceptional Children* 38:469–74.

Fink, A. H., and C. J. Kokaska, eds. 1983. *Career education for behaviorally disordered students.* Reston, Va.: Council for Exceptional Children.

Forness, S., and F. Langdon. 1974. School in a psychiatric hospital. *Journal of Child Psychiatry* 13:562–76.

Forness, S. R. 1979. Clinical criteria for mainstreaming mildly handicapped children. *Psychology in the Schools* 16:508–514.

Forness, S. R., and D. P. Cantwell. 1982. DSM III psychiatric diagnosis and special education. *Journal of Special Education* 16:49–65.

Forness, S. R., E. Sinclair, and A. T. Russell. 1984. Serving children with emotional or behavior disorders: Implications for educational policy. *American Journal of Orthopsychiatry* 54:22–23.

Foster, G. G., J. E. Ysseldyke, and J. H. Reese. 1975. I wouldn't have seen it if I hadn't believed it. *Exceptional Children* 41:469–73.

Foster, H. L. 1974. *Ribbin', jivin', and playing the dozens.* Cambridge, Mass.: Ballinger Publish Co.

Foster, R. M., and D. Flomos. 1978. Anger, disability, and demands on the family. *American Journal of Orthopsychiatry* 48:228–36.

Fraiberg. S. 1980. *Clinical studies in infant mental health: The first year of life.* New York: Basic Books.

Frankel, F., S. R. Forness, S. L. Rowe, and J. Westlake. 1979. Individualizing schedules of instruction for school children with learning and behavior problems. *Psychology in the Schools* 16:270–79.

Fremont, T. S., M. J. Klingsporn, and J. H. Wilson. 1976. Identifying emotional disturbance in children: The professionals differ. *Journal of School Psychology* 14:275–82.

French, A., and I. Berlin. 1971. *Depression in children and adolescents.* New York: Human Sciences Press.

Freud, A. 1946. *The ego and the mechanisms of defense.* New York: International Universities Press.

Friedman, R., ed. 1973. *Family roots of school learning and behavior disorders.* Springfield, Ill.: Charles C. Thomas.

Fuller, G. D. 1978. Current status of biofeedback in clinical practice. *American Psychologist* 33:39–48.

Gadow, K. D. 1979. *Children on medication: A primer for school personnel.* Reston, Va.: Council for Exceptional Children.

Gagne, E. E. 1977. Educating delinquents: A review of research. *Journal of Special Education* 11:13–27.

Gajar, A. 1979. Educable mentally retarded, learning disabled, emotionally disturbed: Similarities and differences. *Exceptional Children* 45:470–71.

Gallagher, P. A. 1970. A synthesis of classroom scheduling techniques for emotionally disturbed children. *Focus on Exceptional Children* 2:1–12.

———. 1978. *Teaching students with behavior disorders: Techniques for classroom instruction.* Denver: Love Publishing Co.

Garber, B. 1972. *Follow-up study of hospitalized adolescents.* New York: Brunner/Mazel.

Gardner, G. G., and K. Olness. 1981. *Hypnosis and hypnotherapy with children.* New York: Grune and Stratton.

Gardner, R. A. 1971. *Therapeutic communication with children: The mutual story-telling technique.* New York: Science House.

Gardner, W. I. 1977. *Learning and behavior characteristics of exceptional children and youth: A humanistic behavioral approach.* Boston: Allyn and Bacon.

Garfield, S. L. 1983. Effectiveness of psychotherapy: The perennial controversy. *Professional Psychology* 14:35–43.

Garfinkel, P. E., and D. M. Garner. *Anorexia nervosa.* New York: Brunner/Mazel.

Garrett, J. E., and N. Brazil. 1979. Categories used for identification and education of exceptional children. *Exceptional Children* 45:291–92.

Gast, D. L., and C. M. Nelson. 1977. Time out in the classroom: Implications for special education. *Exceptional Children* 43:461–64.

Geddes, D. 1980. *Psychomotor individualized education programs.* Boston: Allyn and Bacon.

Geston, E. L., E. L. Cowen, M. A. DeStefano, and R. Gallagher. 1978. Teachers' judgments of class-related and teaching-related problem situations. *Journal of Special Education* 12:171–81.

Gerston, J. C., T. S. Langner, J. C. Eisenberg, O. Simcha-Fagan, and E. D. McCarthy. 1976. Stability and change in types of behavioral disturbance of children and adolescents. *Journal of Abnormal Child Psychology* 4:111–28.

Gickling, E. E., and J. T. Theobald. 1975. Mainstreaming: Affect or effect? *Journal of Special Education* 9:317–28.

Gilliam, J. E. 1979. Contributions and status rankings of educational planning committee participants. *Exceptional Children* 45:466–68.

Gillingham, A., and B. Stillman. 1960. *Remedial training, manual, green.* 7th ed. Cambridge, Mass.: Educator's Publishing Service.

Gillung, T. B., and C. N. Rucker. 1977. Labels and teacher expectations. *Exceptional Children* 43:464–65.

Glasser, W. 1965. *Reality therapy.* New York: Harper and Row.

———. 1969. *Schools without failure.* New York: Harper and Row.

Glavin, J. P., H. C. Quay, F. R. Annesley, and J. S. Werry. 1971. An experimental resource room for behavior-problem children. *Exceptional Children* 38:131–37.

Glovinsky, I. 1979. The use of fairy tales in educational therapy. *Hawthorn Center Bulletin* 5:3–8.

Gold, M. 1958. Power in the classroom. *Sociometry* 21:50–60.

———. 1977. Scholastic experiences, self-esteem, and delinquent behavior: A theory for alternative schools. In *Theoretical perspectives on school crime,* ed. R. Z. Emrick. Washington, D.C.: U. S. Department of Health, Education, and Welfare.

Goldfarb, W., D. Meyers, J. Florsheim, and N. Goldfarb. 1978. *Psychotic children grown up.* New York: Human Sciences Press.

Goldfried, M. R. 1980. Toward the delineation of therapeutic change principles. *American Psychologist* 35:991–99.

Goldstein, A. P. 1980. *Skill streaming the adolescent: A structured learning approach to teaching prosocial skills.* Champaign, Ill.: Research Press.

Goldstein, H. 1974. *Social learning curriculum.* Columbus, O.: Charles E. Merrill Publishing Co.

Goldstein, S., B. Strickland, A. P. Turnbull, and L. Curry. 1980. An observational analysis of the IEP conference. *Exceptional Children* 46:278–86.

Gorenstein, E. 1984. Debating mental illness. *American Psychologist* 39:50–56.

Gossett, J. T., S. B. Lewis, J. M. Lewis, and V. A. Phillips. 1973. Follow-up of adolescents treated in a psychiatric hospital. *American Journal of Orthopsychiatry* 43:602–610.

Graham, S., F. Hudson, N. B. Burdy, and D. Carpenter. 1980. Educational personnel's perceptions of mainstreaming and resource room effectiveness. *Psychology in the Schools* 17:128–34.

Graubard, P. S. 1976. The use of indigenous grouping as the reinforcement agent in teaching disturbed delinquents to learn. In *Conflict in the classroom*, ed. N. Long et al. 3d ed. Belmont, Calif.: Wadsworth.

Graubard, P. and H. Rosenberg. 1974. *Classrooms that work*. New York: E. P. Dutton and Co.

Graybill, D., and H. Gabel. 1978. Relationship of teacher nominations for parent counseling to perceptions of children's behavior problems. *Southern Journal of Educational Research* 12:151–159.

Greenwood, C. R., Walker, H. M., and H. Hops. 1977. Issues in social/interaction/withdrawal assessment. *Exceptional Child* 43:490–502.

Gresham, F. M. 1982. Misguided mainstreaming: The case for social-skills training with handicapped children. *Exceptional Children* 48:422–33.

Grieger, R. M. and H. C. Richards. 1976. Prevalence and structure of behavior symptoms among children in special education and regular settings. *Journal of School Psychology* 14:27–38.

Grimes, C., D. S. Weiss, and G. R. Mazuryk. n.d. School-age day treatment: Concept and evaluation. Toronto, Can.: Thistletown Regional Centre. Mimeo.

Grosenick, J. K., and S. L. Huntze. 1980. *National needs analysis in behavioral disorders: Human resource issues in behavior disorders*. Columbia, Mo.: Department of Special Education, University of Missouri.

Grosenick, J. K., S. L. Huntze, B. Kohan, R. L. Peterson, C. S. Robertshaw, and F. H. Wood. 1981. *Disciplinary exclusion of seriously emotionally disturbed children*. Columbia, Mo.: Department of Special Education, University of Missouri.

———. 1982. *Psychotherapy as a related service: National needs analysis in behavior disorders*. Columbia, Mo.: Department of Special Education, University of Missouri.

Grossman, H. 1972. *Nine rotten lousy kids*. New York: Holt, Rinehart, and Winston.

Guidano, V. F., and G. Liotti. 1983. *Cognitive processes and emotional disorders: A structural approach to psychotherapy*. New York: The Guilford Press.

Guindon, J. 1969. The reeducation process. Paper read at 47th Annual Convention of the Council for Exceptional Children, 1969, at Denver, Colo.

Gump, P., P. Schoeggen, and F. Redl. 1957. The camp milieu and its immediate effects. *Journal of Social Issues* 13:40–46.

Gump, P., and B. Sutton-Smith. 1955. The "it" role in children's games. *The Group* 17:3–8.

Guralnick, M. J. 1976. The value of integrating handicapped and non-handicapped preschool children. *American Journal of Orthopsychiatry* 46:236–45.

———, ed. 1977. *Early intervention and the integration of handicapped and nonhandicapped children*. Baltimore, Md.: University Park Press.

Hallahan, D. P., and J. Kauffman. 1977. Labels, categories, behaviors: ED, LD, and EMR reconsidered. *Journal of Special Education* 11:139–51.

Hallahan, D P., J. W. Lloyd, and L. Stoller. 1982. *Improving attention with self-monitoring: A manual for teachers.* Charlottesville, Va.: Learning Disabilities Institute, University of Virginia.

Hallahan, D. P., ed. 1980. Teaching exceptional children to use cognitive strategies. *Exceptional Education Quarterly* 1.

Halleck, S. 1978. *The treatment of emotional disorders.* New York: Jason Aronson.

Halpern, A. S. 1979. Adolescents and young adults. *Exceptional Children* 45:518–23.

Harasymiw, S. J., and M. D. Horne. 1976. Teacher attitudes toward handicapped children and regular class integration. *Journal of Special Educaton* 10:393–401.

Harding, E. H., J. Bellow, and L. W. Penwell. 1978. Project aftercare: Follow-up to residential treatment. *Behavioral Disorders* 4:13–23.

Haring, G., and E. L. Phillips. 1972. *Analysis and modification of classroom behavior.* New York: Prentice Hall.

Harrington, A. 1972. *Psychopaths.* New York: Simon and Schuster.

Harris, W. J., D. R. King, and R. J. Drummond. 1978. Personality variables of children nominated as emotionally handicapped by classroom teachers. *Psychology in the Schools* 15:361–63.

Harrison, S. I., ed. 1979. *Basic handbook of child psychiatry.* Vol. 3. New York: Basic Books.

Harter, S. 1982. The perceived competence scale for children. *Child Development* 53:87–97.

Hartman, D. P. 1982. *Using observers to study behavior.* New Directions for Methodology of Social and Behavioral Science Publication No. 14. San Francisco: Jossey-Bass.

Haskill, S. C. 1979. A time-references Q-sort technique for evaluating behavioral change. *American Journal of Orthopsychiatry* 49:109–120.

Hauser, C. 1978. Education for mildly handicapped adolescents: Structure and quality of published information from the past decade. *Journal of Special Education* 12:285–301.

———. 1979. Evaluating mainstream programs: Capitalizing on a victory. *Journal of Special Education* 13:107–129.

Havighurst, R. J. 1953. *Human development and education.* New York: Longmans Green.

Heaton, R. C., and D. J. Safer. 1982. Secondary school outcome following a junior high school behavioral program. *Behavior Therapy* 13:226–31.

Henry, J. 1965. *Pathways to madness.* New York: Random House.

Heron, T. E. 1978. Punishment: A review of the literature with implications for the teacher of mainstreamed children. *Journal of Special Education* 12:244–52.

Heron, T. E., and K. C. Harris. 1982. *The educational consultant: Helping professionals, parents, and mainstreamed students.* Rockleigh, N. J.: Allyn and Bacon.

Herr, D. E. 1975. Camp counseling with emotionally disturbed adolescents. *Exceptional children* 41:331–32.

Hersch, C. 1968. The discontent explosion in mental health. *American Psychologist* 23:497–506.

Hersen, M., and D. H. Barlow. 1976. *Single case experimental designs: Strategies for studying behavior change.* New York: Pergamon Press.

Herson, P. 1974. Biasing effects of diagnostic labels and sex of the pupil on teacher's view of pupil's mental health. *Journal of Educational Psychology* 66:117–22.

Hewett, F. M. 1968. *The emotionally disturbed child in the classroom: A developmental strategy for educating children with maladaptive behavior.* Boston: Allyn and Bacon.

Hewett, F. M., and F. D. Taylor. 1980. *The emotionally disturbed child in the classroom: Orchestration process.* 2d ed. Boston: Allyn and Bacon.

Hewett, F. M., F. D. Taylor, and A. A. Artuso. 1969. The Santa Monica project: Evaluation of an engineered classroom design with emotionally disturbed children. *Exceptional Children* 35:523–29.

Hirshoren, A., and G. Heller. 1979. Programs for adolescents with behavior disorders: The state of the art. *Journal of Special Education* 13:275–77.

Hobbs, N. 1968. Sources of gain in psychotherapy. In *Use of interpretation in treatment: Technique and art,* ed. E. F. Hammer. New York: Grune and Stratton.

———. 1974. *The futures of children.* San Francisco: Jossey-Bass.

———. 1981. The role of insight in behavior change: A commentary. *American Journal of Orthopsychiatry* 51:632–35.

———. 1982. *The troubled and troubling child.* San Francisco: Jossey-Bass.

Hobbs, T. R., and J. E. Radka. 1975. A short-term therapeutic camping program for emotionally disturbed adolescent boys. *Adolescence* 10:447–55.

Hoffer, W. 1949. Deceiving the deceiver. In *Searchlights on delinquency,* ed. K. R. Eissler. New York: International Universities Press.

Hoffman, A. D., R. D. Becker, and H. P. Gabriel. 1976. *The hospitalized adolescent: A guide to managing the ill and injured youth.* New York: Free Press.

Hoffman, E. 1976. Children's understanding of emotionally disturbed peers. Ph.D. diss., University of Michigan.

Hoffman, L., ed. 1982. *The evaluation and care of severely disturbed families.* Jamaica, N.Y.: Medical and Scientific Books.

Hoover, T. 1978. A rural program for emotionally handicapped students: Democracy in action teaching. *Exceptional Children* 10:30–34.

Hops, H. 1983. Children's social competence and skill: Current research practices and future directions. *Behavior Therapy* 14:3–18.

Horn, R. E., and A. Cleaves. 1980. *The guide to simulations/games for education and training.* 4th ed. Beverly Hills, Calif.: Sage Publishing.

Hughes, J. H., and J. L. Hurth. In press. *Handicapped children and main-streaming: A mental health perspective.* Washington, D.C.: U.S. Government Printing Office.

Hundert, J. 1982. Some considerations of planning the integration of handicapped children into the mainstream. *Journal of Learning Disabilities* 15:81–83.

Hung, D. W., and M. J. Thelander. 1978. Summer camp treatment program for autistic children. *Exceptional Children* 44:534–36.

Hunter, C. P., and C. E. Myers. 1972. Classroom climate and pupil characteristics in special classes for the educationally handicapped. *Journal of School Psychology* 10:25–32.

Hutton, J. B., and T. G. Roberts. 1982. Relationships of sociometric status and characteristics of emotional disturbance. *Behavioral Disorders* 8:19–24.

Iowa State Department of Education. 1971. *Social and sexual development—A guide for teachers of the handicapped.* Iowa City, Ia.: Iowa State Department of Education.

Jacobs, B. J., and R. Schwertzer. 1979. Conceptualizing structure in a day-treatment program for delinquent adolescents. *American Journal of Orthopsychiatry* 49:246–51.

Janes, C. L., and V. M. Hesselbrock. 1978. Problem children's adult adjustment predicted from teachers' ratings. *American Journal of Orthopsychiatry* 48:300–309.

Janis, I. L. 1983. The role of social support in adherence to stressful decisions. *American Psychologist* 38:143–61.

Jenkins, J., and W. Mayhall. 1976. Development and evaluation of a resource teacher program. *Exceptional Children* 43:21–29.

Jernberg, A. M. 1979. *Theraplay.* San Francisco: Jossey-Bass.

Jersild, A. T. 1952. *In search of self.* New York: Teacher's College, Columbia University.

Jessee, E. H., G. J. Jurkovic, J. Wilkie, and M. Chiglinsky. 1982. Positive reframing with children: Conceptual and clinical considerations. *American Journal of Orthopsychiatry* 52:314–22.

Jessor, R., and S. Jessor. 1977. *Problem behavior and psychosocial development.* New York: Academic Press.

John, R. S., S. A. Mednick, and F. Schulsinger. 1982. Teacher reports as a predictor of schizophrenia and borderline schizophrenia: A baysian analysis. *Journal of Abnormal Psychology* 91:399–413.

Johnson, A. 1949. Sanctions for superego lacunae of adolescents. In *Searchlights on delinquency,* ed. K. R. Eissler. New York: International Universities Press.

Johnson, O. G., and J. W. Bommarito. 1971. *Tests and measurements in child development: a handbook.* San Francisco: Jossey-Bass.

Johnson, R. T., and D. W. Johnson. 1981. Building friendships between handicapped and nonhandicapped students: Effects of cooperative and individualistic instruction. *American Educational Research Journal* 18:415–24.

Joint Commission for Mental Health. 1970. *Crisis in child mental health: Challenge for the 1970s.* New York: Harper and Row.

Jones, J. 1977. Self-help activists talk of joining forces. *APA Monitor* 8:1, 12.

Jones, R. M. 1968. *Fantasy and feeling in education.* New York: Harper and Row.

Jones, V. 1980. *Adolescents with behavior problems.* Boston: Allyn and Bacon.

Kaffman, M. 1979. Hypnosis in child psychiatry. *Current psychiatric therapies* 10:46–51.

Kagan, Jerome. 1982. The emergence of self. *Journal of Child Psychology and Allied Disciplines* 24:363–81.

Kahle, L. R., ed. 1979. *Methods for studying person-situation interactions.* San Francisco: Jossey-Bass.

Kahn, J. H., P. J. Nursten, and H. C. Carroll. 1981. *Unwillingly to school: School phobia or school refusal, a psychosocial problem.* 3d ed. New York: Pergamon Press.

Kalma, S. H. 1976. Sex education within biology classes for hospitalized disturbed adolescents. *Exceptional Children* 42:451–55.

Kamiya, J., T. X. Barber, N. E. Miller, D. Shapiro, and J. Stoyna, eds. 1976–77. *Biofeedback and self-control.* Chicago: Aldine Publishing Co.

Kanner, L. 1962. Emotionally disturbed children: A historical review. *Child Development* 33:97–102.

Kaplan, H. B. 1980. *Deviant behavior in defense of self.* New York: Academic Press.

Kaplan, H., and I. Kaufman. 1978. Sociometric status and behaviors of emotionally disturbed children. *Psychology in the schools* 15:8–13.

Karnes, M. 1979. *Small wonder.* Circle Pines, Minn.: American Guidance Service.

Kashani, J. H., A. Husain, W. O. Shekim, K. K. Hodges, L. Citryn, and D. H. McKnew. 1981. Current perspectives on childhood depression: An overview. *American Journal of Psychiatry* 138:143–53.

Kauffman, J. M. 1980. Where special education for disturbed children is going: A personal view. *Exceptional Children* 46:522–27.

Kaufman, M. J., J. A. Cottlieb, M. B. Agard, and M. B. Kukic. 1975. Mainstreaming: Toward an explication of the construct. In *Alternatives for teaching exceptional children,* ed. E. L. Meyen, G. A. Vergason, and R. J. Whelan. Denver: Love Publishing Company.

Kaye, K. 1983. *The mental and social life of babies: How parents create persons.* Chicago: University of Chicago Press.

Kaye, N. L., and R. Aserlind. 1979. The IEP: The ultimate process. *Journal of Special Education* 13:137–43.

Kazdin, A. E., and A. H. Tuma, eds. 1982. *Single-case research designs.* San Francisco: Jossey-Bass.

Keat, D. B. 1979. *Multimodal therapy with children.* New York: Pergamon Press.

Keating, D. P. 1978. A search for social intelligence. *Journal of Educational Psychology* 70:218–23.

Kegan, R. 1982. *The evolving self.* Cambridge, Mass.: Harvard University Press.

Keller, A., L. H. Ford, and J. A. Meacham. 1978. Dimension of self-concept in preschool children. *Developmental Psychology* 14:483–89.

Kelly, George. 1955. *The psychology of personal constructs.* New York: W. W. Norton.

Kelly, T. J. 1979. Behavioral disorders: Teachers' perceptions. *Exceptional Children* 43:316–18.

Kendall, D. 1971. Towards integration. *Special Education in Canada* (November), 3–16.

Kendall, P. C., and L. E. Wilcox. 1979. Self-control in children: Development of a rating scale. *Journal of Consulting and Clinical Psychology* 47:1020–29.

Keniston, K., and Carnegie Council on Children. 1977. *All our children: The American family under pressure.* New York: Harcourt Brace Jovanovich.

Kent, R. N. and K. D. O'Leary. 1976. A controlled evaluation of behavior modification with conduct problem children. *Journal of Consulting and Clinical Psychology* 44:586–96.

Kerlin, M. A., and W. L. Latham. 1977. Intervention effects of a crisis resource program. *Exceptional Children* 44:32–34.

King, C. H. 1975. The ego and the integration of violence in homocidal youth. *American Journal of Orthopsychiatry* 45:134–45.

Knapczyk, D. R. 1982. Handling physical problems among students with behavioral disorders. *Behavioral Disorders* 7:157–62.

Knoblock, P. 1982. *Teaching and mainstreaming autistic children.* Denver: Love Publishing Company.

Knoff, H. M. 1983. Investigating disproportionate influence and status in multidisciplinary child-study teams. *Exceptional Children* 49:367–70.

Knotting, C. and R. Brozovitch. 1969. A descriptive follow-up study of a public-school program for the emotionally disturbed. Research Report OEG-0-8-085068-3628. Pontiac, Mich., Division of Special Education, Oakland Schools.

Koegel, R. L., A. L. Egel, and A. Rincover, 1981. *Educating and understanding autistic children.* San Diego, Calif.: College-Hill Press.

Kohlberg, L. 1976. Moral stages and moralization. In *Moral development and behavior,* ed. T. Lickona. New York: Holt, Rinehart, and Winston.

———. 1969. Stage and sequence: The cognitive-developmental approach to socialization. In *Handbook of socializaition theory and research,* ed. D. A. Goslin. New York: Rand McNally.

Kolvin, I, R. F. Garside, A. R. Nicol, A. MacMillan, F. Wolstenholme, and I. M. Leitch. *Help starts here: The maladjusted child in the ordinary school.* London: Methuen.

Konopka, Gisela. 1983. Adolescent suicide. *Exceptional Children* 49:390–96.

Kounin, J. S. 1970. *Discipline and group management in classrooms.* New York: Holt, Rinehart, and Winston.

Kounin, J. S., W. V. Frusen, and E. Norton. 1966. Managing emotionally disturbed children in regular classrooms. *Journal of Educational Psychology* 57:1–3.

Kralj, M. M., J. B. Tavormina, J. L. Zimmerman, and W. F. Crayton, n.d. Camping as therapeutic tool for troubled children: A critical review. Department of Psychology, University of Virginia. Typescript.

Kratochwill, T. R. 1977. N-1: An alternative research strategy for school psychologists. *Journal of School Psychology* 15:239–49.

———. 1981. *Selective mutism: Implications for research and treatment.* Hillsdale, N. J.: Erlbaum.

Kulitz, I., B. A. Zaremba, and P. K. Broder, 1979. The link between learning disabilities and juvenile delinquency: Some issues and answers. *Learning Disability Quarterly* 2:2–11.

Kupfer, D. J., T. P. Detre, and J. Koral. 1975. Relationship of certain childhood traits to adult psychotic disorders. *American Journal of Orthopsychiatry* 45:74–80.

Kurtz, P. D., and J. T. Neisworth. 1976. Self-control possibilities for exceptional children. *Exceptional Children* 42:213–17.

Lamb, M. E., and L. R. Sherrod, eds. 1981. *Infant social cognition: Empirical and theoretical considerations.* Hillsdale, N. J.: Erlbaum.

Lambert, N. M., and M. Windmiller. 1977. An exploratory study of temperament traits in a population of children at risk. *Journal of Special Education* 11:37–47.

Laneve, R. S. 1979. Mark Twain School. *Behavioral Disorders* 4:183–92.

LaVietes, R. 1962. The teacher's role in the education of the emotionally disturbed child. *American Journal of Orthopsychiatry* 32:854–62.

Lawlor, E. D. 1976. Hypnotic intervention with "school-phobic" children. *International Journal of Clinical and Experimental Hypnosis* 14:74–86.

Lawrenson, G. M., and A. McKinnon. 1982. A survey of classroom teachers of the emotionally disturbed: Attrition and burnout factors. *Behavioral Disorders* 8:41–49.

Lazarus, A. A. 1981. *The practice of multi-modal therapy.* New York: McGraw-Hill.

Lazerson, D. B. 1980. I must be good if I can teach: Peer tutoring with aggressive and withdrawn children. *Journal of Learning Disabilities* 13:43–48.

Lebsock, M. S., and C. L. Salzberg. 1981. The use of role play and reinforcement procedures in the development of generalized interpersonal behavior with emotionally disturbed-behavior disordered adolescents in a special-education classroom. *Behavioral Disorders* 6:150–63.

Lecky, P. 1961. *Self-consistency: A theory of personality.* N.p.: The Shoestring Press.

Leinhardt, G., and A. Pallay. 1982. Restrictive educational settings: Exile or haven? *Review of Educational Research* 52: 557–78.

Leitenberg, H., ed. 1976. *Handbook of behavior modification and behavior therapy.* Englewood Cliffs, N. J.: Prentice-Hall.

Lerner, M. J. 1980. *The belief in a just world: A fundamental delusion.* New York: Plenum Press.

Leventhal, T., and G. Weinberger. 1975. Evaluation of a large-scale brief therapy program for children. *American Journal of Orthopsychiatry* 45:119–33.

Levine, M., J. W. Hummel, and R. T. Salzer. 1982. Mainstreaming requires something more: The person-environment fit. *Clinical Psychology Review* 2:1–25.

Levine, M. D., S. Clark, and T. Ferb. 1981. The child as a diagnostic participant: Helping students describe their learning disorders. *Journal of Learning Disabilities* 14: 527–30.

Lewis, M., and J. Brooks-Gunn. 1979. *Social cognition and the acquisition of self.* New York: Plenum Press.

Lewis, M., D. O. Lewis, S. S. Shanok, E. Klatskin, and J., R. Osborne. 1980. The undoing of residential treatment. *American Academy of Child Psychiatry* 19:160–70.

Lewis, W. W. 1965. Continuity and intervention in emotional disturbance: A review. *Exceptional Children* 31:465–75.

Lichter, S. O., E. B. Rapien, F. M. Seibert, and M. A. Sklansky. 1962. *The Dropouts.* New York: The Free Press.

Lightfoot, S. L. 1978. *Worlds apart.* New York: Basic Books.

Linniban, P. C. 1977. Adolescent day treatment: A community alternative to institutionalization of the emotionally disturbed adolescent. *American Journal of Orthopsychiatry* 47:679–88.

Linton, T. E. 1969. The European educateur model: An alternative and effective approach to the mental health of children. *The Journal of Special Education* 3:319–27.

Lipsitz, J. 1977. *Growing up forgotten.* Lexington, Mass.: D. C. Heath and Co.

Little, T. L. 1978. The teacher-consultant model: A different perspective. A reaction to symposium 13. *Journal of Special Education* 12:345–56.

Littlesand, D. B. 1977. A behavioral psychodynamic approach to day treatment for emotionally disturbed children. *Child Welfare* 56:612–19.

Loeber, R. 1982. The stability of antisocial and delinquent child behavior: A review. *Child Development* 53:1431–1446.

Long, N. J. 1979. The conflict cycle. *The Pointer* 24:6–11.

Long, N., and W. C. Morse. 1966. Special classes for special and emotional problems in the public schools. In *Sixty-fifth yearbook*, pt. 1. Chicago: National Society for the Study of Education. Un. of Chicago Press.

Long, N. J., W. C. Morse, and R. G. Newman, 1980. *Conflict in the classroom*. 4th ed. Belmont, Calif.: Wadsworth Publishing Co.

Looney, J. G., A. Z. Schwartzberg, A. D. Sorosky, S. C. Feinstein, and P. L. Giovacchini, eds. 1981. *Adolescent psychiatry*. Vol. 8. Chicago: University of Chicago Press.

Lorr, M. 1983. *Cluster analysis for social scientists*. San Francisco: Jossey-Bass.

Lotter, V. 1974. Social adjustment and placement of autistic children in Middlesex: A follow-up study. *Journal of Autism and Childhood Schizophrenia* 4:11–32.

Love, L. R., and J. Kaswan. 1974. *Troubled children: Their families, schools, and treatment*. New York: John Wiley and Sons.

Loven, M. 1978. Four alternative approaches to the family-school liaison role. *Psychology in the Schools* 15: 553–59.

Lynch, W. C., H. Hama, S. Kohn, and N. Miller. 1976–77. Instrumental control of peripheral vasometer responses. In *Biofeedback and self-control*. ed. J. Kamiya et al. Chicago: Aldine Publishing Co.

Lyon, S. 1977. Teacher nonverbal behavior related to perceived pupil social-personal attributes. *Journal of Learning Disabilities* 10:52–56.

MaCaslin, N. 1980. *Creative drama in the classroom*. New York: Longman.

Macdonald, C. 1979. Sex education for emotionally disturbed and learning disabled children. *SEICUS* 1:2; 6.

Macfarlane, J. W. 1963. From infancy to adulthood. *Childhood Education* 39:336–42.

MacMillan, D. L., and M. I. Semmel. 1977. Evaluation of mainstream programs. *Focus on Exceptional Children* 9:1–14.

Macy, D., and J. L. Carter. 1978. Comparison of a mainstream and self-contained special-education program. *Journal of Special Education* 12:304–313.

Mahler, M. 1968. *On human symbiosis and the vicissitudes of individuation*. Vol. 1, *Infantile psychosis*. New York: International Universities Press.

Mahoney, M. J. 1977. Reflections on the cognitive-learning trend in psychotherapy. *American Psychologist* 32:5–13.

Mahoney, M. J., and C. E. Thoresen. 1972. Behavioral self-control: Power to the person. *Educational Researcher* 1:5–7.

Malmquist, C. P. 1978. *Handbook of adolescence*. New York: Lexington Books, D.C. Heath.

Mandel, H. P., F. Werzmann, B. Millan, J. Greenwoh, and D. Speers. 1975. Reaching emotionally disturbed children: "Judo" principles in remedial education. *American Journal of Orthopsychiatry* 45: 867–74.

Mann, D. W., and M. Gold. 1984. *Expelled to a friendlier place: A study of effective alternative schools*. Ann Arbor: University of Michigan Press.

Marcus, L. M. 1977. Patterns of coping in families of psychotic children. *American Journal of Orthopsychiatry* 47:388–99.

Marlow, M., and J. Erreva. 1982. Low lead levels and behavior problems in children. *Behavioral Disorders* 7:163–72.

Marsden, G., and N. Kalter, 1976. Children's understanding of their emotionally disturbed peers: The concept of emotional disturbance. *Psychiatry* 39:227–38.

Martin, J. Z. 1979. The reading counselor: A method of counseling the reading-disabled child. *Journal of Learning Disabilities* 10:17–20.

Mason, E. A. *He comes from another room.* Boston, Mass.: Documentaries for Learning. Film, n.d.

Masterson, J. F., and J. L. Costello. 1980. *From borderline adolescent to functioning adult: The test of time.* New York: Brunner/Mazel.

Matuszek, P., and T. Oakland. 1979. Factors influencing teachers' and psychologists' recommendations regarding special-class placement. *School Psychologist* 17:116–235.

Mayer, M. F., L. H. Richman, and E. A. Balcerzak. 1977. *Group care of children: Crossroads and transitions.* New York: Child Welfare League of America.

McAuley, R., and P. McAuley. 1977. *Child behavior problems.* New York: Free Press.

McCandless, B. R. 1964. *Children, behavior, and development.* New York: Holt, Rinehart, and Winston.

McDonald, J. E., and G. Sheperd. 1976. The autistic child: A challenge for educators. *Psychology in the Schools* 13:248–56.

McDonald, P. L. 1973. Filmloops enhance curriculum for hostile aggressive students. *Teaching Exceptional Children* 5:97–98.

McGee, C. S., J. M. Kauffman, and J. L. Nussen. 1977. Children as therapeutic change agents: Reinforcement intervention paradigms. *Review of Educational Research* 47:451–77.

McKinnon, A. J. 1978. A follow-up and analysis of the effects of placement in classes for emotionally disturbed children in elementary school. Ph.D. diss., University of Michigan.

McMillan, A. 1978. *The language-impaired child in the classroom.* Brooklyn, N.Y.: The League School.

McPhail, P., J. R. Ungood-Thomas, and H. Chapman, 1975. *Life line/Learning to care.* Niles, Ill.: Argus Communications.

McReynolds, P. 1964. *Advances in psychological assessment.* Vol. 3. San Francisco; Jossey-Bass.

Media Fair. *Contraception: A matter of choice.* Vienna, Va., Media Fair. Film, n.d.

———. *Sex roles: Redefining the difference.* Vienna, Va.: Media Fair. Film, n.d.

Medway, F. J., and R. C. Smith. 1978. An examination of contemporary elementary school affective education programs. *Psychology in the Schools* 15:260–69.

Menolascino, F. J. 1980. *Home and school partnerships in exceptional education*. Gaithersburg, Md.: Aspen Systems Corporation.

Menolascino, F. J., and D. R. Eyde. 1979. Biophysical bases of autism. *Behavioral Disorders* 5:41–47.

Mercer, J. R., and J. F. Lewis. 1977. *A system of multicultural pluralistic assessment*. New York: The Psychological Corporation.

Mesinger, J. F. 1982. Alternative education for behavior disordered and delinquent adolescent youth: What works—maybe? *Behavioral Disorders* 7:91–100.

Meyers, J., R. D. Parson, and R. Martin. 1979. *Mental health consultation in the schools*. San Francisco: Jossey-Bass.

Miller, M. L., J. A. Chiles, and V. E. Barnes. 1982. Suicide attempts within a delinquent population. *Journal of Consulting and Clinical Psychiatry* 50:491–98.

Miller, T. L., and D. A. Sabatino. 1978. An evaluation of the teacher consultant model as an approach to mainstreaming. *Exceptional Children* 45:86–91.

Millman, H. L., C. E. Schaefer, and J. J. Cohen. 1981. *Therapies for school behavior problems*. San Francisco: Jossey-Bass.

Minner, S. 1981. Using photography as an adjunctive and creative teaching approach. *Teaching Exceptional Children* 13:145–47.

Minskoff, E. H. 1980a. Teaching approach for developing nonverbal communication skills in students with social perception deficits. *Journal of Learning Disabilities* 13:9–15.

———. 1980b. Teaching approach for developing nonverbal communication skills in students with social perception deficits. Part 2: Proxemic, vacalic, and artifactual cues. *Journal of Learning Disabilities* 13:203–208.

Minuchin, S., P. Chamberlain, and P. Graubard. 1967. A project to teach learning skills to disturbed delinquent children. *American Journal of Orthopsychiatry* 37:558–67.

Mischel, W. 1977. On the future of personality measurement. *American Psychologist* 32:246–55.

———. 1979. On the interface of cognition and personality: Beyond the person-situation debate. *American Psychologist* 34:740–55.

Moore, C., K. G. Morton, and A. Southard. 1983. *A reader's guide for parents of children with mental, physical, or emotional disabilities*. Washington, D.C.: National Maternal and Child Clearinghouse.

Moore, D. R. 1982. Childhood behavior problems: A social learning perspective. In *Psychopathology in childhood*, ed. J. R. Lachenmeyer and M. S. Gibbs. New York: Gardner Press.

Moos, R. H. 1979. *Evaluating educational environments*. San Francisco: Jossey-Bass.

Moos, R. H., and R. Fuhr. 1982. The clinical use of social-ecological concepts: The case of an adolescent girl. *American Journal of Orthopsychiatry* 52:111–22.

Moos, R. H., L. R. Snowden, and J. Kelly. 1979. *Social and psychological research in community settings*. San Franscisco: Jossey-Bass.

Morgan, D. I. 1979. Prevalence and types of handicapping conditions found in juvenile correctional institutions: A national survey. *Journal of Special Education* 13:284–95.

Morgan, S. R. 1979. A model of the empathic process for teachers of emotionally disturbed children. *American Journal of Orthopsychiatry* 49:446–53.

Morris, J. D., and D. Arrant. 1978. Behavior ratings of emotionally disturbed children by teachers, parents, and school psychologists. *Psychology in the Schools* 15:450–455.

Morse, W. C. 1971. *Classroom disturbance: The principal's dilemma.* Reston, Va.: Council for Exceptional Children.

————. 1976. The helping teacher/crisis teacher. *Focus on Exceptional Children* 8:1–11.

————. 1981. Issues in diagnosis and programming for socioemotionally impaired early adolescent's program. In *Education of the early adolescent with behavioral disorders,* ed. D. R. Eyde, F. J. Menolascino, and A. H. Fink. Omaha, Neb.: Nebraska Psychiatric Institute.

————. The place of affective education in special education. *Teaching Exceptional Children* 14:209–211 and entire issue.

Morse, W. C., J. Ardizzone, C. MacDonald, and P. Pasick. 1980. *Affective Education for Special Children and Youth.* Reston, Va.: Council for Exceptional Children.

Morse, W. C., F. B. Bruno, and S. R. Morgan. 1973. *Training teachers for the emotionally disturbed.* Ann Arbor: University of Michigan.

Morse, W. C., R. Cutler, and A. A. Fink. 1964. *Public school classes for the emotionally handicapped: A research analysis.* Washington, D.C.: Council for Exceptional Children.

Morse, W. C., and H. J. Lockett. 1973. A passive-aggressive selective mute. In *Disturbed and troubled children,* ed. Maurice F. Freebill. Flushing, N.Y.: Spectrum Publications.

Morse, W. C., and M. A. Ravlin. 1979. Psychoeducation in the school setting. In *Basic handbook of child psychiatry.* Vol. 3, *Therapeutic interventions,* ed. S. Harrison. New York: Basic Books.

Morse, W. C., and E. R. Small. 1959. Group life space interviewing in a therapeutic camp. *American Journal of Orthopsychiatry* 29:27–44.

Morse, W. C., and J. M. Smith. 1980. *Understanding child variance.* Reston, Va.: Council for Exceptional Children. Videotape training packages.

Moyer, K. E. 1975. The physiology of violence: Allergy and aggression. *Psychology Today* 9:77–79.

Munger, R. L. 1979. The effects of a social cognition preventative program on problem solving, locus of control, and self-control behavior in middle childhood. Ph.D. diss., University of Michigan.

Murphy, L. B. 1974. *Growing up in Garden City.* New York: Child Welfare League of America.

Murphy, B. J., and A. J. Bryan. 1980. Multiple-baseline and multiple-purpose designs: Practical alternatives for special-education assessment and evaluation. *Journal of Special Education* 14:325–35.

Murray, H. A. 1938. *Explorations in personality.* New York: Oxford University Press.

Naiman, D. W. 1975. *Needs of emotionally disturbed hearing-impaired children.* New York: Deafness Research and Training Center.

National Association of State Directors of Special Education. 1978. *Special-education programs for emotionally disturbed adolescents.* Washington, D.C.: National Association of State Directors of Special Education.

Nazzara, J. 1978. *Preparing for the IEP meetings: A workshop for parents.* Reston, Va.: Council for Exceptional Children.

Neill, A. S. 1960. *Summerhill: A radical approach to child rearing.* New York: Hart Publishing Co.

Neisworth, J. T., S. J. Willoughby-Herb, S. J. Bagnato, C. A. Cartwright, and K. W. Lamb. 1980. *Individualized education for preschool exceptional children.* Germantown, Md.: Aspen Systems Corporation.

Nelson, C. M., and J. M. Kauffman. 1977. Educational programming for secondary-age delinquent and maladjusted pupils. *Behavioral Disorders* 2:102–113.

Neuhaus, S. M., J. D. Mowrey, and D. S. Glenwich. 1982. The cooperative learning program: Implementing an ecological approach to the development of alternative psychoeducational programs. *Journal of Clinical Child Psychology* 11:151–56.

Newberger, D. A. 1978. Situational socialization: An effective interaction component of the mainstreaming reintegration construct. *Journal of Special Education* 12:113–23.

Newman, R. G. 1974. *Groups in schools.* New York: Simon and Schuster.

Nickerson, E. T., and K. S. O'Laughlin, eds. 1982. *Helping through action-oriented therapies.* Amherst, Mass.: Human Resources Development Press.

Noll, R. B., and H. Benedict. 1981. Differentiations within classifications of childhood psychoses: A continuing dilemma. *Merrill-Palmer Quarterly* 27:174–95.

Northcutt, J., and G. B. Tipton. 1978. Teaching severely mentally ill and emotionally disturbed adolescents. *Exceptional Children* 45:18–23.

Novak, D. W. 1975. Children's responses to imaginary peers labeled as emotionally disturbed. *Psychology in the Schools* 12:103–106.

Offer, D., R. C. Marohn, and E. Ostrov. 1979. *The psychological world of the juvenile delinquent.* New York: Basic Books.

Oppenheim, R. 1974. *Effective teaching methods for autistic children.* Springfield, Ill.: Thomas.

Orange County Public Schools. 1983. *Model Affective Resource Curriculum.* Orlando, Fl.: Orange County Public Schools.

Ornitz, E. M., and E. R. Ritvo. 1976. The syndrome of autism: A critical review. *American Journal of Psychiatry* 33:609–21.

O'Rourke, R. D. 1977. Troubled children: A new design for learning, teaching. *Exceptional Children* 9:34–36.

Paluszny, M. 1979. *Autism: A practical guide for parents and professionals.* New York: Syracuse University Press.

Parens, H. 1979. *The development of aggression in early childhood.* New York: Jason Aronson.

Parents' Campaign for Handicapped Children and Youth. n.d. *Closer Look.* Washington, D.C.: Parents' Campaign for Handicapped Children and Youth.

Pastor, D. L., and S. M. Swap. 1978. An ecological study of emotionally disturbed preschoolers in special and regular classes. *Exceptional Children* 45:213–15.

Paul, J. L., A. P. Turnbull, and W. M. Cruickshank. 1977. *Mainstreaming: A practical guide.* Syracuse, N.Y.: Syracuse University Press.

Pearl, S. 1979. The responsibility resource rooms and resource center: A program administrator looks at training needs of teachers of emotionally disturbed students in secondary school programs. *Behavioral Disorders* 4:163–67.

Pease, G. A., and V. O. Tyler. 1979. Self-regulation of time-out duration in the modification of disruptive classroom behavior. *Psychology in the Schools* 16:101–105.

Peterson, R. L., R. H. Zabel, C. R. Smith, and M. White. 1983. Cascade of services model and emotionally disabled students. *Exceptional Child* 49:404–408.

Pfeffer, C. R. 1981. Suicidal behavior of children. *Exceptional Children* 48:170–72.

Piaget, J. 1948. *The moral judgment of the child.* Glencoe, Ill.: Free Press.

———. 1952. *The language and thought of the child.* London: Routledge and Kegan Paul.

Piana, D. 1973. *How to talk with children and other people.* New York: John Wiley and Sons.

Pierce, L., and Klein, H. 1982. A comparison of parent and child perception of the child's behavior. *Behavioral Disorders* 7:69–75.

Plutchik, R., and Kellerman, H., eds. 1983. *Emotions in early development.* New York: Academic Press.

Pointer 25 (entire issues).

Poorman, C. 1980. Mainstreaming in reverse with a special friend. *Teaching Exceptional Children* 12:136–43.

Popper, K. R., and J. C. Eccles. 1977. *The self and its brain.* New York: Springer International.

Powers, D. 1980. *Creating environments for troubled children.* Chapel Hill: University of North Carolina Press.

Poznanski, E. D. 1982. The clinical phenomenology of childhood depression. *American Journal of Orthpsychiatry* 52:308–13.

Prentice-Dunn, S., D. R. Wilson, and R. D. Lyman. 1981. Client factors related to outcome in residential and day-treatment program for children. *Journal of Clinical Child Psychology* 10:188–91.

Pressley, M. 1979. Increasing children's self-control through cognitive interventions. *Review of Educational Research* 49:319–70.

Price, M., and L. Goodman. 1980. Individualized education programs: A cost study. *Exceptional Children* 46:446–54.

Prieto, A. G., and A. B. Rutherford. 1977. An ecological assessment technique for behaviorally disordered and learning disabled children. *Journal of Behavioral Disorders* 2:169–75.

Prout, H. T., and D. T. Brown. 1983. *Counseling and psychotherapy with children and adolescents*. Tampa, Fla.: Mariner Publishing Co.

Purvis, J., and S. Somet. 1976. *Music in developmental therapy*. Baltimore, Md.: University Park Press.

Quay, H. C. 1979. Classification. In *Psychopathological disorders of childhood*, ed. H. C. Quay and J. S. Werry. 2d ed. New York: John Wiley and Son.

Quay, H. C., and D. R. Peterson. 1979. *Manual for the behavior problem checklist*. Coral Gables, Fla.: University of Miami.

———. 1983. *Interim manual for the revised behavior problem checklist*. Coral Gables, University of Miami.

Quay, H. D., and J. Galvin. 1970. *The education of behaviorally disordered children in the public-school setting*. Washington, D.C.: U.S. Department of Health, Education, and Welfare.

Rabinovitch, R. D. 1971. Are inpatient hospital services for children obsolete? *Research Bulletin* (Michigan Department of Mental Health) 5:3–18.

———. *Early infantile autism: The clinical picture through adulthood*. Northville, Mich.: Hawthorn Center. Film, 1980.

Raschke, D. 1981. Designing reinforcement surveys: Let the student choose the reward. *Teaching Exceptional Children* 14:82–97.

Raschke, D., S. Stainback, and W. Stainback. 1982. The predictive capabilities of three sources for a promised consequence. *Behavior Disorders* 7:213–18.

Raths, L., M. Harim, and S. Simon. 1966. *Values and teaching*. Columbus, Oh.: Charles E. Merrill.

Raver, S. A. 1979. Preschool integration: Experiences from the classroom. *Teaching Exceptional Children* 12:22–27.

Razeghi, J. A., and S. Davis. 1979. Federal mandates for the handicapped: Vocational education opportunity and employment. *Exceptional Children* 45:353–59.

Recreation for autistic and emotionally disturbed children. 1973. Washington, D.C.: U.S. Government Printing Office.

Redl, F. 1959a. The concept of life-space interviewing. *American Journal of Orthopsychiatry* 29:1–18.

———. 1959b. The concept of a therapeutic milieu. *American Journal of Orthopsychiatry* 29:721–34.

———. 1966. *When we deal with children.* New York: Free Press.

Reid, W. H., ed. 1978. *The psychopath.* New York: Brunner/Mazel.

Reimer, J., D. P. Paolitto, and R. H. Hersh. 1983. *Promoting moral growth.* New York: Longman.

Research and Education Association. 1981. *Handbook of psychiatric rating scales.* New York: Research and Education Association.

Rezmierski, V. 1973. An exploratory study of nonverbal communication between teachers and children: Some theoretical and methodological considerations. Ph.D. diss., University of Michigan.

Rezmierski, V., and N. Shiffler. 1983. Prevalence and persistence of teacher-perceived emotional problems in school-aged youth. Typescript.

Rhodes, W. C., and M. Tracy. 1972. A study of child variance. Vol. 1–2. Ann Arbor: University of Michigan Press.

Ribner, S. 1978. The effects of special-class placement on the self-concept of exceptional children. *Journal of Learning Disabilities* 2:60–64.

Rich, H. L. 1978. A matching model for educating the emotionally disturbed and behaviorally disordered. *Focus on Exceptional Children* 10:1–11.

Richman, N., P. J. Graham, and J. Stevenson. 1982. *Preschool to School.* New York: Academic Press.

Robbins, A., ed. 1980. *Expressive therapy.* New York: Human Sciences Press.

Roberts, M. C., W. B. Beidleman, and S. K. Wurtele. 1981. Children's perceptions of medical and psychological disorders in their peers. *Journal of Clinical Child Psychology* 10:76–78.

Robins, L. N. 1966. *Deviant children grown up. A sociological and psychiatric study of sociopathic personality.* Baltimore: Williams and Wilkins Company.

Rogeners, G. A., R. A. Bednar, and H. Diesenhaus. 1974. The social system and children's behavior problems. *American Journal of Orthopsychiatry* 44:497–502.

Rose, S. D. 1972. *Treating children in groups.* San Francisco: Jossey-Bass.

Rosenberg, M. 1979. *Conceiving the self.* New York: Basic Books.

Ross, A. D. 1981. *Child behavior therapy: Coming of age.* New York: John Wiley and Sons.

Rothman, E. P. 1971. *The angel inside went sour.* New York: David McKay.

———. 1977. *Troubled teachers.* New York: David McKay.

Rubin, E., C. B. Simson, and C. Marcus. 1966. *Between emotionally handicapped children and the elementary school.* Detroit, Mich.: Wayne State University Press.

Ruckhaber, C. J. 1975. Four-year study of a psychological consultation process. *Psychology in the Schools* 12:64–70.

Russell, A., and W. A. Russell. 1979. Using bibliotherapy with emotionally disturbed children. *Teaching Exceptional Children* 11:168–71.

Russell, M. L., and M. S. Roberts. 1979. Behaviorally based decision-making training for children. *Journal of School Psychology* 17:264–69.

Rust, J. O., and L. S. Miller. 1978. Using a control group to evaluate a resource-room program. *Psychology in the Schools* 15:503–506.

Rutter, M., and P. Graham. 1966. Psychiatric disorders in ten-and eleven-year-old children. *Proceedings of the Royal Society of Medicine* 59:382–87.

Rutter, M., and E. Schopler, eds. 1978. *Autism: A reappraisal of concepts and treatment.* New York: Plenum.

Rutter, M., J. Tizard, P. Graham, and K. Whitmore. 1976. Isle of Wight studies, 1964–74. *Psychological Medicine* 6:313–32.

Ryan, V. L., C. A. Krall, and W. F. Hodges. 1976. Self-concept change in behavior modification. *Journal of Consulting and Clinical Psychology* 44:638–45.

Sabatino, D. A., and A. J. Mauser. 1978. *Specialized education in today's secondary schools.* Boston: Allyn and Bacon.

Sabatino, D. A., and T. L. Miller, eds. 1979. *Describing learner characteristics of handicapped children and youth.* New York: Grune and Stratton.

Safer, D. J. 1982. *School programs for disruptive adolescents.* Baltimore, Md.: University Park Press.

Safter, D. J., R. C. Heaton, and F. C. Parker. 1981. A behavioral program for disruptive junior high school students: Results and follow-up. *Journal of Abnormal Child Psychology* 9:483–94.

Safer, N. D. 1980. Implications of minimal competency standards and testing for handicapped students. *Exceptional Children* 46:288–90.

Safer, N. D., M. J. Kaufman, P. A. Morressey, and L. Lewis. 1979. Implementation of IEPs: New teacher roles and requisite support systems. In *Instructional planning for exceptional children,* ed. E. W. Meyen, G. A. Vergason, and R. Whelan. Denver, Colo.: Love Publishing Co.

Salzinger, S., J. Antrobus, and J. Glick, eds. 1980. *The ecosystem of the "sick" child.* New York: Academic Press.

Sanders, S. 1975. Corrective social interactive therapy: Role modeling. *American Journal of Orthopsychiatry* 45:875–83.

Sargent, L. R. 1981. Resource teacher time utilization: An observational study. *Exceptional Children* 47:420–25.

Sarnoff, C. 1976. *Latency.* New York: Jason Aronson.

Sattler, J. M. 1982. *Assessment of children's intelligence and special abilities.* Rockleigh, N.J.: Allyn and Bacon, Longwood Division.

Saul, L. J. 1979. *Childhood emotional patterns and maturity.* New York: Brunner/Mazel.

Saunders, B. T. 1971. The effect of the emotionally disturbed child in the public-school classroom. *Psychology in the Schools* 8:23–26.

Savicki, V., and R. Brown. 1981. *Working with troubled children.* New York: Human Sciences Press.

Schaefer, C. E., J. M. Briesmeister, and M. E. Fitton, eds. 1984. *Family therapy techniques for problem behaviors of children and teenagers*. San Francisco: Jossey-Bass.

Schaefer, C. E., L. Johnson, and J. N. Wherry, eds. 1982. *Group therapies for children and youth*. San Francisco: Jossey-Bass.

Schaefer, C. E., and H. L. Millman, eds. 1977. *Therapies for children*. San Francisco: Jossey-Bass.

Schaefer, C. E., H. L. Millman, and G. F. Levine, eds. 1979. *Therapies for psychosomatic disorders in children*. San Francisco: Jossey-Bass.

Schopler, E. 1978. National society for autistic children definition of the syndrome of autism. *Journal of Autism and Childhood Schizophrenia* 8:162–69.

———. 1978. Prevention of psychosis through alternate education. In *Focus on prevention: The education of children labeled emotionally disturbed*, ed. S. A. Apter. Syracuse, N.Y.: Syracuse University Press.

Schopler, E., S. S. Brehm, M. Kinsbourne, and R. Reichler. 1971. Effect of treatment structure on development in autistic children. *Archives of General Psychiatry* 24:415–21.

Schopler, E., M. Lansing, and L. Waters, eds. 1983. *Teaching activities for autistic children*. Baltimore: University Park Press. (This is one of three volumes that include diagnostic and teaching strategies for home and school.)

Schopler, E., and R. Reichler, eds. 1976. *Psychopathology and child development research and treatment*. New York: Plenum.

Schultz, E. W., and W. Walton. 1979. Biofeedback and self-management of stress in schools. *Pointer* 24:107–113.

Schwikgebel, R., and D. Kolb. 1964. Inducing behavior change in adolescent delinquents. *Behavior Research and Therapy* 1:299–304.

Scott, M. 1980. Ecological theory and methods for research in special education. *Journal of Special Education* 14:279–94.

Segal, J. 1978. *A child's journey*. New York: McGraw-Hill.

Selby, J. W., and L. G. Calhoun. 1980. Psychodidactics: An undervalued and underdeveloped treatment tool of psychological intervention. *Professional Psychology* 11:236–41.

Selfe, L. 1978. *Nadia*. New York: Academic Press.

Semmel, M. J. n.d. *Project prime*. Bloomington, Ind.: Indiana University Center for Innovation in Teaching the Handicapped.

Shearn, D. F., and D. L. Randolph. 1978. Effects of reality therapy methods applied in the classroom. *Psychology in the Schools* 15:79–83.

Shears, L. M., and E. M. Bower. 1974. *Games in education and development*. Springfield, Ill.: Charles C. Thomas.

Shectman, F. 1979. Problems in communicating psychological understanding. *American Psychologist* 34:781–90.

Shepherd, M., B. Oppenheim, and S. Mitchell. 1971. *Childhood behavior and mental health*. New York: Grune and Stratton.

Shore, M. F., and J. L. Massimo. 1979. Fifteen years after treatment: A follow-up study of comprehensive vocationally oriented psychotherapy. *American Journal of Orthopsychiatry* 49:240–45.

Shrauger, J. S., and T. M. Osberg. 1981. The relative accuracy of self-predictions and judgments by others in psychological assessment. *Psychological Bulletin* 90:322–51.

Shultz, E. W., A. Hirshoren, A. B. Manton, and R. A. Henderson. 1971. Special education for the emotionally disturbed. *Exceptional Children* 38:313–19.

Silverman, M. 1979. Beyond the mainstreaming: The special needs of the chronic child patient. *American Journal of Orthopsychiatry* 49:62–68.

Simmons, R., F. Rosenberg, and M. Rosenberg. 1973. Disturbance in self-images at adolescence. *American Sociology Review* 38:553–68.

Simon, S., and R. O'Rourke. 1977. *Values clarification strategies for exceptional children.* Englewood Cliffs, N.J.: Prentice-Hall.

Sindelar, P. T., and S. L. Deno. 1978. The effectiveness of resource programming. *Journal of Special Education* 12:17–28.

Slavson, S. R., and M. Schiffer. 1975. *Group psychotherapies for children.* New York: International Universities Press.

Slingerland Screening Tests. n.d. *Screening tests.* Cambridge, Mass.: Educator's Publishing Service.

Smiley, W. C. 1977. Classification and delinquency: A review. *Behavioral Disorders* 2:184–201.

Smith, B. 1978. Selfhood. *American Psychologist* 33:1053–63.

Smith, C. R. 1977. *Identification of youngsters who are chronically disruptive.* Department of Public Instruction, Special-Education Division, Des Moines, Iowa. Mimeo.

Smith, C. R., M. White, and R. Peterson. 1979. *Reintegration of emotionally disabled pupils.* Des Moines, Ia.: Department of Public Instruction, Special-Education Division.

Smith, J. D., E. A. Polloway, and G. K. West. 1979. Corporal punishment and its implications for exceptional children. *Exceptional Children* 45:264–68.

Smith, M. L., and G. V. Glass. 1977. Meta-analysis of psychotherapy outcome studies. *American Psychologist* 32:752–60.

Smith, R. I. 1978. *The psychopath in society.* New York: Academic Press.

Speers, R. W., and C. Lansing. 1965. *Group therapy in childhood psychosis.* Chapel Hill: University of North Carolina Press.

Spivack, G., J. J. Platt, and M. B. Shure. 1976. *The problem-solving approach to adjustment.* San Francisco: Jossey-Bass.

Spivack, G., and M. Swift. 1973. The classroom behavior of children: A critical review of teacher-administered rating scales. *Journal of Special Education* 7:55–89.

Spoerl, D. T. 1959. *Tensions our children live with: Stories for discussion.* Boston: Beacon Press.

Staub, E. *Positive social behavior and morality.* Vol. 1, *Social and personal influences;* vol. 2, *Socialization and development.* New York: Academic Press.

Stein, M. D., and J. K. Davis, eds. 1982. *Therapies for adolescents.* San Francisco: Jossey-Bass.

Steinhauer, P., and R. Quentin. 1977. *Psychological problems of the child and his family.* Toronto: Ont.: Macmillan of Canada.

Stephens, T. M., and B. L. Braun. 1980. Measures of regular classroom teachers' attitudes toward handicapped children. *Exceptional Children* 46:292–94.

Stewart, J. C. 1978. *Counseling parents of exceptional children.* Columbus, O.: Charles E. Merrill Publishing Co.

Stilivell, W. E., and J. Barclay. 1979. Effects of affective education interventions in the elementary school. *Psychology in the Schools* 16:80–87.

Stott, D. H., N. C. Marston, and S. J. Neill. 1975. *Taxonomy of behavior disturbance.* London: University of London Press.

Strain, P. S., and T. P. Cooke. 1976. *Teaching exceptional children.* New York: Academic Press.

Strain, P. S., T. P. Cooke, and T. Apolloni. 1976. The role of peers in modifying classmates' behavior: A review. *Journal of Special Education* 10:351–57.

Strain, P. S., and R. E. Shores. 1977. Social reciprocity: A review of research and educational implications. *Exceptional Children* 43:526–32.

Strain, P. S., ed. 1981. *The utilization of classroom peers as behavior change agents.* New York: Plenum.

Strang, L., M. D. Smith, and C. M. Rogers. 1978. Social comparison, multiple reference groups, and the self-concepts of academically handicapped children before and after mainstreaming. *Journal of Educational Psychology* 70: 487–97.

Strider, F. D., and M. A. Strider. 1979. Current applications of biofeedback technology to the problems of children and youth. *Behavioral Disorders* 5:53–59.

Stuart, R. B., ed. 1977. *Behavioral self-management: Strategies, techniques, and outcomes.* New York: Brunner/Mazel.

Stumphauzer, J. S. 1979. *Progress in behavior therapy with delinquents.* Springfield, Ill.: Charles C. Thomas.

Swan, A. 1983. Professional socialization and career plans of student teachers. Ph.D. Diss. University of Michigan.

Swap, S. M. 1973. An ecological study of disruptive encounters between pupils and teachers. In *Proceedings, American Psychological Association 81st Annual Convention.* Washington, D.C.: American Psychological Association.

———. 1974. Disturbing classroom behaviors: A developmental and ecological view. *Exceptional Children* 14:163–72.

Swift, M. S., and G. Spivack. 1974. Therapeutic teaching: A review of teaching methods for behaviorally troubled children. *Journal of Special Education* 8:259–89.

Task Force Four. 1972. *Chaos to order.* New York: Child Welfare League of America.

Tavormina, J. B. An evaluation of a therapeutic camp experience on children and their parents. University of Virginia, Department of Psychology. In preparation.

Taylor, S. E. 1983. Adjustment to threatening events: A theory of cognitive adaptation. *American Psychologist* 38:1161–71.

Thomas, A. 1979. Learned helplessness and expectancy factors: Implications for research in learning disabilities. *Review of Educational Research* 49:208–221.

————. 1981. Current trends in developmental theory. *American Journal of Orthopsychiatry* 51:580–609.

Thomas, A., and S. Chess. 1973. *Temperament and development.* New York: Brunner/Mazel, revised edition, 1977.

Thompson, R. H., K. R. White, and D. P. Morgan. 1982. Teacher-student interaction patterns in classrooms with mainstreamed mildly handicapped students. *American Educational Research Journal* 19:220–36.

Thurman, R. L. 1980. Mainstreaming: A concept general educators should embrace. *Educational Forum* 44:285–93.

Thurman, R., and G. J. Yard. 1978. Sex education and the behavioral disordered: A strategy pertinent to parents and professionals. *Behavioral Disorders* 4:53–61.

Thurman, S. K., and M. Lewis. 1979. Children's response to differences: Some possible implications for mainstreaming. *Exceptional Children* 45:468–70.

Tonick, R. H., J. S. Platt, and J. Bowen. 1980. Rural community attitudes toward the handicapped: Implications for mainstreaming. *Exceptional Children* 46:549–50.

Towns, P. 1981. *Educating disturbed adolescents: Theory and practice.* New York: Grunen and Stratton.

Traumontana, M. G. 1980. Critical review of research in psychotherapy outcome with adolescents, 1967–77. *Psychology Bulletin* 88:451–57.

Trinka, N. 1978. Children's conceptualizations of emotional disturbance in peers. Research study, University of Michigan.

Truckenmiller, J. L. 1982. Delinquency, bread and books. *Behavioral Disorders* 7:82–85.

Turnbull, A. P., B. Strickland, and J. C. Brantley. 1982. *Developing and implementing individualized education programs.* 2d ed. Columbus, O.: Charles E. Merrill.

Turnbull, A. P., and H. R. Turnbull. 1978. *Parents speak out: Views from the other side of the two-way mirror.* Columbus, O.: Charles E. Merrill Publishing Co.

Tyler, L. E. 1978. *Individuality.* San Francisco: Jossey-Bass.

————. 1983. *Thinking creatively.* San Francisco: Jossey-Bass.

Vacc, N. A. 1968. A study of emotionally disturbed children in regular and special classes. *Exceptional Children* 35:197–206.

———. 1972. Long-term effects of special-class intervention for emotionally disturbed children. *Exceptional Children* 39:15–22.

———. 1979. Coping with the behaviorally disturbed child in the classroom. *Viewpoints in Teaching and Learning* 55:29–36.

Von Isser, A., H. C. Quay, and C. T. Love. 1980. Interrelationships among three measures of deviant behavior. *Exceptional Children* 46:272–76.

Vorrath, H. H., and L. K. Brendtro. 1974. *Positive peer culture.* Chicago: Aldine Publishing Co.

Wagman, R. 1977. Preliminary report for Washtenaw Community Mental Health Program. Mimeographed. Ann Arbor, Mich.: School of Education, University of Michigan.

Walker, D. K. 1973. *Socioemotional measures for preschool and kindergarten children.* San Francisco: Jossey-Bass.

Walker, H. 1979a. *How to manage the acting-out child.* Rockleigh, N.J.: Allyn and Bacon.

———. 1979b. *The acting-out child: Coping with classroom disruption.* New Jersey: Allyn and Bacon.

———. 1978. Observing and recording child behavior in the classroom: Skills for professionals. *Iowa Perspective* 4:1–9.

Wallbrown, F. H., T. S. Fremont, E. Nelson, J. Wilson, and J. Fisher. 1979. Emotional disturbance or social misperception? An important classroom management question. *Journal of Learning Disabilities* 13:11–14.

Walls, R. T., T. J. Werner, A. Bacon, and T. Zane. 1977. Behavior checklists. In *Behavioral assessment,* ed. J. D. Cone and R. P. Hawkins. New York: Brunner/Mazel.

Wang, M. C., and R. Stiles. 1976. An investigation of children's concept of self-responsibility for their school learning. *American Educational Research Journal* 13:159–79.

Ward, A. J. 1976. *Childhood autism and structural therapy.* Chicago: Nelson-Hall.

Weiner, J. M., ed. 1977. *Psychopharmacology in childhood and adolescence.* New York: Basic Books.

Weinrott, M. R., and R. R. Jones. 1977. Differential effects of demand characteristics on teacher and pupil behavior. *Journal of Educational Psychology* 69:724–29.

Weinstein, L. 1969. Project Re-Ed schools for emotionally disturbed children: Effectiveness as viewed by referring agencies, parents, and teachers. *Exceptional Children* 35:703–711.

———. 1970. *Evaluation of a program for reeducating disturbed children: A follow-up comparison with untreated children.* Research report OEG-2-7-062974-2207. Nashville, Tenn.: George Peabody College for Teachers.

Weintrob, A. 1974. Changing population in adolescent residential treatment: New problems for program and staff. *American Journal of Orthopsychiatry* 44:604–610.

———. 1975. Long-term treatment of the severely disturbed adolescent: Residential treatment vs. hospitalization. *Journal of Child Psychology* 14:436–51.

Werner, E. E., J. M. Bierman, and F. E. French. 1971. *The children of Kauai: A longitudinal study from the prenatal period to age ten.* Honolulu: University of Hawaii Press.

Werner, E. E., and R. S. Smith. 1977. *Kauai's children come of age.* Honolulu: University of Hawaii Press.

Werner, E. E., and R. S. Smith. 1981. *Vulnerable but invincible: A longitudinal study of resilient children and youth.* New York: McGraw-Hill.

Werry, J. S., ed. 1978. *Pediatric psychopharmacology: The use of behavior-modifying drugs in children.* New York: Brunner/Mazel.

West, N. 1980. The effects of mainstreaming on behavior-disordered children. Ph.D. diss., University of Michigan.

Whelan, R. 1977. Human understanding of human behavior. In *Mainstreaming emotionally disturbed children,* ed. A. J. Pappanikou and J. L. Paul. Syracuse, N.Y.: Syracuse University Press.

White, O. R., and N. G. Haring. 1976. *Exceptional teaching: A multimedia training package.* Columbus, O.: Charles E. Merrill.

Wilson, S. J. 1981. A piagetian-based analysis of insight and the interpretative process. *American Journal of Orthopsychiatry* 51:626–31.

Wing, L. 1972. *Autistic children.* New York: Brunner/Mazel.

———, ed. 1976. Early childhood autism: Clinical, educational, and social aspects. 2d ed. Oxford: Pergamon Press.

Wingo, Max. 1974. *Philosophies of education: An introduction.* Lexington, Mass.: D. C. Heath and Co.

Wolman, B. B., ed. 1978. *Handbook of treatment of mental disorders in childhood and adolescence.* New York: Prentice-Hall.

Wood, F. H. 1973. Negotiation and justification: An intervention model. *Exceptional Children* 40:185–90.

———. 1977. *Proceedings of a conference on preparing teachers to foster personal growth in emotionally disturbed children.* Minneapolis: University of Minnesota, Department of Psychoeducational Studies.

Wood, F. H., and C. K. Lakin, eds. 1979. *Disturbing, disordered, or disturbed.* Minneapolis: University of Minnesota, Department of Psychoeducational Studies.

Wood, F. H., and K. C. Lakin, eds. 1978. *Punishment and aversive stimulation in special education: Legal, theoretical, and practical issues in their use with emotionally disturbed children and youth.* Minneapolis: University of Minnesota.

Wood, F. H., and R. H. Zabel. 1978. Making sense of reports on the incidence of behavior disorders/emotional disturbance in school-aged populations. *Psychology in the Schools* 15:45–51.

Wood, F. H., ed. 1980. *Teachers for secondary school students with serious emotional disturbance.* Minneapolis: Advanced Training Institute, University of Minnesota.

Wood, M., and J. Williams. 1977. *Developmental art therapy.* Baltimore, Md.: University Park Press.

——, ed. 1975. *Developmental therapy.* Baltimore, Md.: University Park Press.

Woody, R. H., ed. 1981. *Encyclopedia of clinical assessment.* Vols. 1 and 2. San Francisco: Jossey-Bass.

Workman, E. A., and M. A. Hector. 1978. Behavioral self-control in classroom settings: A review of the literature. *Journal of School Psychology* 16:227–36.

Wrightsman, L. S. 1964. Measurement of philosophies of human nature. *Psychological Reports* 14:743–51.

Wylie, R. 1961. *The self-concept.* Lincoln: University of Nebraska Press.

——. 1974. *The self-concept.* Lincoln: University of Nebraska Press.

——. 1979. *The self-concept.* Vol. 2. Lincoln: University of Nebraska Press.

Yamamoto, K. 1979. Children's rating of stressfulness experiences. *Developmental Psychology* 15:581–82.

Yoshida, R. K., K. S. Fenton, J. P. Maxwell, and M. Kaufman. 1978. Group decision making in the planning process: Myth or reality? *Journal of School Psychology* 16:237–44.

Young, L. 1965. *Life among the giants.* New York: McGraw-Hill.

Ysseldyke, J. E., and R. Algozzine. 1981. Diagnostic classification decisions as a function of referral information. *Journal of Special Education* 15:429–35.

Ysseldyke, J. E., and G. G. Foster. 1978. Bias in teachers' observations of emotionally disturbed and learning disabled children. *Exceptional Children* 44:613–14.

Zabel, R. H. 1979. Recognition of facial expressions by emotionally disturbed and nondisturbed children. *Psychology in the Schools* 16:119–26.

Zabel, R. H., L. W. Boomer, T. R. King. 1984. A model of stress and burnout among teachers of behaviorally disordered students. *Behavioral Disorders* 9:215–21.

Zabel, R. H., and M. K. Zabel. 1981. Factors involved in burnout among teachers of emotionally disturbed and other exceptional children. Paper presented at Council for Exceptional Children Annual Convention, New York City.

Zax, M., E. L. Cowen, J. Rappaport, D. R. Beach, and J. D. Laird. 1969. Study of children identified early as emotionally disturbed. *Journal of Consultation and Clinical Psychology* 32:369–74.

Zeeman, R., and I. Martucci. 1976. The application of classroom meetings to special education. *Exceptional Children* 42:461–62.

Zevin, G., ed. 1979. *The development of self-regulation through private speech.* New York: John Wiley and Sons.

Index

THE EDUCATION AND TREATMENT OF
SOCIOEMOTIONALLY IMPAIRED CHILDREN AND YOUTH

was composed in 10-point Times Roman and leaded 2 points,
with display type in Times Roman, by Coghill Book Typesetting Company, Inc.;
printed sheet-fed offset on 50-pound, acid-free Warren Eggshell Cream,
Smythe–sewn, and bound over binder's boards in Columbia Bayside Chambray,
also adhesive bound with paper covers by Maple-Vail Book Manufacturing Group, Inc.;
with paper covers printed in two colors by Philips Offset Company, Inc.;
and published by

SYRACUSE UNIVERSITY PRESS
SYRACUSE, NEW YORK 13210

E DUE

DAT